Philosophy of Emotion

In this book, Christine Tappolet offers readers a thorough, wide-ranging, and highly accessible introduction to the philosophy of emotions. It covers recent interdisciplinary debates on the nature of emotions as well as standard theories of emotions, such as feeling theories, motivational theories, and evaluative theories. The book includes discussions of the alleged irrationality of emotions, and looks into the question of whether emotions could not, in some cases, contribute positively to theoretical and practical rationality. In addition, the role of emotions in the theory of virtues and the theory of values receives a detailed treatment. Finally, the book turns to the question of how we can regulate and even educate our emotions by engaging with music and with narrative art.

The overall picture of emotions that emerges is one that does justice to the central role that emotions play in our lives, conceiving of emotions as crucial to our grasp of values. As an opinionated introduction, the book doesn't pretend to be neutral but aims to engage readers in contemporary debates. Each chapter closes with questions for further discussion and suggestions for further reading.

Key Features:

- Written for advanced undergraduates, suitable as the main text in a philosophy of emotion course or as a complement to a set of primary readings.
- Includes useful features for student readers like introductions, study questions, and suggestions for further reading in each chapter.
- Considers whether emotions interfere with our reasoning or whether they can, in some cases, help us to be more rational.
- Argues against basic emotion theory and social constructionism that emotions are both shaped by biological forces and social forces.
- Discusses a variety of subjectivist and objectivist approaches, which share the assumption that emotions and values are closely connected.

Christine Tappolet is a Full Professor in the Philosophy Department at the Université de Montréal. Her research interests lie mainly in metaethics, moral psychology, and emotion theory. She has edited a number of volumes, including, with Sarah Stroud, *Weakness of Will and Practical Irrationality* (Oxford University Press, 2003) and with Fabrice Teroni and Anita Konzelmann Ziv, *Shadows of the Soul: Perspective on Negative Emotions* (Routledge, 2018), and has authored three books, including *Emotions, Values, and Agency* (Oxford University Press, 2016).

Routledge Contemporary Introductions to Philosophy
Series editor: Paul K. Moser, Loyola University of Chicago

This innovative, well-structured series is for students who have already done an introductory course in philosophy. Each book introduces a core general subject in contemporary philosophy and offers students an accessible but substantial transition from introductory to higher-level college work in that subject. The series is accessible to non-specialists and each book clearly motivates and expounds the problems and positions introduced. An orientating chapter briefly introduces its topic and reminds readers of any crucial material they need to have retained from a typical introductory course. Considerable attention is given to explaining the central philosophical problems of a subject and the main competing solutions and arguments for those solutions. The primary aim is to educate students in the main problems, positions and arguments of contemporary philosophy rather than to convince students of a single position.

Recently published volumes:

Philosophy of Perception
2nd Edition
William Fish

Business Ethics
Jeffrey Moriarty

Philosophy of Social Science
2nd Edition
Mark Risjord

Philosophy of Psychiatry
Sam Wilkinson

Philosophy of Emotion
A Contemporary Introduction
Christine Tappolet

For a full list of published Routledge Contemporary Introductions to Philosophy, please visit https://www.routledge.com/Routledge-Contemporary-Introductions-to-Philosophy/book-series/SE0111

Philosophy of Emotion

A Contemporary Introduction

Christine Tappolet

Routledge
Taylor & Francis Group

NEW YORK AND LONDON

First published 2023
by Routledge
605 Third Avenue, New York, NY 10158

and by Routledge
4 Park Square, Milton Park, Abingdon, Oxon, OX14 4RN

Routledge is an imprint of the Taylor & Francis Group, an informa business

ISBN: 978-1-138–68743-1 (hbk)
ISBN: 978-1-138–68745-5 (pbk)
ISBN: 978-1-315–54230-0 (ebk)

DOI: 10.4324/9781315542300

Typeset in Times New Roman
by codeMantra

In loving memory of my mother, who filled my childhood with all kinds of colors, puppets, and tales

Contents

Illustrations

Figures

Table

Preface

I started planning this book a while ago, just after having finished my book, *Emotions, Values, and Agency*, which came out in 2016. The idea was not to write a second and simplified version of the 2016 book. What attracted me, on the contrary, was the opportunity to think about new topics, such as the question of why many of us like sad music or why some people – even if not me – are keen to watch thrillers and horror movies.

The aim of this book is to offer an introduction to the philosophy of emotion as it has been developing over the last decades. One of the difficulties inherent to such a project is that recent philosophical theorizing about emotions cannot be considered separately from the discussions of emotions that take place within the many empirical sciences that are concerned with emotions. Think of psychology, neurosciences, and anthropology, for instance. These disciplines all aim at understanding what emotions are and what role they play in our lives. Because of this, a good introduction to the philosophy of emotions cannot but be deeply empirically informed. As the reader will discover, many of the chapters contain detailed discussions of empirical results that have had an impact on the philosophical debates.

In my view, the best way to introduce someone to the philosophy of emotions is to plunge that person into the lively debates that are central to contemporary philosophy of emotions. Moreover, because it will help the reader to get involved in these debates, I do not refrain from taking a stand. Thus, this is very much an opinionated introduction. In fact, some of the claims I defend here are new. For instance, the theory of emotion that is proposed, according to which emotions are to be modelled on the representation of magnitudes, such as distance, is entirely new even though it builds on my previous work on perceptual theories of emotions. Similarly, the suggestion that sad music is attractive because it is liable to cause the emotion of being moved is, as far as I know, a new one. And so is the claim that the calibration of our sentiments that the world affords is of the same kind as the one that results from our engagement with fiction. However, in spite of the fact that the aim is definitely not to remain neutral about controversial issues, I have been careful to present the different positions and arguments in their best light, so as to give as balanced a picture of the issues as possible.

Let me explain how the book is organized. It is divided into four parts. The first part aims at laying out some basic notions so as to prepare the reader for the issues that are discussed in the following parts. Chapter 1 offers an overview of the history of the philosophy of emotions and spells out the central questions, on which philosophers, but also empirical scientists such as psychologists and neuroscientists, have focused. The questions are (a) the question of the essence of emotions, (b) the question of how good or bad emotions are for us, and (c) the question of whether and how we can regulate our emotions. Chapter 2 discusses features that have been generally thought to characterize emotions, such as feelings and motivation, and reviews a number of distinctions, such as that between emotions and moods, which have shaped the discussions in the philosophy of emotions and more generally in affective science. Chapter 3 discusses whether emotions are biologically determined or socially constructed and argues that emotions are shaped by both biological and social forces.

The second part of the book turns to theories of emotions, thus focusing on the question of the essence of emotions. Chapter 4 discusses feeling theories, which involve important insights despite being considered by most to have major shortcomings. Chapter 5 considers motivational theories, including the recent attitudinal theory, and argues that the problem with these approaches is that they fail to properly account for the fact that emotions involve evaluations. Chapter 6 turns to evaluative theories, starting with appraisal theories as found in psychology, followed by the main versions of the evaluative approach in philosophy, that is, judgmental, quasi-judgmental, and perceptual theories. What is proposed is to understand emotions on the model of analog representations of magnitudes, such as distance. On this model, emotions would involve nonconceptual representations of evaluative features.

Part III turns to the normative question of whether emotions are good or bad for us. Chapter 7 considers whether emotions generally interfere with our reasoning or whether they can, in some cases, help us to be more rational in that they have the power not only to cause, but also to justify evaluative beliefs. Chapter 8 takes on the relation between emotions and practical rationality and discusses the role of emotions in actions that appear less than fully rational, such as arational actions, as well as actions that are often considered to be paradigmatically irrational, that is, akratic actions. Chapter 9 deals with the metaethical issue of what evaluative features are and how they are related to emotions, and argues that evaluative features can be thought to be objective features of things even though they are intimately related to the emotions we experience. Finally, Chapter 10 considers the role of emotions in moral motivation and argues that emotions are central to virtues such as compassion or honesty.

Part IV, which consists of two chapters, turns to the regulation question and proposes to discuss this issue in relation to the role of emotions in art. Chapter 11 focuses on music and discusses how listening to music could be instrumental in the regulation of emotions, something which requires a discussion of what emotion regulation involves as well as how exactly music causes emotions. Chapter 12 introduces the notion of sentimental education, that is, the education of our emotional dispositions, and considers how emotional dispositions can be calibrated by our engagement with the real world as well as our engagement with fiction, arguing that there is no significant difference between these two ways of shaping our emotional dispositions.

The growing recognition of the importance of emotions in our lives has given rise to an impressive increase in the research on emotions. In particular, the philosophical literature about emotions has been growing rapidly over the last decades, and so have the different strands of empirical literature about emotions. As a result, it is impossible to cover each and every aspect of the questions that are discussed in this introduction. In fact, even though a wide range of issues is addressed, some questions have been left aside. Among the topics that are not addressed, let me mention enactive theories of emotions. A full discussion of enactive theories of emotions would have required adding a whole chapter to what is already a long book. Moreover, even though enactive theories of emotions have been proposed, such theories are not as yet among the standard and well-understood theories of emotions. Therefore, a discussion of such theories would have been necessarily tentative. Another important topic, which I decided not to address in this introduction, is the role of emotions in politics. There has been a growing interest in how the emotions we feel explain not only our social interactions but also our political stances. As yet, however, the overall picture of the different questions that concern the role of emotions in politics in general, as well as the role of specific emotions such as trust, envy, or indignation, is still in the making, so it seemed premature to include this topic.

I would like to thank Andrew Beck and Marc Stratton at Routledge for their support. Many thanks also to Guillaume Soucy for his work on the Index as well to Max Lewis for his help on the proofs. In addition, let me gratefully acknowledge the financial support of the Social Sciences and Humanities Research Council of Canada. I have been fortunate enough to be able to count on the help of a great many people. Special thanks are owed to the students of my fall 2021 course at Université de Montréal, who read the whole set of chapters. I am grateful for their willingness to play the role of guinea pigs, on which I could test the material before finishing the final version, and for their insightful comments. I am also grateful to Julien Deonna, Rodrigo Diaz, Luc Faucher, Raamy Majeed, Michael Milona, Andrea Scarantino, and Gopal Sreenivasan for reading and commenting on parts of the manuscript, as well as to the participants of the Montreal Affective Lab and in particular to Rodrigo Diaz, Federica Berdini, Ian Gold, Chris Howard, Miriam McCormick, Catherine Rioux, and Jules Solomone-Sehr for their feedback on material from the manuscript. Many thanks, also, to Antoine Panaïoti for his advice concerning Buddhist philosophy. In addition, I owe a big debt of gratitude to Ronald de Sousa, Fabrice Teroni, Jonathan Mitchell, and Hichem Naar, who have taken up the habit of reading drafts of the chapters almost as soon as they came out of the oven, barely cooked. Their insightful comments and questions as well as their constant encouragements were of tremendous help. I am also very grateful to Mauro Rossi, for his readiness to discuss and clarify difficult issues whenever the need arose. Thanks a lot, also, to François Gingras for discussions about music, fiction, and especially the fear of bears and the fear of fear. Finally, this book, and indeed any books and papers I have ever written, would not have been possible without the constant support of my partner, Philippe Zaugg.

PART I

The Philosophy and the Science of Emotions

1 The Philosophy of Emotions

1.1. Preamble

Imagine being confined to an igloo and trying to take notes, "when a lump of slush from the overheated dome [falls] for the third time in as many days into [your] typewriter and [ends your] work for the day" (Briggs 1970, 259). It would seem that the anger and the frustration you feel are quite understandable. Yet, as the anthropologist Jean L. Briggs discovered, this is not a universally shared opinion. In her fascinating book, *Never in Anger* (1970), she describes the emotional life of the Utkuhikhalingmiut (or Utku, as she calls them for brevity), a small Inuit community living in the Arctic tundra northwest of Hudson Bay, where she spent a year and a half sharing the life of a family during the 1960s. As Briggs learned the hard way, the Utku showing their disapproval by ostracizing her, an important norm regulating the life of the community was that one should never become angry. Though they were very tolerant toward the emotional outbursts of young children, the Utku believed that adults should control their emotions. As a result, expressions of emotions such as anger, but also sadness and love, were rare, much rarer than you would see in an average North American family. This might seem a pity. But in the harsh environment with which the Utku had to cope, a norm asking adults to control strong emotions and the violence that comes in their tow clearly makes sense.

Similar norms regarding emotions can be found in many cultures. Indeed, in one form or another, the ideal of a life devoid of emotional upheavals has appeared attractive to many. One can think of ancient Stoicism, a doctrine according to which emotions like fear, anger, or envy were thought to be irrational impulses involving false judgments. Correspondingly, Stoics were advised to free themselves from emotions in order to achieve tranquility of mind. In the same way, Buddhism invites us to forgo hatred as well as desire and love, the attachments that such states involve being incompatible with the liberation of the soul. In contemporary societies too, emotions are often blamed for all sorts of ills. Fear, anger, envy, disgust, and even compassion or love are regularly thought to interfere with our reasoning abilities and our decision-making, thereby making things worse for us and for others.

DOI: 10.4324/9781315542300-2

Even so, emotions are also the object of praise. Fear can help us to avoid danger, just as disgust can prevent the ingestion of noxious substances. In fact, we sometimes seek the experience of negative emotions in ways that seem independent of potential benefits, such as when we practice bungee jumping, listen to sad music, or watch horror movies. Even anger is sometimes considered to be a good thing, because it is thought to help with dealing with opponents, but also because it sometimes seems justified, such as when we speak of "righteous anger". When one considers positive emotions, such as compassion and love, or joy, admiration, and hope, it is even more difficult to deny that emotions can be a good thing. We are keen to experience positive emotions and the pleasure they involve. Indeed, emotions such as joy or love would seem to play a crucial role in a happy life. In fact, it is often thought that a life devoid of emotions, whether positive or negative, would be badly impoverished and barely human. Who would choose to live the life of the *Star Trek* android, Data, who has a super-powerful positronic brain, but who does not experience emotions?

In general, we seem to be ambivalent regarding emotions. On the one hand, we think we should be less emotional, while on the other hand, we want to lead a full and passionate life. Interestingly, this ambivalence does not only manifest itself intellectually, in terms of opposite assessments of our emotions. Our ambivalence often expresses itself emotionally. We fear anger, disgust, love, and indeed fear itself is something we are afraid of. At the same time, we are attracted by emotional experiences, whether these are negative ones such as fear and anger, or positive ones such as love and joy. This is what most of us, whatever our trade, think and feel about emotions, but what about philosophers? Of course, since philosophers cannot help being human beings, what they feel cannot be fundamentally different from what ordinary people feel. Nor can what they think be fundamentally different.

To get a sense of what philosophers have been up to, let me sketch a brief historical overview of the philosophy of emotions. It hardly needs underscoring that this overview is highly selective in that it focuses on a handful of major figures, thereby neglecting arguably equally important contributors to the philosophy of emotions, such as Baruch Spinoza (1632–1677) or Adam Smith (1723–1780). The same is true of contributions from non-European thinkers, such as the Confucian philosopher Mengzi (or Mencius in the Latinized version of the name) (c. 1040–221 BCE) (Mengzi 2008, see Virág 2017; Van Norden 2019; Wong 2019) or the Buddhist philosopher Buddhaghosa (5th century) (Buddhaghosa 1984, see Heim 2013; Tuske 2016). Not to mention the voices of female thinkers, who were not given the chance to leave as permanent a mark in the history of ideas (see Superson 2020).

1.2. Emotions from Plato to Aquinas

Contemporary Western philosophy has its source in Ancient Greece, and so does the philosophy of emotions. In particular, even though neither Plato (c. 429–347 BCE) nor Aristotle (384–322 BCE) developed a complete theory of emotions, they held distinctive views about emotions (or passions, *pathê*, things that we undergo, with respect to which we are passive) and these views have not only influenced thinkers over the last 2,000 years, but they are still influential today (see Price 2009).

Both Plato and Aristotle thought that the human mind or "soul" (*psyche*), as they called it, was divided in parts. According to Plato's *Republic*, the soul is composed of a rational part, reason, and a lower, non-rational part, which is further divided into a passionate part (*thumos*) and an appetitive part (*epithumia*). The passionate part was thought to be the home of anger, shame, indignation, fear, pride, and admiration, while the appetites were taken to involve bodily desires such as hunger and thirst. Given this tripartite division, it is tempting to consider the passionate part as the one exclusively concerned with emotions. This, however, would be an oversimplification. Plato explicitly held that emotions accompany some of the desires which belong to the appetites. In addition, to restrict emotions to the passionate part would be a mistake because Plato locates love for truth and wisdom in the rational part. It is noteworthy that according to Plato, emotions were not purely mental, for he held that both emotions and appetites involve bodily disturbances. Anger, for instance, is thought to involve boiling of the blood upon thinking that one has been wronged.

What is central to Plato's conception of the soul is the possibility of conflict between its different parts. In particular, a specific failure of rationality, called *akrasia* (or weakness of the will), which Plato defined as an action performed in spite of believing or even knowing that the action is bad, is explained in terms of a conflict between an appetite and a rational attitude. To avoid such conflicts, Plato held, quite unsurprisingly, that the rational part of the soul had to prevail. In terms of the allegory of the charioteer leading two winged horses pulling in different directions, which Plato proposed in the *Phaedrus*, the task of reason is to guide the two other parts of the soul, passion and appetite. Nevertheless, Plato considered the passionate part of the soul to be closer and more receptive to reason's influence, compared to the appetites, and he allowed for the possibility of learning to love and hate correctly, so as to avoid conflict between emotional inclination and reason.

A similar hierarchy characterizes Aristotle's conception. But instead of the tripartite division, Aristotle divides the mind in only two parts: the rational and the non-rational soul, comprising emotions. In his *Nichomachean Ethics*, he includes desire or appetite (*epithumia*), along with anger, fear, confidence, envy, joy, love, hatred, longing, emulation, and pity, in his list of emotions. Like Plato, Aristotle thinks of emotions as involving both the soul and the body, the angry person being described as boiling up at the thought of an insult. It is in his *Rhetoric*, a work that explains to orators how to influence people's opinion by arousing their emotions, that Aristotle specifies what he takes emotions to be. More specifically, he gives definitions of a number of emotions, among which are anger, indignation, shame, pity, envy, and fear. Anger, for instance, is defined as a desire for revenge, accompanied with pain, because of a real or imagined slight to oneself or someone close to one. Aristotle thought that anger is not merely painful, for it comes with a certain pleasure, which arises from the expectation of taking revenge. In general, Aristotle held that emotions involve several components: pain or pleasure, an evaluation, such as the belief that there is a slight (or a threat in the case of fear), a motivation, as well as bodily changes.

Like Plato, Aristotle claimed that emotions often are an important source of irrationality. Thus, a conflict between reason and emotion could result in acting against one's better judgment, that is, in *akrasia*. But Aristotle also thought that emotions could have a positive role. Indeed, he thought emotions were central to moral (or ethical – I will use the terms without differentiation) virtues and happiness. According to Aristotle, moral virtues, which he conceived of in terms of habits, crucially involve feeling emotions at the right times, with reference to the right objects and the right people (see Chapter 10). Even anger he considered to be sometimes the proper reaction. Importantly, Aristotle held that being virtuous or vicious was not simply something we find ourselves to be. He thought that the virtues require education, our emotional reactions depending on socially learned patterns we acquire through experience. In the same way you become a good lyre-player from practicing playing the lyre, we become brave by facing up to danger and becoming habituated to feel the right emotions in such circumstances. As we shall see, the idea of an education of our emotions is one that has been very influential (see Chapter 12).

Whereas Aristotle considered properly educated emotions to be essential to virtue and happiness, the Stoics, who founded an important school of thought in Athens in the 3rd century BCE which lasted well into the Roman period, were much more critical of emotions. Their work contains extended discussion of negative emotions such as anger, fear, distress, sorrow, grief, shame, envy, jealousy, and pity, among others. In contrast to Plato and Aristotle, the Stoics did not believe in a partitioned soul. They conceived of the soul as a physical substance (*pneuma*), which is mixed with the body. However, they held that the soul comprised a governing faculty, which was, among other things, the seat of reasoning. Moreover, they considered emotions to be irrational disturbances, which not only had to be controlled, but altogether eradicated. According to Seneca (c. 1 BCE–CE 65), "We shouldn't control anger, but destroy it entirely – for what 'control' is there for a thing that's fundamentally wicked?" (Seneca, *On Anger*, iii. 42, p. 95). Thus, in spite of not dividing the soul into parts, the Stoics upheld a strong opposition between emotions and reasons. This opposition was thought to be the source of *akrasia*, which the Stoics considered to involve swift changes in the soul.

Why did the Stoics object to emotions? The Stoics considered emotions to consist in judgments about the good and the bad and they thought that these judgments were deeply mistaken. Distress, for instance, was held to consist in the erroneous opinion that something bad is present. Indeed, the Stoics conceive of emotions as involving a kind of assent. A person experiencing distress would thus consider that reaction to be the proper one. The problem with emotions, according to the Stoics, is that the judgment in question is grounded in an attachment to a mistaken conception of human life and its place in the world.

The Stoics held that only virtue was intrinsically good, and only virtuous activities were thought to allow for true happiness. Considering anything else, such as one's pleasure or one's pain, as important, was not only wrong, but irrational. It would result in nothing but unhappiness. This is why the Stoics proposed different methods to get rid of emotions, ranging from cognitive therapy involving philosophical reasoning to habituation and even musical therapy.

The Stoics were often ridiculed for their ideal of a being who feels no emotions at all, which seems quite out of reach for normal human beings. In fairness, it has to be stressed that the Stoics did not recommend a life entirely devoid of feelings. They held that it was permissible to feel a kind of proto-emotional reaction as long as one does not assent to it, that is, as long as one does not let it become a full-blown emotion accompanied by an impulse toward action. In addition, they encouraged some mental states which we would nowadays consider to be emotions, such as well-reasoned elation. But even with these concessions to human nature, the Stoic ideal might still seem both psychologically too demanding and overall less than desirable.

Medieval philosophers also had a strong interest in emotions (which they called *passio* or *affectus*). Thomas Aquinas (1225–1274), whose approach was importantly influenced by Aristotle, offered the most extensive medieval treatment of emotions in his *Summa Theologica* (Part II – 1.22–48 and 2.17–36) (see Knuuttila 2004; Perler 2018). Like the Stoics, the main focus of Aquinas and his contemporaries was on the normative question of whether emotions are good or bad. Thus, Aquinas was chiefly interested in whether emotions, such as love, hatred, hope, despair, fear, joy, or anger, are good or bad, or indeed virtues or sins. Aquinas, who thought that emotions are movements of the soul, emphasized the motivational force of emotions. Indeed, he held that emotions are motivations to act. For example, anger is claimed to be a desire for vengeance. He conceived of these motivations as associated with bodily changes and as arising from an estimation of something as pleasurable or painful, or more generally as emotionally relevant. Aquinas calls these categories the "formal objects" of emotions, a notion which, as we shall see in Chapter 2, still plays an important role in the philosophy of emotions. Because the estimations that ground emotions could be erroneous, Aquinas held that they need to be assessed by reason. However, by contrast with the Stoics, whom he explicitly criticized, Aquinas followed Aristotle in holding that emotions should not be eradicated. Emotions, according to Aquinas, should simply be held under control. Thus, Aquinas also followed Aristotle in holding that virtue requires that one feel emotions in accordance with the verdict of reason. Since emotions can resist the commands of reason, Aquinas thought of the control that reason exercises in terms of a kind of "political" power, like the power of a king ruling over free subjects who are able to resist orders. Reflection he thought can not only attenuate an emotion like anger, but make it stop, and the main way to have this effect is by means of getting oneself to imagine what triggers the emotion in a different light. As we shall see in Chapter 11, the strategy of reappraising what causes our emotions is central in contemporary accounts of emotion regulation.

1.3. Modern Philosophy and the Emotions

René Descartes (1596–1650) (see Shapiro 2020), who is generally considered to be the father of modern philosophy, explicitly scorned medieval theories of emotions in his book *The Passions of the Soul* (1649/1989). One of Descartes' main philosophical concerns was the relationship between the mind and the body, which he considered to be distinct substances. According to Descartes, emotions are perceptions, sensations, or commotions of the soul caused by the movements of the animal spirits, minute particles that inform the soul that the body is preparing for action. Emotions thus do not belong to pure mind but they involve both the mind and the body. It is noteworthy that because Descartes also thought that non-human animals have no mind, he considered that these beings are incapable of having emotions and indeed of feeling pain and pleasure. This makes for a stark contrast with his predecessors, who all agreed that non-human animals can have emotions in spite of lacking reason.

The difficult question here is how to explain how the mind and the body interact. To explain how the mental and the bodily components of emotions interact, Descartes developed an account of how the body affects the mind, suggesting that the motions of the body were transmitted by the animal spirits to the mind through a small gland at the base of the brain, the pineal gland. This account is largely considered hopeless. Insofar as the mind is taken to consist in a non-physical substance, postulating what Daniel Dennett calls a "fax machine to the soul" (Dennett 1991, 106) fails to explain how something physical can have a causal impact on the mind.

In spite of his focus on mechanistic explanations of emotions, Descartes' account presents strong affinities with both the Aristotelian and the Stoic tradition. Even though Descartes held that emotions are perceptions, sensations, or commotions of the soul caused by the movements of the animal spirits, he also considered that some emotions involve assessments of the ways in which things may harm or benefit us. Descartes explicitly claimed, for instance, that love, which counts with wonder, hatred, desire, joy, and sadness as the six basic emotions, is caused by a representation of its object as good or beneficial without regard to time, while joy is aroused by the thought of a present good. These emotions are thought to have motivational power, the perceptions of the soul causing desires, such as the desire to join the object of the emotion. What distinguishes an emotion from a value judgment is that when you judge that something is good, you need not only represent that thing as good, for you also need actively to give you assent to that content. Thus, Descartes can allow for cases in which you judge something to be good, while you react to that thing with sadness, representing it as bad without assenting to that content. As we shall see in Chapter 6, such cases of "recalcitrant emotions" (D'Arms and Jacobson 2003) have been prominent in contemporary debates concerning the nature of emotions.

Descartes also held that emotions differ from judgments in that they are liable to be deeply misleading. They often distort our grasp of reality, making us believe that things are better or worse than they really are. Because of this,

Descartes thought it was important to control one's emotions, even if the control we have over our emotion is not a direct one. However, Descartes held that it was up to us to give or withhold one's assent to an initial emotional reaction. Interestingly, Descartes thought that what makes indirect control over our emotional reaction possible is nothing but an emotion: the emotion of self-esteem, which is based on the thought that one freely exercises one's will. Another point that is worthy of attention is that Descartes claimed that there are several ways to change one's emotional reactions. We can for instance attempt to imagine the object of one's emotion in a different light. Merely thinking about something can also result in an emotional response, which Descartes called an "intellectual" emotion, and which can be used to counteract an initial response. According to Descartes, another way to change or weaken our emotions is to train ourselves by getting habituated to what arouses us.

Another major figure of the modern period, David Hume (1711–1776), took it upon himself to overhaul the traditional rationalist conception of emotions (see Cohon 2018). Instead of worrying about how we could gain control over putative irrational emotions, Hume boldly claimed that emotions should take the lead. He famously proposed in his *Treatise of Human Nature* that "reason is, and ought only to be the slave of the passions" (Hume 1739–1740/2000, Book 2, Part 3, Section 3). The role Hume attributed to reason is the useful but subservient one of providing information about the world and in particular about the means to achieve our ends, where these ends are given by the emotions we feel. Because Hume considered the faculty of reason to have no motivational power on its own, he concluded that this faculty is not in a position to resist the impulse of emotions. Any attempt to resist such an impulse has to come from a conflicting emotion. And because at least in the *Treatise*, Hume held that emotions, unlike judgments, do not consist in representations of things and therefore fail to be assessable as rational or irrational, reason cannot influence our emotions by correcting them. It is noteworthy that in a later work, *Of the Standard of Taste* (1757/1985a), Hume changed his mind regarding the thesis that emotions do not consist in representations. In the *Treatise*, however, Hume claimed that "'Tis not contrary to reason to prefer the destruction of the whole world to the scratching of my finger" (Hume 1739–1740/2000, Book 2, Part 3, Section 3). It needs to be underscored, however, that even if Hume held that emotions and preferences cannot be irrational, he did not believe that there is nothing wrong with the destruction of the whole world. Indeed, because contemplating the possibility of the destruction of the world is a source of displeasure and moral disapproval, Hume would have strongly condemned such a preference.

According to Hume, there are two kinds of emotions. The first are the "direct passions". These include desire, aversion, hope, grief, joy, hope, fear, despair, and what Hume calls "security" (the opposite of fear), and are what he calls "impressions", or "sensations" in our terms. They are caused by the experience, or the thought, of good or bad, which Hume considered to be the same as the experience, or the thought, of pleasure or pain. The so-called "indirect passions" include pride, humility (or shame), ambition, vanity, love, hatred, envy, pity, malice, and generosity. They are also impressions that involve the experience (or the thought) of pain or pleasure, but they require additional thoughts. Thus, pride in the beauty of one's house, say, is a kind of pleasure, which is directed at oneself and is caused by the thought that we own the house. We feel pride when the idea we have of ourselves is positive, and shame when it is negative. Thus, both direct and indirect emotions involve evaluations of their objects. Given this, there is less distance between Hume's account of emotions and the ones proposed by his predecessors than one might have thought initially. What marks Hume out is therefore not so much his account of the nature of emotions, but the way he conceives of the relationship of emotions and the faculty of reason.

The inversion of the traditional relation between reason and emotion is particularly significant for Hume's "moral sentimentalism", as his anti-rationalist stance has come to be known. According to Hume, moral evaluations arise from our emotions, and not from reason. It is on the basis of the pleasure or displeasure we take when considering people and their actions that we make moral judgments regarding the value of their characters. Thus, we consider someone to be virtuous insofar as disinterested contemplation of their character produces approval, where approval is nothing but a kind of pleasure. This pleasure Hume thought to be mediated by a mechanism he called "sympathy", which results in feeling pleasure (or displeasure) at the sight of pleasure (or displeasure). Given this mechanism, what happens when we consider a trait that tends to benefit others, such as benevolence, is that we tend to feel pleasure, thereby approving that trait. Importantly, Hume thought that our emotional reactions could be misleading. When considering the character of an enemy, for instance, we would tend to have a biased reaction, which would prevent us from arriving at a fair assessment. Hume thus recommended that we adopt a kind of neutral point of view, which is taken to enable us to correct our emotions, or at least to correct the judgments we make on the basis of these emotions.

Another major figure of the modern era, Immanuel Kant (1724–1804), sets himself up against Hume's conception of morality (see Wilson and Denis 2018). By contrast to Hume, who thought that morality is grounded in human nature and more specifically in the emotions we feel toward others, Kant held that the foundation of morality lies in reason, a faculty that we by definition share with all rational beings, and which can be practical, in the sense that reason can determine the will and thereby result in action. Morality is grounded in the autonomy of the will, where an autonomous will is one that gives itself its own law. To do so, the will has to disregard any attractive features that objects of the will may possess. The reason for this is that to consider these features would consist in being motivated by our "inclinations", which Kant considers to be foreign to our proper self. In his view, to be governed by our inclinations would amount to reducing our will to slavery, so to speak. It would make our will "heteronomous", instead of autonomous and free. Therefore, our "inclinations", including our emotions, have to be put aside. As a result, virtue is considered to involve control over one's emotions and more generally one's inclinations. It is only in this way that we can be autonomous agents, who by obeying reason fulfill our moral duties.

To motivate his rationalism, Kant voiced a number of criticisms against the claim that morality should be grounded in emotions. Basically, Kant thought that emotions, which he took to be motivations, are too shaky a ground to play any fundamental role. In his *Groundwork of the Metaphysics of Morals* (1785/1996), he argues that such "empirical principles" cannot ground moral laws that hold for all rational beings, because they depend on the nature of human beings, which might be different from that of other rational beings. Similarly, Kant notes that there are important differences between the feelings people have. As he puts it, "there are endless differences of degrees between different kinds of feelings", from which he concludes that "feelings can't give us a uniform standard of good and bad" (Kant 1785/1996, 4: 442). Independently of the difficult question of the scope of moral principles, that is, of whether or not moral principles hold universally, one might wonder whether Kant's condemnation of emotions on the basis of their contingency and their variability is fair. After all, our rational abilities are also contingent upon our nature, and the conclusions we reach in our reasonings not only vary a lot depending on the circumstances, but they often lead us astray.

Notwithstanding his rejection of the Humean claim that morality is grounded in the sentiments, Kant is less negative regarding emotions than one might think. A first point to stress is that Kant grants a central role to one particular emotion, namely, *respect* for the moral law. According to him, such an emotion, which arises from the contemplation of the moral law, involves the consciousness of the subordination of one's will to that law. More generally, Kant held that for beings like us, a feeling of pleasure or delight in the fulfillment of one's duty is required. Furthermore, as Kant noted in later works (see for instance, Kant 1797/2018), certain moral emotions, such as love of human beings or compassion and respect for oneself, are ones it is our duty to cultivate. Finally, in his work on aesthetic judgments, Kant argues that emotions are central to our appreciation of beauty and the sublime. Even so, and in strong contrast with what Hume held, Kant considered that action performed from duty alone has genuine moral worth.

The take-home lesson of this brief overview of what are often considered to be major milestones in the philosophy of emotions is that interest in emotions has given rise to nuanced and sophisticated theories. Bearing in mind the concerns that philosophers of the past have expressed over the years in quite different historical and social contexts, let us turn to the question of what a philosophical enquiry about emotions should be taken to achieve. What, in other terms, are the central questions that organize this field of enquiry?

1.4. The Central Questions

The question most contemporary philosophers would consider to be central is the one that William James raised in the very title of his famous paper: "What Is an Emotion?" (1884). Clearly, much of the work of philosophers, both in the past and today, focuses on this question. To answer it, they try to develop a theory that aims at spelling out what emotions consist in, so as to be able to distinguish emotions from other states, like itches or migraines and more generally other psychological states. Put differently, their aim is to specify the nature or *essence* of emotions. Now, as we have seen, many philosophers of the past – and this is also true of contemporary philosophers – thought that emotions involve different components. According to Aristotle, for instance, emotions involve pains and pleasures, evaluations, motivations, as well as bodily changes. The question of the essence of emotions, thus, is whether any of these components is essential to emotions, and if so which one is, or if there are several of them, which ones are essential to emotions. If several components are involved in emotions, the further question is how they hang together. Furthermore, because there are distinct kinds of emotions, which seem to differ importantly – think about the differences between fear and pride, or between disgust and hope – answers to the question of what emotions are might well depend on the kind of emotion that is considered. Indeed, one task that the philosophy of emotion takes on is to spell out the differences between the different kinds of emotions, so as to explain what demarcates them.

However, as should be obvious from the historical sketch, the question of what emotions are is not the only one that triggered the interest of philosophers. Indeed, it is far from obvious that it is the main one. Philosophers of the past, just like ordinary people, have all had a sense that emotions can both be good and bad for us. From Plato to Kant, most philosophers agreed that at least some emotions, if not all emotions, need to be educated or at least controlled, while some, like the Stoics, even thought that we should get rid of most emotions altogether. However, even the most radical critics of emotions held that some emotions – well-reasoned elation for the Stoics, respect for the moral law for Kant – were essential to the good life. Moreover, even the thinkers who were most enthusiastic about emotions could not help but take note that some emotions make us miserable. Thus, both Aristotle and Hume thought that some emotions, such as shame or hatred, involve pain. And even Hume had to make room for the fact that emotions can lead us to error.

This ambivalence regarding emotions is testimony to the complexity of the subject-matter, emotions coming in all sorts of forms and colors. But what it indicates, above all, is that the main interest philosophers have had when thinking about emotions is not the question of what emotions are, but rather the *normative question* of whether emotions are good or bad for us. In other words, the question is that of the function of emotions, a question that is central in contemporary debates. More precisely, because of the variety of emotions, the question on which philosophers focused was whether this or that emotion is good or bad for us. Because emotions are susceptible to being good or bad for us in different ways – fear might help us to deal with dangers, while compassion might make us morally better persons, for instance – what has to be determined is in what ways a particular kind of emotion, such as fear or compassion, or indeed, specific emotional episodes, might be good or bad for us. In any case, it is with an eye to the normative question that philosophers of the past developed accounts of what emotions are. If theories of emotions were thought to be of interest, it was mainly because such theories could help answer the normative question.

One important focus of historical theories of emotions concerns the regulation of emotions, that is, the influence we can have on the emotions we experience, whether by educating, controlling, or indeed eradicating them. Even if it is less central in their accounts, this question of the regulation of emotions has also attracted the interest of contemporary philosophers. The question is whether it is possible to change our emotional reactions, and if so, how we should go about it. Obviously, this question is intimately related to the normative question. It is only insofar as emotions can be good or bad for us that there is a need for regulation. It is noteworthy that interest in the essence of emotions can be seen as being partly motivated by the question of whether and how emotions can be regulated. Put in another way, one question that theories of emotions can help clarify is to what extent and how we can educate, control, or maybe even suppress our emotional reactions. As we have seen, philosophers of the past have made several intriguing suggestions as to how we should deal with our emotions, and this is also something that is of interest to contemporary philosophers, along with contemporary psychologists.

In a nutshell, philosophers have been interested in three interrelated questions:

a) *The essence question:* What is the essence of emotions?
b) *The normative question:* Are emotions good or bad for us?
c) *The regulation question:* Can we regulate our emotions, and if so, how?

The normative question is the one that has most practical import. Because interest in the first and the third question appears to depend on whether one sees emotions as good or bad for us, there is reason to think that the normative question is the chief one. This does not entail that the other questions lack importance. Clearly, the essence question is the more fundamental one. Knowing what emotions are is crucial if one wants to understand in what ways emotions can be good or bad for us. The question of the essence is also crucial to get a grasp on the question of whether and how we can regulate our emotions. The importance of the third question lies in the fact that knowing how we can regulate our emotions, assuming it is something feasible, is a key practical question, with which we all have to deal.

So far, we have focused on what philosophers are interested in. Indeed, the discussion mainly concerned contemporary western philosophy and its historical sources. But philosophers are far from being the only ones who are interested in emotions. Outside philosophy, a great many disciplines, ranging from the social sciences to the life sciences, have contributed to the understanding of emotions, not to mention the rich insights that are afforded by art and in particular by literature. One important question is how these different strands of inquiry are related to each other. Let us turn to the question of the relevance of scientific approaches to emotions.

1.5. The Relevance of Scientific Results

A great many scientific disciplines are concerned with emotions. One can think of biology, psychology, psychiatry, neurosciences, anthropology, sociology, and history. A good question, therefore, is how these different perspectives are connected. More pointedly, what should philosophers do in light of the work in these other disciplines? Should they simply hand over the topic to the social and life sciences, just as philosophers of the past handed over to biology questions regarding the functioning of organisms? Or somewhat more ambitiously, because the different sciences do not speak with one voice, philosophers might see their role as being that of bringing together different scientific perspectives in order to propose a unified account of emotions, possibly working out some hidden implications from scientific premises. Many philosophers would balk at both these suggestions. But the question is what philosophy can bring to the table to justify its place as a distinct approach to the emotions.

There are two points that philosophers might try to make here. The first is that philosophy uses distinctive methods to investigate emotions. The second is that philosophy is interested in a different set of questions regarding emotions. Accordingly, one could claim that philosophers not only have their own subject-matter but that they would also have their own methods to investigate that subject-matter (for such a line of defense, see Roberts 2003). As a result, philosophers wouldn't need to pay much attention to what is done in other disciplines – polite curiosity would be quite enough. Can these two claims be defended?

Let us start with the methodological issue. The meta-philosophical question of what philosophical methods consist in is controversial, but most would agree that the main tools of philosophy are the following: conceptual analysis, thought experiments, introspection, and observation. One might wonder whether these tools are likely to be sharp enough to yield reliable results, and I shall come back to this shortly. Whatever the verdict concerning their reliability, the tools in question will surely appear very different from experimental methods and the statistical results they yield, which are essential to most social and life sciences. There are pertinent differences between philosophical and scientific methods – even philosophers who are into experimental philosophy and thus use questionnaires to see how terms are used by the general public have, in general, no use for microscopes or for Magnetic Resonance Imaging scanners. Even so, the divide between philosophical and scientific methods should not be exaggerated.

Quite generally, there is reason to think that the methods that characterize sciences are not as deeply different from philosophical methods as one might first think. Even if scientific observation is much more systematic than anything that philosophers could envisage, there is arguably no essential difference insofar as both can be thought of as more or less systematic ways to conduct everyday observation (see Haack 2003). Insofar as introspection can be taken to be a kind of observation, there would again be no deep divide between philosophical and scientific methods. Finally, while most philosophers heavily rely on conceptual analysis and thought experiments, such tools also seem essential to scientific investigation. Obviously, it would be difficult to conceive of testable hypotheses without some conceptual clarification, and to clarify the concepts at stake, it would seem necessary to think about examples and counterexamples. At best, there are therefore only differences of emphasis between philosophical and scientific methods, and it is not clear that such differences provide enough to consider philosophy as a distinct perspective on emotions.

What about the point regarding the proprietary subject-matter? Emotions are complex phenomena, so it seems plausible that different disciplines are interested in different aspects of emotions. Neurosciences focus on the brain and more generally on the nervous systems in order to specify the underpinnings of emotions; evolutionary biology looks into the response mechanisms that might have helped our ancestors to spread their genes; anthropology is interested in the various social norms that regulate emotions, and so forth for each discipline. Given this, it is tempting to think that the philosophy of emotions has its own specific interest to pursue. To assess this suggestion, let us look back at the three central questions, which I introduced in the previous section. Would any of these questions be specifically philosophical?

The essence question might seem to be one that only philosophers would care about. Are essences not philosophical creatures? One should not be misled by the terminology here, however. The question of what emotions consist in is central to the philosophy of emotions, and philosophers have spared no efforts to address it, but it is surely not one that is of no interest to other disciplines. How could one even start setting up scientific experiments regarding emotions without presupposing some rough account of what emotions are? Indeed, emotion theories from many disciplines explicitly attempt to explain what emotions are, different scientific disciplines favoring distinct kinds of accounts. In any case, the essence question is not specifically philosophical.

What about the normative question? Because scientists often view normative questions as dubiously unscientific, this question has a good chance of being of interest only to philosophers. In particular, questions regarding how emotions might make us morally better or worse persons are questions that not only have preoccupied philosophers for centuries, but are also ones for which philosophers seem better placed than others, ethics being a traditional philosophical discipline. However, it hardly needs emphasizing that making progress on such questions is likely to require input from outside of philosophy. For instance, questions regarding how emotions influence judgments, which surely belong to psychology, are clearly relevant to understanding how emotions affect our moral character. Similarly, whether or not emotions allow us to deal with challenges in our environment needs to be assessed empirically. Given this, the normative question might well be specifically philosophical, but it nonetheless needs to be addressed with an eye on empirical findings.

The situation is not much different in the case of the regulation question. This question is one that is undeniably central to philosophical inquiries into emotions, but it also one that has been a major focus in psychology, as well as in psychiatry and neurosciences, so that there is no way to argue that it is specifically philosophical. The upshot is that the regulation question is one that philosophers have no choice but to address in collaboration with other disciplines.

In short, even if it can be agreed that the normative question is specifically philosophical, neither alleged methodological differences nor specific interests warrant the claim that philosophers can go about their business on their own, without the help of researchers from other disciplines. Thus, we can see that an interdisciplinary approach to emotions has to be favored.

Scientists might argue that even the idea of an interdisciplinary approach that includes philosophy as one of the disciplines seems unwarranted. As I mentioned, there are worries regarding the tools that philosophers bring to the table. Are these tools sufficiently reliable or should we try to dispense with conceptual analysis, thought experiments, introspection, and lay observation? An obvious consideration that speaks in favor of considering these tools in a positive light is that, as we have seen, there is arguably no big divide between philosophical and scientific methods. Insofar as scientists use basically the same tools there is no reason to dismiss the philosophical approach.

To better understand why philosophical methods should not be frowned upon, let me say a word about *conceptual analysis*. The basic idea is that philosophers have to try to cut concepts into pieces so as to specify the fundamental concepts out of which the complex concepts are built. The model here is that of chemical analysis, which aims at specifying the fundamental elements out of which complex elements are made. Now, as is commonly recognized, most ordinary concepts resist this kind of treatment. Thus, it is often a better idea to try simply to spell out the conceptual ties between concepts. Importantly, this task of *conceptual elucidation*, as it has become known, does not aim at reducing a concept to other, more fundamental concepts. Conceptual elucidations yield conceptual truths, that is, propositions that are true in virtue of the concepts that they involve. Good examples of such truths are the proposition that yellow is a color, the proposition that if something is heavier than an elephant it cannot be lighter than this elephant, and the proposition that knowledge entails truth, such that if you know that the earth is round, then it is true that the earth is round. An interesting feature of such truths is that they do not aim at neutrally registering the usages of terms. This is because unlike dictionaries, conceptual analysis and also conceptual elucidation concern not words and sentences, but concepts and thoughts. But it is also because the putative conceptual truths often cannot all be true at the same time. To resolve tensions between putative conceptual truths and also to account for counterexamples, some act of balancing is necessary, a certain number of putative claims being liable to be rejected as misleading.

The process at stake can be usefully compared to the method of reflective equilibrium, which John Rawls proposed in his milestone work, *A Theory of Justice* (1971). Rawls argued that to obtain justified ethical beliefs, you need to start with your considered ethical judgments and work from there to a coherent set of ethical beliefs that form a theory. Similarly, to get to conceptual truths, you need to start with the putative conceptual truths – or *platitudes*, as they are sometimes called – which flow from the meaning of concepts and thus correspond to our intuitive account of a given subject-matter. When you hit upon a tension or a counterexample to a hypothesis, you adjust the platitudes, modifying or rejecting them so as to obtain a coherent set of platitudes (Jackson 1998). As I hope to make clear in the following chapters, this method can be fruitful when applied to emotions, for instance when applied to the connections between concepts for emotions and evaluative concepts (see Chapter 9).

Quite generally, it has to be underscored that philosophical thinking can be and has been very fruitfully applied to all of the three main questions concerning emotions. Philosophers have developed sophisticated theories of what emotions are. They have had insightful things to say about how emotions influence, whether in a good or a bad way, our thoughts and our actions, and about how emotions are related to values and virtues. And even though philosophers had less to say about the regulation question, some of their suggestions, such as the influence of literature on empathy, have proven very influential. Indeed, philosophers are far from having losing interest in emotions and, as will be obvious to anyone who follows the current debates, they continue to contribute importantly to our understanding of emotions.

1.6. Taking Stock

Emotions play an important role in our lives, but as we have seen it is not clear whether this role is a positive or a negative one. Mainly because they worried about the negative impact of emotions, philosophers of the past, from Plato and Aristotle to Descartes and Kant, have been keen to understand what emotions are and how we could regulate what we feel. Contemporary philosophers similarly focus on the question of the essence of emotions, which can be seen as the most fundamental one regarding emotions, but they also have a strong interest in the normative question of whether emotions are good or bad for us, for instance by positively or negatively affecting our ability to reason. Even if the regulation question has attracted less attention among philosophers in recent times, it is nonetheless of high practical importance. Since philosophy is not the only discipline interested in the essence and the regulation questions, philosophers cannot but work hand in hand with empirical scientists to make progress on these questions. And as we have seen, even the normative question is one that needs empirically informed reflection. The next chapter turns to the task of clarifying key concepts in the philosophy of emotions as well as in the sciences that look into emotions.

1.7. Summary

- Both ordinary people and philosophers seem ambivalent regarding emotions: emotions are seen as bad for us in several ways, but they are also considered to be essential to a good and ethical life.
- Philosophers of the past were keenly interested in the nature and role of emotions, as well as their relationship to reason. A common thought was that emotions can be a source of irrationality, so that they had to be regulated.
- Philosophy of emotions can usefully be understood as organized around three main questions: (a) the essence question, concerning the nature of

emotions, (b) the normative question, concerning the benefits and harms of emotions, and (c) the regulation question, concerning how emotions could be educated, controlled, or, if needed, eradicated.

- Scientific results are relevant to the philosophy of emotions because the sciences are concerned with the essence question and the regulation question; even the normative question, which can be considered to be specifically philosophical, needs empirical input.
- The methods used in philosophy – conceptual analysis or elucidation, thought experiments, introspection and observation – are not fundamentally distinct from scientific methods, even if the emphasis is different.

1.8. Study Questions

1. Remember your last fit of anger. Did you find it painful or pleasurable, or maybe both painful and pleasurable?
2. How do you feel about emotions in general? Are there particular kinds of emotions that are especially worrisome or especially desirable?
3. What is specific about the methods we use in the philosophy of emotion and are these methods sufficiently reliable when applied to emotions?

1.9. Further Readings

Aristotle. 2007. *Rhetorics*. Translated by William Rhys Roberts. Oxford: Clarendon Press, book II.

Descartes, René. 1649/1989. *The Passions of the Soul*. Translated by Stephen H. Voss. Indianapolis, IN: Hackett Publishing Company.

Hume, David. 1739–1740/2000. *A Treatise of Human Nature*. Edited by David Fate Norton and Mary J. Norton. 3 vols. Oxford: Clarendon Press, book II.

Hume, David. 1757/1985a. "Of the Standard of Taste." In *Essays: Moral, Political and Literary*, edited by Eugene F. Miller, 231–258 Indianapolis, IN: Liberty Fund.

Kant, Immanuel. 1785/1996. *Groundwork of the Metaphysics of Morals*. Translated by Mary J. Gregor. Cambridge: Cambridge University Press.

Lyons, William. 1999. "The Cognition-Emotion Debate: A Bit of History." In *Handbook of Cognition and Emotion*, edited by Tim Dalgleish and Mick J. Power, 21–44. Chichester: John Wiley & Sons.

Plato. 1974. *The Republic*. Indianapolis, IN: Hackett Publishing Company, book IV.

Roberts, Robert C. 2003. *Emotions: An Essay in Aid of Moral Psychology*. Cambridge: Cambridge University Press, chap. 1.

Seneca. 2010. *Anger, Mercy, Revenge*. Translated by Robert A. Kaster and Martha C. Nussbaum. Chicago: University of Chicago Press.

Wong, David B. 2019. "Moral Sentimentalism in Early Confucian Thought." In *Ethical Sentimentalism: New Perspectives*, edited by Remy Debes and Karsten R. Stueber, 230–249. Cambridge: Cambridge University Press.

2　The Affective Domain

2.1. Introduction

Think back to what went through your mind the morning of April 15, 2019, the day a massive blaze ravaged Notre-Dame Cathedral in Paris. For me this is a flashbulb memory. I woke up on what seemed a more or less ordinary morning. I was in a rather good mood and happy to see that the weather was clear, even if still feeling somewhat sleepy and confused, as well as being a bit hungry; when I took my shower, I tried to remember a dream while also feeling pleasure at the flow of the warm water; and then, when I sipped my tea and checked the news, I started thinking about the tasks of the day – I worried about how I should start a new chapter and decided to use an example, paying little attention to the radio. This is when the news hit me: a fire had partly destroyed Notre-Dame Cathedral. I reacted with surprise and horror, and was suddenly fully awake; and when I looked at the pictures of the falling spire and the destroyed roofs, a sense of sadness at the loss of these beautiful and historically charged structures overcame me as I imagined walking by the scene of devastation.

As this example makes clear, our inner life consists in a stream of intermingling mental phenomena: feeling in a mood, being happy, seeing something, feeling sleepy, feeling confused, feeling hungry, remembering something, feeling pleasure, thinking about something, worrying about something, deciding to do something, starting with surprise and horror, feeling fully awake, looking at something, being sad, imagining doing something, to consider only the ones mentioned in the previous paragraph. On the face of it, it is not obvious that these mental phenomena lend themselves to classification into clearly distinct categories.

Yet, as should be clear from our historical survey (in Chapter 1), the fact that our mental life has this stream-like quality has not discouraged philosophers of the past from proposing big divisions, such as the one between the rational part and the non-rational part of the soul we find in Aristotle. Indeed, it is still common in contemporary philosophy to oppose what pertains to the faculty of reason, one the one hand, and what belongs to emotions or more generally to affects, on the other.

DOI: 10.4324/9781315542300-3

Indeed, this weatherworn opposition between reason and affects has taken on new, more empirical clothes. Psychologists have thus proposed to divide cognitive processes in two types, the ones that belong to the Intuitive System (or System 1), and which involve fast, automatic, but largely inflexible treatment of information, and ones that are part of the Reasoning System (or System 2), which are supposed to be slow and deliberative. More controversially, some consider the Reasoning System to be generally smarter, at least when it does not get fooled by the atavistic Intuitive System (see Kahneman 2011, for instance).

So-called *dual-process theories of cognition*, which divide the mind into two types of processes, are not without their critics, but in some form or other they are accepted by a large majority of psychologists and economists, as well as outside these disciplines. It is rather the question of how exactly to spell out the distinction between different kinds of cognitive systems or processes that gives rise to debates. According to a plausible conception, the distinction should be thought of in terms of two types of cognitive processes, *intuitive processes* and *reflective processes* (Evans and Stanovich 2013). According to this conception, the difference between the intuitive processes and reflective processes is that the latter crucially involve controlled attention and the manipulation of information in working memory, while the latter make minimal demands on working memory, which is tantamount to saying that they do not require controlled attention. The other features, such as rapidity, lack of consciousness and automaticity in the case of intuitive processes, tend to be correlated, but they need not be present. Importantly, processes of the two kinds can result in correct answers, and whether they do so depend largely on the kind of environment in which they are deployed. Thus, even if both intuitive and reflective processes can lead to mistakes, both are smart in their own way.

Emotional, and more generally affective, processes are most often considered to belong to the family of intuitive processes. But things might well be more complicated. Even if emotions are generally taken to be passive states that depend on quick, automatic processes, they are often thought to involve consciousness. However, insofar this is also true of sensory perception, which can be taken to consist in intuitive processes, this feature of emotions is compatible with considering emotional processes to count as intuitive processes. In any case, it is not obvious that all emotional processes fall on the side of intuitive processes. Some emotions, such as indignation and guilt, appear to depend on judgments, which are states that are likely to involve controlled attention. The question is what the exact relationship between judgments and such emotions consists in. If the judgments are not required each time the emotion is experienced, then there is no pressure to count such emotions as involving reflective processes (see Chapter 3 and Chapter 6). A general question is how processes of one type interact with processes of the other type, for instance in the case of acquiring skills, such as when we learn to play the piano. This question is particularly interesting in the case of emotions, for the question of how reasoning influences emotions is crucial for understanding how we might regulate our emotional reactions (see Chapter 11 and Chapter 12).

To start clearing things up, this chapter introduces the standard distinctions within the affective domain. One important question is how emotions differ from other types of affects. But first what are affects, exactly? The term "affect" derives from the Latin *affectus*, which means "being acted on, being influenced", and which medieval philosophers used to refer to emotions (see Chapter 1, Section 2). In contemporary debates, the concept of affect, which is central in so-called "affective sciences", a recent field of inquiry that brings together psychologists, neuroscientists, anthropologists, and philosophers, among others, is a general concept that refers to emotions and similar phenomena. Thus, affects are generally taken to involve emotions, moods, sentiments, desires, as well as pleasures and displeasures or pains. More generally, affects are thought to be mental phenomena that are typically characterized by both feeling and motivation. The question, then, is how emotions differ from other phenomena of this kind. Let us begin by looking at the main characteristics of emotions, starting with feeling and motivation.

2.2. Feeling and Motivation

Consider the fear you experience when looking down from a high cliff that plunges into the sea. Such a fear surely counts as a prototypical case of emotion, as much as does the disgust you feel at the sight of the carcass of a decaying crab, the anger at negligent tourists who left their garbage behind, the joy when you think that your friends will be joining you for a swim, the sadness when you suspect that they have decided not to come, or the surprise when you see that they have already arrived. As these examples make manifest, emotions come in different kinds.

In fact, there is a great variety of terms that refer to what appear to be distinct kinds of emotion, ranging from the ones I used in the previous examples – "fear", "disgust", "anger", "joy", "sadness", "surprise" – which seem to refer to emotions which we share with some non-human animals, to ones that appear characteristically human, like "indignation", "shame", "guilt", "respect", "admiration", "awe", "grief", "hope", "amusement", and "relief". This is anything but a complete list of English emotion terms, let alone of terms from all known languages and cultures. In fact, a complete list of emotion terms is likely to be remarkably long. For instance, Anna Wierzbicka (1999) discusses more than 50 emotion terms from the English lexicon, as well as a great many terms from other languages and cultures. Now, since what is true of some of these emotions need not be generally true of emotions, and also because some emotions seem less prototypical – think of amusement or awe, for instance – it is a good idea to start with cases that clearly count as prototypical emotions. Therefore, the discussion in this chapter will mainly focus on fear, disgust, anger, happiness (or joy), sadness, and surprise. (As we shall see in Chapter 3, this is the initial list of so-called *basic emotions* proposed by Paul Ekman (1972).) In fact, because even among examples of emotions that are prototypical, there might be cases that fail to display all the typical features, it will be useful to limit the discussion to typical cases of these six kinds of emotion. Our question, then, is the following: what is true of emotional responses such as your fear when looking down the cliff?

In line with the assumption that emotions are affective phenomena, which as we have just seen are generally considered to be typically characterized by feeling and motivation, a first thesis that seems undeniably true is that to undergo an episode of fear as illustrated by the example of the cliff, is something that involves feelings. And the same appears true of disgust, anger, joy, sadness, and surprise. The thesis that emotions like these involve feelings is generally accepted by philosophers of the past as well as by many contemporary philosophers (see Deonna and Teroni 2012, for instance). As we shall discuss, feelings have been considered so important to emotions that some theorists have proposed to identify emotions with feelings (see Chapter 4).

In general, it seems true that when you are afraid, you typically feel afraid, just as when you are disgusted, you feel disgusted, and so forth for anger, joy, sadness, and surprise. The idea is that there is something "it is like" to undergo fear, just as there is something "it is like" to be disgusted by the crab or to be angry at the tourists. Put differently, emotions like fear or disgust are thought at least typically to have what philosophers call *phenomenal properties*. The distinctive feelings that are involved in emotions are often thought to be closely related to physiological changes, such as the racing of your heart, as well as psychological changes, such as shifts in your attention that come with your fear. What is felt seems to depend on the kind of emotion one considers – compare the feeling of disgust with that of happiness, for instance – but a good question is whether each kind of emotion is characterized by distinctive phenomenal properties. One might also wonder what is common to emotions such as fear, disgust, and sadness, which seem to involve negative, unpleasant feelings, by contrast to joy, which seems to involve positive or pleasant feelings. In any case, it appears that what is distinctive of the phenomenal properties of emotions is that they are *valenced*. Fear, disgust, anger, and sadness appear to involve negative feelings, while joy, hope or pride appear to involve positive feelings. In general, it seems that emotions are either positively or negatively valenced. Interestingly, surprise appears a bit of an outsider here, for it seems that it can be both positive or negative depending on whether the surprise is good or bad. However, surprise is arguably a mildly negative emotion, but which can either be followed by positive or negative emotions, depending on the situation. The question is how to account for valence, and more generally for the nature of distinctive phenomenal properties of emotions. In any case, the following claim seems plausible:

(Phenomenology) Episodes of emotion typically have phenomenal properties.

An interesting point to note is that in spite of its plausibility it is not obvious that this claim amounts to a conceptual truth, that is, a truth that holds in virtue of the concepts that are involved. In contrast to the thesis that birds typically have wings, say, it seems possible to question whether emotions typically involve feelings. If you find a sparrow that lacks wings, there is something wrong with that sparrow, but there is nothing wrong with the concept of sparrow, let alone the concept of bird. The wingless sparrow is simply not a good exemplar of its species, just as a penguin is not a typical bird. By contrast, it does not seem to flow from the concept of emotion that there is something wrong with an emotion that does not involve feelings. In reply, it can be pointed out that learning the concept *emotion*, as well as the concepts of particular kinds of emotions, crucially depends on how it feels to experience such states. When teaching to a child what fear is, we point towards episodes of fear undergone by others, but we mainly highlight the feelings experienced in fearsome circumstances, such as when the child hears thunder or is confronted by a growling dog. What seems to follow is that the claim that emotions typically have phenomenal properties is a putative conceptual truth, and whether it should count as a genuine conceptual truth requires reflection.

Even so, the stronger claim that an episode of emotion not only typically, but necessarily involves phenomenal qualities surely fails to be a conceptual truth. There seems to be no blatant contradiction in the thought that someone undergoes an episode of fear, which involves all the characteristics that are typical of such episodes, while not experiencing any associated feelings. This raises the controversial question whether emotions can be unconscious, to which we will return (see Chapter 4). Whatever the verdict regarding the possibility of unconscious emotions, however, it can be agreed that unconscious emotions do not count as typical. Therefore, their existence would not threaten the thesis under consideration, namely, that emotions typically involve feelings.

In line as well with the assumption that emotions are affective phenomena, the second thesis that will strike many as plausible is that episodes of emotion such as fear and disgust at least typically involve motivations. As we shall discuss (see Chapter 5), this thesis is particularly popular among psychologists (Frijda 1986), but it is also generally accepted by philosophers (Scarantino 2014). When you feel fear when looking down from a cliff, you will instinctively move back to a safer spot, your disgust at the crab will motivate you to turn away and block your nose, and your anger at the tourists is likely to come with an urge to call them names or take some action to encourage them to change their behavior. What thus seems plausible is the following thesis:

(Motivation) Episodes of emotion typically involve motivations.

Again, it is noteworthy that this thesis does not obviously seem to consist in a conceptual truth. It is not obvious that someone who denies the claim that emotions typically involve motivations fails to understand the concept of emotion. The claim seems at best to constitute a putative conceptual truth. In any case, the stronger thesis according to which emotions necessarily involve motivations is open to question. There seems to be no contradiction in saying that you can experience an emotion of fear, disgust, or anger that lacks any motivational pull. Against this, it might be argued that the etymology of the term "emotion" makes it clear that there must be a tie to motivation. The term goes back to the Old French *emouvoir*, which means to stir up, itself going back to the Latin *emovere*, meaning to move out, remove, agitate, from *ex-* (out) and *movere* (to move). However, the idea of a movement from the inside could also be thought to refer to the expression of emotions. More generally, arguments based on the etymology of terms fail to be conclusive, given that the terms acquire new meanings over time. It should also be underscored that some kinds of emotions, such as admiration, do not seem to have close ties to motivation (see Chapter 5). So, it is not obvious that the thesis in question should be taken to be generally true of all kinds of emotions. In the case of emotions such as fear, disgust or, anger, however, the thesis regarding motivation appears difficult to deny. Episodes of such emotions typically come with a tendency to act in certain ways.

2.3. The Objects of Emotions

A third thesis that many philosophers have underlined is that such episodes of emotions are about something or other. You are afraid of falling from the cliff, you are disgusted by the crab, you are angry at the tourists, you feel joy at the thought that your friends are joining you for a swim, you are sad that they might have decided not to come, and surprised by the fact that they have arrived. The term standardly used in the philosophy of emotions to refer to these things is that of "intentional object". But note that the term "intentional" has little to do with the ordinary meaning of the word "intentional" as used to describe actions, such as when we say "her action was perfectly intentional" in the sense, roughly, that it was not by mistake that she acted the way she did. In the sense we are interested in, intentionality concerns the "directedness" or "aboutness" of our mental states. The claim that emotions have intentional objects has been considered to be central by a great many philosophers (see Brentano 1874/1995; Kenny 1963/2003; Lyons 1980). Here is how we can formulate the thesis that episodes of emotions at least typically are about something or other:

(Intentionality) Episodes of emotion typically have intentional objects.

According to this thesis, emotions would share an important feature with beliefs and desires, which also have intentionality as an essential mark. Consider beliefs. You believe that it rains, where your belief is about the fact that it rains. Similarly, desires have intentionality. You desire that the sun shine, where your desire is about the state of affairs that the sun shines.

In contrast to beliefs, however, emotions can take a variety of intentional objects (Deonna and Teroni 2012 and Scarantino and de Sousa 2018). You can be angry that there is garbage on the beach. In such a case, the intentional object of your emotion is a state of affairs. But emotions can also concern particular objects or events. You can be afraid of a wolf, disgusted by the decaying crab, or angry at your friend's behavior, just as you can be surprised by the arrival of your friends. Such intentional objects can be actual and concrete entities, which you perceive, such as the wolf or the crab, but they can be merely possible, such as when you fear a possibly upcoming storm. Indeed, the storm may never materialize, so that your fear will never concern something actual. They can also be abstract, such as when you are surprised by a new hypothesis. Finally, emotions can have classes of things or general entities as their intentional objects. You can not only fear a particular wolf you encounter on a hiking trail, but also a pack of wolves or even all wolves in the world, just as you can be disgusted with humankind in general.

Often, the intentional object of an emotion is also its cause. Your fear of the wolf is caused by the wolf, which you see on the trail. It is important to keep in mind, however, that the intentional object of emotion need not be identical to its cause (see de Sousa 1987). Your anger at a colleague's jocular attitude might be caused by the frustration of having missed an important deadline. In that case, the cause of your anger is the frustration, which is itself caused by the missing of the deadline. Other cases involve intentional objects which lack causal power, such as when what you are afraid of is an upcoming event or a fiction.

Nevertheless, emotions are generally thought to have causes that involve their intentional objects. Consider again the fear you feel when confronting a wolf. Your fear clearly depends on the fact that you see the wolf on the trail. Had you not perceived the wolf, you would not have had a fear reaction. Seeing the wolf on the trail is thus the cause of your emotion. Similarly, hearing or smelling a wolf in the vicinity can cause your fear. But emotions need not depend on sensory perception. Believing that there is a wolf on the trail without perceiving the animal can be sufficient to trigger fear. Indeed, remembering something or imagining that something will happen can cause an emotional episode. Imagining that your friends will bring a dessert can cause you to feel joy, while remembering the loss of an acquaintance might cause sadness. Because such causes involve cognitive states, such as perceptions and beliefs, this kind of cause is often called the "cognitive basis" of your emotion (see Mulligan 1998; Deonna and Teroni 2012).

As is made manifest by the examples we discussed, the thesis that emotions have intentional objects is difficult to deny. It thus seems to be a claim that is well placed to count as a conceptual truth. Again, however, it is far from clear that the intentionality thesis is a conceptual truth. Maybe when you consider cases such as fear or disgust it is true that they typically involve intentional objects. But it is not clear that someone who denies that emotions typically involve intentional objects fails to grasp the concept of emotion. As such, the concept *emotion* does not appear to rule out cases in which there is no intentional object. Thus, there seems to be no contradiction in saying that one feels an emotion but that what one feels is not about anything. In fact, even if the claim that emotions have intentional object is commonly accepted, some have raised doubts about it (Griffiths 1997, 28). Consider happiness. Is it not possible to feel happy without this feeling being about something or other? In the same way, it seems that we are sometimes anxious even if there is nothing specific we are anxious about. There are two possible ways to respond to such considerations.

According to the first, the claim that emotions have intentional object is one that allows for exceptions. As a result, the claim that emotions have intentional objects would not be generally true, so its status as conceptual truth would be ruled out. Thus, according to some philosophers, there are objectless emotions (Goldie 2000 and Price 2006). An alleged example of such objectless emotions is that of an experience of fear that wakes you up in the middle of the night. You look into the dark, at the shape of the curtain, you listen to the noise, but there is no specific object of which you are afraid.

Such cases are interesting, but on reflection, it is not entirely clear that the fear that is experienced fails to have an object. It might be argued that you are afraid of the dark as well as the curtain and of the noise. Even more plausibly, it can be held that what you are afraid of is simply something that you have not yet identified. If so, the emotion would not be objectless; it would be directed at something even if as yet, you don't know what it is. Even so, not all alleged cases of objectless emotions can be treated as cases involving intentional objects that are not identified. When you feel happy but there seems nothing your happiness is directed towards, it does not seem that there is something not yet identified that is the intentional object of your happiness.

Let us look, therefore, at the second line of response, which is in fact the standard one. It consists in holding on to the thesis that all emotions have intentional objects, while maintaining that the alleged objectless affective states are of a different kind: they are *moods*, not emotions. To embrace this claim would amount to adopting a terminology according to which emotions are *by definition* directed at intentional objects. There might good reason to adopt such a terminology and thus to accept as a conceptual truth of the claim that fear, anger, etc., have intentional objects. For one thing, it would make it possible to carve out a class of affective states that share an important feature, namely, intentionality. As we will shortly see (in Section 2.7), this issue is complicated, for according to some, moods are in fact nothing but kinds of emotions. Moreover, the question whether they have intentional objects is debated.

2.4. Emotions and Evaluations

A fourth characteristic of emotions that is often underlined is that emotions are, in some way or other, connected to appraisals or evaluations. As we have seen, this thesis is accepted by many historical figures in the philosophy of emotions (see Chapter 1). This thesis is also popular in psychology (see Lazarus 1991), but it is particularly prominent among contemporary philosophers (for instance Nussbaum 2001), some of whom hold that appraisals or evaluations constitute the core of emotions (see Chapter 6). Consider again your fear when looking down the cliff. It seems plausible to say that in some way or other, your fear involves an assessment of danger (or threat or fearsomeness). Similarly, when you experience disgust at the rotten crab it seems that your disgust involves a negative assessment of the crab as contaminated (or foul or disgusting). It clearly seems to be generally true of episodes of all kinds of emotions that they involve evaluations. A good question, to which we will return in Chapter 6, is what the exact role of evaluations in emotions consists in. Are they the causes of emotions or do they possibly constitute essential components of emotions? In any case, most would agree with the following thesis:

(Evaluation) Episodes of emotion typically involve appraisals.

In the same way as for the other theses we have seen, it is not clear that this thesis regarding evaluation is a conceptual truth. It seems possible to raise the question whether it is really the case that an emotion of fear, say, involves an evaluation, and this does not seem to boil down to the question of whether what we have is a good or a bad exemplar of fear. Again, this does not entail that the thesis in question is incorrect. What it entails is that its truth does not flow from the ordinary concept of emotion, in the sense that the concept of emotion does not carry the notion of appraisal (or evaluation) on its sleeve. It is at best a putative conceptual truth. In spite of this, as we shall discuss in great detail, there appear to be conceptual ties between specific kinds of emotions and evaluative concepts (see Chapter 9). It is for example difficult to deny that the notion of fear and that of the fearsome, or the concept of disgust and that of the disgusting, are conceptually tied. Such claims might seem too circular to be of interest, but as I will argue, there are reasons to believe that they encapsulate important insights into emotions and their relation to values. In any case, the conceptual ties between specific emotion concepts and evaluative concepts give support to the thesis regarding the involvement of appraisals in emotions.

It is worth mentioning that sometimes, we use terms like "fear", "anger", etc. in a derivative way, which focusses on the appraisal content, leaving aside the other aspects of emotional episodes that we have considered. For example, we can say that you are afraid of the neighbor's dog meaning only that you believe that dog is dangerous or fearsome, for you are not undergoing any emotion and there is nothing that you feel. In such a case, the state that is attributed is simply an evaluative belief or an evaluative stance. In the same way, you can say that you are angry at some politician without feeling anything, meaning simply that you find that particular politician offensive. To mark this usage of emotion terms, one might say that they refer to *evaluative stances*, by contrast to emotional episodes.

The way philosophers have generally understood the thesis concerning appraisal is in terms of some kind of criteria for emotions. The idea is that danger (or fearsomeness) is by definition what episodes of fear aim at. By contrast, disgust would be concerned with contamination (or disgustingness), and so forth for each kind of emotion. The term used to describe the evaluative properties that play this regulative role is that of "formal object". As we have seen in the previous chapter, the notion of formal object goes back to medieval philosophy and, in particular, to Aquinas (see Chapter 1, Section 2). In contemporary philosophy, this notion has been revived by Anthony Kenny (1963/2003; see also Lyons 1980; de Sousa 1987; Teroni 2007).

In general, formal objects of emotions are understood as what determines when an emotion is fitting or not. For instance, an episode of fear towards something is fitting when that thing is dangerous, while an episode of disgust is fitting when its intentional object is contaminated. Given this, there seems to be a close relationship between appraisals and formal objects, appraisals being often understood to involve the attribution of a formal object to what the emotion is about. Several questions arise concerning how exactly to conceive of the formal objects of emotions and their relationship to appraisals, depending on how one conceives of the role of appraisals (see Chapter 6). However, there is a wide agreement that emotional episodes are tied to formal objects. Hence the following thesis can be proposed:

(Formal objects) Episodes of emotion typically have formal objects.

Again, because the concept of emotion and that of formal object appear quite distant, it might seem difficult to see how this thesis consists in a conceptual truth. However, insofar as the notion of formal object is a technical one, it can easily be built into its meaning that emotional episodes typically have formal objects.

It should be underscored that emotions are connected to evaluations in yet another way: they can themselves be assessed in evaluative terms. As we just saw, emotions can be thought to be fitting or not, depending on the nature of their intentional object. Disgust, we have seen, would be fitting when it is about something that is contaminated. What fittingness consists in is a controversial question, which we will consider in detail (see Chapter 9). But fittingness is only one dimension in which emotions can be assessed. In fact, there is a variety of assessments that concern emotions. Remember the Stoics (Chapter 1, Section 2) and their complaint about the irrationality of emotions. This evidently consists in a negative evaluation of emotions as irrational, but emotions can be, and indeed sometimes are, praised for their rationality. Emotions are also criticized or praised depending on whether they are useful or not to the person who experiences them, that is, on whether or not they have *prudential* value in that they promote people's interest. Finally, emotions are often the target of moral blame and moral praise, whether this is so because of the consequences of the emotions or because of some of their intrinsic features, such as when one considers anger to be a morally ugly emotion quite independently of its potential effects. In addition to assessments in terms of fittingness, we thus also assess emotions in terms of their rationality (or irrationality), of their prudential value (or lack thereof), as well as their moral or ethical character (see Chapter 7 and Chapter 8).

There surely are other sorts of assessments of emotions, but the four I have introduced are the most significant. A good question is how exactly to conceive of these different dimensions, assuming that they really are distinct from each other. One might also wonder whether or not these assessments depend on cultural or individual contexts. What kind of emotion is considered appropriate, for instance, is likely to depend on cultural norms, and it might also depend on whose emotions are considered. In many cultures, what is expected from people depends on their social role, as teachers or judges, say, or on their gender. In North America, for instance, men who express sadness or fear are viewed as "unmanly", while women are expected to express less anger, compared to men (Brody 1999). The hard question here is whether or not there are objective facts, such as objective moral facts, that transcend cultural norms regarding emotions.

2.5. The Temporal Shape of Emotions

Episodes such as your fear when looking down the cliff are short-lived. The same is true of the disgust at the decaying crab, the anger at the tourist, the joy at the thought of your friends' expected arrival, the sadness when you suspect they will not come, and the surprise at seeing they have already arrived. Such emotional episodes last for seconds or minutes. Thus, it seems plausible to hold the following thesis:

(Temporality) Episodes of emotion are typically short-lived.

This thesis is often taken for granted by both psychologists (for instance Ekman 1994) and philosophers (for instance Ben-Ze'ev 2001). However, it should be noted again that it is less than obvious that the claim that episodes of emotions are typically short-lived consists in a conceptual truth. In any case, it is doubtful that emotions necessarily have to be short-lived. When you consider surprise, it seems indeed impossible to imagine a case of surprise felt for hours in a row. Thus, the emotion of surprise appears necessarily short-lived. Nevertheless, an emotion of fear or anger or even more obviously of sadness that lasts for long periods – not seconds or minutes, but days, months or even years – does not necessarily seem to consist in a defective exemplar of its species. If you are unlucky enough to live close to a source of danger, you can experience fear for an extended period of time, and this is something that will affect you night and days, interfering with your sleep. Similarly, sadness at an important loss can last for weeks or even months. Even if emotional episodes can last for longer stretches of time, it nonetheless seems true that they typically tend to be relatively short-lived, in particular when compared to more lasting features, such as character traits and temperaments, which are stable over long stretches of our lives.

The question about the temporality of emotional episodes is connected to subtle but fundamental issues regarding the ontology of emotions, that is, issues regarding the basic category of entities to which emotions belong (Naar Forthcoming). There are three basic options regarding the ontological status of emotions, depending on how one conceives of the way emotions occupy time. According to the first option, to experience fear when confronting a wolf, say, is to be in a certain *state*, namely a mental state (see Roberts 2003; Prinz 2004).

There is a beginning and end to this state and there might be different elements that manifest the state, such as feelings or motivations, but as such, the state of fear persists during all the time that you are afraid of the wolf. Because states are not dynamic but emotions seem to wax and wane, and more generally because emotions appear to involve changes, some theorists have proposed that emotions are not states, but events or processes. Thus, according to a second option, the fear you experience at the wolf could consist in an *event*, such as the explosion of a volcano, an earthquake, or a hike (see Jaworski 2018). Events have shorter or longer durations, depending on the kind of event that is considered, they can be simple or complex, they can be characterized by different phases, and they have distinctive causes and distinctive effects. Emotions could thus be considered to be events involving feelings and physiological changes, which are caused by appraisals and which result in motivations. The third option is to conceive of emotions as *processes*, such as corrosion, photosynthesis or digestion, which unfold over time, involve different components and have a specific outcome. On this model, episodes of emotions are thought to be complex and dynamic processes, which involve a variety of components, such as evaluative, motivational or physiological components, which causally interact (see Robinson 2005; Goldie 2011).

For the sake of simplicity, I will assume here that to undergo an emotional episode is to be in a mental state. For example, to feel fear when looking down the cliff is to be characterized by a specific mental state. A good question is whether an account of emotions in terms of mental states can make room for the waning and waxing of emotions as well as the interaction between different components of emotional episodes. There is reason to believe that the answer is positive. Thus, one can hold that the mental states in question interact with a number of events and processes, such as physiological changes, feelings or motivations, the interplay of which account for the dynamics of emotional episodes (for this view, see Soteriou 2018).

In any case, whether the fear you feel when confronting the wolf should be considered a state, event, or process. What is uncontroversial is that such a fear is different from a number of other emotional phenomena and more generally from other affective phenomena. Before considering what is distinctive of emotional episodes, it will prove useful briefly to take stock. We have reviewed several claims regarding typical episodes of prototypical emotion, such as fear, disgust, anger, happiness, sadness, and surprise. The upshot of the discussion is that such episodes, which tend to be relatively short-lived, typically involve feelings, motivations, and intentional objects, as well as appraisals and formal objects. With these characteristics in mind, let us turn to emotional dispositions.

2.6. Emotional Dispositions

A very common distinction in the philosophy of emotions is that between so-called *occurrent emotions*, as they are often called, or an *emotional episode*, on the one hand, and *emotional dispositions*, on the other (see Kenny 1963/2003;

Lyons 1980; Deonna and Teroni 2012). The basic idea is that there is a contrast between an emotional episode such as the fear you experience at a particular time, on the one hand, and being disposed to undergo such emotional episodes in given circumstances. Consider the disgust you experience when you see a decaying crab. This experience is clearly distinct from the disposition to experience disgust when you are confronted with decaying corpses and other similar objects, like rotten cabbage in your fridge. On the one hand, there is an emotion that you experience in a particular context, while on the other, what you have is an underlying state that gives rise to emotional episodes, but which is distinct from such episodes.

As the disgust case makes clear, it seems that emotional episodes always depend on emotional dispositions. In other terms, the emotions you experience are the manifestation of underlying dispositions, just as the breaking of a vase is the manifestation of its fragility. In some cases, emotional dispositions lead to emotions that make your life difficult or are even considered pathological, such as when you are claustrophobic, so that you are disposed to feel extreme fear whenever you find yourself in a confined space. But emotional dispositions need not lead to anything problematic, for you might well be disposed to feel fear directed at things that are such as to merit a fear reaction, so that your reactions will be nothing less than fully adjusted to the world.

One important difference between an emotional episode of fear and its underlying disposition concerns its temporality. As we have seen, emotional episodes tend to be rather short-lived. It follows that they occur at a certain time, while emotional dispositions do not take place at a certain time. Thus, they can be considered to be states that are standing. Even so, emotional dispositions can be acquired and lost, so that they characterize persons for a given duration, often for long periods of their life, but not necessarily for the entire stretch of their life. You might become claustrophobic after having been trapped in an elevator when a teenager, and this phobia might well be one with which you have to cope for the rest of your life. Importantly, however, you might succeed in rooting out your phobia, so it would be wrong to believe that emotional dispositions cannot change. The good news is that in spite of being standing states, emotional dispositions are somewhat plastic (for more on this, see Chapters 3 and 12).

Another difference between emotional episodes and emotional dispositions is that as we have seen, the former typically involve phenomenal properties while the former do not, according to most accounts, come with phenomenal properties. The disposition to feel disgust at decaying corpses will only involve feelings when it manifests itself, that is, only when you are confronted with a decaying corpse and feel disgust. In the same way, it might be argued that emotional dispositions only involve the other features of emotions indirectly, because their manifestations involve these features. Thus, emotional dispositions would involve motivations only insofar as their manifestations involve motivations, they would only involve intentional objects insofar as their manifestations involve intentional objects, and they would involve appraisals only insofar as their manifestations would. According to another possible account, however, emotional dispositions can be thought to involve representations regarding kinds of objects and kinds of responses. For instance, the disposition to feel disgust would involve an implicit representation that decaying crabs and other similar objects, such as decaying corpses or rotten cabbages, should trigger a disgust reaction. If so, emotional dispositions would consist in standing states that involve representations and hence would possess intentional objects of their own.

In any case, it is often thought that because emotional dispositions can at least in part be understood in terms of emotional episodes, emotional episodes should be the primary focus of philosophers. This is not to say, of course, that emotional dispositions are not interesting in their own right, particularly because changing them is fundamental to changes in our emotional responses (see Chapter 12). In any case, it is very common to use the term "emotion" to refer to emotional episodes, and this is also how I will use the term (for a different use, see Wollheim 1999; Goldie 2000).

It is commonly agreed that there are different kinds of emotional dispositions (see Broad 1954; Frijda 1994a; Deonna and Teroni 2012). Some emotional dispositions concern one kind of emotion and are thus called "singletrack dispositions". By contrast, other emotional dispositions involve several kinds of emotions. Such multitrack dispositions are often called "sentiments". The disposition to experience disgust at certain types of things and claustrophobia are examples of singletrack dispositions. A good example of multitrack dispositions is the sentiment of love, understood as the disposition to undergo a number of emotions of different kinds, depending on how things stand – joy when you are close to the beloved, sadness when being separated from them, worried when they are in danger, angry at someone who insulted them, proud of their achievements, etc. (see Naar 2013b). Moral sentiments, such as moral disapproval, are often thought to consist in multitrack dispositions or else to consist in standing states that involve multitrack dispositions. For you morally to disapprove of lying, on such an account, involves being disposed to feel to guilt or remorse if you lie, to feel anger or indignation if another person lies, to feel admiration for someone who never lies, and so on (Prinz 2007).

Sentiments such as love are focused on people or types of things. Other emotional dispositions have values as their focus. Consider honesty. An honest person will be disposed, among other things, to undergo a number of emotions. Insofar as honest persons value truth, they will be disposed to be distressed or angered by dishonesty, to despise those who succeed by dishonest means, to admire those who are honest in spite of the risks they take, to be delighted when honesty triumphs, and so on (see Chapter 10). Now, honesty is commonly considered to be a morally admirable trait, a virtue. According to an influential account, which goes back to Aristotle, virtues as well as vices involve such multitrack emotional dispositions, in addition to other kinds of dispositions, such as dispositions that lead to actions. But multitrack emotional dispositions that focus on values need not amount to virtues or vices. If you are a facetious individual, for instance, you will focus on the value of amusement. You will be disposed to treat even serious things with humor, so you will tend to feel amusement when attending serious events, to rejoice when others feel amusement at serious events, to regret that things are taken seriously, and so on. Dispositions such as honesty and facetiousness are generally considered to be *character traits*, that is, traits that taken together make up the person you are.

We have seen that there are reasons to distinguish between emotional episodes and different kinds of emotional dispositions, that is, singletrack dispositions, such as the disposition to feel fear when confronting dogs, multitrack dispositions that concern objects or persons, such as the sentiment of love, and multitrack dispositions that are focused on values, such as the character trait of honesty. Now, a further concept that is commonly thought to be distinct is that of mood. Let us therefore turn to the question of what moods are and how they are related to emotional episodes – or for short, *emotions*, as I will say from now on.

2.7. Moods

Prototypical examples of moods include anxiety, irritability, elation, and sadness. As should be obvious from this enumeration, there seems to be a straightforward correlation between such states and emotional episodes. Fear and anxiety, anger and irritability, happiness, and elation and the emotion of sadness and the mood of sadness undeniably form pairs. Do all moods have matching emotions? The answer might well be negative, for it is not clear that there is a mood corresponding to the emotion of disgust, and it is quite clear that there is no mood that would correspond to surprise. In fact, some kinds of moods, such as laziness or impatience, do not seem to have an emotional correlate. In any case, moods and emotions appear to be distinct, but closely correlated phenomena. Indeed, moods and emotions appear to share important features.

The first point to note is that moods and emotions are both characterized by similar phenomenal properties. For instance, when you are anxious, what you feel is reminiscent of what you feel when you experience fear, and when you are irritable, what you feel is reminiscent of what you feel when you are angry. As is often underlined, one aspect that distinguishes moods from emotions is that the feelings that characterize moods involve a kind of diffuseness (see Frijda 1994a). This diffuseness is sometimes explained in terms of the claim that moods seem less intense, compared to emotions. Indeed, it can seem that moods differ from emotions merely in terms of intensity and duration, moods being thought to last longer than typical emotions. Now, is it surely true that being in an irritable mood involves less intense feelings than experiencing anger, but one should not forget that moods allow for important variations in intensity, ranging from low-intensity anxiety to extreme anxiety, for instance. By contrast, emotions need not be intense. You can feel mild fear when you think of the prospect of meeting a new colleague, for instance. Moreover, moods can be, and often are, fleeting – your irritability on waking up after a short night might disappear as soon as you have had your first coffee – and, as we have seen, emotions need not be short-lived.

An important difference between moods and emotions, which has been underscored by many, is that the former do not seem to directly motivate action.

As we have seen, an experience of fear typically comes with a motivation. By contrast, the mood of anxiety typically seems to fail to involve motivation even if it usually gives rise to expressive behavior, such a drumming the table with your finger out of irritability (see Goldie 2000). In fact, moods are generally thought to have far-reaching, global effects on our psychological lives (see Price 2006). Mood influences what we think, notably in that there is a marked tendency to make mood-congruent judgments, and they also have an impact on attentional processes, memory tasks, and categorization tasks.

The most striking difference between moods and emotions, however, concerns their intentionality. By contrast with emotions, moods do not seem to be directed at particular objects. When you are in an irritable mood, you are not irritable about or towards something. All the same, it is not clear that moods entirely lack intentional objects. Moods seem to concern things globally. To put it paradoxically, moods seem to be both about nothing and everything (Goldie 2000).

To account for these features, some theorists have proposed that moods are not occurrent but dispositional states (see Griffiths 1997). As noted by many, the problem with this approach is that it cannot make room for the fact that moods involve feelings (see Prinz 2004). Thus, according to the approach that is most popular among philosophers, moods are not dispositional but occurrent states. The difference with emotions would come from intentionality. By contrast with emotions, which would concern specific objects, moods would concern more general objects, such as the world as a whole, or maybe more plausibly, most things in your environment (see Solomon 1976/1993; Prinz 2004). On such an account, it is natural to assume that moods, like emotions, involve appraisals and formal objects. Indeed, the formal objects of moods and emotions would be correlated. For instance, the mood of anxiety and fear would both have danger as their formal objects, and the appraisals that are involved would concern dangerousness. One difficulty with this view is that as a result, most moods would have to be considered as involving an error (Deonna and Teroni 2012). Surely the world is rarely such as to be entirely dangerous. Furthermore, it would seem that we can feel emotions regarding pretty general objects. As we have seen, we can be afraid of a pack of wolves and we can despise humankind. Thus, it is not clear that when you fear the world, or most things in your environment, you are experiencing a mood and not an ordinary emotion.

There might be better ways to spell out the characteristic intentionality of moods, for instance in terms of epistemically undetermined objects (Rossi 2021) or else of likelihoods (Price 2006) or of evaluative possibilities (Tappolet 2018), but because moods involve feelings, it seems clear is that they must be occurrent states. Given this, it is natural to accept that in addition to occurrent mood states, there are dispositional mood states. An example of such a mood propensity would be the tendency to feel anxiety. Such mood propensities appear to define the *temperament* of individuals. If you have a happy temperament, for instance, you will tend often to feel moods of happiness. And it goes without saying that this will also result in you tending to feel emotions of joy or happiness.

With this in mind, let us look back at the question we raised when considering the intentionality of emotions. We asked whether all emotions have intentional objects and considered putative exceptions, like happiness. Happiness and anxiety, we said, could be about nothing in particular. To avoid such counterexamples, we considered the possibility of ruling them out by stating that such states are moods, not emotions. Emotions would by definitional fiat be states that have intentional objects. Now, one might wonder whether our discussion of moods constitutes a threat to this strategy. It might seem as if the strategy depends on an understanding of moods as dispositional states, which lack intentional objects. As we have seen, however, accounts of moods in terms of dispositions are not satisfactory. On reflection, however, the strategy is not threatened. It is perfectly consistent to adopt this strategy regarding the use of the term "emotions" while holding that states like the feeling of happiness are kinds of mood, which are not about something or other in particular, but which concern a different kind of object, such as the world.

There are other affective phenomena in addition to those we have discussed so far. Desires, pleasures, displeasures, and pains are often mentioned in lists of affects. As we will see when considering motivational theories of emotions, desires and emotions are generally taken to differ in terms of their direction of fit (Searle 1983). Desires have a world-to-mind direction of fit, in the sense that it is the world that has to change in order to fit the desire, while emotions have a mind-to-world direction of fit, which means that it is the emotion that has to fit how things are (see Chapter 5). What about pleasures and displeasures? Some pleasures and displeasures clearly seem to consist in emotions. One can be pleased or displeased by the weather just as one can hope that the weather will improve or fear that it will deteriorate. Indeed, being pleased or displeased by something or other appears to bear the main hallmarks of emotions. Such states involve feelings and they concern intentional objects, which are appraised positively or negatively, so that it is likely that some motivation will ensue. Moreover, it is plausible to hold that being pleasurable or displeasurable are the formal objects of pleasures and displeasures. All this seems to apply to *sensory* pleasures and displeasures. Consider the pleasure you take in the taste of an espresso. It is plausible to claim that pleasures of this kind are in fact affective states that concern sensations and their pleasurableness (Rossi 2018). Similarly, states such as the displeasure in touching an icy surface are plausibly taken to concern sensations and their displeasurableness. Maybe sensory pleasures and sensory displeasures are not full-blown emotions, but they seem to share important features with emotions. Whether this conclusion holds for pain depends on how one conceives of the relation between pain and displeasure. Because some pains allegedly do not hurt, there is reason to doubt that pains are identical to sensory displeasures (see Grahek 2007; Bain 2014).

Before closing this chapter, let me say something about what might give the impression of a big lacuna in the account so far: *passions*. Now, as most of the terms we have discussed in this chapter – think of "affect", "emotion" and "sentiment", for instance – the term "passion" not only has a rich history but it also had several meanings over the centuries. Contemporary theorists often consider the term to be merely an ancient way to refer to emotions, one that emphasizes the passivity of such states. What should not be overlooked is that in ordinary language the term "passion" can refer to an intense and barely controllable emotion or desire, such as when we speak of love in terms of an all-consuming passion. In addition, the term can refer to a durable interest, which plays a central role in a person's life, such as when we say that you have a passion for music or for philosophy.

2.8. Taking Stock

In order to home in on affective states and more precisely on emotions, we looked at several claims that are commonly thought to be true of emotions. We concluded that it is plausible that prototypical emotions, such as fear and anger, typically involve phenomenal properties and motivations. We also saw that episodes of such emotions typically have intentional objects, which are appraised in evaluative terms – what we fear, for instance, being appraised as dangerous. Evaluative properties like that of being dangerous are generally considered to constitute the formal objects of emotions, in the sense that they determine when an emotion is fitting or not. Accordingly, it seems true that emotions typically have formal objects. Finally, we saw that typical emotions such as fear and anger are plausibly taken to be short-lived. These claims might not be true in virtue of the concepts they involve, but they are nonetheless highly plausible. Indeed, they appear to constitute putative conceptual truths. We also saw that emotional dispositions, or "sentiments", differ from emotional episodes in that the former do not come with phenomenal properties and typically last for longer periods of time. As to moods, they differ from emotions in terms of the kind of intentional object they take. Moods seem to be both about nothing in particular and everything.

Now that we have a better idea of what emotions typically involve, we are ready to tackle a question that is particularly intricate, namely, the question of whether emotions are determined by culture or by nature.

2.9. Summary

- According to dual process theories, intuitive processes differ from reflective processes. Even if emotions are usually considered to belong to the intuitive side, a good question is where to locate emotions that depend on thoughts.
- Episodes of prototypical emotions, such as fear, anger, etc., typically involve feelings, motivations, intentional objects, appraisals, and formal objects. Moreover, they tend to be rather short-lived, even if they often last for more than seconds or minutes.
- Emotional episodes – or for short "emotions" – are occurrent states, by contrast with emotional dispositions.

- Emotional dispositions can be singletrack or multitrack. A singletrack emotional disposition consists in the disposition to experience a particular kind of emotion, such as fear, on certain occasions. Multitrack dispositions, which are often called "sentiments", involve several kinds of emotions; they can concern things or persons, but they can also concern values.
- Moods are typically characterized by affective feelings, but they differ from emotions in that they do not seem to be about particular objects. According to many, moods concern global objects, such as the world.
- Temperaments can be thought to be mood propensities.

2.10. Study Questions

1. Should we count hunger as an affective state, and if so, should hunger be considered to be an emotion? If not, what are the differences between hunger and prototypical emotions?
2. If fear can be felt for days or months, what should we say about the times when you are asleep? Can you be afraid and more generally have emotions only when you are awake?
3. Do all kinds of emotions correspond to kinds of moods? For instance, is there a mood that corresponds to the emotion of disgust?

2.11. Further Readings

Ben-Ze'ev, Aaron. 2001. *The Subtlety of Emotions*. Cambridge, MA: MIT Press, chap. 3.

Deonna, Julien A., and Klaus R. Scherer. 2010. "The Case of the Disappearing Intentional Object: Constraints on a Definition of Emotion." *Emotion Review* 2 (1):44–52.

Deonna, Julien A., and Fabrice Teroni. 2012. *The Emotions: A Philosophical Introduction*. Abingdon: Routledge, chap. 1.

Ekman, Paul. 1994. "Moods, Emotions, and Traits." In *The Nature of Emotion: Fundamental Questions*, edited by Paul Ekman and Richard J. Davidson, 56–58. New York: Oxford University Press.

Evans, Jonathan St. B. T., and Keith E. Stanovich. 2013. "Dual-Process Theories of Higher Cognition: Advancing the Debate." *Perspectives on Psychological Science* 8 (3):223–241.

Frijda, Nico H. 1994a. "Varieties of Affect: Emotions and Episodes, Moods and Sentiments." In *The Nature of Emotion: Fundamental Questions*, edited by Paul Ekman and Richard J. Davidson, 59–67. Oxford: Oxford University Press.

Naar, Hichem. Forthcoming. "What Ontology for Emotions?" In *Routledge Handbook of Emotion Theory*, edited by Andrea Scarantino. New York: Routledge.

Price, Carolyn. 2006. "Affect Without Object: Moods and Objectless Emotions." *European Journal of Analytic Philosophy* 2 (1):49–68.

Rossi, Mauro. 2018. "Happiness, Pleasures, and Emotions." *Philosophical Psychology* 31 (6):898–919.

Teroni, Fabrice. 2007. "Emotions and Formal Objects." *Dialectica* 61 (3):395–415.

3   Are Emotions Social Constructs?

3.1. Introduction

Imagine you travel through space and time to the small Italian city of Verona as it was in the Renaissance, the scene of one of the most celebrated couples, Romeo and Juliet. Their story is that of love at first sight, of intense and tragic romance. When Romeo Montague and Juliet Capulet, both in their teens, first catch a glimpse of each other, they instantly fall in love. It takes them less than 24 hours secretly to marry, despite the violent feud that divides the two families. They can spend only one night together before tragedy unfolds. Forced by her family to consent to marrying someone else, Juliet takes a potion to induce a deathlike coma. Mistaking Juliet's coma for death, Romeo commits suicide, upon which Juliet stabs herself out of despair. End of the story.

Our fascination with such dramatic narratives is something that should give us pause (we will come back to this question in Chapter 12). In any case, such stories tell us a lot about our shared conceptions of love and the way these conceptions change over time and across cultures. Obviously, our conceptions of what love involves have a history. What about love itself, one might wonder? It would seem that the love is a natural phenomenon, which universally characterizes human beings. But is this really so? Against the claim that love is pancultural, some hold that love is, in fact, a social invention. According to C. S. Lewis (1936; see also Bloch 1992), for instance, the birth of romantic love can be located in late 11th-century southern France, within a specific social and cultural context, in which court troubadours composed songs to celebrate the bravery of knights who were seeking to please their mistresses. What has come to be known as "courtly love" comes with a number of rules, which codify what we say, think and do when in love. For instance, courtly love strictly rules out loving more than one person. Similarly, true love is taken to involve jealousy – "he who is not jealous cannot love", as the saying goes. On Lewis' account, Guinevere and Lancelot of the Lake, the dragon-slaying Knight of the Round Table, but also Juliet and Romeo, and you and your lover, follow similar rules, unwittingly impersonating the script spelled out by the troubadours.

Quite generally, one can wonder whether affective states, as distinct from our conceptions of such states, are the products of culture. Maybe affective states are

DOI: 10.4324/9781315542300-4

like money or gender, that is, aggregates of basic elements that hang together in virtue of conventional and largely arbitrary rules disseminated by culture. The question, in other words, is whether affective states are *social constructs*. This question arises for each of the different kinds of affective state. In particular, it can be raised for both emotional episodes, such as the fear you felt the other day when looking down from a cliff, and emotional dispositions, whether they be simple, such as your disposition to be afraid of heights, or multitrack, such as the love Juliet feels for Romeo. In this chapter, the focus will mainly be on emotional episodes.

Social constructionism with regard to affective states contrasts with *biological determinism*, the view that the emotions we feel depend on innate features of our psychology, which are conceived as the result of evolutionary selection. As the discussion will show, neither the arguments for biological determinism nor the ones for social constructionism are convincing. Unsurprisingly, the truth lies somewhere in the middle. The emotions we feel are the product of both nature and culture, and the question is how these two forces interact.

3.2. Biological Determinism

Unlike social constructionism, biological determinism claims that there are pancultural emotional kinds, which are present in all human populations. According to biological determinism, emotions of this kind depend on psychological dispositions written into our genetic makeup. On this account, which goes back to Darwin's work on the universality of emotional expression (Darwin 1872), pancultural emotional dispositions are evolutionary adaptations, which result from natural selection. Even if at the periphery, our emotions are subject to a good measure of cultural influence, biological determinism holds that the core of our emotional dispositions is fixed by natural selection. The corresponding emotional episodes are thought to constitute efficient ways to meet the challenges our ancestors faced in the Pleistocene, thus helping them to promote their genes. These challenges include "[f]ighting, falling in love, escaping predators, confronting sexual infidelity, experiencing a failure-driven loss in status, responding to the death of a family member [...]" (Tooby and Cosmides 2000, 92; see also Ekman 1999).

There are two main sorts of biological determinist accounts, depending on the intended scope of the theory. The first is *basic emotion theory*, which dates back to the 1970s and is associated with psychologists Paul Ekman (1972) and Caroll Izard (1971), neurologist Jaak Panksepp (1998) as well as philosophers Paul Griffiths (1997) and Andrea Scarantino (2014), among others. Basic emotion theorists hold that biological determinism is true of only of a limited number of emotional kinds, the *basic emotions*, which we share with other animals. By contrast, evolutionary psychologists, such as Robert Frank (1988) or John Tooby and Leda Cosmides (1990, 2000), favor evolutionary accounts not only of basic emotions, but also of *nonbasic emotions*, or so-called *higher cognitive emotions*, such as love, jealousy or guilt, which they regard as unique to our species.

Let us focus first on basic emotion theory. Ekman's initial list of basic emotional kinds was limited to six items: anger, disgust, fear, happiness, sadness, and surprise (Ekman 1972). It is noteworthy that Ekman later proposed a longer list of 15 basic emotional kinds: amusement, anger, contempt, contentment, disgust, embarrassment, excitement, fear, guilt, pride in achievement, relief, sadness, satisfaction, sensory pleasure, and shame (Ekman 1999). Panksepp proposed a less orthodox list of seven items: care, fear, lust, panic, play, rage, and seeking (Panksepp 2000), while Izard's list comprised ten items: anger, contempt, disgust, distress, fear, guilt, interest, joy, shame, and surprise (Izard 1971).

On all these accounts, it is crucial to distinguish between basic and nonbasic emotions. This distinction raises the question whether the two kinds of states are sufficiently similar to belong to the same family. Paul Griffiths (1997), for one, holds that basic emotions and nonbasic emotions are too different to belong to the same natural kind. Against this claim, most theorists agree that basic and nonbasic emotions share enough features to count as belonging to the same general psychological category, whether or not this corresponds to a natural kind (see Roberts 2003; Prinz 2004; Deonna and Teroni 2012). Obviously, the question, to which we will return, of whether basic and nonbasic emotions belong to the same category depends on how the two are taken to relate to each to other (see Section 3.7.).

According to basic emotions theorists, basic emotional episodes are taken to consist in reflex-like cascades of complex and coordinated changes, which result from automatic appraisals. These changes include facial and vocal expressions, action tendencies, physiological changes at the level of the autonomic nervous system, such as increased heartbeat, as well as retrieval of memories and expectations. The theory holds that the underlying *affect programs*, which give rise to emotional episodes, are associated with hardwired neural circuits. Basic emotion theory emphasizes the specific action tendencies of each basic emotion type. Fear, for instance, is seen as involving action tendencies like flight or freeze, while anger is claimed to involve attack.

In general, these affect programs are thought to be mostly fixed and automatic, but biological determinists can allow for a certain amount of flexibility in the responses. Indeed, relatively flexible action tendencies appear more adaptive, compared to fixed patterns of responses (Nesse 1990; Griffiths 1997). Thus, biological determinists can agree that the environment plays a role in shaping our emotions. Biological determinists can also agree that cultures partly shape how we react. For instance, Ekman holds that the facial expression of emotions depends on culturally determined norms. An influential study thus shows that the facial expression of Japanese and American subjects watching a film featuring surgical procedures aimed at triggering disgust showed equal disgust when the subjects were left alone, but the Japanese subjects showed less disgust when in the presence of an authority figure. Facial expression thus appears to depend on *display rules* (Ekman and Friesen 1971).

Furthermore, biological determinists commonly agree that the elicitors of basic emotions depend on both the environment and the culture of individuals.

What caused fear in our hunter-gatherer ancestors, such as angry mammoths and other wild animals, is obviously different from what causes fear in our culture, since mammoths are extinct and at least the urban ones among us rarely come face to face with wild animals roaming freely. By contrast, we have to deal with careless drivers, nuclear weapons, and climate change. However, biological determinists hold that each basic emotion depends on an appraisal mechanism that is set to evaluate a small group of stimuli in certain ways – babies seem predisposed to be afraid of loud noises, for instance (Damasio 1994). Because individuals are naturally predisposed to learn to react in certain ways to certain conditions, a number of eliciting conditions can easily be added to innate stimuli (Öhman and Mineka 2001). As a result of this kind of *learning preparedness* (Seligman 1970), we would easily learn to associate spiders and heights with fear, by contrast with historically more recent stimuli like electrical outlets and guns, which are less easily associated with fear. Moreover, once the correlations between spiders and fear are in place, they would be more difficult to undo, compared to the ones between electrical outlets or guns and fear. Similarly, rhesus monkeys easily learn to be afraid of snakes after having observed fear reactions to snakes by other rhesus monkeys, but they fail to do so when the fear reactions are directed at a flower or a toy rabbit (Öhman and Mineka 2001).

Let us look at the evidence for basic emotion theory.

3.3. The Evidence for Basic Emotion Theory

The strongest support for pancultural emotions comes from studies on facial expressions. Other bodies of evidence, which involve neurological considerations and genetic inheritance considerations, remain controversial (see Prinz 2004, chap. 5; Barrett 2006). Let us thus consider the former. In a particularly famous study, Ekman and his collaborator Wallace Friesen (1971) investigated facial expressions among the Fore people, a preliterate group in the highlands of Papua New Guinea, which had only little contact with Western culture before the study. After having been told stories about various emotion-eliciting events, such as the death of a child or an encounter with a friend, the Fore subjects had to select one among three photographs of stereotyped facial expressions as mimicked by actors. The Fore subjects, which involved 189 adults and 130 children, had to select the expression that best fit the story – a frowning face for the story about the death of a child, for instance. The study involved stories and facial expressions for the six basic emotions postulated by Ekman (see Figure 3.1). The Fore subjects' choices did not significantly differ from the choices made by American subjects even if they tended to fail to distinguish between the expression of surprise and that of fear. Only a bit less than half of the adult Fore subjects chose the expression of fear when the face expressing surprise was among the three options from which to choose, though 80 percent of them made the "right" choice when the face expressing surprise was not an alternative. In general, 68 percent of the subjects selected the "right" facial expressions for surprise-eliciting stories, 79 percent did so for sadness-eliciting stories, and

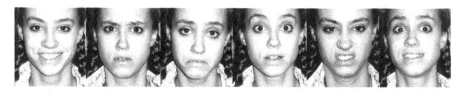

Figure 3.1 Facial expressions of joy, anger, sadness, surprise, disgust, and fear (Prinz 2004, 107).

92 percent did so for happiness-eliciting stories. From this and a number of similar studies, Ekman concluded that the facial expressions of basic emotions are pancultural and hence that basic emotions themselves are pancultural. These results strongly suggest that basic emotions are innate, since innateness seems the best explanation for their being pancultural.

These conclusions from research on facial expression have been the object of sustained criticism. The main worries relate to the methodology that is used. As psychologist James Russell (1994; see also Gendron, Crivelli, and Barrett 2018) has argued, the problem is that studies like the one with the Fore rely on forced-choice: the subject had to choose between a set of only three facial expressions – one correct and two incorrect ones – something which obviously reinforces the impression of agreement with Western choices. If emotions were pancultural, one would expect a higher percentage of cross-cultural agreement than those observed in such studies, given the forced-choice method. Studies letting the subject choose any emotion term to describe a facial expression resulted in much weaker correlations.

In reply, Ekman (1994) argued that agreement across culture is nonetheless much more important than if the correlations between emotions and facial expression were purely arbitrary. This seems plausible. At least to a certain extent, at least a number of emotions appear typically accompanied by characteristic facial expressions. But the problem is that the conclusion that this claim warrants is weaker than what basic emotions theory needs. As Jesse Prinz makes clear (2004; see also Reisenzein, Studtmann, and Horstmann 2013), what follows from the claim that the correlation between emotions and facial expression is not purely arbitrary is only that emotions have a biological basis, in the sense that their development is partly constrained by emotion-specific neural structures, a claim which is considerably weaker than what basic emotion theorists hold.

Another criticism focuses on the function of facial expressions. Basic emotion theorists agree that the function of a smile or a pout is to communicate to others how we feel – happy or disgusted, as the case might be. Given this, one might wonder why natural selection would have favored automatic expressions of emotions. It is surely neither in your interest nor in your genes' interest to show your competitors that you are afraid of them. Indeed, facial expressions vary much more than basic emotion theorists might have thought. Olympic athletes, for instance, do not tend to smile just after winning a gold medal, but they do so when they stand on the podium and face the audience (Fernàndez-Dols and

Ruis-Belda 1995). According to Alan Fridlund (1994), this kind of evidence shows that smiling is not the expression of happiness. The commonalities we find in facial expression, Fridlund argues, can be accounted for by social learning involving imitation.

In reply to these objections, Ekman (1997) has argued that social approval might well be an elicitor of happiness, so that we can expect the athlete to express genuine happiness on the podium. The main point he makes, however, is that facial expression can serve to communicate what one intends to do precisely because these expressions have a tight connection to what we feel. If we did not tend to smile to express happiness, it would be a mystery that this is what athletes do when they face the audience. This reply seems reasonable, but again it appears insufficient to defend basic emotion theory. The reason is that this explanation of how facial expressions have the function to communicate our intentions is perfectly compatible with the claim that facial expressions are the product of both a natural, innate tendency and social learning. Such a dual influence does not rule out a connection between what we feel and what we express, which can account for the communicative function of facial expressions.

Basic emotion theorists assume that the elicitation of each type of emotion comes with a specific neural pattern and specific bodily changes at the level of the autonomic nervous system. In a striking study, Ekman and his colleagues (1983) attempted to gather evidence for the so-called *facial feedback hypothesis*, which holds that the facial expressions of basic emotions induce specific bodily changes. They gave muscle-by-muscle instructions to subjects so that they could form the facial expressions of basic emotions and asked the subjects to hold each of these expressions for ten seconds. Remarkably, merely mimicking the facial expressions of basic emotions resulted in bodily changes. Ekman reported that the expressions of anger, fear, and sadness correlated with a faster heart rate compared to the expressions of happiness, surprise, and disgust, while the expression of fear and sadness came with colder finger temperature compared to the expression of anger. By contrast, skin conductance and arm tension did not distinguish the several expressions. Similar results were confirmed in different studies, and a meta-analysis concluded that the effect of facial feedback on emotional experience is significant if small (Coles, Larsen, and Lench 2019).

What can we conclude from such studies? As Lisa Feldman Barrett (2017) notes, Ekman's study fails to show that each kind of emotion has its own bodily pattern. More generally, Barrett argues that the comparison of studies attempting to correlate emotions and bodily changes by directly triggering emotions via horror movies, for instance, suggests that types of emotions do not correlate with specific patterns. She points out that different studies found different patterns of bodily changes for each basic emotion.

The question to raise here is how much variation can reasonably be expected. Fear, for instance, allows for subtypes, such as panic in the case of imminent attack and anxiety in the case of impending danger, which come with very different responses, including flight, fight, and freeze, depending on the context (Nesse 1990; Prinz 2004). Because these responses depend on distinct bodily changes, one should not expect that fear comes with exactly the same type of bodily pattern. Even so, pattern classification performed by machine-learning algorithms suggests that there are distinct patterns of bodily responses corresponding to emotions such as surprise, fear, anger, and sadness (Kragel and LaBar 2013; but see Siegel et al. 2018).

Much the same is true of studies that attempt to show that emotions have specific patterns in the brain. The amygdala has long been considered the hub of fear (Ledoux 1996), but this primitive brain structure is also involved in anger, disgust, sadness, and happiness, as shown in the meta-analysis conducted by a student of Barrett, Kristen Lindquist (Lindquist et al. 2012). As such, this does not rule out that basic emotions correlate with neural patterns. However, Barrett holds that more generally, the comparison of neurological studies strongly suggests that emotion types fail to correlate with specific brain patterns.

A plausible suggestion here is that instead of looking for a single pattern for each emotion type, one should look out for patterns of patterns, thereby making room for a good measure of variability. Even so, the evidence for neural correlates is mixed. As in the case of bodily correlates, pattern classification methods have been used to show that there are correlated patterns in the brain corresponding to emotions such as surprise, fear, anger, and sadness (Kragel and LaBar 2016). It would be premature, however, to conclude that biological determinism is warranted (Díaz 2019). The main reason is that the similarities among brain activations that form the patterns are consistent with an account of emotion according to which cultural influences affect not merely the surface but the core of emotions.

Another source of evidence for basic emotion theory comes from studies regarding the emotions of nonhuman animals and human infants. There is evidence that human infants have facial expressions of emotions such as fear or happiness, and this is true even if they are born blind (Matsumoto and Willingham 2009). Moreover, facial and especially bodily expression of emotions as well as typical motivation show impressive continuity across human and nonhuman animals. As Darwin (1872) observed and as we can readily see on dogs and cats, the hair of both human and nonhuman animals bristles when in fear. Similarly, fear comes with flight, fight, or freeze behavior, as well as with tonic immobility, a reaction that involves a slowing down of cardiac activity and respiration, as well as a decrease in bodily temperature, and which results in a paralysis that is close to death even though consciousness is maintained. These behaviors characterize both human and nonhuman fears. For instance, tonic immobility, which is common in human beings when they face severe danger, has been observed in a number of mammals, birds, fish, and insects (Archer 1979).

However, even if there are important continuities between nonhuman animals, human infants and adult human facial expressions and behaviors, this fails to show that basic emotions are innate structures that we share with other species. First, it is not obvious that the facial expressions of human infants have the same function as the corresponding adult expressions. The expression that corresponds to adult surprise, for instance, is observed in infants viewing familiar stimuli (Camras 1994). Similarly, what we observe in nonhuman animals are important similarities, but this does not warrant the conclusion that nonhuman emotions are identical with human emotions. What these similarities entail is only that our emotions are close cousins to those emotions of other animals.

The general lesson to draw from these different arguments is, as Prinz (2004) notes, that biology has a significant impact on human emotions, but that nothing rules out that culture also has a significant impact, one that might well go beyond what basic emotion theorists acknowledge. It might well be the case that the core of emotions, and not only their soft outer parts, is subject to cultural influences.

What about the arguments offered by evolutionary psychologists?

3.4. The Evidence from Evolutionary Psychology

As we have seen, evolutionary psychologists have a more ambitious program. What they envisage are evolutionary accounts not only of a limited set of emotions, but of all our emotions, including emotions that are arguably unique to humans. Thus, John Tooby and Leda Cosmides hold that it follows from adaptive thinking that "[e]ach functionally distinct emotion state – fear of predators, guilt, sexual jealousy, rage, grief, and so on – will correspond to an integrated mode of operation that functions as a solution designed to take advantage of the recurrent situation or triggering condition to which that emotion corresponds" (2000, 101). Even if Tooby and Cosmides are sympathetic to basic affect theory, their account aims at covering emotions that are unlike the reflex-like basic emotions in that they are integrated into cognitive processes and planned action.

This approach is well illustrated by Robert Frank's (1988) account of romantic love. According to Frank, who is, incidentally, an economist, emotions are *irruptive motivations*, which serve the interest of individuals by allowing them to overcome cooperation problems. Emotions do so by committing us to courses of actions that seem irrational in terms of personal interest, but which in fact allow us to promote our long-term interest. More specifically, Frank holds that romantic love is nature's solution what he calls "the commitment problem". When we try to find a partner, we can never be sure that the one we consider is the best we can find. Of course, much the same is true of any possible partner. Thus, given the risk of losing out by investing in a relationship without harvesting as much reward as we can, it is rational to prefer not to commit to a relationship. However, by failing to commit, we reduce the chance that our genes replicate. As a result, the sad fact is that individuals who were unable to commit themselves to a relationship died out. By contrast, the individuals who were equipped with a solution to the commitment problem, that is, individuals who were disposed to romantic love, flourished and spread their genes. Put differently, nature's solution to the commitment problem involved in personal relations consists in making us fall in love, thereby inducing long-term commitment and making us forget about the possibility of better partners. By creating a kind of illusion, romantic love thus tends to increase the reproduction of our genes. And that is why we are born equipped with a tendency to fall in love. As a result, Frank concludes that romantic love must be an innate emotion kind found in any human beings. It is noteworthy that a similar account is offered by the anthropologist Helen Fisher (2004), who holds that romantic love is a fundamental drive that evolved because it allows men and women to focus their mating attention on a preferred individual, thereby minimizing courtship time and energy.

Is this account convincing? An important problem with Frank's evolutionary story about romantic love is that it concludes that love is an evolutionary adaptation from the observation that it is useful to be equipped with love. However, as Paul Griffiths (1997) explains, such an inference is not warranted. The general problem with explanations offered by evolutionary psychology is that it is as easy to come up with a story about how a useful feature could have resulted from natural selection as it is hard to support the claim that a feature is actually the product of natural selection. In fact, stories about adaptations work as inferences to the best explanations. The idea is that the best explanation of why we have a useful feature is that it results from natural selection. The difficulty, however, is that alternative explanations, which do not appeal to natural selection, are very often just as good. Evolutionary adaptation stories, often called "just-so stories", are explanations that *would* explain some observed trait *if* the assumption that the trait results from selection were true. However, when alternative stories explain the observed trait equally well, there is no reason to embrace the evolutionary explanation.

Independently of this, however, there are problems with Frank's account. It might seem that this account degrades love in that it reduces it to a useful device, but in fact, as Jesse Prinz notes (2004), the worry is rather that Frank assumes a Western conception of love. The idea that love involves a desire for long-term commitment, in particular, is not one that is panculturally shared. In Chinese culture, for instance, love is associated with short-term affairs, as opposed to the kind of attitudes encouraged in marriage, such as trust and friendship. If there is any truth in the Chinese conception of love, then love need not come with a desire for long-term relationship. In the absence of such a desire, however, love will not solve any commitment problem. Maybe romantic love solves the commitment problem in the West, but given the cultural variations in what love involves, there is no reason to assume that love is the product of natural selection.

More generally, evolutionary psychologists have a hard time showing that the explanations they offer are the best ones. In many cases, there are at least equally good explanations on offer. For instance, Prinz (2004) considers jealousy and discusses several alternative explanations to the one favored by evolutionary psychologists, according to which these emotions evolved to maximize the success of our genes. Evolutionary psychologists explain the alleged prevalence of jealousy in women by the thought that women tend to care about emotional infidelity because this helps to ensure that their male partners help rear their children, thus promoting their genes. By contrast, because men can never be certain to be the father of a child, the theory holds that men care more about sexual infidelity. However, this pattern can well be explained by appealing to economic differences. In most cultures, men have more economic power. As a result, emotional infidelity comes to a higher cost to women than to men. Men would thus prefer emotional infidelity to sexual infidelity, assuming men and women value sex equally.

To show that an evolutionary explanation of a particular emotion is not the best, it is necessary to compare it with its contenders. Because this has to be done with each emotion, this strategy cannot easily be put in place. However, a more general problem for evolutionary psychology is that this approach needs to assume that emotions closely correlate with classes of eliciting stimuli. For the explanations to work, it must be the case that the eliciting conditions that caused an emotion like fear or jealousy in the Pleistocene are roughly the same now. The problem, as stressed by Griffiths (1997), is that emotions do not embody knowledge of the past in such a determinate form. A theory needs to make room, as does, for instance, the basic emotion theory, for the fact that even if appraisal mechanisms might be set to evaluate a small group of stimuli in certain ways, the class of relevant stimuli changes depending on the learning path of individuals.

Evolutionary psychology postulates little cross-cultural variability in our emotional reactions. The main problem with the account offered by evolutionary psychology, thus, is that human emotions vary importantly across cultures. As Prinz (2004) reports, an emotion like jealousy varies considerably depending on the culture in which individuals are born. For instance, Toda people, a small ethnic group who live in the Nilgiri Mountains in India and who practiced fraternal polyandry, that is, a practice in which one woman is married to all the brothers of a family, showed little jealousy for within-group sexual infidelity (Hupka 1991). Even more strikingly, the Samoans are reported to live a life free of anger but also of sexual jealousy (Mead 1928). Such examples are the main motivation behind social constructionism, to which we turn now.

3.5. Social Constructionism

Let me start with a clarification. Even if there are affinities between the two approaches, *social constructionism* has to be distinguished from another brand of constructionism, namely, *psychological constructionism*, a theory defended by James Russell (2003; see also Moors 2017). According to Russell, emotions are made of psychological building blocks that are not specific to emotions. The central building block is *core affect*, a state that psychological constructionists define in terms of hedonic value, which ranges from extreme pleasantness to extreme unpleasantness, and level of arousal, which ranges from deactivation, such as sleep, to high activation, such as frantic excitement. Other building blocks include appraisal, facial expressions, changes in the autonomic nervous system, and actions. The idea is that an emotion like anger, say, consists in a specific pattern of such building blocks, centrally involving specific levels of hedonic value and arousal value. This account of what constitutes emotions is clearly distinct from social constructionism. Indeed, insofar as the psychological mechanisms that produce the different elements that constitute an emotion are common to human beings, cross-cultural variability is not to be expected. There might be differences at the level of how a society conceptualizes specific patterns of building blocks, but as such the patterns exist independently of our conceptualizations.

Social constructionists, by contrast, oppose both versions of biological determinism and hold that emotions allow for much more variability than biological determinism can account for. According to social constructionism, emotions are *social constructs*, in the sense that they are the product of social practices. Emotions would thus be on a par with money and gender, which are widely agreed to be social constructs. The social constructionist theory of emotion emerged in the 1980s. Its main advocates are psychologist James Averill (1980), anthropologist Catherine Lutz (1988) and philosophers Rom Harré (1986) and Claire Armon-Jones (1985, 1986). Social constructionism is still a live research program in the theory of emotions, as shown for instance by recent work by sociologist Martin Aranguren (2017), who argues that social constructionism need not assume that emotions depend on language, because culture need not depend on language either, thus making room for animal emotions within a constructionist account.

Social constructionism comes in two main versions. According to *social role constructionism*, emotions are the enactment of *transitory social roles*, which follow scripts that spell out how a person should respond in a given social context (Averill 1980). These scripts, or social norms, consist in normative beliefs and expectations that are shared within a society. The enactment of such an emotional social role results in an *emotional syndrome*. A syndrome is a set of coordinated responses that correspond to the script, any of which may constitute a particular emotion, even if none is essential to that emotion. These responses include appraisals, typical behavior, physiological arousal, and subjective experience. Part of these responses are biologically determined, but they count as emotions only insofar as the individual incorporated them into an emotional role. One important point is that in spite of what the metaphors of roles and of enactment suggests, the individual who enacts an emotional role takes their responses to be out of their control. They are self-deceived about this, but this is part of a general strategy to cope with the environment. Interestingly, this suggestion is reminiscent of the account proposed by the existentialist philosopher Jean-Paul Sartre (1962), according to whom emotions are essentially self-deceived, "magical" actions we perform to change the world. When we faint out of fear, for instance, we aim at removing the object of our fear by removing our consciousness of that object.

The social role theory obviously allows for extensive cross-cultural variability. For example, members of our society have internalized the rule that anger befits a situation in which there is an offense and that insulting you consists in an offending behavior, so that if someone insults you, you ought to flare up in anger. The content of such rules depends on what a social group considers to constitute an offense – does forgetting about a birthday make for an offense, one might ask – thus allowing for considerable variability. The rules concerning one emotion can differ even more drastically. For instance, as we saw (in Chapter 1), members of the Utku culture, who shun anger, have internalized a rule according to which very little, if anything at all, merits anger (Briggs 1970).

On the social role theory of emotions, enacting a role can involve the application of an emotion concept, such as the concept of anger, to oneself, but it does not require this. By contrast, a more radical version of social constructionism has been advocated by Claire Armon-Jones (1986) and Rom Harré (1986), who hold that to experience anger, you need to grasp the concept of anger and to apply it to your own experience. According to Armon-Jones, "agents cannot be said to feel an emotion (E) unless they have a grasp of the concept E and can apply this concept to their own experience on appropriate occasions" (1986, 37; see also Barrett 2017).

According to the version of social constructionism that emphasizes the role of concepts – *conceptual ascription constructionism,* for short – what counts as an emotion of anger in one society need not be considered anger in another society. Indeed, someone who lacks the concept of anger, possibly because the concept is not available in the culture of that person, cannot experience that particular kind of emotion. In the same way, nonhuman animals who lack conceptual skills cannot experience any emotions. Moreover, the rules that govern the application of emotion concepts can, but need not, involve reference to bodily changes. As a result, bodily changes are not considered essential to emotions. Indeed, both versions of constructionism claim that emotions lack essences and hold that none of the application conditions of an emotion concept is necessary.

Does either of these two versions of social constructivism offer a convincing account of emotions?

3.6. The Evidence for Social Constructionism

Stanley Schachter and Jerome Singer (1962; see also Lindquist and Barrett 2008) conducted an influential study aimed at testing a version of conceptual ascription constructionism, according to which emotions involve unspecific physiological arousal plus a cognitive label, which the subjects attribute to themselves. According to this hypothesis, labeling your state of physiological arousal as anger, joy, or fear, say, determines what emotion you feel. The study involved injecting subjects with epinephrine, a substance that triggers heightened autonomic response, thereby causing subjects to feel accelerated breathing and increase in blood pressure and heart rate. The subjects were all told that the substance was a vitamin supplement to test their eyesight, but some – the epinephrine informed group – were informed about the likely side effects of the injection, while those in the epinephrine ignorant group were not told anything about such side effects. The participants were placed in a waiting room after the injection, and there, a stooge interacted with them, either displaying anger or euphoria.

According to this study, the stooge had a different impact depending on the information given to the participants. In particular, the subjects in the epinephrine ignorant group, who had no explanation for their symptoms, reacted differently in the two conditions, showing negative responses in the anger condition and positive responses, such as amusement, in the euphoria condition. By contrast, the subject in the epinephrine informed group exhibited little responses in either condition. According to Schachter and Singer, these findings support their hypothesis that we label our arousal states in terms of the cues in the environment. Given roughly identical arousal, the participants gave different interpretations of these conditions, hence experiencing different emotions.

What should we think of this study? The main problem is that nothing rules out that the epinephrine ignorant subjects simply misattributed anger or euphoria to themselves, where this misattribution caused them to behave in the relevant ways without feeling any particular emotion. As Griffiths (1997) notes, it is well known that we are prone to confabulation, and it is plausible that subjects simply confabulated being in an emotional state. Prinz (2004) underscores a further problem. One surprising result is that subjects in both the euphoria and the anger condition, whether or not they were informed about the side effects, reported that they were happy when filling a questionnaire at the end of experiment. Given this, it is not clear that the behaviors observed in the anger condition were the manifestation of any negative emotion. As a result, one cannot take this study to be conclusive.

Both versions of social constructionism predict important cross-cultural differences among the emotions that are experienced. Indeed, social constructionists take evidence for cross-cultural variability to vindicate their account. Thus, they point out the fact that anthropological and cross-cultural linguistic studies suggest that many emotions are picked out by terms that are difficult to translate into other languages and thus appear to be specific to particular cultures. A striking example of an emotion that appears culturally specific is the Japanese *amae*, a pleasant feeling of dependence on another's person good will and affection, typically exemplified by what infants experience when with their parents (Doi 1973). There is no equivalent term in English, so it might well seem that *amae* is not something that we can conceptualize, let alone experience. A second example that is often discussed is what the people who live on Ifaluk, a Micronesian atoll in the Pacific Ocean, call *song*, which is a kind of anger that comes with moralistic overtones and no disposition to revenge (Lutz 1988). Again, there is no English equivalent of this term, so this suggests that *song* refers to an emotion that cannot be experienced by people who have been socialized in a culture like ours, in which anger is in general taken to involve a desire for revenge. Finally, consider one of the key words of Russian culture, *toska*, which roughly translates as melancholy-cum-yearning, but in fact appears to blend many more aspects, since it can be translated by terms as varied as "melancholy", "anguish", "pangs", "depression", "ennui", "boredom", "longing", "yearning", "nostalgia", and "homesickness", to name just a few (Wierzbicka 1992, 1999).

As these examples illustrate, there are emotions that appear completely different from the ones with which we are familiar in Western culture. There are many more examples of what seems a limitless diversity in emotional responses. Simply considering the Ifaluk people studied by Lutz (1988) there are many other terms that have no English equivalent, apart from *song*. Consider for instance *baiu* (romantic love/happiness), *ker* (happiness/excitement), *fago* (love/compassion/sadness), *metagu* (fear/anxiety), *rus* (panic/fright/surprise), *tang* (grief/frustration), *lugument* (discomfort/guilt), and *bosu* (jealousy/excitment). It is clear that the emotional landscape the Ifaluk navigate is significantly different from the one with which we are familiar. Given this important diversity in emotional landscapes, social constructionism appears clearly plausible.

A first question is whether this kind of evidence supports social constructionism about emotions in general or whether it only warrants constructionism about a subset of emotion. After all, Ifaluk people have terms that translate directly into English. This is for instance the case of *niyabut* (disgust), *bobo* (disappointment), and *maluwelu* (calmness) (Lutz 1988). Thus, the evidence from anthropology and linguistics does not rule out that at least some emotions are cross-cultural. At best, this kind of evidence supports a limited version of social constructionism.

However, even in the cases in which there is no one-to-one translation of an emotion term, the question that arises is whether a difference in vocabulary entails that emotions are social constructs. Apparent cross-cultural differences might in the end turn out to be merely verbal (Prinz 2004). The important question, thus, is whether individuals can experience emotions like *amae*, *song* and *toska* outside of the cultural context of these concepts. On the face of it, it would seem that even if there is no English term for *amae*, we can, and in all likelihood do sometimes, experience, pleasant feelings towards people on whom we depend.

The difference between Western and Japanese cultures seems to concern the importance assigned to this emotion, *amae* being considered central to Japanese culture. The emphasis on *amae* starkly contrasts with Western values such as independence and autonomy. In this context, it is useful to introduce the distinction between *hypercognized* and *hypocognized* emotions introduced by the anthropologist Robert Levy (1984). Emotions that are hypercognized within a culture are strongly emphasized and valued by members of that culture, while hypocognized emotions are ignored, disvalued or repressed within the relevant culture. Clearly, *amae* appears to be *hypercognized* in Japanese culture, even if it is *hypocognized* in the context of Western culture. Of course, ignoring, devaluing or repressing a type of emotion is far from making it impossible to experience exactly that kind of emotion. Clearly, similar considerations apply to *song* and *toska*. The mere fact that there is no equivalent of these terms in a given language does not entail that these emotions cannot be experienced by speakers of that language.

In general, terminological differences need not entail differences at the level of the emotions, so the evidence from anthropology and linguistics is insufficient to establish that emotions are social constructs. However, social constructionists, and in particular those who defend the social role version of the theory, are likely to respond that this criticism misses a crucial point. Emotions, unlike natural phenomena, come with rafts of socially disseminated rules.

Consider romantic love again. According to social role constructionists, romantic love as we know it consists in behavior that conforms to a set of culturally specific rules, which have a history (Lewis 1936; Averill 1985; Beall and Sternberg 1995). One prominent rule that dates back to courtly love is that romantic love concerns two individuals, specifically a man and a woman. Similarly, romantic love is thought to be exclusive and therefore normatively to involve jealousy. As the history of romantic love shows, no such rule is pancultural. In Victorian England, falling in love involves admiration, while sexual attraction was considered irrelevant if not shameful. More recently, romantic love has come to be thought of as an intimate attachment that includes sexual desire by definition. The contemporary belief that romantic love is a suitable basis for marriage is also far from generally shared, many cultures viewing romantic love as a threat to long-term relationships. More generally, the claim that romantic love only concerns heterosexual relationships, that it needs to be exclusive, and that it should result in marriage has come under scrutiny. As a result new forms of romantic love, such as polyamory, which involves many-to-many relationships, are starting to emerge (Jenkins 2017). It is hence uncontroversial to claim that the scripts for romantic love vary from one cultural context to another. Much the same is true of other emotions, including those that count as basic according to basic emotion theorists. Again recall Jean Briggs' book, *Never in Anger*, which describes the Utku's emotional life and in particular the norm prohibiting anger that regulates their life (Briggs 1970). Obviously, the Utku script for anger is deeply different from the one with which we are familiar.

The question is whether cross-cultural variations in scripts entails that emotions are social constructs. A first point to note here is that the presence of norms regarding something does not entail that this thing is a social construct. There are social and moral norms prohibiting various actions, such as causing pain to others. However, the act of causing pain is surely is not a social construct. In the same way, the fact that there are socially constructed norms governing love does not entail that love is a social construct. Indeed, while it is likely that such norms will affect when love is felt, when it will be expressed, or what kind of behavior will result, these consequences are not in any way necessary. The reason is that norms can well be flouted. The example of the Utku prohibition against anger is a case in point. As Briggs reports, one of the Utku community told her that when an Utku became angry, "it's something to remember, but a kapluna [white American] can get angry in the morning and be over it by afternoon" (1970, 261).

Do we have to conclude that the core of emotions is entirely isolated from cultural influence?

3.7. The Plasticity of Emotions

We have seen that neither the arguments in favor of biological determinism nor the ones in favor of social constructionism are conclusive. This suggests that the truth lies somewhere in the middle. Emotional dispositions but also emotional episodes are shaped by both biological and cultural forces. To understand how these two forces interact, let us look at ways that culture can shape our emotions.

It is noteworthy that everyone in the debate accepts that emotional dispositions are importantly plastic in that they are shaped not only by our environment but also by culture. By teaching what one has to be afraid of or what ought to trigger anger, culture influences what stimuli are likely to cause emotions, something even basic emotion theorists are ready to accept. How exactly this is achieved is a good question, to which we will return (see Chapter 12). Another point that is not contentious is that culturally specific display rules have an impact on facial and bodily expressions of emotions. It also appears uncontroversial that culture influences what action follows from an emotion, be it only because the kinds of actions that are feasible depends on the social context. Picking up your cellphone to call for help is not a course of action that was an option in the Pleistocene. Culture can also encourage some types of motivation over others, for instance by disseminating specific examples of emotional action. The motivation to marry when in love, which is central to many romantic plots in Western culture, is a good example of this kind of influence. In all these ways, culture shapes the causes and effects of our emotions.

In addition, two mechanisms that importantly shape the emotions we feel have been proposed in the literature. The first mechanism, which has been put forward by Robert Plutchik (1980; see also Prinz 2004) is *blending*. Blending is the process of morphing together two or more emotional responses into a single and unified emotional response, which shares aspects of its several ingredients. One can agree with Griffiths (1997) that not all nonbasic emotion types result from blending basic emotions, but as he acknowledges, this does not rule out that some types of emotion are blends. Thus, *fago* seems to blend love, compassion and sadness. Similarly, *toska* might also be a blend involving a number of negative emotion types, such as sadness, fear, and longing. As these examples illustrate, culture clearly has an influence on blends. So, even if it is not impossible to feel *amae*, *fago* or *toska* panculturally, specific cultures encourage specific blends, making them readily available for individuals in that culture.

The second mechanism is *cognitive elaboration*. The mechanism of cognitive elaboration modifies an emotional type by combining it with a cognitive component, such as a belief, to form a new emotional type. This mechanism is invoked to explain how basic emotions give rise to nonbasic emotions (Johnson-Laird and Oatley 2000). The idea is that nonbasic emotions consist in a combination of a basic emotion *plus* a belief. *Amae*, for instance, can be considered to involve joy at the thought of dependency. Similarly, indignation would consist in a cognitive elaboration of anger, which involves the belief that there is an injustice, whereas guilt could be seen as a kind of distress that depends on the belief that one has done something wrong. According to Johnson-Laird and Oatley (2000), some cognitive elaborations are more complex. They argue that romantic love as we know it in our society involves sexual desire and happiness, both of which they consider to be basic emotions, which is combined with an idealization of the loved one, an altruistic desire as well as a longing when apart.

A good question here is whether the emotional kinds that result from cognitive elaboration necessarily involve the belief on which the elaboration process depends. Johnson-Laird and Oatley (2000), for instance, hold that nonbasic emotions always include a conscious cognitive evaluation. The alternative is to hold with Prinz (2004) that the cognitive component is only necessary to acquire the disposition to experience nonbasic emotion. Once the learning or *recalibration* process is over, you can experience the resulting nonbasic emotion independently of the belief that was involved in the cognitive elaboration mechanism. This appears to be plausible in light of the fact that emotions like indignation or guilt allow for recalcitrance. The case of guilt is particularly striking: you can feel guilt while at the same time believing that you have done nothing wrong. Suppose you are climbing Mount Everest, and your group is hit by an avalanche. As it turns out, you are the only survivor of an avalanche. In such circumstances, you might well feel *survivor's guilt*, as we say, even if there is nothing you could have done to prevent the death of your comrades. This clearly suggests that you do not need to believe that you did something wrong to feel *survivor's* guilt (we will get back to such cases of recalcitrance in Chapter 6).

What matters for our purposes is that in both scenarios, culture plays a central role in the mechanism of cognitive elaboration. First, many of the beliefs that are involved in cognitive elaboration are importantly shaped by culture. Consider the belief regarding injustice, which is thought to be involved in indignation. The concept of injustice is one that we learn when being socialized into a culture and, as a result, what is considered to be an injustice varies from culture to culture. Moreover, culture plays a role in cognitive elaboration by fostering specific combinations of emotions and beliefs. For instance, a culture in which the concept of injustice does not exist, or in which that concept fails to be prominent, will be a culture in which the emotional repertoire is not likely to contain indignation.

Biological determinists might agree with all of these points and insist that by contrast with nonbasic emotions, basic emotions are neither blends nor cognitive elaborations. On the contrary, basic emotions would be the raw material that feeds into the mechanisms of blending and of cognitive elaboration. The cultural influences would only be superficial, for they would concern the causes and effects of basic emotions, such as the actions that come in the wake of emotions. The problem with this reasoning, however, is that is assumes that cultural influences on the causes and the effects of emotions are necessarily superficial. If there is a natural core that is left intact, the question is what this core might well be. It is far from clear that emotions are built like avocados, with a soft, cultural mass organized around a hard natural core (Goldie 2000; see also Faucher and Tappolet 2008).

Whether or not culture is considered to influence only the causes and effects of basic emotions, the influence is far from negligible. By changing what we are afraid of or what we are disgusted about, culture makes an important contribution to what we feel. Similarly, by having an impact on the expression of emotions and on what we are motivated to do, culture shapes our emotional responses in important ways. In these ways, culture influences our emotional dispositions and hence the emotions we feel. This plasticity at the level of our emotional dispositions should be welcome, for it makes room for the possibility of an education of our emotions, a topic to which we will return (see Chapter 12).

3.8. Taking Stock

We looked into the arguments for biological determinism as well as the arguments for social constructionism. The upshot of our discussion is that emotions are the product of both nature and culture. The disposition to feel fear, for instance, has evolved because it proved useful to our ancestors, but what we fear, how we express fear and what we are motivated to do when afraid depends largely on the culture in which we are immersed. As we saw, it seems open to biological determinists to hold that cultural influences are only superficial because they would concern only the causes and effects of emotions, leaving the core untouched. However, it is plausible that emotions are instead seamless products of the interaction of nature and culture. The question that needs to be considered in order to make progress is what counts as the essence of emotions, by contrast to their causes and effects.

3.9. Summary

- Biological determinism holds that at least some emotion types depend on pancultural psychological traits that are written into our genetic makeup because they are evolutionary adaptations, which helped our ancestors to face challenges such as escaping predators.
- According to basic emotion theory, only a limited number of our emotion types are biologically determined. Such basic emotions are thought to involve affects programs, that is, reflex-like cascades of coordinated changes, which are associated with hardwired neural circuits.
- By contrast, evolutionary psychologists hold that all emotions are adaptations.
- The evidence for basic emotions theory, which comprises studies of facial expressions, studies of neural patterns and bodily changes, as well as observations regarding the continuity between adult emotions and emotions in non-human animals and infants, shows at best that biology has a significant impact on human emotions.
- The evidence from evolutionary psychology is also less than convincing. The main problem with the claim that an emotion like love or guilt is an adaptation is that it flies in the face of the cross-cultural variability in our emotional reactions.
- By contrast, social constructionism holds that emotions are social constructs, either because they are the enactment of social roles, as social role constructionism claims, or because they hold that to experience an emotion, it is necessary to apply to oneself the relevant emotion concept, as conceptual ascription constructionism argues.
- The main evidence for concept application constructionism, which comes from the Schachter and Singer study, can be criticized on several counts, most significantly because it does not rule out that the subjects were confabulating.

- Evidence from cross-cultural variability is impressive, but it is not clear that this shows more than the obvious fact that emotion vocabulary differs across cultures.
- The evidence for social constructionism based on the fact that emotions come with socially disseminated rules also fails to show that emotions themselves are social constructs, the main reason for this being that rules can be disregarded.
- The bottom line is that both biological and cultural forces shape our emotional dispositions.

3.10. Study Questions

1. What is love? Is it a social construct, a blend, a cognitive elaboration?
2. Can animals have emotions and, if so, what would this entail for the debate between biological determinism and social constructionism?
3. Have you ever felt *amae, song* or *toska*? If so, is it possible to experience an emotion without being aware that one experiences that specific kind of emotion?

3.11. Further Readings

Armon-Jones, Claire. 1986. "The Thesis of Constructionism." In *The Social Construction of Emotions*, edited by Rom Harré, 32–56. Oxford: Blackwell.

Averill, James R. 1985. "The Social Construction of Emotion: With Special Reference to Love." In *The Social Construction of the Person*, edited by Kenneth J. Gergen and Keith E. Davis, 89–109. New York: Springer-Verlag.

de Sousa, Ronald. 2015. *Love: A Very Short Introduction*. Oxford: Oxford University Press.

Ekman, Paul. 1999. "Basic Emotions." In *Handbook of Cognition and Emotion*, edited by Tim Dalgleish and Mick J. Power, 45–60. Chichester: Wiley.

Goldie, Peter. 2000. *The Emotions: A Philosophical Exploration*. Oxford: Oxford University Press, chap. 4.

Panksepp, Jaak. 2000. "Emotions as Natural Kinds in the Brain." In *Handbook of Emotions*, 2nd ed., edited by Michael Lewis and Jeannette M. Haviland-Jones, 137–156. New York: Guilford Press.

Prinz, Jesse J. 2004. *Gut Reactions: A Perceptual Theory of the Emotions*. New York: Oxford University Press, chaps. 5 and 6.

Russell, James A. 2003. "Core Affect and the Psychological Construction of Emotion." *Psychological Review* 110 (1):145–172.

Scarantino, Andrea, and Paul Griffiths. 2011. "Don't Give Up on Basic Emotions." *Emotion Review* 3 (4):444–454.

Tooby, John, and Leda Cosmides. 2000. "Evolutionary Psychology and the Emotions." In *Handbook of Emotion*, 2nd ed., edited by Michael Lewis and Jeannette M. Haviland-Jones, 91–116. New York: Guilford Press.

PART II
Theories of Emotions

4   Feeling Theories

4.1. Introduction

What is the core of emotions? A first step to answer that question is to remind ourselves of what we established in Chapter 2. What emerged from our discussion is that episodes of prototypical emotions, such as fear or disgust, tend to be rather short-lived states, which typically involve feelings, motivations, intentional objects, appraisals, and formal objects. This is a useful preliminary characterization of emotions, which serves not only to underline their status as affective states but also to distinguish emotions from other affective states, such as sentiments or moods. Indeed, this characterization will help in assessing theories of emotions since they can reasonably be required to account for these typical features. But as such, the preliminary characterization will not serve to settle the debate regarding the core of emotions. The reason is that this characterization leaves open what emotions consist in.

What we need to establish is what elements of this preliminary characterization, if any, are essential to emotions, not to mention that elements that we have not yet considered could turn out to be essential to emotions. Put otherwise, we need to address the first of the three central questions in the philosophy of emotions we posited in Chapter 1, namely, the question of the essence of emotions. What we need is a theory of emotions. This is what we will consider in the three following chapters, in which we will look at the main approaches in the theory of emotions. These are *feeling theories*, *motivational theories*, and *evaluative theories*.

A question that might arise here is whether the accounts we considered in the last chapter, such as basic emotion theories or social role constructionism, should not be added to this list of three. Surely, they count as theories of emotions. The reason why the accounts we considered in the last chapter do not figure in the list of the main approaches in the theory of emotions is that these accounts are best interpreted as lying at a different level of generality. Their claims are compatible with several specific emotion theories. This is particularly obvious in the case of basic emotion theories. You can be a basic emotion theorist and hold that emotions essentially are motivations, which result from natural selection and are thus written into our genetic makeup. Basic emotion theories are

DOI: 10.4324/9781315542300-6

also compatible with the claim that emotions essentially are evaluations. Finally, even if this may be a less obvious combination, a basic emotion theorist could also hold that the essence of basic emotions are feelings. Put otherwise, feelings would constitute the core of the cascade of the affects programs that result from natural selection.

Things are less straightforward with social constructionist accounts, but as such, the claim that emotions are social constructs is compatible with any of the three main theories of emotions. Thus, one can hold that evaluations involve culturally specific evaluative concepts, so that the claim that emotions are evaluations would entail that emotions are social constructs. One can also hold that motivations or feelings are social constructs, so social constructionism rules out neither motivational theories nor feeling theories. As we saw in the last chapter, however, social constructionists are in fact prone to deny that emotions have essences, thereby denying the very possibility of developing a positive theory of emotion.

We will begin with feeling theories, an approach that has been historically prominent, and which has a strong intuitive appeal. Even so, feeling theories are the target of important objections and few subscribe to this approach nowadays. Discussing these objections, however, will allow us to deepen our understanding of what emotions are. Before we turn to the presentation of feeling theories, however, let us look at the main challenges that face theories of emotions quite generally.

4.2. The Challenges to Emotion Theories

As we have just seen, a theory of emotions aims at spelling out the essence of emotions. Minimally, such a theory has two demarcation challenges. The first is to show what, if anything, demarcates emotions from states that are not emotions, such as itches or migraines. If nothing demarcates emotions from other kinds of states, the theory has at least to explain away the intuition that emotions constitute a distinctive kind of state. The second task is to spell out what, if anything, demarcates different kinds of emotion. Again, if there is no distinction between different kinds of emotion, the theory has to explain away the fact we intuitively make distinctions between states such as fear, disgust, anger, or admiration.

In general, a theory of emotions has the task to account for, or else explain away, the intuitions we have regarding emotions. Thus, in addition to the intuition that emotions are distinctive states and the intuition that there are different kinds of emotion, the theory also has to account for our intuitions regarding the features that typically characterize prototypical emotions that we have spelled out in Chapter 2. It has to make room for the fact that emotions such as fear or disgust tend to be rather short-lived states, which typically involve feelings and motivations, as well as for the fact that such emotions typically are about intentional objects that are appraised in terms of evaluative concepts.

From the start, it needs emphasizing that the task of spelling out a theory of emotions is tricky. Indeed, it might seem that emotions are just too messy a terrain to allow for theories. As we have seen, there are very different kinds of emotion. Even if one considers that basic and nonbasic emotions are sufficiently similar to belong to the same psychological type, it has to be granted that what is true of fear, say, might well not be true of admiration or awe, for instance. Indeed, what is true of the fear you feel towards an attacking bear might be different from the fear you feel for a fictional character, such as Anna Karenina (see Chapter 12). In any case, the best strategy is the one we followed in Chapter 2, that is, the strategy of focusing first on a limited number of paradigmatic emotions, such as fear, anger or sadness, in order to develop a satisfactory account. The first step is to provide a convincing theory of such states, while the second step is to see whether it generalizes to other kinds of emotion.

It is worth noting that this strategy is neutral with respect to the question of whether some emotions are prototypical, so that other emotions need not share all of their features, or whether every state that counts as an emotion shares the same features as the paradigmatic cases. The strategy is equally neutral with respect to the question of whether the concept of emotions is a *prototype concept*, in the sense that membership in the category depends on the similarity to the paradigmatic examples of the category (Fehr and Russell 1984; Ben-Ze'ev 2001). As a result, the set of what counts as an emotion would not have clear-cut boundaries, some states, such as awe or tranquility maybe, being considered too different from the paradigmatic examples to fully count as emotions.

Another fact that makes it tricky to develop a theory of emotions is that emotions are complex phenomena, which involve several components. Consider a typical episode of sadness. You are at the airport and you are watching the plane on which your sweetheart is leaving for a year abroad. As the plane disappears into the clouds, intense sadness overcomes you. A number of interconnected elements are involved here. There is the sight of the plane taking your sweetheart away and the realization that you will not see your friend anytime soon. As you take in this information, you appraise, however implicitly, the situation as a terrible loss. In addition, a number of physiological changes involving the autonomous nervous system will occur. Your blood pressure will increase in correlation with an increased bodily activation and tears will start to flow. While you start crying, your face will adopt a typical expression, your eyebrows forming an inverted 'V' that matches the pout of your lips, the lower lip pushing the upper lip up, while the upper lip corners turn down. Your bodily posture will also change. After having stretched your neck to see the plane disappear into the clouds, your head will bend over and your shoulders will curve forward. You will also undergo a kind of experience, as if something were tearing you apart. A number of thoughts will quickly cross your mind. You might wonder why you agreed to the separation and you might conclude that you will never survive not seeing your sweetheart for so long. Memories of when your parents left you behind for a vacation might come back to you. More generally, your attention will focus on similarly sad things and the whole world will start looking grey and empty. Finally, your sadness is likely to come with a motivation, such as the urge to run after the plane or to board the next flight in order to reunite with your sweetheart, but eventually, you will go back home and withdraw from the outer world.

Whatever the exact details, a typical episode of sadness, and indeed any typical emotion episode, appears to involve the following components:

a) an informational component (the realization that your sweetheart is leaving you);
b) an evaluative component (the appraisal of the departure as a loss);
c) a physiological component (the increase in blood pressure, etc.);
d) an expressive component (the facial expression and the bodily posture);
e) a phenomenological component (the feeling of being torn apart);
f) a cognitive component (the thoughts crossing your mind and the focus of attention);
g) and finally, a motivational component (the urge to withdraw from the world).

We are familiar with a number of these components, since we encountered them when trying to specify what is characteristic of typical episodes of emotions (see Chapter 2). As we saw, such emotions typically involve feelings, motivations, and appraisals. The question that a theory of emotion needs to tackle is whether any of the components on the above list is essential to emotions. Is the core of your sadness a feeling, a motivation, or an appraisal? Or is this sadness a state that involves several of these components? The question is what component, if any, is essential to your sadness and, more generally, to emotions. This is what Prinz (2004) calls the "problem of parts".

Very different answers have been offered. Social constructionists tend to be skeptical about the existence of essences. As we have seen, Averill (1980), for one, holds that no element in what he called an "emotional syndrome", that is, what results from the enactment of a script, is essential. Similarly, one could deny that any component of the above list of components is essential. This denial need not come with a constructionist account. An interesting alternative is to claim that the concept of emotion is a family resemblance concept. This notion, which can be traced back to Ludwig Wittgenstein (1953), is meant to capture the fact that the items in a category might be like the members of a family, where you find similarities in features such as the color of the eyes, facial expressions, and temperaments between many members even if no set of features characterizes all the members. In the same way, one could say that even if each emotion shares a number of features with some other emotions, no set of features characterizes all emotions. Thus, what an emotion theorist could do, at best, is to list the partial similarities among emotions. This is for instance what Jon Elster (1999) proposes, his account of emotions consisting in a list of features which is similar to the above list of components, but none of which is considered to be necessary. However, before settling for such a deflationary account, the prospects of more ambitious accounts of emotions have to be considered. It is only if theories according to which emotions have essential features fail that we would have a reason to opt for a more modest account in terms of family resemblance.

Among these more ambitious accounts, there are two main kinds. These are *pure* and *hybrid* theories. According to pure theories, the essence of emotions is one single kind of thing, such as feelings for feeling theories. Pure theories do not deny that emotions involve other components, but they claim that these components need not be present. The other components are seen as contingent, for instance because they are typical but not necessary causes or effects of emotions. Thus, a feeling theorist can accept that emotions cause motivations. Strictly speaking, however, a state can count as an emotion even if it does not involve such a contingent component. Hybrid theories, by contrast, hold that emotions are constituted by a set of correlated things. Aristotle's account of emotions, which we discussed in Chapter 1, is often interpreted as a hybrid theory, since according to Aristotle emotions involve pain or pleasure, an evaluation, and a motivation as well as bodily changes. The important question for hybrid theories is what makes the several elements hold together. Following the suggestions of basic emotion theorists who embrace hybrid theories – and yes, this is another possible combination between biological determinism and views about the essence of emotions – one common answer to that question is to appeal to an evolutionary account of emotions and their function.

In this chapter, we will examine accounts according to which emotions essentially are feelings. As we saw in Chapter 2, it can be agreed that emotions typically involve phenomenal properties. Put differently, there is typically "something it is like" to be sad or to be afraid. Feeling theorists hold that feelings are not only typically present in emotions. They argue that emotions are nothing over and above feelings. There are different ways to develop this intuition, depending on how one understands the notion of feeling. The main distinction is between theories that hold that the feelings at stake are bodily feelings (James 1884), on the one hand, and theories that deny that the feelings at stake are bodily (Whiting 2009), on the other. Because it is the most influential account, we will mainly discuss James' version of the feeling theory. As we will see, however, parts of the discussion also concern feeling theories in general, as well as, more specifically, versions of that approach that deny that feelings are bodily.

4.3. William James' Bodily Feeling Theory

According to feeling theories, emotions are distinctive conscious experiences, that is, states that are essentially felt. Such theories have been defended by prominent historical figures. In particular, Descartes (1649/1989) is generally thought to have held a feeling theory on account of his claim that emotions are perceptions, sensations, or commotions of the soul caused by the movements of the animal spirits, the minute particles that inform the soul about bodily changes. In the same way, Hume's (1739–1740/2000) claim that emotions are sensations caused by the experience or the thought of pleasure or pain places him among feeling theorists.

Recent debates have focused on the version of the feeling theory offered by William James (1884, 1890).[1] Even though this theory has been the target of important objections, it has also been remarkably influential. Neuroscientist Antonio Damasio (1994), who counts as a neo-Jamesian, takes up important insights from James to build his account of the feelings involved in emotions. Interestingly, other neo-Jamesians include motivational theorists, such as Julien Deonna and Fabrice Teroni (2012), as well as evaluative theorists, such as Jesse Prinz (2004) and Uriah Kriegel (2014).

In a way that is reminiscent of Descartes' account, James emphasizes the role of bodily changes. Focusing first on what he calls "coarser" emotions, such as grief, fear, rage, or love, which he took obviously to involve bodily changes, James argues that all kinds of emotions, including the "subtler" emotions, such as moral, intellectual, and aesthetic feelings, have bodily feelings as an essential ingredient. In a nutshell, James' view is that emotions are bodily feelings of a kind.

The kind of feelings that for James constitute emotions are feelings of bodily changes caused by the perception, the memory, or the thought of some "exciting" fact, such as the perception of an approaching bear. These changes, which do not require a dedicated brain process, involve both internal changes in the viscera, such as the quickening of the heartbeat, external bodily changes such as crying or frowning, and motivational changes and even actions, such as the impulse to strike and the action of striking. As James puts it, *"the entire organism may be called a sounding-board*, which every change of consciousness, however slight, may make reverberate."* (1890, 450, italics in the original) This variety of the bodily changes involved in emotions plus the possible permutations and combinations they allow makes it possible, according to James, to account for every "shade of emotions", as he puts it.

James' account inverts the causal chain that seems natural. According to a natural thought, what comes first is the perception of some fact, where this perception causes the emotion, which then itself causes the bodily changes. You see the approaching bear, and this perception causes fear in you, something that then causes your heart to race. According to James, this commonsensical picture has to be replaced by the view that the perception causes the bodily changes. As he famously puts it: "My theory [...] is that *the bodily changes follow directly the perception of the exciting fact, and that our feeling of the same changes as they occur* IS *the emotion.*" (1890, 450, italics and capitalization in the original, see also 1884) As James illustrates his theory, we feel sorry because we cry, angry because we strike, afraid because we tremble, and not the reverse.

A point that is worth clarifying is that James' theory is not merely a theory about the feelings involved in emotions, as opposed to the emotions themselves. His claim concerns the nature of emotions, the thesis being that emotions, whether they are of the "coarser" or the "subtler" kind, are constituted by feelings of bodily changes. Thus, the causal chain postulated by James is one that starts with the perception, or the memory or thought, as James makes clear, of some fact – what James calls the exciting fact – which causes the bodily changes that give rise to the emotion understood as the feeling of these bodily changes.

Because James holds that all bodily changes are felt, even if only obscurely, one might think his theory is not a feeling theory, but a hybrid theory, which holds that both bodily feelings and bodily changes are essential to emotions. However, James allows that in pathological cases, it is sufficient to have a hallucination of bodily feelings to undergo an emotion. This claim anticipates a thesis proposed by Damasio (1994), according to which the pathway to emotions can follow what he calls an "as if loop". Damasio holds than emotions can occur in the absence of bodily changes, because the brain centers ordinarily associated with the bodily changes can be activated in the absence of these changes. As a result, it feels as if you were undergoing bodily changes. Thus, imagining a threatening bear might cause changes in the brain centers associated with the quickening of the heartbeat, etc., without triggering any real bodily changes. Given the possibility of a dissociation between bodily feelings and bodily changes envisaged by James, there is thus good reason to consider that James' theory is a feeling theory and not a hybrid theory.

It is noteworthy that because James allows for bodily feelings that fail to correlate with bodily changes, his account is immune to the objection, levelled by Walter Cannon (1927; see also Cobos et al. 2002) in his early critique of James, according to which patients with spinal cord injuries who have no feedback from their bodily changes, nonetheless have emotions. The bodily feeling theory can allow that in the case of spinal cord injuries, the causal chain that leads to the bodily feelings follow the "as if loop". This claim does not, of course, entail that all emotions are caused in that way, so it is consistent with studies that suggest on the contrary that spinal cord patients report subdued emotional experiences at least for some emotions – sadness, interestingly, was not affected – in proportion to the degradation of bodily feedback (Hohmann 1966).

According to James, the bodily changes are typically automatic reactions. Indeed, he holds that instinctive reactions and emotional reactions belong to the same class, that is, the class of impulses. James claims that emotions such as fear of heights are reactions that are called forth in advance of, and often in direct opposition to, the verdict of our reason. However, James allows for considerable individual differences in emotional reactions. How we react to situations depends on our individual history and our personal interest, but also on our social environment; what we count as an insult, for instance, depends on our education.

Moreover, James thought that even if we have no direct control over our emotions, we can control them indirectly, by controlling the bodily changes over which we have voluntary control. Thus, we can increase our panic by running away from the danger, we can make our sorrow more acute by sobbing or we can sit in a moping posture and sigh to induce melancholy. But we can also diminish our emotions, such as when we count to ten to reduce the intensity of our anger. In general, his view of "moral education", as he calls it, is that "if we wish to conquer undesirable emotional tendencies in ourselves, we must assiduously, and in the first instance, cold-bloodedly, go through the *outward motions* of those contrary dispositions we prefer to cultivate" (1884, 198, see also 1890).

4.4. The Arguments for the Bodily Feeling Theory

Why think that emotions are bodily feelings? The main attraction of James' theory is that it focuses on the component of emotions that we generally think to be most central, namely feelings. In case you would doubt this, there is empirical confirmation of this claim. Panksepp (2000) tested folk intuitions about the importance of different components of emotions, that is, facial expressions, vocal expressions, feelings states, cognitive changes, and autonomic changes. According to the results, feelings had the highest overall rating, close to 4 on a scale of 5, even if cognitive changes and autonomic changes were not far behind. This accounts for the intuitive appeal of the theory, but the question, of course, is whether feelings, and in particular bodily feelings, are not only typical, but essential to emotions.

According to James, one important consideration in favor of his account of emotion is that the theory makes a valid prediction. The theory predicts that voluntary bodily changes affect our emotions and it seems that we can agree with James that this is true. Casual observation suggests that we can indeed affect the strength of our fear by running away or that we can reduce our anger by counting to ten. Moreover, as we have seen (in Chapter 3) facial feedback studies show that mimicking facial expressions results in bodily changes and has an impact on emotional experience. For instance, moving the corner of your lips upward so as to form a smile causes you to feel happy, and in general, facial feedback can both modulate as well as initiate emotional experience (Zajonc 1984; and for a recent meta-analysis, see Coles, Larsen, and Lench 2019). Do these findings really provide evidence for the bodily feeling hypothesis? A first point to note is that the facial feedback studies concern only a limited range of emotions. Nicholas Coles and his colleagues (2019), for instance, focus on anger, disgust, fear, happiness, sadness and surprise. As a result, the current evidence does not provide evidence for the bodily feeling theory as an account of all emotions. More damagingly, these results are perfectly consistent with alternative accounts of emotions, such as an account according to which emotions consist in bodily changes. Thus one could hold that the intentional bodily movements cause the emotions understood as bodily changes, which then cause the bodily feelings. Indeed, the result from feedback studies might well be consistent with evaluative theories, according to which emotions essentially are evaluations or appraisals, for it is not ruled out that facial feedback can cause feelings by activating an appraisal via associative processing (Smith and Kirby 2004). The idea is that your smile induces a positive appraisal of things, which then causes you to experience happiness. In sum, the evidence from facial feedback, and more generally from the fact that intentional movement causes emotional experience, falls short of establishing the bodily feeling theory.

What needs to be emphasized at the start is that James does not take the thesis that emotions are bodily feelings to be a conceptual truth. He thus countenances the possibility that pure bodiless spirits have emotions. On the contrary, he considers that his account is an empirical hypothesis. Even so, the main argument James proposes for his view is not empirical. The so-called *subtraction argument* consists in a thought experiment, which aims at establishing a conceptual truth, namely that what we call an emotion necessarily involves bodily feelings. James asks us to imagine a strong emotion and to mentally abstract from it all the bodily feelings. According to James, what we are left with is not an emotion anymore, but a cold and neutral state of feeling-less cognition:

> What kind of emotion of fear would be left, if the feeling neither of quickened heart-beats nor of shallow breathing, neither of trembling lips nor of weakened limbs, neither of gooseflesh nor of visceral stirrings, were present, it is quite impossible for me to think. [...] In like manner of grief: what would it be without its tears, its sobs, its suffocation of the heart, its pang in the breast-bone? A feelingless cognition that certain circumstances are deplorable, and nothing more.
>
> (1884, 193–194)

Before discussing this thought experiment, let us pause to note that according to James what is left after the bodily feelings are taken away is what we now would call an evaluative judgment – the judgment that something is deplorable. This is an intuitive suggestion, which anticipates evaluative theories of emotion, but what is remarkable is that James does not seem to notice how strange it is to make this suggestion within the framework of his theory. Nothing in his account of emotions and of their causes involves something evaluative. It is thus entirely mysterious how an evaluative judgment would result from the subtraction of the feelings involved in an emotion.

Is this thought experiment convincing? One might object that because James holds that all bodily changes are felt, he fails to clearly distinguish between two questions. First, the question of what is left if you abstract bodily feelings, whether or not these are correlated to bodily movements, and second the question of what is left if you abstract bodily movements, whether or not these are felt. Intuitively, it seems more difficult to imagine intense anger, say, in the absence of bodily movements than to imagine intense anger involving bodily movements but no bodily feelings. In any case, because it does not keep apart these two questions, it is not clear that the subtraction argument establishes a bodily feeling theory instead of a theory that equates emotions with bodily movements.

Another difficulty with the thought experiment is spelled out in terms of strong emotions. As the philosopher David Irons (1894) noted in an early discussion of James' theory, it can at best show that the bodily feeling theory is true of this particular class of emotions. Indeed, the thought experiment is much less plausible when transposed to other cases. Thus, it is surely less obvious that a state of mild anger or of faint fear from which we have mentally subtracted bodily feelings fails to count as an emotion. Maybe the feeling theorist could reply that we have the intuition that bodily feelings are not necessary for mild emotions because the intensity of emotions correlates with the importance of the bodily changes, and obviously, this correlation is well accounted for by the bodily feeling theory. However, it is far from clear that even occurrences of intense admiration, regret, or hope need to come with bodily feelings. In such cases, the thought experiment fails to convince. If such emotions need not involve bodily feelings, surely one can abstract from such feelings without having to conclude that what is left is not an emotion anymore. In fairness, it has to be admitted that James considers moral, intellectual, or aesthetic pleasures and argues that unless they involve bodily feelings, they are nothing but judgments, not emotions. But it would be arbitrary to hold that admiration, regret, or hope are not emotions simply because they do not need to involve bodily feelings. Moreover, a recent set of studies testing intuitions regarding the subtraction argument suggests that most people consider that emotions such as fear, sadness, and anger survive the subtraction process and thus persist even if the bodily feelings disappear (Díaz 2022). These results suggest that bodily feelings are not taken to be essential to emotions.

Let us turn to the main objections to James' feeling theory, starting with two objections regarding demarcation.

4.5. Two Objections from Demarcation

A first objection to the bodily feeling theory is that it arguably fails to demarcate emotions from other kinds of states. In particular, it is not obvious that it can account for the difference between emotions and bodily feelings that have nothing to do with emotions (see Irons 1894 among others). We can for instance feel an increase in our heart rate while jogging without experiencing any emotion. It seems reasonable, thus, to infer that it is only insofar as bodily feelings are involved in emotions as specified independently that such feelings become emotional. Any attempt to identify emotions with bodily feelings would thus be bound to fail.

In reply to this objection, it is possible to appeal to the studies regarding the correlations between patterns of bodily and neural changes and emotions. As we have seen in the last chapter, pattern classification by machine-learning algorithms suggests that there are distinct patterns of bodily responses corresponding to a number of emotion kinds, such as surprise, fear, anger, and sadness (Kragel and LaBar 2013; but see Siegel et al. 2018). These results do not cover all kinds of emotions, but one might argue that the emotions that correlate to such patterns are the building blocks of all our emotions. One could then demarcate emotions from other kinds of states by appealing to the conjunction of the specific bodily patterns. Because it depends on the success of pattern classification studies, whether or nor not such a general strategy works is partly an empirical question.

There are also conceptual problems with this reply, however. A first problem is that by establishing that emotions correlate with bodily patterns, one has not yet established that whenever your body instantiates such a pattern, you undergo an emotion. One important ingredient, that is, feelings, might be missing. A second and related problem is that given the focus on bodily patterns, the strategy falls short of establishing that a feeling theory allows for demarcation. It is a further and unwarranted step to argue that the family of bodily patterns in question has to come with distinctive feelings. Finally, as the bodily feeling theory allows for cases in which the feelings do not correspond to bodily changes – remember that the pathway to emotions can follow an "as if loop" in which the brain center associated with the bodily changes is activated in the absence of these changes – using bodily patterns as a demarcation criterion will fail to account for at least some cases of emotions recognized by the theory.

These very same pattern classification studies might be thought to work better as a reply to a second and influential objection to the bodily feeling theory, namely that it lacks the resources to demarcate different kinds of emotions (see Cannon 1927; Bedford 1956–1957 among others). The objection is that different kinds of emotions can be associated with the same bodily changes. Consider fear and rage, for instance. According to Walter Cannon (1927), the bodily feelings characteristic of fear are not distinct from the ones that are characteristic of rage because the same kind of bodily changes can underlie both fear and rage. Indeed, Cannon holds that because bodily changes are too uniform to allow for useful demarcation, fear and rage would feel just the same as chilliness, hypoglycemia, and fever. This should remind us of the Schachter and Singer (1962) experiment we discussed in the previous chapter, and which aimed to show that states of unspecific arousal need to be categorized in terms of emotion labels to count as occurrences of specific emotion types, such as anger. As we have seen, there is ground to resist this conclusion because nothing rules out that the subjects misattributed the emotions to themselves.

In any case, if we are to believe the pattern classification studies, however, Cannon's thesis is incorrect. According to such studies, there are specific bodily patterns corresponding to at least some emotion types. In particular fear, and anger, which surely counts as a mild form of rage, are associated with distinct patterns. Now, even if we suppose that bodily patterns allow for the demarcation of a number of emotions, the question is again how this strategy generalizes to all kinds of emotion. Moreover, because the claim is that there are distinct bodily patterns for distinct kinds of emotion, the strategy does establish that the bodily feeling theory is vindicated. What is missing here is a reason to think that there cannot be a dissociation between bodily patterns and bodily feelings. Indeed, as Errol Bedford (1956–1957) has stressed, there seems to be little difference, in terms of phenomenal qualities, between what you feel when you experience indignation and when you experience annoyance. Finally, using bodily patterns to demarcate kinds of emotion gives, again, the wrong verdict in cases in which the bodily feelings are activated independently of the bodily changes.

4.6. The Objection from Unconscious Emotions

Another important objection to the bodily feeling theory, and indeed to any theory that holds that feelings are essential to emotions, is that it seems, intuitively, that emotions, and more specifically emotional episodes, need not come with bodily feelings. It is worth clarifying that this worry concerns emotional episodes and not emotional disposition. That emotional dispositions need not involve feelings is not a problem for feeling theories. It is not a problem either that when emotional dispositions involve feeling, these might be different kinds of feelings, depending on the particular emotional state that manifests the

disposition. Thus, it would not be a problem for feeling theories that the sentiment of love involves the feeling of joy when you are close to the beloved, the
feeling of sadness when separated from them, worried when they are in danger,
etc. The bodily feeling theory as well as feeling theories in general concern emotional episodes and not emotional dispositions. What would be a problem for
feeling theories, therefore, is that an episode of fear or of happiness, say, fails to
involve feelings.

The question is whether there can be emotional episodes without feelings,
whatever the type of feeling at stake. If there can be emotions without feelings,
it follows that there can be unconscious emotions. Not surprisingly, the question
whether emotional episodes can be unconscious is controversial. The father of
psychoanalysis, Sigmund Freud, explained much of what we do in terms of
unconscious motivations, but he is famous for having doubted that unconscious
emotions are possible. In his terms, "[i]t is surely the essence of emotion that
we should be aware of it, i.e., that it should become known to consciousness"
(1915/1984, 179). Many, be they psychologists, neuroscientists or philosophers,
have followed Freud in doubting that emotions can be unconscious (see for
instance Clore 1994; Ledoux 1994; Deonna and Teroni 2012). By contrast,
others hold that even if emotions typically involve feelings, they can well be
unconscious (see for instance Damasio 1994; Prinz 2004; Scherer 2004).

One thing to make clear is that the sense in which emotions could be unconscious if they can lack feelings is that the consciousness at stake is so-called
phenomenal consciousness, as distinct from *access consciousness* (Block 1995). As
Ned Block explains, the phenomenally conscious aspect of a state amounts to
what is experienced, to what it is like to be in that state, while access consciousness concerns the access to information. Block argues that in the case of "blindsight", a condition that is caused by damage to the primary visual cortex, the
patients have access to the information in their visual field, but what they lack is
phenomenal consciousness. From the point of view of the patients, it seems as
if they see nothing, even if they are able to reliably answer questions about the
features of the stimulus.

Now, everyone in the debate agrees that emotions can be such that we lack
access consciousness to them, in the sense that we might lack information about
our own emotions. As many have underlined, you can easily be irritated by a
friend without realizing that you are, just as you can be afraid without noticing
that you are. In neither case does it follow that you do not experience anything,
so such cases do not threaten the bodily feeling theory. The question is whether
emotions necessarily involve phenomenal consciousness.

As we have discussed (in Chapter 2), it can also be agreed that it is not in virtue
of the concept of emotion that emotions have to involve feelings. This makes
for a difference between the concept of an itch, for instance, and the concept
of emotion. One strategy to defend the necessity of feelings is to assume that
this is the default position and then work your way to the conclusion that this is
indeed the case by explaining away all apparent cases of unconscious emotions.
Thus, Deonna and Teroni (2012) argue that emotions can be unconscious in

many senses of that word even if they are never unconscious in the phenomenal consciousness sense of the term. For instance, you can experience anger while having your attention taken up by something else. Or else you can experience guilt without realizing that what you feel is guilt, maybe because you have not given any thought to the nature of the feelings you experience. These scenarios are, of course, entirely compatible with the claim that your anger and your guilt involve feelings. The shortcoming of this strategy is that it does not rule out possible cases of emotions that fail to involve feelings.

A more ambitious argument for the thesis that emotions necessarily involve feelings has been proposed by the psychologist Gerald Clore (1994). According to Clore the function of emotions is such that emotions need to be conscious. What is that function? Clore holds that emotions have the function to inform the individual about the nature and importance of events as well as to motivate the individual accordingly. To do so, emotions need to capture the attention of the person who undergoes the emotion, something that requires conscious experience. To assess the argument, one would need to take a stand on the function of emotions. However, the argument fails even if one grants the premise regarding the function of emotion. As Prinz (2004) argues, the reason is that emotions could well inform and motivate individuals without grabbing the attention and without involving feelings. Carrying information and influencing motivation are functions that can be performed below the threshold of conscious experience. Indeed, emotions could even have a role to play in directing attention without being conscious.

In reply, it might be argued that the feelings we experience in emotions have a specific function, which is distinct from the dual function of emotions postulated by Clore. What seems likely is that emotional feelings have a special role in that they allow the conscious and reflexive monitoring of our emotions (Scherer 2004). For instance, it seems it is only on condition that emotions involve feelings that they could have an impact on conscious deliberation. Now, the thesis that feelings have a monitoring function is quite plausible. The problem, however, is that this thesis is perfectly compatible with the claim that emotions typically but far from necessarily involve feelings. That emotional feelings are a useful feature of emotions, which allow their monitoring, does not entail that they are necessarily present in emotions.

A good question when assessing the bodily feeling theory is whether James is right to claim that the feelings that are involved in emotions are bodily feelings. As Carolyn Price (2015; see also Solomon 2007; Kriegel 2014) argues, James' account of the phenomenology of emotion is much too narrow. In addition to bodily changes, what affects the way it feels to be afraid, for instance, involves the way your attention is focused on the object of your fear, the way your thoughts seem to race as memories and images come to mind, as well as sensory information that you take in from the scene around you. In addition, one might hold with James Russell (2003) that emotional feelings include not only the feelings of bodily activation, but also pleasures and displeasures, states that are surely distinct from purely bodily feelings.

Now, even if it is obviously incompatible with James' own account, one might well think that the richness and diversity of emotional feelings might not be a problem for a feeling theorist. A feeling theorist surely can claim that emotions consists not merely in bodily feelings, but in a felt experience that integrates a variety of feelings. However, embracing this enriched conception of emotional feeling in all likelihood involves recognizing a feature of emotions that is incompatible with the original account. This feature is the intentionality of emotions, one of the typical characteristics of prototypical emotions. What typically happens when you are afraid is that your attention is directed toward what you fear and this *aboutness* of your experience is something that colors this very experience. What you feel when your attention is focused on your body and you focus on your cardiac rhythm is completely different from what you experience when you focus on the object of your fear, and it is the latter that is characteristic of emotional episodes.

These observations take us to the next set of objections, for the strongest and most widely accepted objection to bodily feeling theory and, more generally, to feeling theories presses exactly this point.

4.7. The Objections from Intentionality and from Motivation

The main objection to feeling theories in general is that they fail to make room for the intentionality of emotions (see Pitcher 1965; Solomon 1976/1993 among others). More precisely, it is aimed equally at those versions of the approach that take the feelings to be about bodily changes, and those which can be traced back to Hume (1739–1740/2000; see Whiting 2009) and according to which the feelings at stake are purely phenomenal states that lack intentional objects. According to this line of argument, feeling theories either deny the intentionality of emotions or else they misplace this intentionality. They are forced to deny that emotions have intentional objects if they understand feelings to consist in states that lack intentional objects. According to a version of the theory, which goes back to Hume's denial that emotions have representational content, your fear at the sight of a bear would not be about the bear. Alternatively, and this is most common interpretation of James' theory, one can hold that bodily feelings are directed at bodily changes in that they represent these changes. But on that interpretation, it is clear that the theory misplaces the intentional object of emotions. It entails that your fear has bodily feelings and not the bear as its intentional object.

Both the denial and the misplacing of intentionality are clearly problematic as such. But they make for a further problem. What is entailed is that emotions cannot be assessed in terms of their rationality (Pitcher 1965). When you feel fear at the sight of an innocuous teddy bear, say, it seems natural to criticize your fear as being irrational. There are different ways to understand what is involved in this kind of criticism, but according to one conception, it amounts to the accusation of misrepresenting the object of fear as dangerous. The problem is that neither of the two versions of the feeling theory can make room for this kind of assessment. On the version of the feeling theory according to which emotions have no intentional object, emotions cannot be criticized for misrepresenting their objects. On the version according to which emotions are about bodily changes, the only misrepresentation that can be envisaged concerns how these bodily changes are represented.

A first reply to this objection consists in digging one's heels in and arguing that emotions as such are non-intentional states, even though they can be part of complex states that involve intentional thoughts (Whiting 2009). Following this suggestion, being afraid of a bear would be a complex state that consist in a belief, such as the belief that there is a bear nearby, plus a non-intentional emotional state. The important point, according to this reply, is that being afraid of the bear would not in itself be an emotion. Only the non-intentional state would count as an emotion. If we mistake the complex state for an emotion, it is simply because we conflate it with its emotional component. On reflection, there is room for doubt here. The difficulty, of course, is that the claim that a state such as that of being afraid of a bear is not emotion flies in the face of the ordinary usage of the term "emotion". Moreover, there would be no room on this account for the fact that we criticize our emotions in terms of their rationality.

A more concessive reply to the objection from intentionality is to appeal to the causes of emotions. On the bodily feeling theory, what causes the bodily changes that cause your feelings is itself caused by perceptions, memories or thoughts. It might thus be claimed that your fear is about the bear because it is the effect of your perception of the bear. The emotion would inherit, so to speak, its intentional object from its cognitive basis. This line of reply is not very convincing, however. Clearly, we are not inclined to use the same strategy in similar cases (Price 2015). If hot weather causes you to have a migraine, this does not tend to make it the case that your migraine is about the weather conditions.

It seems unnecessary, at this stage, to consider further objections to James' theory or more generally to feeling theories, but because it reveals another important gap in feeling theories, let us look at a final objection to this approach. The objection is that the bodily feeling theory misrepresents how emotions relate to action. When you run away in a desperate attempt to outrun the bear that frightens you, what you do can be explained by your emotion. Your emotion motivates your action and causally explains it. As Irons (1894) suggests, it is likely that it is only insofar as emotions have intentional objects – that they are "feeling towards" objects, to use his expression – that they have the potential to explain what we do. This appears plausible because what we do consists not in mere activation but in acting toward things. Accordingly, it is difficult to see how a feeling theory can make room for the explanation of action in terms of emotions. This is an obvious difficulty for an account which holds that emotions are non-intentional feelings. But it is also a problem for the bodily feeling account. In fact, this is not something that would have worried James. As he is fully aware, the bodily feeling theory inverts the commonly accepted conception. On this account, the perception of the bear causes the bodily changes and these changes cause the feelings that constitute the fear. Thus, your fear itself does nothing in terms of the explanation of what you do. As we will see, the main attraction of motivational theories, to which we will turn in the next chapter, is that they propose to restore the commonsensical picture and make room for action explanation in terms of emotions.

4.8. Taking Stock

In sum, we have little reason, to embrace the bodily feeling theory as well as strong reasons to reject it. Indeed, insofar as feelings are conceived as being either about bodily changes or as nonintentional states, feeling theories in general and not only the bodily feeling theory will falter on the objection from intentionality and the objection from motivation. Let us therefore turn to accounts that aim at improving on feeling theories, starting with motivational theories.

4.9. Summary

- Theories of emotions such as feeling theories, motivational theories, and evaluative theories, which address the question of the essence of emotions, lie at a different level of generality, compared to basic emotion theories and to social role constructionism, so that the latter are compatible with several emotion theories.
- Theories of emotions have to meet several challenges. They have to demarcate emotions from other kinds of states, and emotion kinds from other emotion kinds. Moreover, they have to account for the intuitions we have regarding emotions.
- Understanding emotions is difficult because of the variety and complexity of emotions, which typically involve several components: an informational component, an evaluative component, a physiological component, an expressive component, a phenomenological component, a mental component, and finally a motivational component.
- Depending on whether the theory allows for one or more components, it will count as pure or as hybrid.
- According to the most prominent feeling theory, i.e., James' bodily feeling theory, emotions are bodily feelings, that is, feelings of internal and external bodily changes, including motivational changes and actions, which are caused by the perception, the memory, or the thought of something.
- The main argument in favor of the theory, which involves a thought experiment asking us to subtract feelings from an emotional episode, is problematic because it does not clearly distinguish between bodily feelings and bodily changes and because it is plausible only for strong emotions.
- It is not clear that the bodily feeling theory can meet the demarcation challenges even if one accepts that bodily changes might be sufficient to demarcate emotions from other kinds of states, and emotion kinds for other emotion kinds.
- As the possibility of unconscious emotions shows, feelings, whether bodily or of another kind, do not appear to be necessary for emotions.
- The strongest objections to bodily feeling and more generally to feeling theories is that such theories fail to make room for the intentionality of emotions. Such

theories are either forced to deny the intentionality of emotions or they misplace their intentionality by claiming that emotions represent bodily changes.

• Finally, feeling theories are not in a position to account for the commonsensical thought that emotions causally explain actions.

4.10. Study Questions

1. What are you left with if you subtract bodily feelings but not bodily movements for an emotional episode?
2. Think of Wall-E. Can robots experience emotions, such as fear? If not, why not?
3. Would a hybrid theory do well to include bodily feelings as one of its essential components?

Note

1 This view is often called the "James-Lange theory", because the Danish physician Karl Georg Lange (1885/1922) is thought to have discovered it independently. Lange agreed that some emotions, such as sorrow, delight, fear, and anger, are sensations of bodily changes, but he had a different view of what these changes involved, and unlike James, he thought that some emotions, such as love, hatred or contempt, include thoughts (see Livingston 2019).

4.11. Further Readings

Clore, Genald L. 1994. "Why Emotions Are Never Unconscious." In *The Nature of Emotions: Fundamental Questions*, edited by Paul Ekman and Richard J. Davidson, 285–292. New York: Oxford University Press.

Damasio, Antonio. 1994. *Descartes' Error: Emotion, Reason and the Human Brain*. New York: Gossett/Putnam, chap. 7.

Deigh, John. 2014. "William James and the Rise of the Scientific Study of Emotion." *Emotion Review* 6 (1):4–12.

Deonna, Julien A., and Fabrice Teroni. 2016. "Getting Bodily Feelings into Emotional Experience in the Right Way." *Emotion Review* 9 (1):55–63.

Díaz, Rodrigo. 2022. "Emotions and the body: Testing the Subtraction Argument." *Philosophical Psychology* 35 (1):47–65.

Ellsworth, Phoebe C. 1994. "William James and Emotion: Is a Century of Fame Worth a Century of Misunderstanding?" *Psychological Review* 101 (2):222–229.

Frijda, Nico. 2005. "Emotion experience." *Cognition and Emotion* 19 (4):473–497.

James, William. 1884. "What Is an Emotion?" *Mind* 9:188–205.

Ratcliffe, Matthew. 2005. "William James on Emotion and Intentionality." *International Journal of Philosophical Studies* 13 (2):179–202.

Reisenzein, Rainer, and Achim Stephan. 2014. "More on James and the Physical Basis of Emotion." *Emotion Review* 6 (1):35–46.

5 Motivational Theories

5.1. Introduction

Consider a case of fear felt by one of those cute and furry marmots that you can easily observe when going for a hike in the Rockies. When the marmot sees an eagle circling high up in the air, it immediately freezes, but it will also whistle in order to alert the other marmots in the colony. When the eagle comes closer, the marmot will start running, usually toward its burrow, before disappearing into the hole. If the predator comes close enough, the marmot will fight back. Finally, if the eagle manages to get hold of it, the marmot is likely to fall into tonic immobility, a kind of paralysis that is close to death, apart from the fact that the animal remains conscious. As this case nicely illustrates, an emotion like fear typically involves motivation. As is also made clear by this case, the motivations involved in emotions are flexible enough to adapt to a changing context, so that it can motivate an individual to behave differently, depending, for instance, on the distance of a predator.

As we have seen in the last chapter, one important objection to feeling theories is that such theories cannot make room for the fact that emotions can cause actions and provide explanations of what we, or marmots, do when feeling fear. Because they hold that motivation is the core of emotions, motivational theories, which have made a recent comeback in philosophical debates, constitute a clear improvement on feeling theories. The question is whether motivations really are essential to emotions. Moreover, it has to be seen whether motivational theories are in a position to meet the other challenges that a theory of emotion has to meet. Are such theories able to demarcate emotions from states that are not emotions? Can they provide an account of what distinguishes different kinds of emotions? Finally, can such theories make room, or else explain away, the other typical features of emotions, such as, in particular, their intentionality?

Motivation has been considered to be an essential component of emotions by many historical figures. In his *Rhetoric*, Aristotle (2007), for instance, argued that an emotion like anger involves a desire for revenge. Indeed, according to some, such as Aquinas (1268–1273/1981) and Kant (1785/1996), emotions consist in motivational states. In their wake, John Dewey suggested that instead of the Jamesian conception of emotions as feelings, an emotion should be viewed as a

DOI: 10.4324/9781315542300-7

"mode of behavior which is purposive" (1985, 15) and which involves a readiness to act in certain ways. Contemporary psychologists have also emphasized the role of motivation in emotion. Robert Plutchik (1980), for instance, proposed that each basic emotion corresponds to a different pattern of adaptive behavior, such as withdrawal and escape aimed at protection in the case of fear. In general, as we have seen in Chapter 3, basic emotion theorists hold that the affect programs which constitute emotions involve action tendencies (see for instance Ekman 1999).

Because it constitutes the best worked out version of this approach, we will start our discussion by looking at the account spelled out by the psychologist Nico Frijda (Frijda 1986, 2007, 2010), which we will call the "simple motivational theory" to differentiate it from more complex versions of the motivational theories, according to which emotions also involve evaluations. Frijda's account has had a strong influence on recent theories of emotion developed by philosophers, such as Andrea Scarantino's "pushme-pullyu" version of the motivational theory (2014), and Deonna and Teroni's attitudinal theory (2012), both of which we will also discuss in this chapter. The upshot of our discussion is that emotions need not involve motivations, but even if one assumes that they do, it is necessary to take them to involve evaluative representations.

5.2. The Simple Motivational Theory

Frijda's starting point is that emotional behavior and, more generally, emotional experience suggest that emotional episodes involve urges to act. Accordingly, he holds that the best way to understand emotions like fear or anger is to regard them as being types of "action tendencies". This is a term that Frijda borrows from Magda Arnold (1960), a psychologist who pioneered appraisal theories (see Chapter 6). According to Arnold an emotion is a "felt tendency toward anything intuitively appraised as good (beneficial), or away from anything intuitively appraised as bad (harmful)" (Arnold 1960, 171). Frijda understands action tendencies in terms of what he calls "action readiness". Action tendencies, he holds, are "states of action readiness to execute a given kind of action" (1986, 70). Moreover, he defines the given kind of action by appealing to specific goals, or "end result aimed at or achieved" (1986, 70).

Each action tendency involves a readiness for a variety of actions aimed at the same overall goal. Frijda gives the example of the action tendency he associates with anger and consisting in "readiness for attacking, spitting, insulting, turning one's back, or slandering, whichever of these appear possible or appropriate at a given moment" (1986, 71). The goal of anger, Frijda suggests, is "to regain control or freedom of action – generally to remove obstruction" (1986, 89). What particular action results is something that depends on the specific context, so that the account in terms of action tendency allows for considerable flexibility. As such, this account is more plausible compared to one that would suggest that emotions consist in rigid action tendencies, such as reflexes, which automatically result in stereotypical behavior. Indeed, because the action tendencies involved in emotions can be counteracted, Frijda holds that they sometimes fail to manifest themselves in full-fledged action. In general, however, the actions associated with emotions include full-fledged action, like flight or attack, and expressive behavior, including vocal and facial expressions, but also mental actions, such as thinking about flight or attack.

According to Frijda, emotion kinds can be identified with specific action tendencies: anger is an action tendency aimed at removing obstruction, whereas fear is an action tendency of avoidance aimed at protection, and disgust one of rejecting also aimed at protection. As those examples illustrate, the action tendencies constituting specific kinds of emotions correspond to specific goals. Because emotions aim at establishing, maintaining, or disrupting a relationship with the environment, Frijda emphasizes the relational aspect of the action tendencies constituting emotions. In his terms, "[f]ocused states of action readiness – that is, action tendencies – involve readiness to establish, maintain, or modify relationships" (Frijda 2007, 33).

One difficulty is that in contrast with emotions such as anger, fear, or disgust, some emotions do not appear to have specific goals. Consider the joy you feel upon being informed that a friend has finally recovered from a long illness. This joy need not result in any particular type of action aimed at a specific goal. According to Frijda, an emotion like joy involves instead an activation state, which he describes as a kind of action readiness with no specific goal. As Frijda suggests in a later work (2010; see also Scarantino 2014), the action readiness that constitutes joy might be considered to involve a generic goal: the goal to relate with the world in general. Other emotions, such as sadness or grief, are also difficult to account for in terms of action readiness. The reason is that they seem to tend to reduce any tendencies to perform actions. Frijda, who calls such emotions "null states", suggest that they involve the opposite goal to *not* relate in general. Accordingly, he holds that such emotions can nonetheless be considered to consist in states of action readiness, this time with the goal to not relate.

Putting these points together, Frijda thesis is that "*emotions* [...] *can be defined as modes of relational action readiness, either in the form of tendencies to establish, maintain, or disrupt a relationship with the environment or the form of modes of relational readiness as such*" (Frijda 1986, 71, italics in the original). As Scarantino (2014) suggests, insofar as the modes of relational readiness involved in emotions such as joy or sadness involve a generic, unfocussed goal, emotions can be understood in terms of either specific or generic, unfocussed action or inaction tendencies.

Now, if emotions are states of action readiness, a good question is what distinguishes them from other states of action readiness, such as the tendency to fall asleep after lunch. Frijda's answer to this question consists in focusing on the urge-like nature of emotions (see also Scarantino 2014). He holds that the states of action readiness that constitute emotions are marked out by what he calls "control precedence". What Frijda means is that the states of action readiness that constitute emotions have the character of urges or impulses in that they "clamor for attention and for execution" (1986, 78). In general, states of action readiness become prioritized in that they tend to take precedence over other action tendencies, for instance by interrupting what we do. Control precedence also involves the preemption of cognitive capacities such as memory, inference, or perception. Moreover, control precedence means that the states of action readiness involve bodily preparation for the implementation of at least some of the actions associated with the goal of the action tendency. To illustrate control precedence, consider again the frightened marmot. Given its fear, the marmot will hastily interrupt whatever it was doing and focus its visual attention on the eagle, taking in information about the predator, while its heart will start racing so that it will be ready to run away or to fight back, depending on the proximity of the danger.

According to the simple motivational theory, then, emotions consist in relatively flexible action (or inaction) tendencies, which are understood in terms of states of action (or inaction) readiness, which have either specific or generic goals, and which manifest control precedence. How convincing is this account of emotions? Let us first look at the arguments in favor of this approach.

5.3. Two Arguments for the Simple Motivational Theory

Clearly, fear, anger, and disgust, are good candidates for a motivational theory of emotions. Such emotions clearly involve motivations of some kind. Again, as in the case of feelings, it does not seem true that this holds because of the concepts that are involved. The question, then, is whether there are good arguments in favor of Frijda's account.

Before considering two arguments in favor of the simple motivational theory, let us note that this theory is well placed to account for a number of the typical features of emotions other than their motivational component. It has no problem, in particular, to account for the fact that emotions typically involve feelings. The reason is that it is plausible that action tendencies understood as states of action readiness typically involve feelings. Note that this does not entail that feelings are necessarily present. Since emotions can result in mental actions with no distinctive bodily signatures, emotions need not be associated with feelings. Thus, the simple motivational theory can hold that emotions typically, but not necessarily involve feelings. The motivational theory can also easily account for the fact that emotional episodes tend to have a short duration. The reason is that it is plausible to hold that action tendencies manifesting control precedence tend to have a relatively short duration.

The first argument in favor of the simple motivational theory appeals to the function of emotions. As we have seen when discussing whether there can be unconscious emotions, it can be argued that the function of emotion is that of informing the individual about the nature and the importance of events, as well as to motivate individuals accordingly (Clore 1994b). Indeed, that is how Frijda himself thinks of the function of emotions. In his terms, "[t]he function of emotions is to signal events that are relevant to the individual's concerns, and to motivate behavior to deal with those events" (Frijda 1994b, 121). We have seen that there is no need to assume that emotions are conscious in order to fulfill such a function. By contrast, it is obviously difficult to deny that emotions need to involve motivation in order to fulfill the function of motivating individuals.

To fully assess this argument, we would again need to take a stand on whether this is indeed the function of emotions. Even if we grant that this is a plausible claim, however, it is not clear that the argument can take us all the way to motivational theories, let alone to Frijda's version of this approach. The main reason for this is that emotions could play a significant role in motivation without being themselves motivations. As we will see in the next chapter, one can hold that emotions consist in appraisals or evaluations, which are states that can cause motivations. Thus, emotions could fulfill the motivational function without involving motivations as constituents. It is also noteworthy that both Clore and Frijda postulate a dual function that involves both what can be described as an evaluative component and a motivational component. In addition to playing a role in motivation, emotions have the function to inform about the importance of events or to signal events that are relevant to one's concerns, that is, the function to evaluate events. This is a point to which we will come back.

Let us turn to a second argument in favor of motivational theories. This argument, which has been developed by Scarantino (2014), grants that other accounts of emotions can explain their motivational function. The aim of the argument is to show that only motivational theories that invoke flexible action tendencies with control precedence can account for *how* we act when we are experiencing emotions. Scarantino highlights three hallmarks of emotional actions: *impulsivity*, *flexibility*, and *bodily underpinnings*. Following Frijda (2010), he explains impulsivity in terms of a sense of urge, a preference for acting earlier rather than later, as well as the "shortsightedness" of such action, that is, the fact that they are based on reduced information gathering as well as on information processing biases. What is characteristic of the flexibility of emotional actions is that even if there is a range of different things that we do out of an emotion like fear or anger, there are constraints to what can be envisaged in terms of action when you are afraid or angry. The last feature of emotional actions is that they typically come with concurrent bodily changes, such as changes in facial and vocal expressions as well as changes in the autonomic nervous system.

To make his point vivid, Scarantino asks us to consider two characters, Regular Matt, who feels emotions like you and me, and Twin Matt, who is a marine and is trained to not become afraid in dangerous circumstances. Both are visiting a circus when a tiger escapes from its enclosure. Regular Matt's action manifest impulsivity, constrained flexibility, and bodily underpinnings. He trembles and sweats, forgets where the closest exit is located, mistakes a shadow for another tiger, and when he faces the tiger, he remembers he should stand still but cannot help himself running up a tree that is well within reach of the tiger. By contrast, Twin Matt, who believes the tiger is dangerous and desires to get away from that danger, coldly assesses the situation, calmly goes for the closest exit, and when facing the tiger, remains motionless as the tiger approaches.

We can agree that an account in terms of action tendencies has no difficulty explaining the difference between Regular Matt's emotional action and Twin Matt's cold action. Yet, it is not clear that the argument succeeds in establishing that emotions have action tendencies as essential components. The problem is that the argument arguably fails to generalize. It is plausible for a limited range of emotions, such strong forms of fear, anger, and disgust, but it is far from obvious when emotions in general are considered. It seems that actions resulting from mild forms of these emotions need not manifest impulsivity, constrained flexibility, and bodily underpinnings. Suppose that it is not a grown-up tiger, but a tiger cub, that escaped. You might be slightly fearful that it might jump at you and scratch you, and so, you slowly walk away. Your action might not count as emotional in the sense of being impulsive, but in the strict sense, it is an emotional action because it is caused by an emotion. Mild emotions are emotions too, after all. The motivational theorist might reply that there are degrees of impulsiveness and that if your action is emotional, it nonetheless has to manifest some impulsiveness. However, it seems that some kinds of emotions cause actions that are not particularly impulsive. This is the case of admiration, for instance. When you admire a hilly landscape stretching in front of you, you might be motivated to take a picture. But surely your action need not be impulsive, and neither does your motivation involve constrained flexibility or be marked by bodily underpinnings. In the same way, when you are motivated to help someone because you feel compassion for that person, your action need not manifest the hallmarks of emotional actions, such as impulsivity.

The upshot is that the arguments in favor of the simple motivational theory can be resisted. In addition, as we will now discuss, there are important objections to that approach.

5.4. The Objections from Demarcation

Let us first look at how the simple motivational theory deals with the two demarcation challenges. The theory might seem well placed to account for the difference between emotions and states that are not emotions. As we have seen, it holds that the action tendencies that constitute emotions are marked by control precedence and by a certain flexibility. The urge-like character distinguishes emotions from non-emotional motivations, such as the tendency to fall asleep after lunch. The flexibility of the motivation makes a difference with potentially very intense action tendencies such as thirst or hunger as well as reflexes. What you are inclined to do when you are thirsty is just one kind of action, namely drinking, even if what you drink will depend on the context, and similarly when you are hungry, you will be motivated to eat all sorts of things, but the kind of action that is envisaged is of just one kind, namely, eating. In the same way, a reflex such as that of closing one's eyes when an object approaches might be very pressing, but it clearly fails to manifest flexibility.

A first problem with this way of demarcating emotions, however, is that mild emotions, such as light fear, will fail to count as an emotion insofar as they lack sufficient control precedence. The motivations associated with such emotions need not tend to take precedence over other action tendencies, they need not involve much in terms of the preemption of cognitive capacities, and the bodily preparation might be minimal. One possibility here is to insist that there is some vagueness in what counts as an emotion (Scarantino 2014). Let us grant that there might be some vagueness involved. However, the problem is that there are cases of mild emotional episodes which have low control precedence but which nonetheless clearly count as emotions. You might be a bit afraid of how your boss will take your derogatory comment, but this fear might well lack significant control precedence, so that it will systematically lose out to other motivations, such as the desire to humiliate your boss. Nonetheless, your mild fear surely counts as an emotion.

A second problem is that some emotions, such as admiration, relief, and regret, arguably are not closely connected to motivation. As a result, they will not count as emotions on the proposed criteria. Consider again admiration. Even if admiration sometimes involves action tendencies, there is reason to doubt that this is always the case. It seems that you can well admire a landscape without being motivated in any way. You might go for a hike to see the landscape from a different point of view, but you might just as well stay where you are. As the landscape example suggests, one can hold that when you admire something, you are motivated to contemplate it. Another suggestion, made by Deonna and Teroni (2012), is that admiration involves the motivation to explore what one admires. Admiration would consist in "feeling the way one's body opens up to sustained and expanding exploration" (Deonna and Teroni 2012, 81). It is not obvious, however, that admiration needs to come with any of these motivations. You can, it would seem, admire the landscape without being motivated to contemplate or to explore it (Tappolet 2016).

Similar remarks apply to relief and regret. Consider the deep relief you feel after you have nearly lost a friend to a terrible disease. You will think to yourself how good it is that your friend survived, but apart from that, it is hard to see what action tendency your relief involves. In reply, the motivational theorist could claim that the tendency to have this thought is already sufficient to attribute to an action tendency. The problem, however, is that it is difficult to see how emotions could involve tendencies to make such evaluative judgments if they do not involve appraisals. As stated, the motivational theory would thus be incomplete. Similar remarks apply to regret. If you regret that five years ago, you decided to study law while, in fact, philosophy would have been more interesting, there is little in terms of what you can do. There simply is no way to undo your past decision. Thus, there appears to be no action (or inaction) tendency and no goal that is associated with regret. Maybe regret can incline you to ruminate over what you have done, but again, it is not clear that this is always the case.

What about the demarcation between kinds of emotions? It is clearly problematic to appeal only to action tendencies. After all, we are prone to attack both when afraid and when angry, and we tend to avoid what we are afraid of as much as we tend to avoid what disgusts us. Indeed, avoiding someone can also be a way to express anger. The motivational theorist will argue that one has to appeal to the goals at which the different action tendencies aim. When afraid, what we do has the goal of protecting ourselves from harm, while according to Frijda (1986; see also Scarantino 2014), the goal of anger is the removal of obstruction, and that of disgust the removal of some object. Thus, even if the actions involved in action tendencies of fear, anger, and disgust can be the same, their goals are sufficiently different to mark the difference between the two kinds of emotions. Is this really so?

Emotions that are not closely connected to motivation are as much a problem here as they are concerning the demarcation between emotions and states that are not emotions. If admiration, relief, and regret are not associated with action tendencies and goals, the simple motivational theory will have no way to differentiate them. Another problem, however, is that on the simple motivational theory different emotions appear to share the same goal. As Frijda (1986) notes, fear and disgust both share protection as their function. Indeed, it would seem the goal of removing obstruction that is associated with anger can also be understood as involving a kind of protection, that is, protection from obstruction. What needs to be added to differentiate the action tendencies of fear, disgust, and anger is a specification of the protection at stake. In the case of fear, one seeks protection from danger, whereas in the case of disgust one seeks protection from contamination, and with anger, the goal is protection from obstruction. Because "obstructive", "dangerous" and "contaminated" are evaluative expressions, however, it follows that one has to appeal to evaluations in order to demarcate emotions. As such, it might seem fine for a motivational theorist to allow evaluative expressions in the description of action tendencies. The question, however, is whether it is possible for someone to have such an action tendency without representing the evaluative feature in question. Can you be motivated to protect yourself from danger without representing what you fear as dangerous? It seems the answer is that you cannot. But if you cannot, it follows that emotions must involve evaluations in addition to motivations.

In a similar way, Robert Roberts (2003) asks us to consider a case of anger at a colleague and points out that this anger can trigger a huge variety of actions, ranging from a dirty look and smiling contemptuously to shouldering the colleague into the gutter. Now, none of these actions need to express anger, for the dirty look could result from disgust, the smile could express contempt and shouldering into the gutter might be required to save the colleague from falling crockery. Roberts argues that the actions correlated with anger have to be defined as ways of punishing an offender. Thus, punishing an offender (and not merely the removal of obstruction, as Frijda had it) would be the unifying goal of the different actions we tend to do when in anger. The problem, according to Roberts, is that to have this kind of goal, it is necessary that the agent see the situation as offensive. Because he claims that seeing the situation as offensive requires feeling anger, Roberts concludes that "the proposal to define emotions as readiness for action seems to reverse the conceptual priorities [...]" (2003, 169). Whether or not one accepts this last point, what follows from the argument is that the motivation involved in emotions depends on evaluations.

The conclusion that emotions must involve evaluations also follows from problems that arise because emotions have intentional objects, to which we now turn.

5.5. The Objections from Intentionality

As we have seen, the simple motivational theory can account for a number of typical features of emotions, such as the fact that they typically involve feelings. What is more problematic is to account for the intentionality of emotions. When you fear a tiger, your fear is about the tiger, the tiger being the intentional object of your emotion. The problem is that insofar as action tendencies are behavioral tendencies, they do not appear to be about anything. Your tendency to run is not about running any more than the stone's tendency to fall is about falling. In reply, one could argue that one has to conceive of action tendencies as mental states, such as desires, that have intentional objects. When you desire to have a drink, your desire is about having a drink. Having a drink is the intentional object of your desire. Thus, if one understands the action tendency to run away from the tiger as the desire to run away, this action tendency has an intentional object, namely your running.

Because motivational theorists seem to understand action tendencies merely in bodily terms, it is not obvious that they would welcome this suggestion. Even if they would, however, the problem is that the intentional object would not be the correct one. When you are afraid of the tiger and you are motivated to run away, your emotion is about the tiger, not the running. The desire to run away, however, has the running as its intentional object. You could of course also be afraid of running, but that is quite a different emotion from being afraid of the tiger. In reply, the motivational theorist can invoke the goals of the action tendency, such as the protection from danger. Put otherwise, safety is what you desire. Thus, the intentional object of your emotion would be safety and more precisely safety from the tiger. The problem, again, is that this is not what intuitively appears to be the intentional object of your fear, namely, the tiger.

A second objection that involves intentionality is that the motivational theory cannot account for the fact that emotions are about things such as dangers, contaminations, obstructions, or offenses. It is not only that fear involves motivations that aim at dealing with such danger. Fear involves a representation of danger, an evaluation of something, such as the situation or the tiger, as dangerous. Indeed, as we have seen, once one grants that fear involves the motivation to protect oneself from danger, it seems that one has to accept that fears also involve a representation of what you fear as dangerous. The objection, thus, is that insofar as it holds that emotions consist in nothing but motivations, the simple motivational theory is at best incomplete.

Another way to make the point is to make use of the distinction between so-called *directions of fit* (Searle 1983). Desires have a world-to-mind direction of fit, in the sense that the world has to change in order to fit what is desired. If in the middle of summer, you desire that it snow (and you live in Montréal and not in Nunavut), your desire will be satisfied on the condition that the world changes and it starts snowing. Your desire aims at being realized, and this requires that the world changes accordingly. By contrast, beliefs have the opposite direction of fit, which is that of mind-to-world. It is your belief that has to try to match how things are in the world. For example, your belief that it snows fits the world on condition that it really snows. This direction of fit is closely connected to the idea of truth conditions. If it snows, your belief that it snows will be true, but if it does not snow – remember, it's the middle of summer in Montréal – your belief will be false.

Now, on the simple motivational theory, emotions have a world-to-mind direction of fit. That is, they have the same direction of fit as desires. The problem, however, is that emotions appear to have the other direction of fit. Even if we would maybe not say that emotions can be true or false (but see de Sousa 2011), emotions are generally considered to be assessable in terms of their correctness. Thus, we standardly assess emotions in terms of how they represent evaluative facts, such as facts regarding danger or contamination. When you are afraid of a small innocuous spider that crawls up your arm, your friend is likely to remark that you should not be afraid because there is no danger. Put otherwise, your fear involves a misrepresentation of the spider as dangerous. This kind of criticism presupposes that emotions are like beliefs in that they have a mind-to-world direction of fit. Your fear involves the representation of the spider as dangerous, and thus involves an evaluation of the spider as dangerous. It follows that the simple motivational theory is, at best, incomplete. Even if one grants that emotions involve motivations, it has to be accepted that they also involve evaluations.

In reply, one could try to deny that emotions involve evaluations. However, the task to explain away the current practice of assessing emotions in terms of how they represent evaluative facts is daunting. A more concessive reply is to grant that evaluations need to be involved, but to deny that they constitute essential components of emotions. It thus can be argued with Frijda (1986) that these evaluations are merely the causes of emotions, not their essences. The main problem with this suggestion is that it does not account for the centrality of evaluations in emotions. Thus, the claim that emotions are caused by evaluations cannot make room for the fact that we assess our emotions themselves, and not their causes, in terms of how they fit the world (see Chapter 6).

An even more concessive reply is to opt for a hybrid theory, according to which emotions combine an evaluative and a motivational component. The most straightforward way of combining these two elements is to hold that fear consists in a belief that there is danger plus a desire to stay safe. As Scarantino (2014) argues, the problem with this suggestion is that because beliefs and desires do not typically involve feelings, this suggestion fails to account for the fact that emotions typically involve feelings. However, to remedy this problem, it can be held that the motivational elements are action tendencies, which typically involve feelings. According to a sophisticated version of this approach – but note that it is a bit unclear whether or not it really should count as a hybrid theory – emotions consist in states that are both evaluative and motivational, in the sense that they represent how things are in terms of their values and they motivate accordingly (Scarantino 2014). Emotions would be states that have both directions of fit, so-called "pushmi-pullyu" representations, to use Ruth Millikan's expression (2004), which at the same time represent facts and involve goals. Such a theory nicely handles the second objection from intentionality, and it is also well placed to handle the objections from demarcation according to which we need to assume that emotions involve evaluations in order to account for the difference between kinds of emotion. As we shall see, it nonetheless shares some of the problems of the simple motivational theory.

The third reply consists in denying that the evaluative component needs to be cashed out in terms of an evaluative representation. Thus, the attitudinal theory developed by Deonna and Teroni (2012) holds that if emotions involve evaluations, it is because they are motivations. Let us examine the attitudinal theory.

5.6. The Attitudinal Theory

Deonna and Teroni (2012, 2014, 2015) follow Frijda in taking states of action readiness to be central to emotions, but they also take on board James' emphasis on feelings. Their starting point is that "emotions are intimately connected with types of action readiness or, more precisely, felt action readiness" (2012, 79). Thus, they hold that emotions have to be understood in terms of feelings of action readiness. In anger, for instance, we feel the way our body is prepared for hostile activity. In shame, we feel our body poised to hide from the gaze of others. In disgust, we feel our body poised to prevent the object of disgust coming into contact with it. In contrast with the simple motivational theory, Deonna and Teroni hold that these states of action readiness consist in bodily attitudes toward intentional objects. According to them, the feelings of action readiness are bodily feelings, but they are not directed toward our body. Instead, these feelings of action readiness are directed toward things in the world. As they put it, "the bodily changes involved in emotions are felt by the subject as distinctive attitudes that are (at least typically) directed towards external objects" (Deonna and Teroni 2014, 27). The fact that emotions have intentional objects is thus built into the theory. As a result, the attitudinal theory has no trouble accounting for this aspect of the intentionality of emotions.

Importantly, Deonna and Teroni hold that emotions involve evaluations. The feeling of action readiness is not only directed at an intentional object, but it also involves an experience of its intentional object as being dangerous, offensive, etc. This, according to them, follows from the fact that emotions involve states of action readiness. "Fear of the dog", they write, "is an experience of the dog as dangerous, precisely because it consists in feeling the body's readiness to act so as to diminish the dog's likely impact on it (flight, preemptive attack, etc.) [...]" (Deonna and Teroni 2012, 81). They hold that because of this, fear has correctness conditions which can be spelled out in terms of danger. Thus, they add that "the felt attitude is correct if and only if the dog is dangerous" (Deonna and Teroni 2012, ibid.). This is another attractive feature of the proposed theory, which makes it possible for the theory to account for the second aspect of the intentionality of emotions, that is, the fact that emotions are about dangers, contaminations, offenses, etc., and can be assessed in terms of whether they fit evaluative facts.

What has to be underscored, and this is the tricky part, is that Deonna and Teroni do not understand the evaluative component to consist in a representation. Being afraid of a dog, according to them, does not involve a representation of the dog as dangerous. According to their account, fear consists in an *evaluative attitude* and not in an *evaluative representation*. The notion of attitude here is in fact a technical notion. The distinction that is important to understand is that of *attitude* versus *content* (see Searle 1983). Attitudes are mental states that are directed at contents. Standard examples of attitudes are believing, desiring, or supposing, which we have toward contents. Thus, we can believe that it snows, just as we can believe that it rains. One feature of attitudes is that we can have distinct attitudes toward the same content. We might believe that is snows, we might desire that it snows, or we might suppose that it snows. These different attitudes are characterized in terms of specific constitutive aims.[1] The attitude of belief, for instance, aims at truth and a belief can be assessed as incorrect when it fails to be true. Now, emotions are also often cited as examples of attitudes. In the same way as we can believe that it snows, desire that it snows, or suppose that it snows, we can have different emotions that concern the same content. We can for instance fear that it snows, we can be angry that it snows, or we can be amused that it snows. Or else we can fear the dog, be angry at the dog, or be amused by the dog.

Taking these observations regarding attitudes as their starting point, Deonna and Teroni's suggestion is that emotions form a particular family of attitudes, namely, *evaluative attitudes*. Fear, for instance is an evaluative attitude, which we have toward content such as dogs and tigers, or else, states of affairs, such as that it might snow. Such attitudes are evaluative because their constitutive aim is evaluative. Thus, fear is an attitude that has danger as its constitutive aim, while anger is tied to the constitutive aim of offensiveness, and disgust to contamination or disgustingness. This suggestion contrasts with the claim that emotions are or essentially involve attitudes that have evaluative contents, whether these attitudes are taken to be judgments or perceptions, for instance. To put it differently, the way the attitudinal theory understands the evaluative character of emotions contrasts with standard evaluative theories of emotions, according to which emotions involve evaluative judgments or perceptions, which consist in evaluative representations.

In sum, then, the attitudinal theory holds that emotions are feelings of action readiness, which have to be understood as evaluative attitudes directed toward intentional objects. The attitudinal theory shares the virtues of the simple motivational theory. In particular, it has no problem accounting for the fact that emotional motivation can be impulsive. However, the attitudinal theory clearly improves on the simple motivational theory by holding that emotions are directed at intentional objects and involve evaluations. In spite of this, the theory nonetheless shares some important weaknesses of the simple motivational theory. Before we consider these weaknesses, let us first look at an important argument in favor of the attitudinal theory.

5.7. An Argument for the Attitudinal Theory

As we will better understand in the next chapter, Deonna and Teroni's account is motivated by the desire to improve on evaluative theories, and in particular to improve on so-called *perceptual theories*. A good part of its attractiveness, according to them, is that the attitudinal theory accounts for the evaluative dimension of emotions without falling prey to the alleged difficulties of standard evaluative theories. In particular, Deonna and Teroni (2012, 2014, 2015) hold that, unlike its competitors, the attitudinal theory can account for one important feature of emotions. This feature is that different emotions can be directed at the same content. As we have seen, you can fear that it snows, angry that it snows, or hope that it snows, to mention only a few possibilities. According to the attitudinal theory, this is just to be expected, since emotions are attitudes that can share contents. The problem with competing theories, according to Deonna and Teroni, is that they cannot account for this fact.

The competing theories that Deonna and Teroni consider are evaluative theories, but the problem can also be formulated as one that concerns the simple motivational theory. Consider a case in which two persons feel differently toward the same object. I fear the dog, but you are angry at the dog, maybe because the dog disobeyed your orders. Now, on the simple motivational theory, this amounts to having motivations of different kinds, characterized by different goals. Fear is a motivation that aims at protection from danger, while anger is a motivation that aims at protection from offense. Now when you compare the content of the two motivations, it is clear that they have different contents. The content of one motivation is the protection from danger, while the content of the other is protection from offense. As a result, the content of my fear is distinct from the content of your anger. But this appears wrong, considered that both emotions are about the very same dog.

What can be questioned in this argument, however, is that different kinds of emotions can share the exact same content (Rossi and Tappolet 2019). It has to be granted, of course, that my fear and your anger have the same intentional object, namely, the dog – a fact that the simple motivational theory has a hard time to account for, but this is neither here nor there. The question is whether these two emotions share more than their intentional object. In contrast with what Deonna and Teroni hold, there is arguably more to the content involved in an emotion than their intentional objects. According to evaluative theories, in particular, emotions involve a representation that has an evaluative content, that is, the representation of its intentional object as having an evaluative feature. Thus, the content of emotions consists in an intentional object plus an evaluative feature. My fear involves the representation of the dog as dangerous, while your anger involves the representation of the same dog as offensive or obstructive. Even though the two emotions share their intentional object, their full contents, which involve evaluative features, are distinct. The problem, then, is that the argument for the attitudinal theory simply assumes that apart from their intentional object, there is no additional element in the content of emotion. This amounts to begging the question.

5.8. Objections to the Attitudinal Theory

A first issue with the attitudinal theory concerns its emphasis on feelings. As we saw when discussing feeling theories, emotions are typically felt, but it is far from clear that this is necessarily the case. This might not be a fatal problem for the attitudinal theory, however, for it is possible to envisage an account according to which evaluative attitudes are understood not in terms of feelings, but in terms of motivational states of action readiness that are typically but not necessarily felt. A good question is whether a revision of the attitudinal theory on those lines could make room for the fact that emotions have intentional objects, but let us leave this issue to the side.

A more difficult problem is that just like the simple motivational theory, the attitudinal theory faces counterexamples. As we have seen, some emotions, such as admiration, relief, or regret, appear to be only distantly related to action tendencies and more generally to motivations (see Mitchell 2020). As we saw above, it is not obvious that admiration always involves a motivation, be it that of contemplating or of exploring what one admires. It is worth underscoring that insofar as they take motivations to constitute the essence of emotions, such cases make for a major problem for any kind of motivational theory, including Scarantino's pushmi-pullyu version.

Another problem that the attitudinal theory shares with the simply motivational theory concerns the demarcation between different kinds of emotions. As we have seen, it is necessary to appeal to evaluative terms in order to differentiate the action tendencies that constitute the different kinds of emotions. In the case of fear, one seeks protection from danger, whereas in the case of disgust, the action tendency is aimed at protection from contamination, and both "dangerous" and "contaminated" are evaluative terms. As we have seen, the problem for the simple motivational theory is that to have such a motivation, it appears necessary to represent the evaluative feature in question. It does not seem possible, for instance, to be motivated to protect yourself from danger without representing what you fear as dangerous. Now, it might seem that the attitudinal theory does not face that problem. After all, the theory can appeal to the constitutive aim of the different evaluative attitudes, such as danger in the case of fear, offense in the case of anger, or loss in the case of sadness (Deonna and Teroni 2014).

The problem, however, is that according to the attitudinal theory, the evaluative nature of the attitudes is derived from the underlying states of action readiness. Deonna and Teroni hold that being afraid of the dog is an evaluative attitude precisely because it consists in feeling the body's readiness to diminish the dog's likely impact on it. The question is whether the felt action readiness is a motivation that already involves evaluation (Ballard 2021). Do we not aim at diminishing the dog's impact on our body because we consider it to be dangerous? If the answer is yes, it is hard to see how we could do so without representing the dog as dangerous. Obviously, we need to see the dog's impacting our body as dangerous in order to be motivated to diminish that impact because it is dangerous. Hence, in spite of what the attitudinal theory holds, emotions would involve evaluative representations. If the answer is no, it is difficult to see how the theory demarcates the different kinds of emotions. As such, the motivation of diminishing a dog's impact on our body could be one that is associated with disgust – the aim would be to avoid being contaminated by the dog, which we can imagine to be a harmless Chihuahua covered in slime. Or it could be associated with pity – the aim would be to avoid harming the smallish and fragile dog that would be seriously harmed if it ran into you. There appears to be no choice but to allow that the motivations that constitute the emotions presuppose evaluative representations. This is bad news for the attitudinal theory, since this is exactly what the theory denies.

A further difficulty concerns the direction of fit of emotions. According to Deonna and Teroni, the attitudinal theory can make room for the thought that emotions have a mind-to-world direction of fit, that is, that emotions can be assessed in terms of how they correspond to real dangers, offenses, etc., in the world. What Deonna and Teroni hold is that it is because emotions are evaluative attitudes, which have evaluative constitutive aims, that evaluative features enter the correctness conditions of emotions. The model here is that of belief. Recall that the constitutive aim of belief is truth. Now, a belief can be criticized as incorrect when it fails to be true. Put differently, a belief is correct on the condition that its content is true. Thus, truth enters the correctness conditions of belief simply in virtue of being the constitutive aim of that kind of attitude. The suggestion is that emotions exhibit the same pattern. Fear, for instance, has danger as its constitutive aim and it is because of this that danger figures in the correctness condition of fear. As a result, fear would be correct on condition that its content – that is its intentional object – is dangerous.

The problem is that it is an open question whether the way the attitudinal theory proposes to understand the correctness conditions of emotions is successful (Rossi and Tappolet 2019). The question, in fact, is whether the attitudinal theory can account for the mind-to-world direction of fit of emotions, that is, for the fact that emotions are correct or not depending on how the world is in terms of evaluative features. Arguably, if emotions are thought to be correct insofar as they correspond to how the world is in terms of evaluative features, it follows that emotions involve evaluative representations. To see this, consider again beliefs. To say that beliefs are correct insofar as they correspond to how things are is to say that they represent how things are. Your belief that the sky is blue is correct insofar as it corresponds to how the sky is, namely blue. To say that your belief has these correctness conditions is just to say that the belief represents the sky as blue. Similarly, if your fear of the dog is correct insofar as it corresponds to how the dog is, namely dangerous, your fear must represent the dog as being dangerous.

In fact, the difficulty for the attitudinal theory is that its starting point is that the core of emotions is constituted by felt states of action readiness, that is, motivational states. We were told that being afraid of the dog is an experience of the animal as dangerous because fear consists in a felt readiness to deal with the danger. Because it is a motivation, being ready to deal with the danger arguably has a world-to-mind direction of fit. The world has to fit the desire and the desire is satisfied if the danger is dealt with. Moreover, if we say that the motivation is correct, it is not in terms of matching the world, but in terms of being useful – clearly, dealing with the danger is useful, since it promotes your well-being. But if so, asking whether an emotion is correct could not consist in asking whether its intentional object has the corresponding evaluative feature. It would rather consist in asking whether the emotion is useful.

A final problem with the attitudinal theory, and indeed with all motivational theories spelled out in terms of action readiness, is that the proposed picture of emotional motivation lacks plausibility. Even if such theories allow for a good amount of flexibility, they are committed to the implausible view that the motivational effects of emotions are nonetheless importantly limited. Consider again fear. According to Deonna and Teroni, to fear something involves our body's readiness to act so as to diminish the feared object's impact by fleeing, fighting, etc. Thus, fear involves behavioral dispositions, which tend to result in a limited range of actions, such as fleeing and fighting, or else freezing and hiding. As we saw at the outset, it makes sense to describe the marmot's behavior in terms of such behavioral dispositions, at least on condition that the dispositions at stake are complex enough to account for the variety of context-dependent behaviors that we can observe in marmots. However, in the case of human beings, an account in terms of behavioral dispositions will clearly not do. We sometimes run away or attack out of fear, but what we do when we experience fear is much more varied.

As Gerald Clore notes, "the direct effects of emotions are motivational rather than behavioral. One can achieve more agreement about the likely goals of [...] fearful [...] persons than about their likely behaviors" (1994a, 111; see also de Sousa 1987). Fear, according to Clore, comes with bodily activation that facilitates action, but this falls short of an action tendency. Fear rather involves a desire to avoid harm, but whether this goal is achieved by selling one's stock, listening to the weather report, or by running away will depend on the particular context. In addition to the influence of the context, it is also important to recognize that the deliberation of the agent is an important factor in determining what will be done out of fear. In the terms used by Prinz (2004), who distinguishes between dispositions that move us to action, or "action-commands", and what he calls "motives", emotions are not action-commands, but motives, in the sense that they give us reasons for action. Thus, emotions may prepare us for action via bodily activation, but what is needed for emotion to result in action is that the agent deliberates and takes a decision. As a result, actions resulting from emotions may manifest the hallmarks of emotional action, such as impulsivity – and this is something that can be explained in terms of the bodily activation mentioned by Clore – but they certainly do not have always to do so. If this argument is on the right lines, it follows that all the theories that place states of action readiness at the core of emotions, and this includes the attitudinal theory, the simple motivational theory, and the pushmi-pullyu version of the motivational theory, fail to account for the way emotions motivate us.

5.9. Taking Stock

Motivational theories, which hold that motivations constitute the core of emotions, improve on feeling theories in that they can easily account for the fact that emotions provide explanations of our actions. However, several objections to the different versions of motivational theories we discussed strongly suggest that emotions involve evaluative representations. The next chapter turns to theories according to which evaluations are central to emotions.

5.10. Summary

- According to the simple motivational theory defended by Frijda, emotions are relatively flexible action (or inaction) tendencies, which have either specific or generic goals, and which manifest control precedence.
- This account is well placed to account for several typical features of emotions, but the argument in favor of the simple motivational theory, or indeed of any motivational theory, that appeals to the function of emotions is unconvincing, because rival theories, such as evaluative theories, can also account for the role of emotion in motivation.
- The argument for the simple motivational theory that appeals to specific features of emotional actions, such as impulsivity, also fails, and the reason is that not all emotional actions are characterized by these features.
- Given the possibility of mild emotions, but also of emotions that are not tightly connected to motivation, such as admiration, the simple motivational theory has trouble demarcating emotions from other kinds of states.
- For the same reason, the simple motivational theory also has trouble differentiating kinds of emotions; moreover, to account for the difference between emotions having goals that are described in evaluative terms, such as the protection from danger, it is likely that the theory has to accept that emotions involve evaluative representations.
- The simple motivational theory has a hard time making room for both the fact that our emotions are about intentional objects, such as tigers and dogs, and the fact that emotions are about dangers, contaminations, etc., in the sense that they are correct on condition their intentional objects are dangerous, contaminated, etc.
- The pushmi-pullyu version of the motivational theory as defended by Scarantino deals with these problems by accepting that emotions are states that involve both representations and motivations. Because it holds that

action tendencies are the core of emotions, it faces some of the difficulties of the simple motivational theory.

- The attitudinal theory aims at accounting for both the fact that emotions have intentional objects and the fact that they involve evaluations without accepting that emotions involve evaluative representations. This theory holds that emotions are feelings of action readiness, which have to be understood as evaluative attitudes directed toward intentional objects.
- The main argument for the attitudinal theory, which claims that only this theory can account for the fact that different emotions can have exactly the same content, fails to convince because it assumes without argument that there is no further content to emotions in addition to their intentional objects.
- The attitudinal theory arguably shares some of the difficulties with the simple motivational theory, such as the fact that some kinds of emotions are not closely connected to motivation.
- Similarly, it is not clear that the attitudinal theory can differentiate emotion kinds without accepting that emotions involve evaluative representations.
- Another problem is that it is not clear that the attitudinal theory can make room for the fact that we assess emotions in terms of how they correspond to features of the world, such as dangers or offenses.
- Finally, the attitudinal theory, as well as other theories in terms of action readiness, proposes what is arguably an unconvincing picture of emotional motivation, which fails to make room for the variety of actions motivated by emotions.

5.11. Study Questions

1. Do emotions regarding the past (such as anger at one's ancestors) involve motivations? If they do, are such motivations necessarily involved in these emotions?
2. Suppose you admire a work of art, such as a painting. What will you tend to do? And are these action tendencies to be found in all cases of admiration?
3. Does anger have a goal? And if so, what is it? The removal of obstruction, the punishment of an offender, or something else?

Note

1 These constitutive aims are often referred to as "formal objects", but for the sake of clarity, we will reserve that term for the evaluative features in terms of which emotions are assessed (see Chapter 2).

5.12. Further Readings

Ballard, Brian Scott. 2021. "Content and the Fittingness of Emotions." *Philosophical Quarterly* 71 (4):845–863.

Deonna, Julien A., and Fabrice Teroni. 2015. "Emotions as Attitudes." *Dialectica* 69 (3):293–311.

Dokic, Jérôme, and Stéphane Lemaire. 2015. "Are Emotions Evaluative Modes?" *Dialectica* 69 (3):271–292.

Frijda, Nico H. 1986. *The Emotions*. Cambridge: Cambridge University Press, chap. 2.

Mitchell, Jonathan. 2020. "The Bodily-Attitudinal Theory of Emotion." *Philosophical Studies* 178 (8):2635–2663.

Pacherie, Elisabeth. 2001. "The Role of Emotions in the Explanation of Action." *European Review of Philosophy* 5:55–90.

Reisenzein, Rainer. 1996. "Emotional Action Generation." In *Processes of the Molar Regulation of Behavior*, edited by Wolfgang Battmann and Dutke Stephan, 151–165. Lengerich: Pabst Science.

Rossi, Mauro, and Christine Tappolet. 2019. "What Kind of Evaluative States Are Emotions? The Attitudinal Theory vs. the Perceptual Theory of Emotions." *Canadian Journal of Philosophy* 49 (4):544–563.

Scarantino, Andrea. 2014. "The Motivational Theory of Emotions." In *Moral Psychology and Human Agency*, edited by Daniel Jacobson and Justin D'Arms, 156–185. New York: Oxford University Press.

Scherer, Klaus R. 1994. "Emotion Serves to Decouple Stimulus and Response." In *The Nature of Emotion: Fundamental Questions*, edited by Paul Ekman and Richard J. Davidson, 127–130. New York: Oxford University Press.

6   Evaluative Theories

6.1. Introduction

Recall the marmot that was afraid of the eagle circling in the air. If we apply the main lesson drawn from our discussion of motivational theories in the previous chapter to this case, we have to assume that the marmot evaluates the eagle as dangerous. A first set of questions that arise concerns the relation between the evaluation and the marmot's fear. Is the relation a causal one, the evaluation being the cause of the emotion? Is it a constitutive relation, so that the emotion fully or partly consists in the evaluation? Could it be both a causal and a constitutive relation? A second set of questions concerns the nature of this evaluation. As we have seen in the previous chapter, there are reasons to take the evaluations to consist in representations. The marmot represents the eagle as dangerous. This claim, however, leaves many possibilities open. The evaluation could for instance consist in a judgment that the eagle is dangerous, but it could also consist in other kinds of representational states, such as the perception of the eagle as dangerous. As we will see, evaluative theories come in quite different versions, depending on how they answer these questions.

Evaluative theories are often traced back to the Stoics, such as Seneca. As we have seen in Chapter 1, the Stoics held that emotions consist in judgments about the good and the bad. They also thought that these judgments were for the most part deeply mistaken and irrational, but this is a claim that sets them apart from other evaluative theorists. Going further back, Plato and Aristotle already thought that emotions depend on evaluations. Plato, for one, viewed anger as involving the boiling of the blood upon thinking that one has been wronged, whereas Aristotle defined anger as a painful desire for revenge caused by the thought of a slight. Indeed, the claim that at least some emotions have evaluations as necessary or at least typical causes is a common one in the history of emotion theories. It was held by Aquinas, Descartes, and Hume, among others.

Evaluative theories have made a comeback both in philosophy and in psychology, starting in the late 1950s. On the basis of their rejection of feeling theories, philosophers such as C. D. Broad (1954), Errol Bedford (1956–1957) and Anthony Kenny (1963/2003) defended the view that emotions consist in evaluations of a

DOI: 10.4324/9781315542300-8

particular kind, while William Lyons argues that emotions have evaluations as causes (1980). Quite independently and as part of the cognitivist revolution that replaced behaviorism, psychologists such as Magda Arnold (1960) and Richard Lazarus (1991) defended so-called *appraisal theories* of emotions and argued that emotions are caused by appraisals. Both the *constitutive version* of the evaluative approach according to which emotions are (at least partly) evaluations, and its *causal version*, which holds that emotions are caused by evaluation, have contemporary advocates.

Because it has been particularly influential both in psychology and in philosophy, we will start our exploration of evaluative theories with a discussion of appraisal theories as defended by Arnold (1960), Lazarus (1991) and Klaus Scherer (1984, 2005, 2009). We will see that the causal thesis at the heart of this approach is compatible with all three kinds of theories of emotions. After this, we will turn to so-called *judgmental theories*, which are advocated by Robert Solomon (1976/1993, 2003, 2007) and Martha Nussbaum (2001), as well as what has become known as *quasi-judgmental theories*, as developed by Patricia Greenspan (1988) and Robert Roberts (2003). In spite of their many attractions, judgmental and quasi-judgmental theories face important objections, so our discussion will focus on *perceptual theories*, such as defended by Sabine Döring (2003) and Jesse Prinz (2004), among others. The upshot of our discussion is that we need an account that makes room for the differences between sensory perceptions and emotions. The chapter will close with a sketch of a new approach, which I will call the "receptive theory".

6.2. Appraisal Theories

Arnold (1960) introduced the notion of *appraisal* in order to explain how emotions are caused. According to her, to appraise something consists in seeing it as affecting oneself in some way that matters. The process of appraisal determines the significance of a situation for an individual. Arnold thought of emotions as resulting from the appraisal of things as good (or beneficial) or bad (or harmful). In a way reminiscent of the Stoics, Arnold thought that appraisals comprise several dimensions. Arnold's scheme comprises three dimensions. The eliciting circumstances can be evaluated as good or bad, as present or absent, but also as easy to attain or to avoid. The appraisal that causes fear, for instance, is one of an event as bad, absent but possible in the future, as well as hard to avoid. By contrast, the appraisal that causes joy characterizes the event as good, present, and easy to maintain.

If one thinks of anger and disgust, which both concern things that are bad, present, and difficult to avoid, it becomes clear that the three dimensions postulated by Arnold are not sufficient to differentiate kinds of emotions. The obvious way to improve on Arnold's account consists in adding dimensions of appraisals. This is exactly what Lazarus (1991) proposed. Lazarus emphasized well-being in his understanding of the notion of appraisal. Seeing well-being as depending on the environmental conditions as well as on the person's beliefs and goals, he claims that "[t]he task of appraisals is to integrate the two sets of antecedent variables – personality and environmental – into a relational meaning based on the relevance of what is happening for the person's well-being" (1991, 39). Accordingly, appraisals, which can be either conscious and deliberate or not, are defined as consisting in evaluations of the significance of what is happening for a person's well-being.

Lazarus distinguishes six dimensions of appraisal, which belong to two broad categories. In the first category of so-called *primary appraisal* components, there is (a) *goal relevance*, (b) *goal congruency and incongruency*, and (c) *type of ego-involvement*. In the second category, that of *secondary appraisal* components, there is (d) *blame or credit*, (e) *coping potential*, and (f) *future expectations*. The process of appraisal thus starts with the question of whether something is relevant to your goals. If not, no emotion is triggered. If it is relevant, the next question is whether that thing thwarts or facilitates your goals. In the latter case, a positive emotion follows, but in the former, the emotion will be negative. The third question that arises is how you are involved in the situation. Lazarus distinguishes different types of ego-involvements, among which are self-esteem and social esteem. The dimension of blame or credit concerns the question of who, if anyone, is accountable. An interesting feature of Lazarus' account is that he stresses the importance of the coping potential. The dimension of future expectancy, finally, has to do with the question of whether things are likely to change for the better or the worse, in the sense of becoming more, or less, congruent to your goals.

According to Lazarus, the complex appraisals corresponding to kinds of emotions are captured by what he calls "core relational themes", a concept that has been influential in recent discussions (see Prinz 2004; Solomon 2007; Scarantino 2014). A core relational theme "summarizes the personal harms and benefits residing in each person-environment relationship" (Lazarus 1991, 39). Each kind of emotion has its distinctive core relational theme. In the case anger, for instance, the core relational theme is defined as "a demeaning offence against me and mine", while the core relational theme for fright is that of "facing an immediate, concrete, and overwhelming physical danger", and for sadness, "having experienced an irrevocable loss" (Lazarus 1991, 122). It is noteworthy that according to Lazarus you do not have to explicitly evaluate something in terms of core relational themes to experience the emotions.

One of the attractions of Lazarus' theory is that it allows him to distinguish 15 different kinds of emotion: anger, anxiety, fright, guilt, shame, sadness, envy, jealousy, disgust, happiness, pride, relief, hope, love, and compassion. Scherer's version of the appraisal theory is even more ambitious. In his 2009 paper, he distinguishes a dozen dimensions divided into four main categories, that is, *relevance, implication, coping potential*, and *normative significance*. The so-called "stimulus evaluation checks", as Scherer calls them, which we perform in appraising events might be complex, but they are thought to consist in a "very rapidly occurring evaluation process that can occur on several levels of processing, ranging from automatic and implicit to conscious conceptual or propositional evaluations" (2005, 701). Interestingly, Scherer does not assume the existence of a limited set of emotion kinds. On the contrary, because of the multiple ways the appraisal dimensions combine and interact over time, he suggests that there might be "an infinite number of different types of emotion episodes" (2009, 1316). However, some particularly adaptive patterns of appraisals are expected to be more frequent. One example is anger, which involves "an appraisal profile that includes novelty, high goal relevance, other agent and intent, high outcome probability, dissonant expectation, goal obstructiveness, high urgency, high control and power, as well as injustice and immorality" (2009, 1316).

A distinction that is important in this context is that between the process of appraisal and appraisal understood as the result of that process. The common thread among the different appraisal theories is that a process of appraisal plays a crucial causal role in emotions. But what are emotions, on these accounts? Appraisal theorists in fact favor different theories of emotions. Arnold (1960), for one, subscribes to a motivational theory since she holds that emotions are felt action tendencies caused by appraisals. More precisely, appraisals give rise to attraction and aversion, and emotions are identified with such felt tendency *toward* what is appraised as good or *away* from what is appraised as bad. By contrast, Lazarus (1991) advocates a hybrid account, according to which emotions consist in a complex process that involves a cause and its effect, where the cause is the appraisal, and the effect, a combination of an action tendency, physiological change and subjective affect. Interestingly, a structurally similar account has been proposed in philosophy by Jenefer Robinson (2005), who holds that an emotion is a process that starts with a non-cognitive and automatic appraisal, which triggers characteristic physiological and behavioral changes as well as cognitive monitoring of the situation. Scherer, for his part, defines emotion in terms of "an episode of interrelated, synchronized changes" (2005, 697) in all or most of five subsystems, so that an emotional episode comprises up to five components: an appraisal, autonomic physiological changes, action tendencies, facial and vocal expressions, plus subjective feelings.

In fact, the thesis that the process of appraisal plays an essential causal role in emotions is compatible with the main kinds of emotion theories. Feeling theorists and motivational theorists can readily accept this causal thesis. Evaluative theorists holding that emotions consist in evaluation can also accept this causal thesis. Indeed, it hardly can be denied that insofar as they consist in evaluations, emotions result from a process of appraisal, understood as a mechanism that results in evaluations.

A distinct approach consists in holding that emotions are caused not by appraisal processes, but by appraisals themselves. Emotions, on this approach, can be seen as reactions to the way we appraise things. While close to Arnold's motivational theory, this approach has been mainly defended by philosophers (Mulligan 2009; Müller 2019; Massin Forthcoming). According to what are known as "reactive theories", emotions are attitudes that arise in reaction to prior evaluations, where these evaluations are conceived as feelings or perceptions of values. A good question here is whether these evaluations can coherently be thought to be distinct, non-emotional states (see Mitchell 2019). What could a feeling or a perception of danger amount to if not fear? In any case, there is reason to hold that appraisals, understood as states that consist in evaluative representations, have to be involved as constituents and not merely as causes of emotions. This is because it is only insofar as emotions consists in states that are evaluative representations that they themselves can be assessed in terms of how they represent things. It is only insofar as fear consists in a representation of danger that it can be assessed as fitting in case there is danger or as unfitting in case there is no danger. Merely being caused by an appraisal is not sufficient for this. Or this at least is the case if the evaluation that causes the emotion fails to transmit its representational properties to the emotion. For if it manages to transmit its representational properties to the emotion, the emotion will consist in nothing less than an evaluative representation.

Let us therefore turn to the accounts that make evaluations central to emotions by claiming that emotions consist in evaluative representations. There are several ways to understand this constitutive claim and we will start with so-called judgmental and quasi-judgmental accounts.

6.3. Judgmental and Quasi-Judgmental Theories

According to philosophers such as Solomon (1976/1993, 2003) and Nussbaum (2001), emotions consist in evaluative judgments. Thus, Solomon writes: "An emotion is an evaluative (or a 'normative') judgment [...]" (1976/1993, 126). Similarly, Nussbaum argues that "[e]motions are appraisals or value judgments, which ascribe to things and person outside the person's own control great importance for that person's own flourishing" (2001, 4). According to these authors, being angry is to judge that someone has wronged or offended you, being afraid is to judge that there is danger, while being sad is to judge that you have suffered a loss. Each kind of emotion consists in a distinctive kind of evaluative judgment.

By making evaluation central to emotions, judgmental theories constitute a clear improvement on feeling and motivational theories. Given that judgments have intentional objects, judgmental theories easily make room for the fact that our emotions have intentional objects. Your fear is about the tiger just as your judgment that the tiger is dangerous is about the tiger. Moreover, because the judgments in question are evaluative, such theories have no difficulties accounting for the fact that our emotions can be assessed as correct or incorrect depending on how they fit the evaluative features of their objects. Clearly, insofar as fear is the judgment that there is danger, it can be assessed as correct or not depending on whether there is danger. Thus, by contrast to motivational theories, judgmental theories rightly assume that emotions have a mind-to-world direction of fit.

In spite of this, another virtue of judgmental theories is that they can easily account for the fact that emotions have a close tie to motivation. As Deonna and Teroni note (2012), judgmental theories can invoke the fact that what we are motivated to do often depends on our evaluative judgments. Indeed, our evaluative judgments explain much of what we do. Thus, if you desire to be safe from the tiger, this can readily be explained by your fear, given that your fear consists in your judgment that the tiger is dangerous. By involving evaluative judgments, our emotions can thus be considered to constitute *explanatory reasons* for what we do.

One could wonder, at this stage, whether judgmental theories have the means to meet the two demarcation challenges. An important advantage of this approach is that it has no problem differentiating kinds of emotions. This is so because judgmental theories can appeal to the different evaluative judgments and more specifically the evaluative concepts that are involved in the judgments at stake to individuate emotions. Judgmental theories can hold that fear is what concerns danger, while anger concerns the offensive, disgust the contaminated, and so forth for each kind of emotion.

The task of demarcating emotions from states that are not emotions is much less obvious, however. What makes the demarcation of emotions and states that are not emotions difficult is that you can make an evaluative judgment without undergoing an emotion. To judge that there is danger is not necessarily to feel fear. Thus, the judgmental theorist owes us a story about what marks emotions from evaluative judgments that do not count as emotions. A common reply here is to claim that in addition to evaluative judgments, emotions involve feelings. The resulting "add-on" theory, to use Peter Goldie's term (2000, 40), is problematic in that it treats feelings as mere icing on the cake. In contrast to what "add-on theorists" suggest, the feelings that are typically experienced when we experience emotions cannot be pulled apart from the evaluative content of the emotion. The idea is that it is *in virtue* of feeling afraid of the tiger that fear allows you to be aware of the tiger and its dangerousness. At this level, there seems to be no difference with the case of color perception. When you see a red poppy and thus visually are aware of the poppy and its color, you do so in virtue of having a visual experience with a distinctive phenomenology, as of a red poppy. The representational content of your experience cannot be severed from the way it is like visually to experience a red poppy. As will become clear, this is a point that militates in favor of perceptual theories.

A standard objection to judgmental theories comes from fact that emotions can conflict with our evaluative judgments (Rorty 1978; Greenspan 1988; Helm 2001). This is what happens in case of *recalcitrant emotions*, to use Justin D'Arms and Daniel Jacobson's expression (2003), such as when you are afraid of a tiny spider while at the same time judging that this spider is not dangerous in any way. Of course, you might be wrong about the spider – suppose it is a tiny tarantula, for instance – and your fear could thus well be perfectly fitting. Whether the emotion or the evaluative judgment is correct, what matters is that there can be such a conflict. If emotions necessarily involve evaluative judgment, we would have to conclude that you suffer from acute irrationality. By contrast, we regularly have recalcitrant emotions and even if they can be considered to involve some irrationality, the kind of irrationality involved in recalcitrant emotions is surely less acute than the one involved in making contradictory judgments.

Quasi-judgmental theories have been developed directly in response to this objection. Instead of evaluative judgments, quasi-judgmental theories focus on states that do not involve a commitment to their own truth. According to Patricia Greenspan (1988), emotions are "compounds of two elements: affective states of comfort or discomfort and evaluative propositions spelling out their intentional content. Fear, for instance, may be viewed as involving discomfort at the fact – or the presumed or imagined fact (I shall say 'the thought') – that danger looms" (1988, 4). On Greenspan's account, thus, emotions are feelings of comfort or discomfort at evaluative thoughts we entertain without holding them to be true. Similarly, Robert Roberts (2003) holds that emotions are concern-based evaluative construals. A construal, in this context, consists in a way of grasping something or seeing something in terms of something else. To illustrate his account, Roberts explains that

> fear, for example, is not just construing one's present situation as involving a threat to one's well-being or someone's else's well-being [...]: it is, rather, construing one's present situation as involving a threat to something [...] in such a way that an active concern for one's own or someone else's well-being is impinged on by the impression of that threat [...].
>
> (2003, 101)

Now, the advantage of such quasi-judgmental accounts is that no contradiction arises when there is a conflict between emotions and evaluative judgments. You can easily judge that the tiger is not dangerous while entertaining the thought that it is or else construing it as dangerous. There is no more contradiction here than when you believe something while at the same time you imagine the contrary. Clearly, imagining that the rain has stopped and the sun is out is perfectly compatible with believing, and indeed knowing, that it rains.

As Bennett Helm (2001) pointed out, the problem with this solution to the problem of recalcitrance is that it fails to account for the fact that there is nonetheless some irrationality involved in recalcitrant emotions. Even if the irrationality involved in such cases is not as acute as the one that characterizes contradictory judgments, there is nonetheless some irrationality involved in cases of recalcitrance. Something clearly goes wrong when you fear a spider while at the same time you judge that the spider is not dangerous. Even if you do not flout a norm that forbids having contradictory judgments, there is nonetheless some weaker form of irrationality at stake.

Another well-established objection to judgmental but also to quasi-judgmental theories concerns the content of the states in question. The objection, in a nutshell, is that they make emotions too demanding in terms of cognitive capacities (see for intance Deigh 1994). According to a standard account of judgments, making a judgment involves possessing the concepts that feature in its content. Thus, to judge that the lake is cerulean, you need to possess both the concept of lake and the color concept *cerulean*. It helps, for instance, to know that cerulean is a kind of deep blue. Similarly, to make quasi-judgments, such as when one entertains the thought that the lake is cerulean or one construes the lake as cerulean, requires that you possess the concepts that are involved. The problem, now, is that it clearly seems possible to experience emotions without possessing much in terms of concepts. Consider infants and nonhuman animals. Because infants and nonhuman animals lack linguistic abilities, which are usually taken to correlate with the possession of concepts, there are reasons to think that infants and nonhuman animals lack the ability to make judgments or quasi-judgments. *A fortiori*, infants and nonhuman animals would lack the ability to make evaluative judgments involving concepts such as *dangerous, offensive* or, *disgusting*, not to mention similar evaluative thoughts or construals. But as the marmot's fear of the eagle or the fear of loud noises newborn babies experience show, it appears that nonhuman animals and infants experience emotions such as fear, and the same seems true of anger and disgust.

This objection depends on the theories of judgment and of concepts that one favors, and since these are difficult issues, there is room for debate. In reply, several moves are possible. One move that is popular is to argue for a minimal notion of judgment or quasi-judgment, which allows the attribution of judgments and quasi-judgments to infants and nonhuman animals. In a later publication, Solomon for instance suggests that the bodily feelings involved in emotions are a species of judgment, which he calls "judgment of the body" (2003, 191–192; see also Nussbaum 2001; Roberts 2003). As Scarantino (2010) notes, the problem with the strategy of stretching the notion of judgment in order to accommodate counterexamples is problematic, for it threatens to result in an unfalsifiable theory. A second move consists in the denial either that prelinguistic creatures have emotions or that the emotions they have are exactly the same as the ones we have (see Naar 2019). If one wants to make room for the intuition that we share some emotions with nonhuman animals, however, one can turn to perceptual theories of emotions, which arguably share all the virtues of judgmental and quasi-judgmental accounts without suffering from their shortcomings. Let us have a closer look at what is often considered to be the leading contemporary approach.

6.4. Perceptual Theories

The basic intuition that motivates perceptual theories is that emotions share many important features with sensory perceptions. Compare the visual experience of a red poppy and feeling anger at your neighbor because he plucked a flower from your garden without asking for permission. Here is a list of the main analogies between the visual and the emotional experience:

a) A first analogy is that each experience appears to have an intentional object. In the visual case, it is the poppy and in the anger case, it is the neighbor.

b) A second analogy is that on standard representionalist views of perception both visual experiences and emotions have representational content: they represent their intentional object as being a certain way. The visual experience represents the poppy as red and the anger represents the neighbor's action as offensive.

c) A third analogy is that because both sorts of experiences have a mind-to-world direction of fit, it follows that both experiences have correctness conditions. Your visual experience of the poppy and its color is correct on condition that the poppy is red, while your anger is correct if your neighbor's action was offensive. These first three points of analogy do not make a difference with judgment or quasi-judgments, but the next ones do.

d) A fourth analogy is that unlike the way judgments are standardly conceived of (but see Strawson 1994; Kriegel 2014), experiences of both kinds have phenomenal properties. There is a way it is like to see the red poppy, and similarly, there is at least typically a way it is like to experience anger.

e) A fifth analogy is that neither visual nor emotional experiences are directly subject to the will. You cannot see a red poppy simply because you decide to see a red poppy, any more than you can be angry simply upon deciding to be angry. To put it otherwise, experiences of both types are automatically elicited or passive. In both cases, you nonetheless have some indirect control. It is possible to make it the case that you see red poppies, but it takes some steps, like finding a field of poppies and looking at it. In the same way, you have indirect control over our emotions. You can take a deep breath or go for a walk to attenuate your anger, and you can also get yourself to feel sad by intentionally thinking about sad events.

f) Another analogy is that both sensory experiences and emotions can conflict with judgments. Thus, if you wear red-tinted glasses when looking at a white poppy, you may make the correct judgment that the poppy is white even if at the same time you see it as red. As we have seen, this kind of conflict is common in the case of emotions. You might feel anger toward your neighbor even if at the same time you judge that he has not slighted you in any way, possibly because you realize there are so many flowers that taking one makes little difference.

g) In part because there can be conflicts between what we see and what we judge, sensory experiences are often taken to be nonconceptual, in the sense that the content of such states is not constrained by the conceptual abilities of the subject (see Crane 1992). Thus, by contrast to what is true of the judgment that the poppy is red, you need to possess neither the concept *red* nor the concept *poppy* to have a visual experience of the red poppy. The general idea is that states that involve conceptual contents, such as judgments, are akin to sentences, which are composed of words, while sensory perceptions are similar to iconic representations, such as pictures, whose content cannot fully be captured by words. That sensory experiences have nonconceptual content is plausible for several reasons (for an overview, see Bermúdez and Cahen 2015). One of these is that the assumption that sensory experience but not judgment has nonconceptual contents nicely explains why sensory experience can easily conflict with judgments. Consider the famous Müller-Lyer illusion (Figure 6.1.)

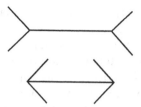

Figure 6.1 The Müller-Lyer illusion

You see the lines as having different lengths even if you judge (and know) that they are of the same length. That this can be so is entirely non-mysterious if the two states involve different modes of representation. There is no contradiction in seeing the line as having different lengths while at the same time judging that they have the same length. The nonconceptual character of visual perceptions makes for a further analogy between sensory perceptions and emotions, for not only is this assumption plausible in light of recalcitrant emotions, but as we have seen, emotions can be felt by beings, such infants and nonhuman animals, who do not, it seems, possess concepts (Tappolet 2020).

This *argument by analogy* (see de Sousa 1987; Prinz 2006; Tappolet 2012) has given rise to a variety of accounts emphasizing the similarities between emotions and sensory perceptions. The core idea is that emotions have the same kind of relation to evaluative features as color perceptions have to colors or more generally sensory perceptions have to sensory features. The way sensory perceptions represent sensory features would be significantly similar to the way emotions represent evaluative features. This core idea can be spelled out in quite different ways.

A first distinction between such accounts is between literal versions, which hold that emotions are literally kinds of perceptions, and weaker, non-literal versions. Some, like Prinz (2004, 2006), go so far as to hold that emotions literally are a sort of sensory perception. Prinz argues that emotions exhibit the properties that characterize paradigm cases of sensory perceptions, and this is why he concludes that emotions are a form of sensory perception. This appears to be an unnecessarily strong claim, for it seems difficult to deny that there are important differences between sensory perceptions and emotions. For one thing, it appears clear that by contrast to sensory perception, there are no sense organs underlying emotions (de Sousa 1987). Another way to think of emotions as being perceptions consists in acknowledging that there are important differences between emotions and sensory perceptions while nonetheless maintaining that the two share sufficient characteristics to both count as perceptions. Thus, Sabine Döring (2003, 2007; see also Tappolet 2016) holds that emotions are not sensory perceptions, but *affective perceptions*. According to Döring, what "makes it an affective perception is its feeling dimension, which is also called its 'affect'" (2003, 223).

In contrast to these literal readings of the analogy, non-literal versions hold that emotions are importantly similar to but in the end crucially different from genuine perceptual experiences (de Sousa 1987; Goldie 2000; Helm 2001; Mitchell

2021). Ronald de Sousa, for one, writes that "emotions are best regarded as a kind of perception, the object of which are what I call *axiological properties*" (1987, 45). But even if he thinks that emotions share important features with perceptions and can be viewed as providing information about evaluative (or as he calls them "axiological") features, de Sousa denies that emotions are perceptual experiences in any literal sense. For his part, Goldie argues that emotions should be understood in terms of "feeling toward", that is, essentially intentional mental states, which have a special sort of emotionally laden content (Goldie 2000, 4; see also Kriegel 2014). "Feeling fear toward something", according to Goldie, "is thinking of it as dangerous in that special way which involves feeling fear" (2000, 36). Spelling out this idea, Jonathan Mitchell (2021) argues that emotional experiences are feelings of favoring and disfavoring that we hold toward values. Finally, Bennett Helm claims that emotions are felt evaluations. In his view, "to feel an emotion is to feel the target of that emotion as having a certain kind of import – that is, to be pleased by things going well or pained by things going poorly" (2001, 60). Nevertheless, these authors all resist the suggestion that emotions are perceptual states. The central claim of non-literal versions of the perceptual account can be expressed by the claim that emotions are not perceptions, but *quasi-perceptions*.

A second distinction is between direct and indirect versions of the perceptual approach. According to the former, emotions are direct perceptual (or quasi-perceptual) representations of evaluative features. Being afraid would consist in perceiving something as dangerous. More precisely, because emotions can misfire – you can be afraid of innocuous things or be amused by bad jokes – emotions are better described in terms of perceptual experiences. Thus, being afraid would consist in having the perceptual experience of the tiger as dangerous (Tappolet 2016). Importantly, to make a difference with judgmental and quasi-judgmental theories, the content of this experience has to be thought to be nonconceptual. Thus, you do not have to possess the concept of a tiger or the concept of danger to fear the tiger.

On the indirect versions, by contrast, the representation of evaluative features is mediated by some other type of representation. Prinz (2004, 2006) has developed a well-known literal version of this idea. Prinz' theory brings together James' account of emotions in terms of bodily feelings and Lazarus' appraisal theory. Emotions, as Prinz nicely puts it, are "embodied appraisals" (Prinz 2004, 51). Why does Prinz hold that emotions are embodied appraisals? The important point to understand is that according to Prinz, emotions are appraisals in virtue of being bodily feelings, that is, perceptions of bodily changes. He claims that, "[t]here is a sense in which emotions allow us to perceive matters of concern, and they do so by registering changes in the body" (2006, 158). Central to Prinz's conception of emotions is an account of representation according to which a mental state represents that which it has the function of reliably detecting (Dretske 1988). On the basis of this, Prinz argues that emotions represent core relational themes – that is, evaluative features – because the bodily changes we perceive when experiencing emotions have, according to him, the function to reliably detect things, such as danger, contamination, or loss. More specifically, drawing on evolutionary accounts of emotions, Prinz claims that these bodily feelings have been selected by evolution to correlate with such features. Fear, for instance, would represent danger because the bodily feelings involved in fear have the biological function of correlating with danger, thus allowing the reliable detection of danger, something that surely had and still has considerable survival value.

A good question here is whether one should prefer indirect over direct versions of the perceptual account. Whatever the general answer to that question is, Prinz's embodied appraisal theory has been criticized on several counts. As mentioned, a first problem is that the account relies on the disputable claim that emotions necessarily involve bodily feelings. A further worry, which is spelled out by Deonna and Teroni (2012), comes from the phenomenology of emotions. Their observation is that when we feel fear, danger appears to be given to us as what we feel when experiencing fear, not as anything else. They ask: "is danger not given to us through fear precisely as danger, in the sense that the phenomenology of fear is what makes this evaluative aspect of the world manifest to us?" (2012, 73). The answer, in their mind, is a positive one, and that certainly seems right. The thesis that how it feels to undergo emotions is essential to what emotions allow us to be aware of is common to most perceptual theorists. For example, it is the feeling of fear that allows us to be aware of the dangerousness of a situation, while the feeling of anger makes manifest to us the offensiveness of a situation. The problem for the embodied appraisal theory is that there appears to be a mismatch when the feelings at stake are bodily feelings. Whatever danger feels like, it surely does not feel like bodily changes. As a result, it would be difficult to maintain that bodily feelings allow us to be aware of the evaluative features of things.

The upshot is that direct versions of the perceptual account appear to have the upper hand. But is the perceptual approach convincing at all? Let us look at its literal versions.

6.5. For and against Literal Perceptual Theories

Consider the claim that emotions are perceptual experiences of things as having evaluative features. It should be clear that a theory of emotions along these lines is well placed to account for the typical features of emotions as relatively short-lived states that typically involve feelings, motivations, intentional objects, appraisals, and formal objects. The last three features do not need any explanation. The close tie to motivation is easily accounted for, given the type of content at stake. Just as judgmental theorists can hold that what we are motivated to do depends on our evaluative judgments, the advocate of the perceptual approach can appeal to evaluative contents to explain why we are typically motivated to act on the basis of our emotions.

One worry here is that literal accounts have to deny that emotions can be unconscious, but as we have seen, there seems to be no reason to deny that some of our emotions are unconscious. However, perceptual theorists can accept this possibility. The case would not be different from so-called cases of *blindsight*, in which subjects can register colors and shapes of a stimulus without being aware of seeing it, as is made manifest by their ability to give correct answers when asked to make guesses (see Weiskrantz 1986).

In general, it seems that literal perceptual accounts have all the virtues of judgmental theories without suffering from their shortcomings. Thus, because they assume that the perceptual experiences of things as having evaluative features need not involve concepts, the perceptual approach has no problem accounting for the fact that infants and nonhuman animals can experience emotions. Nor do they seem to have a problem with respect to the possibility of recalcitrance, since it is only to be expected that emotions and evaluative beliefs can conflict. As we will see shortly, this might not be the bottom line regarding recalcitrance, however.

In any case, regarding the demarcation challenges, literal perceptual theories have as little problem as judgmental theories accounting for the difference between emotions, since they can also appeal to the different evaluative features represented by emotions. Finally, a perceptual theory along these lines has a plausible suggestion concerning the difference between emotions and non-emotions. In a nutshell, the suggestion is that emotions are *typically felt evaluations*. The idea is that thinking of emotions as nonconceptual perceptual experiences that are typically felt marks them out from other kinds of evaluative states, such as evaluative judgments.

All this might sound too good to be true. And indeed, there are a great many objections to literal versions of the perceptual approach. We have seen the argument from analogy that supports such theories. The objections against these theories arise because there is also a list of striking differences between emotions and sensory perceptions (see Salmela 2011; Deonna and Teroni 2012; Brady 2013). Let us consider the main differences that have been discussed.

A point we already have mentioned is that it is doubtful that organs underlie emotions. Relatedly, emotions but not sensory perceptions depend on cognitive bases. To feel anger at your neighbor because he plucked a poppy from your garden, you need to be aware of what he has done, for instance because you saw the neighbor pluck the poppy. In that case, seeing the neighbor pluck the flower is the cognitive base of your anger. By contrast, seeing your neighbor pluck a flower requires no antecedent mental state. Another related point is that while sensory perceptions are required to be caused by the objects and properties that are perceived or else such perceptions cannot be accurate, emotions are not subject to a similar causal constraint. You can regret that dinosaurs died out even if you have never been in causal contact with any of them, and you arguably can feel compassion for fictional characters, such as Anna Karenina or Harry Potter.

Furthermore, even if both emotions and sensory perceptions have phenomenal properties, the phenomenology of emotions appears significantly different from that of sensory perception. One point that is often emphasized is that to describe what it is like to see a vase of red poppies, say, what we do is to refer to what we see, that is, the vase of poppies and their colors. In particular, we normally do not refer to properties of the visual experience itself. This is what is called the *transparency* of perception. By contrast, when trying to describe what it is like to experience anger at your neighbor, you might give details about what awful thing the neighbor did, but you might just as well focus on your feelings, such as your increased blood pressure as you feel as if your blood is boiling.

Another point of contrast is that emotions, but not sensory perceptions, appear to be influenced by psychological factors, such as expectations, projects or preferences. If you have the project to go for a hike you might fear that it will rain, but if you are worried that your garden suffers from a drought, you will hope that it rains. Moreover, as we have seen in Chapter 3, what we are afraid of or angry at depends on the socio-cultural context. By contrast, the shapes and colors we see seem largely immune to socio-cultural influences. These influences in part explain another difference between emotions and sensory perceptions. What we are disposed to see does not change much in the course of a lifetime. Not so with emotions: our emotional dispositions are plastic in that they are open to changes over the lifetime of individuals. This is made clear by the fact that we can get rid of a spider phobia, for instance. As a result, emotional dispositions can be educated (see Chapter 12), while it is far from clear that sensory perceptions are liable to the same kind of changes.

Finally, emotions and sensory perceptions appear to differ concerning rationality assessments. A point that has been discussed at great length concerns recalcitrant emotions. As we have seen, recalcitrant emotions have been used to argue against judgmental theories. The problem was that such theories are forced to say that such cases involve contradictions, so that one would have to attribute a stark form of irrationality to what seems a rather benign and common phenomenon. However, as Helm (2001, 2015) argues, recalcitrant emotions have also been thought to constitute a problem for perceptual theories. This is so because emotions that conflict with evaluative judgment are thought to involve some kind of irrationality nonetheless. As such, they would seem distinct from cases of visual illusions, where no irrationality is involved. A related point is that in the case of emotions, but not in that of sensory perceptions, we can ask why you feel that emotion. If you are angry at your neighbor, it makes sense to ask for the reasons for your anger. In most contexts, by contrasts, sensory perceptions are not open to "why questions", as they are sometimes called. It clearly appears strange to ask for the reason why you see a poppy as red.

In view of this long list of differences between emotions and sensory perceptions, it might well seem that we should reject at least the literal versions of the theory. But maybe that is being too hasty. A first point is that some of the alleged differences might well be overstated. Indeed, the list relies on a conception of sensory perception that might be questioned. It has been argued, for instance, that sensory perception is cognitively penetrable, and if so, it could well be that the fact that emotions depend on psychological factors does not mark them off (MacPherson 2012; Siegel 2017). Because some important differences are likely to persist, this kind of strategy would probably need to be complemented by an argument to the effect that one should adopt a liberal account of what counts as perception, according to which perceptual experiences are allowed to differ from sensory states (Tappolet 2016). On such a suggestion, perceptions need not depend on organs, perceptions can have cognitive bases, perceptions need not be subject to a causal constraint, perceptions can lack transparency, perceptions can be influenced by psychological factors, perceptions can be plastic, they can be assessed as irrational, and they are open to "why questions".

The other strategy is to grant that the analogy between emotions and sensory perceptions is only partial. At best, emotions are quasi-perceptions. In the next section, we will explore a new version of this kind of approach.

6.6. The Receptive Theory

Let us recap. Direct and literal versions of the perceptual approach hold that emotions are affective and nonconceptual perceptual experiences of things as having evaluative features. The problem with this suggestion is that there are a number of important differences between perceptual experiences and emotions. The crucial point to understand in order to move forward is to recognize that nonconceptual mental states need not be perceptual in the strict sense of lying at the sensory periphery. They can be located at a higher level of the cognitive architecture.

The suggestion is to model emotions on analog magnitude representations, such as analog representations of numbers, durations, or temperatures. Consider number representations. As Jacob Beck (2012, 2019) explains, there are good reasons to think that animals such as pigeons, rats, and monkeys, but also human beings when they are not counting explicitly, are able to represent numbers by using analog representations, which do not involve conceptual contents. Pigeons, for instance, are able to count the number of times they peck on a key with considerable accuracy, even if there are good reasons not to attribute conceptually articulated contents to the pigeons' state. Rather, they appear to use analog representations of numbers.

To see what analog representations are, consider a watch with rotating hands. Such a watch displays an analog representation of the time, by contrast with the digital representation of time you find on your phone. Quite generally, analog representations can be defined as representations that tend to be continuous and that mirror what they represent, in the sense that they share structural features with what they represent. As time marches on, the hands on the watch turn. Because analog representations fail to behave like representations that have conceptual contents in that they do not allow for the systematic recombination of their contents, there are reasons to take analog representations to involve nonconceptual contents, that is, contents that do not have concepts as constituents (see Beck 2012). Thus, in what follows, we will assume that analog representations involve nonconceptual contents.

Now, as Beck (2012) argues, nonconceptual representations of magnitudes can occur at one remove from perception understood in the strict sense. In particular, if you take causal contact with the objects or property to be the mark of perception, you have to conclude that analog representations need not be perceptual states in any strict sense. One important reason for this is that because analog magnitude representations can be stored in memory, they can be activated in the absence of the stimuli they represent. The second reason is that analog magnitude representations can be amodal, in the sense that they are not tied to a specific sensory modality, such as vision, hearing, smell, or taste. Thus, we are able to estimate the sum of visually presented dots and aurally presented tones without having the time explicitly to count the stimuli, which suggests that such amodal number representations are analog.

Perceptual theorists of any persuasion can and should agree that emotions consist in analog representations of things as having evaluative features. What gives plausibility to this thought is that evaluative features are, quite obviously, a kind of magnitude in that they allow for degrees – things can be more or less dangerous, offensive or disgusting. Thus, it appears plausible that emotions mirror the evaluative features they represent in that they co-vary with such features (Tappolet 2020).

The difference with literal accounts, however, is that on the present suggestions, emotions are thought to be removed from the sensory periphery. Thus, they would not count as perceptions in any strict sense. As should be obvious in light of the fact that emotions have cognitive bases, there are good reasons to adopt this thesis. Like analog magnitude representations, emotions can be activated in the absence of causal contact with the stimuli. We can feel fear simply because we remember a fierce tiger or because we are told that there is a tiger loose in the neighborhood. Moreover, it is clear that emotions are not tied to specific sensory modality. Your fear can be based on seeing something, but also on hearing, smelling, or tasting it, just as it can be based on a belief or a memory.

The suggestion, then, is that emotions are analog representations of things as having evaluative features, which do not lie at the sensory periphery. This *receptive theory*[1] – as one might call it because emotions are thought to involve a reaction to cognitive bases (hence the "re") but also to be relevantly similar to perceptions (hence the "ceptive") – has a number of advantages.

The receptive theory holds on to the main virtues of literal perceptual accounts. It takes emotions to be representations that can be assessed in terms of their fittingness. Because emotions concern evaluative features, the theory can explain how emotions play a motivational role. For the same reason, it has no more difficulty with the demarcation between kinds of emotions than literal versions or indeed judgmental and quasi-judgmental theories have. Given the assumption that the content of representations matches their format, it follows that emotions have nonconceptual contents. The receptive theory would thus have no problem to account for the fact that beings, such as nonhuman animals, who lack concepts have emotions.

Nor need the receptive theory worry about recalcitrance. The problem was to make room for the irrationality involved in a conflict between emotions and judgments, such as when you are afraid of a spider that you judge to be innocuous. One might hold that even for the literal perceptual theorist, there is some tension involved, since, after all, it cannot be the case that both the emotion and the judgment present things as they are. However, the same kind of tension seems to be present in the case of sensory illusions. Imagine you are on a canoe trip and look at your paddle, which is plunged into water. It surely cannot be that both your visual experience of the paddle as bent and the judgment that it is straight are accurate representations of how things are. Either the paddle is bent or it is not. In spite of this, however, it would be strange to say that your visual experience of the paddle is irrational. Thus, the question is how to explain the difference between the visual case and the emotional case. A plausible suggestion is to appeal to the fact that emotions, but not sensory experiences, are, as we have seen, plastic (Tappolet 2016). Because we can learn not to fear spiders, but we cannot learn not to see the objects plunged in water as straight, it makes sense to assess emotions, but not visual experiences, in terms of irrationality. Of course, it could well be the case that it is the emotion, and not the judgment, that gets things right. Even so, your emotion will seem to you to be incorrect, so that you will deem it to be irrational, something that makes sense to believe, given that you can take steps to change your emotional dispositions. In any case, the nice thing is that the receptive theory can spell out this story regarding recalcitrance without having to worry about the distance it introduces between emotions and perceptions.

The receptive theory is tailored to account for several important differences between emotions and sensory perceptions. Because emotions are thought to be removed from the sensory periphery, the account has no worries regarding the absence of corresponding organs, the dependence on cognitive bases, as well as the fact that emotions need not be causally correlated with their objects. Similarly, the emphasis on the cognitive bases of emotions allows the theory to make room for the fact that emotions are shaped by cultural and social factors, and, more generally, for the plasticity of emotional dispositions. In a nutshell, what happens in such learning processes is that different sets of cognitive bases get associated with different emotional reactions (see Chapter 12).

Another attractive feature of the receptive theory is that the emphasis on cognitive bases allows the theory easily to account for the fact that emotions can be open to so-called *why questions*. This is because the cognitive basis of an emotion can be considered to explain the emotion they cause. The reason for which you feel fear upon seeing a tiger, on this suggestion, is that you have seen a tiger. The visual experience of the tiger, thus, explains why you feel fear. As we will see, this experience can also justify your fear (see Chapter 7).

All this seems promising, but before concluding that we should adopt the receptive theory, we need to address one important issue with the suggestion that emotions are analog representations that do not count as literal perceptions. The question is whether on this account, we can make room for the fact that emotions are typically felt. To put it differently, can analog representations that are removed from the sensory periphery have a phenomenology? On the face of it, there appears to be no reason to deny that they can. Accordingly, the receptive theory can hold that analog representations of things as having evaluative features are typically felt. Subtle questions arise as how to characterize these feelings. The most plausible suggestion seems to be that affective feelings are built up from a number of correlated phenomenal properties, such as the ones that may be involved in the cognitive bases of emotions, those that arise from bodily changes when such changes occur, as well as the ones that come from how our attention is engaged. One might wonder whether the resulting experience lacks transparency. One indication that such experiences are at least partly transparent is that we tend to describe our emotions in terms of evaluative features. As Mitchell (2021) reports, it appears natural to specify anger in terms of being aware of someone as annoying, for instance. Given this, it appears plausible that the feelings at stake allow us to be aware of the evaluative features of things. If this is on the right lines, the receptive theory can hold on to the claim that emotions are typically felt evaluations.

6.7. Taking Stock

The upshot of our discussion so far is that the essence of emotions is constituted by evaluative representations. There are several ways to spell out this idea, but the most attractive one holds that emotions consists in analog representations, which have evaluative contents that are nonconceptual. These representations share many features with sensory perceptions, but they are not perceptions in any literal sense, for they depend on cognitive bases and are thus located at a higher level of the cognitive architecture. This "receptive theory" has a lot going for it. In the next chapters, it will become clear that this approach and more generally perceptual theories, whether literal or non-literal, fit well with a number of claims regarding how emotions get assessed.

6.8. Summary

- Among evaluative theories, appraisal theories as developed by psychologists focus on different dimensions of appraisals, such as goal relevance or coping potential. Appraisal theorists disagree on what emotions are, but agree that emotions are caused by appraisal processes, a claim that is compatible with feeling, motivational, and evaluative theories.
- Reactive theories hold that emotions are reactions to prior evaluations, where these feelings or perceptions of values are taken to be distinct from emotions. The main problem is that such theories struggle to account for the fact that emotions themselves, as distinct from their causes, can be assessed in terms of how they represent things.
- Judgmental and quasi-judgmental theories, by contrast, make evaluations central to emotions. In spite of a number of advantages, these two approaches appear to have important shortcomings. It is not obvious that they can demarcate emotions from other kinds of states, they struggle to make room

for recalcitrance, and they appear forced to deny the possibility of emotions in infants and nonhuman animals.

- Perceptual theories, which are based on the many analogies between emotions and sensory perceptions, hold that emotions are evaluative perceptions – this is what the literal versions of the approach hold – or quasi-perceptions–as the non-literal versions have it. In contrast with direct versions of the approach, indirect versions claim that there is an intermediary step.

- The embodied appraisal theory, a literal indirect perceptual account according to which emotions represent evaluative features in virtue of being bodily feelings, faces a number of difficulties. Since it holds that emotions are bodily feelings, the theory has to deny the intuition that it is in virtue of what we feel that we are aware of evaluative features.

- Literal and direct perceptual theories that hold that emotions are, quite literally, affective perceptual experiences, have important advantages. They have no difficulties accounting for the fact that emotions are states that typically involve feelings, motivations, intentional objects, appraisals, and formal objects. They have no difficulties either with the demarcation between types of emotion, and they can hold that emotions are typically felt evaluations. The problem, however, is that there are important differences between emotions and sensory perceptions.

- Instead of holding that one has to opt for a liberal conception of what counts as a perception, one can suggest that emotions are like perceptions in being analog representations that have nonconceptual contents, but are unlike perceptions in the strict sense, because by having cognitive bases, they are removed from the sensory periphery. This receptive theory shares all the virtues of literal perceptual theories, but not their shortcomings, since it is tailored to account for the differences between emotions and sensory perceptions.

6.9. Study Questions

1. Can nonhuman animals feel all the kinds of emotions human feel, and if not, how do you explain this?
2. How would you describe what it feels like to be disgusted by rotten leftovers in your fridge?
3. Have you ever felt emotions that conflict with your evaluative judgments, and if so how would you describe what happens in such cases?

Note

1 I owe this name to Mauro Rossi.

6.10. Further Readings

Brady, Michael S. 2013. *Emotional Insight: The Epistemic Role of Emotional Experience.* Oxford: Oxford University Press, chap. 2.

D'Arms, Justin, and Daniel Jacobson. 2003. "The Significance of Recalcitrant Emotion (or Anti-Quasi-Judgmentalism)." In *Philosophy and the Emotions*, edited by Anthony Hatzimoysis, 127–145. Cambridge: Cambridge University Press.

Döring, Sabine A. 2003. "Explaining Action by Emotion." *Philosophical Quarterly* 53 (211):214–230.

Greenspan, Patricia. 1988. *Emotions and Reasons: An Enquiry into Emotional Justification.* London: Routledge, chaps. 1 & 2.

Helm, Bennett W. 2015. "Emotions and Recalcitrance: Reevaluating the Perceptual Model." *Dialectica* 69 (3):417–433.

Montague, Michelle. 2009. "The Logic, Intentionality, and Phenomenology of Emotion." *Philosophical Studies* 145 (2):171–192.

Moors, Agnes. 2013. "On the Causal Role of Appraisal in Emotion." *Emotion Review* 5 (2):132–140.

Nussbaum, Martha C. 2001. *Upheavals of Thought: The Intelligence of Emotions.* Cambridge: Cambridge University Press, chap. 1.

Scarantino, Andrea. 2010. "Insights and Blindspots of the Cognitivist Theory of Emotions." *The British Journal for the Philosophy of Science* 61:729–768.

Scherer, Klaus. 2009. "The Dynamic Architecture of Emotion: Evidence for the Component Process Model." *Cognition and Emotion* 23:1307–1351.

PART III
Normativity and the Emotions

7 Emotions and Theoretical Rationality

7.1. Introduction

Ancient mythology is ripe with drama, but maybe the most stirring story is that of Medea as told by Euripides. Having been betrayed by her husband Jason, who marries another woman despite all that she did to help him in his quest for the Golden Fleece, Medea's rage moves her to take a bloody revenge. Aiming to hurt Jason, Medea poisons her rival and her rival's father, after which she murders the two sons she had with Jason. What is deeply tragic is that she understands the dreadfulness of what she plans to do. In her own words: "The horror of my evil overwhelms me. Horror of what I'll do. Angry passions have mastered me – emotions of misrule that destroy men" (Euripides 2011, verses 1053–1056).

Such scenarios bolster the picture of emotions as negative forces, which have to be controlled by reason, if not entirely suppressed. This dark picture is deeply ingrained in philosophical thinking. Indeed, philosophers have traditionally accused emotions of interfering with the faculty of reason and thus fostering all sorts of irrationality and immorality. As we saw in Chapter 1, both Plato and Aristotle held that emotions could give rise to akratic actions, that is, actions done against one's better judgment. Even more drastically, the Stoics recommended that we free ourselves from most of our emotions, which they considered to consist in erroneous judgments that mislead us.

This negative conception of emotions is still very much alive in contemporary thought, where emotions are often depicted as distorting proper reasoning. As mentioned in Chapter 2, it is common to divide cognitive processes in two kinds. On the one hand, you have reflective processes, which are often slow and deliberative and which involve controlled attention, while, on the other hand, you have intuitive processes, which do not require controlled attention and are generally faster as well as automatic. Now, a common line regarding this division is that intuitive processes, which are taken to include emotional processes, tend to yield only quick and dirty outputs, which disrupt reflective processes. The function of the reflective processes, hence, would be to check and if necessary override the intuitive processes.

In the wake of the evaluative turn that started in the 1950s, however, emotion theorists have argued that this traditional conception has to be replaced by a

DOI: 10.4324/9781315542300-10

more positive account of emotions. Indeed, following the work of philosopher Ronald de Sousa (1987) and that of neuroscientist Antonio Damasio (1994), a consensus that is favorable to emotions has established itself among emotion theorists, be they philosophers, psychologists, or neuroscientists. Most contemporary emotion theorists now hold that emotions are far from being an obstacle to rationality and morality. Indeed, they hold that emotions are essential to the proper functioning of both theoretical and practical rationality, just as they are essential to good motivation. In brief, our emotions allow us to be better at thinking and acting.

The question is whether this new consensus does not make for too rosy a picture of emotions. Clearly, Medea's rage – a kind of anger that is both intense and uncontrolled – does not fit well into the proposed picture, and much the same appears to be true of emotions such as hatred, jealousy, envy, and spite. Moreover, particular instances of generally useful emotion kinds also appear problematic. As we have seen when discussing Matt's fear of the tiger (Chapter 5), fear can interfere with one's ability to deal with danger. The general question at stake is, as we have called it, the *normative question* (Chapter 1): are emotions, whether as types or as particular instances, good or bad for us? Because there are different ways in which emotions can be good or bad for us, this very general question splits into several sub-questions.

There is, first, the broad question of how emotions affect how we think. It might seem obvious that emotions hinder good reasoning, thus interfering with theoretical rationality. It seems clear, for instance, that Medea's rage clouds her judgment. Interestingly, however, the horror she feels at the thought of killing her children seems to play a key role in getting her to understand the evil she plans. And in fact, a great many emotion theorists hold that emotions play a central role in the acquisition of epistemic justification, knowledge, and understanding of values (see Elgin 1996; Döring 2003; Deonna and Teroni 2012a; Silva 2021, among others). Indeed, those who defend the view that emotions play a central role in epistemic justification often argue that emotions or more generally affective states are indispensable for the knowledge of values (see Johnston 2001, for instance). Reason alone would not be enough fully to grasp the dangerousness of a situation or the admirable nature of a mountain view.

A second question is how emotions affect our practical rationality, that is, the rationality that concerns what we do. The case of Medea is particularly instructive here in that the action that results from her rage is something she considers to be evil. Such a conflict between one's motivation and one's judgment, which is characteristic of akratic action, constitutes a kind of irrationality that is often considered paradigmatic of practical irrationality. In spite of such cases, philosophers have argued that emotions can, under certain circumstances, help us to be more rational in that they allow us to grasp our practical reasons (see for instance Arpaly 2000; Jones 2003; Tappolet 2003).

A third question, finally, concerns how emotions affect what we do, be it with respect to prudence, in the sense that the good of the agent is at stake, or to morality, where the good of other beings is at stake. It would seem that Medea's rage results in actions that are threatening both her own good and the good of others, so that one can consider them as bad from both the point of view of prudence and from the point of view of morality. Again, many have argued that emotions are nonetheless essential to good decision making and to morality.

In this chapter, we will consider how emotions affect the rationality of what we think, while the next chapter will look into the role of emotion in practical rationality. We will turn to prudence and morality, and more generally to the role of emotion in ethics in Chapter 10, following a discussion of the nature of values in Chapter 9. These are questions that are interesting in themselves, but exploring these debates will also allow us to deepen our understanding of what emotions are. How one conceives of these debates depends on the particular account of emotion that is favored.

7.2. The Justification of Evaluative Beliefs

Even if emotions need not be caused by evaluative judgments, even if they need not be constituted even partly by evaluative judgments, and even if emotions can conflict with evaluative judgments, it is commonly acknowledged that emotions often cause evaluative judgments or else evaluative beliefs, where a belief can be understood as the standing representation that disposes you to make the correlated judgment. Thus, if you feel admiration for your friend Sarah, this admiration is likely to result in the judgment or the belief that Sarah is admirable. A view that has recently become popular is that in addition to causing evaluative beliefs, emotions can justify evaluative beliefs. Note that this claim could be framed in terms of evaluative judgments, but to simplify I will focus on beliefs. Your admiration would not only cause the belief, it would also justify that belief, given certain conditions. It would constitute an epistemic reason for the evaluative belief. The kind of justification that is envisaged here is epistemic justification, that is, justification that is tied to knowledge and truth, by contrast to other kinds of justification, such as prudential or moral justification. Basically, one can think of epistemically justified beliefs as beliefs that are permitted from an epistemic point of view.

The claim that emotions can confer this kind of justification to evaluative belief comes in different flavors, which depend in part on the general epistemological framework that is assumed. Epistemologist Catherine Elgin, who favors coherentism, writes that "[a]bsent specific reasons to distrust them, cognitive deliverances of emotions are initially tenable" (1996, 150, see also 2008). According to Elgin, full tenability or justification depends on the integration and indeed the contribution of the emotion to a coherent cognitive system, that is, a system that is in reflective equilibrium, so that its different components support each other. As she puts it "[n]o more than other insights are deliverances of emotions certain. They are initially tenable but must promote reflective equilibrium to qualify as fully tenable" (Elgin 1996, 155). Deonna and Teroni (2012a) also hold that emotions have conditional justificatory power, but this power does not depend on the contribution to a coherent cognitive system but on some states that justify emotions. Thus, they write that "justified emotions are suffi-cient to justify evaluative judgments" (2012a, 120). According to them, it only insofar as the cognitive bases of emotions justify them that emotions result in justified beliefs.

The most discussed suggestion, however, is that the epistemic force of emotions is of the same kind as that of sensory perceptions. Döring, who as we have seen defends the view that emotions are affective perceptions (see Chapter 6), writes that as a consequence of the view that emotions resemble sensory perceptions in having an intentional content that is representational, "an emotion can jus-tify a belief. Like a perception, it can do so by its representational content non-inferentially justifying the content of that belief" (Döring 2003, 215; see also Milona 2016; Tappolet 2016).

Let us have a look at the case of sensory perception. The basic idea, which is widely accepted, is that sensory perceptions have the power to confer justi-fication on beliefs. Importantly, the kind of justification provided by sensory perceptions is taken to be *basic* or *immediate*, because it does not depend on some other state that would justify the sensory perception. Furthermore, when you have the perceptual experience as of a red poppy, you are *prima facie* justi-fied in believing that the poppy you see is red (see Audi 2011), where this *prima facie* justification is immediate. *Prima facie* justification – literally, justification at first sight – is justification that prevails unless *defeated*. If you also believe that the flower is illuminated by red light, for instance, the belief that the poppy is red will be *prima facie* justified, but it will not be *ultima facie* justified, that is, justi-fied *all things considered*. The belief about the red light functions as a *defeater* of the reason provided by your visual experience. The defeater undermines the reason you have to trust your visual experience. In other cases, defeaters consist in reasons to believe that your visual belief is false, for instance because an expert told you that all poppies in the world are yellow. From this, you can infer that your visual experience must be misleading you, so in the end you have a defeater that undermines the reason you have for the belief. If the *prima facie* justifi-cation for your belief is not defeated, your belief is *ultima facie* justified. This does not entail, however, that *ultima facie* justification guarantees truth. On most accounts, you can have that kind of justification for a belief that happens to be false. Insofar as knowledge requires truth, *ultima facie* justification thus falls short of knowledge. For instance, you can believe that the poppy is red and be *ultima facie* justified in this belief, because nothing you know or believe indicates that your visual experience is misleading you, but your belief is unfortunately mistaken, for in fact the poppy is a white one. Thus, you clearly do not know that the poppy is red – it is not.

It is possible to favor a perceptual account of emotions without holding the view that emotions have the same justificatory power as sensory perception. Maybe emotions have some particular feature that prevents them from having any justificatory power. In spite of this, embracing an account of emotions that underlines the analogies with sensory perceptions makes it natural to tell a similar story in the case of emotions. Indeed, this kind of epistemological account has sometimes been considered to be central to the perceptual approach, so that an attack on the epistemological account was thought to consist in the best way to dismount perceptual theories (see Brady 2013).

Let us hence focus at first on the thesis that emotions provide immediate *prima facie* justification for evaluative beliefs. To clarify this *justification thesis*, as we will call it, let us consider a case of disgust. The thesis is that if your belief that a piece of cheese is disgusting is based on the disgust you feel at the cheese, then this belief is *prima facie* justified, and it is so immediately, without any help from mental states that justify it. In the absence of defeaters – such as the belief that you are unwell and that any food would trigger disgust in you – the belief that the cheese is disgusting is *ultima facie* justified. It is thus epistemically permissible for you to believe that the cheese is disgusting. It is worth stressing here that in this context, defeaters are understood as beliefs about conditions that interfere, and not as the interfering conditions themselves. Accordingly, to say that there are no defeaters is to say that as far as you are aware, nothing indicates that your disgust is misleading you or that the belief about the disgustingness of the cheese might be false. If you believe that you are unwell or that cheese of this kind looks disgusting but is not, in fact, disgusting, you should, by contrast, not put any trust in what you feel.

Here is how one can spell out the justification conditions of the belief that something is disgusting:

Your belief that x is disgusting is *prima facie* justified if

a)   you feel disgust towards x;
b)   your belief is based on your disgust.

If there are no defeaters, this belief will be *ultima facie* justified (see Tappolet 2016). Again, this does not entail that the belief is true, for unknown to you, your emotion might nonetheless mislead you.

In general, then, the justification thesis holds that if you base your evaluative belief on the emotions you feel, you are *prima facie* justified in believing that the object of your emotion has the correlated evaluative feature. Note that the reason why it is only a conditional claim, by contrast to a biconditional one, is that there can be other ways to get to justified evaluative beliefs. You might be *prima facie* justified to believe that something is disgusting because you remember that it triggered disgust in you the other day or because someone trustworthy told you that it was.

On the face of it, the justification thesis is intuitive. As Robert Cowan (2016) notes, the idea that emotions can reveal to us the evaluative features of things, such as when guilt is a way we realize the moral import of what we have done, appears plausible. Moreover, as we have seen, the justification thesis gets support from perceptual accounts. This is true even in the case of what I argued is the best version of such accounts, namely, the receptive theory. Although that account insists on the differences between emotions and sensory perceptions, it nonetheless holds that emotions are felt representations of evaluative features.

In particular, the receptive theory holds that the feelings we experience makes us aware of the evaluative features of things. Given this, it is natural to hold that the emotions we feel play a central role in the justification of evaluative beliefs, one that is analogous to the role sensory perceptions play in the justification of perceptual beliefs.

The justification thesis is generally coupled with the claim that emotions are epistemically indispensable to our knowledge of values. Were it not for the emotions we feel, we would be blind, so to speak, to values. In Mark Johnston's words, "[i]f one has never been moved or affected by the determinate ways in which things are beautiful or charming or erotic or banal or sublime or horrific or appealing, then one is ignorant of the relevant determinate values" (2001, 183; see also Döring 2003). According to Johnston, it is thus only if we experience emotions that we can make detailed evaluative discriminations.

The thesis that emotions are epistemically indispensable to our knowledge of evaluative features is plausible. In this respect, the case of values appears to be similar to that of colors (see Pelser 2014). In a famous thought experiment, Frank Jackson (1982) asks us to imagine the case of Mary the scientist, who is forced to live in a black and white room. Mary has all the imaginable scientific knowledge regarding colors. For instance, she knows the neurophysiology of vision and the physics of wavelengths. But because she has not seen any color, there is something crucial she does not know. When she is released from the black and white room, she will learn how colors look. Before seeing a blue sky, she did not know how blue looks, and given this, she was not able to attribute colors on the basis of her visual experiences. Similarly, someone who has never felt amusement seems to be ignorant of something essential regarding amusingness. To grasp the amusing nature of a joke, it seems surely necessary to feel amusement at the joke, and this appears true of all the evaluative features that constitute the formal objects of emotions.

The epistemic indispensability thesis suggests that emotions can provide immediate *prima facie* justification. Consider the case of amusement. What would seem uncontroversial is that if you have not felt the relevant emotions you would not be in a good position to form justified beliefs regarding the amusingness of the joke. At best, you would have to rely on information provided by others or else make use of some improbable principles that correlate non-evaluative features of jokes with their amusingness. By contrast, emotions would put you in what seems a prime position to have *prima facie* justified evaluative belief. This, however, does not necessarily entail that emotions are the only way to acquire justified evaluative beliefs. After all, Mary the scientist can have justified beliefs about the color of the sky based on the scientific knowledge she had before venturing into the colored world. Nor does this entail that when you base your belief on your emotions, you really have *prima facie* justification for these beliefs. Simply put, maybe emotions are simply not sufficiently trustworthy to do the work.

The question, thus, is whether the justification thesis is true. There has recently been a barrage of objections raised against the idea that emotions provide even immediate *prima facie* justification, let alone immediate *ultima facie* justification. In the next sections, we will look at the main objections against the justification thesis.

7.3. The Objection from Reliability

Maybe the major concern here is that emotions do not appear to be reliable sources of information. On the contrary, it is easy to think of examples of emotions that bias our evaluative beliefs. As Peter Goldie puts it, it would seem that "our emotions can and do profoundly distort our view of things" (2004, 249), for instance by getting us to focus on what appears to confirm what we feel. When we are afraid, for example, we tend to focus on information that justifies our fear, leaving aside what could prove us wrong in our assumption that there is danger. The claim that emotions can bias our judgments is also empirically confirmed. In a well-known study, Thalia Wheatly and Jonathan Haidt (2005) showed that subjects who were given a post-hypnotic suggestion to experience disgust whenever they would read an arbitrary word, such as "often", tended to be more severe in their moral assessment of characters when the vignettes involved the terms associated with the disgust reaction. The disgust reactions of the subjects obviously did not put them in a good position to make moral judgments.

Now, it is uncontroversial that emotions can occasionally bias us. The difficult question is whether emotions are in general unreliable, in the sense that, more often than not, they lead to incorrect evaluative assessments. Assessing the reliability of our cognitive capacities is not easy. Consider the question of how you would go about checking that your senses are, more often than not, yielding correct results. In fact, you could not but appeal to sense perception itself to do so, for instance by looking at something in better light to see whether it is really what it appears to be. In the case of our epistemic access to evaluative properties such as dangerousness or disgustingness, the task appears even less obvious. One difficulty is that you might not be sure of how to set the conditions so as to avoid having a biased reaction. In the case of sensory perception, we have a good grasp of what conditions are conducive to accurate observation, but things are certainly much less clear in the case of emotions. Indeed, the deep question that arises is whether there is anything out there in terms of values, which would be sufficiently objective for the question of whether emotions can be reliable even to make sense. We will turn to this last question in the next chapter so let us put it aside for now.

In any case, two main strategies can be envisaged to deal with the reliability objection. The first one consists in arguing that emotions, or at least particular kinds of emotions, are sufficiently reliable to have justificatory power. Let us start by noticing that evolutionary considerations might help bolster the case for the reliability of emotions (see Elgin 2008). If emotions, or at least a number of them, allowed our ancestors to face challenges such as attacks by ferocious predators, emotions must have provided relatively accurate information about evaluative features such as dangerousness. Given this, a limited number of emotions could be defended against the unreliability accusation. The question, however, is whether the emotions we feel in the contemporary setting are likewise reliable. After all, the world we inhabit is non-trivially different from that of our Pleistocene ancestors. What we would need here is a reason to believe that the shaping of our emotions by culture results in emotions that are, more often than not, accurate, and it is not clear that such a reason can be found.

In any case, a good strategy might consist in lowering the expectations and pointing out that there is no need to hold that all emotions of all kinds are reliable all the time, whatever the context. Instead, one can argue that what is at stake is the limited reliability of specific types of emotions regarding a particular range of cases. As Deonna and Teroni (2012b) suggest, your anger disposition might be generally unreliable, but at the same time, it might well be reliably tracking for particular kinds of offences, such as slight-to-honor based offences.

Moreover, it should be noted that the kind of reliability that is needed might well be minimal. Sense perception is far from one hundred percent reliable, and we make all sorts of mistakes on account of our sensory perceptions. But even a low kind of reliability that provides information that is sometimes badly mistaken is preferable to having no information at all. In the same way, it would seem sufficient that emotions are minimally reliable in that when we put our trust in them, we find ourselves with beliefs that are only slightly more often correct than if we were merely guessing. If we put the bar that low in terms of reliability, and if we consider only reliability that is limited to a specific domain, it would seem that the objection from reliability should not be that difficult to meet.

Because these considerations might not be sufficient to make the case that emotions are sufficiently reliable to provide even *prima facie* justification, it is useful to look at the second strategy. Let us thus assume that emotions are, in general, unreliable sources of information. The thing to notice is that this assumption does not condemn the justification thesis. The reason is that one might question the *reliabilist* assumption according to which only reliable sources of information can provide *prima facie* justification. These are complicated and hotly debated epistemological issues, but what should be made clear is that according to many epistemologists, justification need not depend on something *external*, like the reliability of the source of information. Thus, according to *evidentialism*, having a perceptual experience as of something being the case is sufficient to ensure *prima facie* justification (see Lyons 2016). In contrast to *reliabilism*, the account of justification according to which beliefs have to result from reliable belief acquisition processes in order to be justified, evidentialism is an *internalist* account in that the justification is provided by experiences, that is, by states of which you are aware.

Suggesting that one has to opt for this kind of evidentialist epistemology might make it seem that one has no room to account for the fact that emotions can be unreliable. However, once that picture is in place, a further point can be made. It consists in underlining that reliability considerations will figure prominently in the justification conditions, given that having reasons to believe that one's emotions are unreliable will constitute a defeater. Consider a case of fear. If you have reason to believe that the fear you feel when you see a spider is unreliable because you know all too well that you have a spider phobia, then your belief that the spider is dangerous will not be *ultima facie* justified. It might appear to you as if the spider is dangerous, but this will not be sufficient to provide *ultima facie* justification for your belief.

In general, if as far as you know, all your emotions are unreliable, you would not get further than *prima facie* justification. For each *prima facie* justification provided by an emotion, you would have a defeater that prevents you from ever having *ultima facie* justification. This would not be good news, but on the other hand, it would not falsify the justification thesis. However, things are probably not that bleak. What seems plausible, rather, is that depending on the cases, we might have reasons to think that an emotion misleads us while in other cases nothing might indicate that we should not trust what we feel. Moreover, even if there will remain difficult cases, we can often work out which conditions are such as to interfere with our emotions. Knowing that you have a spider phobia, for instance, makes it clear that you should not trust the fear you feel when seeing a spider.

One important point here is that it is not as if we know in advance, in some *a priori* way, what conditions constitute interferences. Rather, it is through experience and by comparing what we feel with what others feel that we can understand what conditions are favorable and what conditions are not (see Tappolet 2016). Thus, if you feel disgust at some piece of blue, moldy cheese, but your French friends tell you that this is how the cheese is supposed to look, you might conclude that your disgust is misleading you, so that you will reconsider the belief that this piece of cheese is disgusting. The situation is not different from the case of sensory perception, where you often rely on the opinion of others to assess whether you should trust your experience. Thus, when you enter a warm room after a hike in the snow, you will feel very hot, so that it will seem to you that the temperature is very high. But as your friends who have not left the room will tell you, this is a case in which you should not trust your heat sensation. In general, the search for defeaters is one we best conduct not in isolation, but with others.

A final point here is that if we do not allow emotions as our (albeit defeasible) starting points in thinking about things like amusingness, disgustingness, or offensiveness, it is difficult to see where we would start instead. To see why, let us consider another prominent objection to the justification thesis.

7.4. The Objection from Why-Questions

One striking difference between emotions and sensory perceptions is that the latter, but not the former, appear to admit of so-called *why-questions*. If you feel anger at a friend, we can ask why that is so. When asking this question, we might be interested in the cause of your emotion – what did the friend do to trigger your anger? The answer might thus be that you are angry because the friend took your bicycle without asking for permission. But it seems that we can also be interested in normative why-questions. If it is common knowledge that the friend took your bicycle without asking for permission, asking why you are angry raises the normative question of whether what the friend did really justifies anger. After all, one might wonder whether taking your bicycle without asking for permission really is offensive. The question is whether anger would be fitting. Finally, it would seem that we can also ask whether you are justified in your anger, given what you are aware of and what you believe. Does the way you take things to be justify your anger even if in fact you are wrong to believe that your friend took the bicycle? By contrast, such normative why-questions do not appear to make much sense when raised regarding sensory perceptions. In most contexts, we would not ask what would justify, in any sense of the term, having the visual experience of a red poppy when looking at a red poppy. You simply have the experience, and it is not in need of any justification.

Given this apparent asymmetry between emotions and sensory perceptions, Michael Brady (2013) argues that emotions are not well placed to provide even *prima facie* justification. The thought is that by contrast to sensory perceptions, emotions cannot function as "regress-blockers", in the sense that they cannot stop the quest for justification. As a result, it would be wrong to believe that emotions provide *prima facie* justification, let alone *ultima facie* justification.

Brady (2013) grants that in some cases, why-questions do not arise. The feeling of disgust triggered by a shank of venison gives you, he argues, sufficient reason to believe that it is unappetizing. In such cases, then, Brady has no issue with the justification thesis, and since it is sufficient to vindicate the thesis that emotions can provide justification in some cases this might appear to settle the issue. According to Brady, however, things are typically much less favorable. When you feel fear upon hearing a noise downstairs in the middle of the night, you prick your ears to see whether or not your fear is justified – you try to determine whether there is an intruder downstairs or whether it is simply your spouse coming home from the pub. In such a case, why-questions loom large, and it would seem ill-advised to rely on your fear and to conclude that there is danger.

In general, it would seem that emotions often invite why-questions, and this is surely something that needs explaining. As Jonathan Mitchell (2017) notes, what can be argued here is that emotions differ from sensory perceptions in that things are more complicated in the case of emotions, so that when we reflect upon our emotions, we are often less sure as to whether we should trust what we feel. Consider fear for oneself. In such a case, you need to have some idea as to whether something is harmful to you in particular, given your specific vulnerabilities, and this makes the assessment more difficult. Another point here is that when we feel an emotion and therefore form an evaluative belief, we are often not quite sure what exactly triggered the emotion. Suppose you are walking home in the dark and start feeling frightened. You might not know what exactly it is that frightens you, and this might raise the question as to whether there is really something to fear.

However, it is at best controversial that we most often fail to take our emotions at face value. Brady holds that we are typically moved to discover whether our emotions are justified, and notes that this "reflect[s] the fact that in normal circumstances it would usually be *impermissible* for us to take our emotional experience at face value or to think that the need for justification is silenced" (Brady 2013, 88). There is empirical evidence that we do at least sometimes base our beliefs on what we feel. Thus, Clore and Gasper (2000) propose that feelings are sometimes experienced as evidence for beliefs that are consistent with such feelings. They explain that "[e]vidence from the sensations of feeling may be treated like sensory evidence from the external environment, so that something both believed propositionally and also felt emotionally may seem especially valid" (2000, 25). As Adam Pelser (2014) stresses, it seems in fact that we often take our emotions at face value. Maybe this is not what we ought to do, but we often do it nonetheless, so there it seems difficult to argue from the lack of trust we put in our emotions to the putative lack of justificatory power of emotions.

But are we right to put our trust into our emotions? One important difference between emotions and sensory experiences might, in fact, affect their justificatory power. As we have seen, emotions but not sensory experiences have cognitive bases. Because of this, it would seem that emotions have epistemic justification conditions. If you base your fear on the unjustified belief that there is a tiger on the loose in the neighborhood – you have read it on Facebook and you are fully aware that you should not put any trust in what you read on online social media – your fear seems to lack epistemic justification. On the other hand, if your fear is based on the justified belief that there is a tiger on the loose – a trustworthy person informed you of that fact – the fear appears justified even if in fact, your belief is false and there is no tiger to fear.

Given this, it can be argued that emotion cannot function as a regress-blocker. The thought is that if emotions are in need for justification, then they cannot constitute basic or immediate justification. At best, they transmit the justification they receive from whatever states, whether these are beliefs or sensory experience, that justify them. Indeed, if that is the case, it would seem that emotions are epistemically superfluous (see Goldie 2004; Brady 2013). Evaluative beliefs could just as well get their justification on the basis of the states that justify the emotions. All the justificatory work would be done by these other states.

A concessive reply consists in agreeing that whatever justifies emotions also justifies evaluative beliefs, while defending that emotions nonetheless play a special role in the justification of evaluative beliefs. Thus, Deonna and Teroni (2012a) argue that emotions constitute a privileged epistemic route to our knowledge of value even if whatever can justify an emotion is also sufficient to justify the corresponding evaluative belief. Emotions, they hold, are justified by their cognitive bases. Simplifying a bit, they hold that the justification of an emotion depends on whether the properties you seem to be aware of – the dog's sharp teeth and short temperament, etc. – are such that they constitute (or would constitute in case it is merely a seeming) an instance of the relevant evaluative feature – dangerousness in this instance. Provided it is itself justified, an emotion would be able to justify the relevant evaluative belief. Indeed, because emotions allow us to be aware of the relevance of facts that are difficult consciously to articulate and may be inaccessible to us independently of what we feel, emotions would provide a privileged route to justified beliefs. Thus, emotions might not be regress-blocker and they would not be epistemically indispensable, but they would nonetheless be epistemically crucial.

One question here is whether these conditions for the justification of emotions are plausible. A first point here is that one might want to add as a condition that the cognitive bases be justified. If you believe that there is a tiger on the loose in the neighborhood because you have read this on Facebook and as you are well aware, this is not a good source of information, surely your fear appears to lack justification. As Pelser (2014) argues, we can criticize emotions because they are based on unjustified beliefs. According to Pelser, the justification of emotions thus depends on both the fact that the cognitive basis does not lack justification *plus* the fact that if that cognitive basis were true, then the emotion would be accurate. Furthermore, one can ask whether the justification conditions of one's emotion do not need to include the general belief that tigers on the loose are dangerous, which affords a bridge between the non-evaluative and the evaluative (see Smith 2014; Echeverri 2019). This, in any case, would seem necessary to justify the belief that the tiger is dangerous, and if whatever justifies emotions can also justify the corresponding evaluative belief then one should surely conclude that the justification conditions spelled out by Deonna and Teroni are incomplete.

The main problem, however, is that it is not obvious that emotions and beliefs are on a par in terms of justification. It is clearly a rational requirement of beliefs that we are permitted to believe only what we have good epistemic reason to believe. Our beliefs are thus required to be supported by sensory perceptions or by justified beliefs. But it is not as clear that there is a similar requirement for emotions, so that we are permitted to feel only the emotions that are backed by further mental states. Suppose you see the tiger approaching and this causes you to be afraid of the tiger. It is far from clear that this emotion is in need of epistemic support from the visual experience of the tiger approaching. After all, you might not realize that what you see is an approaching tiger. It is even more obvious that your fear needs no support from any belief of yours. In particular, you are not required to believe that approaching tigers are dangerous, and this is because in most cases, emotions fail to involve such beliefs. Instead, you simply have a disposition to fear approaching tigers and similar animals, and even if one grants that dispositions involve implicit representations, it is hard to see, at least from an internalist point of view, how a state of which you are not aware could have justificatory force.

Given this, one might be tempted to argue that emotions do not, in fact, have justification conditions. Thus, there would be no asymmetry between emotions and sensory perceptions. The problem with this strategy, however, is to explain how it can be the case that some emotions appear to lack justification, such as when you base your emotion on an unjustified belief.

A second strategy in reply to the accusation of epistemic superfluity looks more promising. It consists in arguing that emotions can be regress-blockers even if, *in some sense*, they are open to why-questions. One way to go here is to deny that the sense in which emotions can be justified or unjustified is the same in which beliefs can be justified or unjustified. Michael Milona (2016; also see Cowan 2016) thus argues that in whatever sense emotions can be unjustified, sensory perception can also be unjustified. When looking at an illusion, for instance, you might well know that things are not as they visually appear to be. In such a case, your visual experience in some sense lacks "justification", because you have reasons to think that it is not accurate. The crucial point to stress is that this story would be compatible with the claim that perceptual experiences are regress-blockers in that they provide immediate *prima facie* justification. Transposed to emotions, one can then hold that emotions can be regress-blockers in that they provide *prima facie* justification. The question that arises, however, is whether this suggestion does not overstretch the notion of justification.

A third and more plausible reply consists in agreeing that emotions differ from sensory perceptions in that the former but not the latter have justification conditions, while holding that emotions are, by default, justified. Until proven guilty, emotions can be trusted. Therefore, the *prima facie* justification conditions of evaluative beliefs would not be affected by the fact that you sometimes have reasons to think that what you feel should not be trusted. If you realize that your emotion is based on beliefs that lack justification, for instance, the evaluative belief will not be *ultima facie* justified. In favorable cases, when such defeaters do not kick in, you will be *ultima facie* justified in your evaluative belief, and that justification will not depend on prior beliefs, so it will be immediate. One might wonder whether on this suggestion, emotions will not have to be considered epistemically superfluous. After all, it seems that whatever confers the default justification to emotions should also be in a position to justify evaluative beliefs. It would be a mistake to reason in this way, however. What is sufficient for justification by default for an emotion is, in all likelihood, very different from what is necessary for the justification of evaluative beliefs. It can thus be argued that being felt is sufficient for default justification.

One question that might arise here is whether we should not prefer the other, non-emotional route to the justification of evaluative beliefs. Surely, if you have the justified beliefs that there is a tiger on the loose and that tigers on the loose are dangerous, your belief that the tiger is dangerous will be in pretty good epistemic shape. The question here is how you form the belief that tigers on the loose are dangerous. Arguably, this generalization is inductively based on specific beliefs about the dangerousness of particular tigers or similar animals. The question, thus, is how you arrive at these specific beliefs. Interestingly, a good suggestion here is that it is thanks to specific instances of emotions, felt by you or by others, that you can conclude that tigers on the loose are dangerous. The situation would be similar to the belief that ripe tomatoes are red, a belief that is based, canonically, on the visual experiences you have when looking at ripe tomatoes. There might be some other route to the general belief, but if, as perceptual theories hold, emotions are at least partly similar to sensory perceptions, it would seem that such routes would inevitably lead back to the emotions we feel.

In any case, if this argument is on the right lines, the justification thesis does not appear to be threatened by the fact that emotions allow for why-questions. Insofar as emotions are justified by default, they can both confer justification to beliefs and be open to why-questions. Let us turn to a third line of argument against the justification thesis.

7.5. The Objection from the Focus of Attention

It is generally accepted by both by psychologists (see Wells and Matthews 1994), neuroscientists (see Damasio 1994), but also philosophers (see de Sousa 1987; Faucher and Tappolet 2002; Brady 2013) that emotions have a close relationship to attentional phenomena. It is hard to deny, for instance, that when you are afraid of an attacking tiger, your attention will be focused on that tiger. In the same way, when you feel anger at your sister, your attention tends to center on her and on what she has done. Attention is often compared to a spotlight that illuminates some part of a scene while leaving the rest in the dark, and which can be maintained on a spot, moved from one element to another as well as change its focus so as to zoom in or out, lighting up smaller or larger portions of a scene. How are we to understand these metaphors? William James (1890) held of attention that "[f]ocalisation, concentration of consciousness are of its essence. It implies withdrawal from things in order to deal effectively with others" (1890, 403–404). Following James, attention is generally understood as involving selectivity in information processing. For instance, when you visually focus on a poppy, you will notice more things about the flower than if your gaze is focused on the field of flowers before you.

Now, that emotions have this kind of effect on attention would seem at first sight to be good news for the justification thesis and more generally for perceptual accounts of emotions. It makes sense that emotions direct our attention towards objects that are represented as having evaluative features. Against this, Brady (2013) argues that because emotions not only direct our attention, but tend to capture and consume attention, their function is not to justify evaluative beliefs but to motivate the search for reasons for and against such beliefs. This he sees as an important epistemic feat of emotions: "one of the important things that attentional persistence can do is to enhance our representation of potentially significant objects and events, precisely by enabling us to discover reasons which bear on the accuracy of our initial emotional appraisals" (2013, 93). By doing so, emotions promote the reassessment of their object, thus enabling us to go from rough initial emotional appraisals to evaluative judgments that are based on a better understanding of situations.

Why would the fact that emotions allow us to collect information about the object of our emotions conflict with the justification thesis? Brady's idea is that emotions themselves rule out taking our initial emotional appraisal at face value. As he explains, he holds that "emotions themselves [...] *raise*, rather than silence, the justificatory question, through keeping our attention focused on the emotional object or event and by moving us to seek out considerations that bear on whether this object or event really is as it emotionally appears to be" (2013, 97). This claim appears plausible when you think of the example of someone who experiences fear upon hearing a noise at night. The fear appears to function as an alarm bell, signaling that there might be danger. By inducing a state of alertness, your fear will allow you to focus entirely on whether or not there is an intruder and thus on whether or not there is danger.

This example is striking, but the question is whether emotions and the attentional phenomena they involve generally raise rather than silence the justificatory question. As Brady (2013) notes, a rival proposal is that the point of attentional persistence is to monitor what is taken to be dangerous. When you focus on the approaching tiger, surely you are not interested in whether the appearance of acute danger might be false. Rather, you try to determine what the tiger is up to, in order to see how you could escape. Your working assumption, thus, is that the tiger is dangerous. Now, Brady anticipates this objection and argues that the hypothesis in question is in fact compatible with the claim that emotions have the function to motivate the reappraisal of the object. The claim concerning reappraisal would follow from the thesis that the maintenance of attention facilitates monitoring. Surely, it can be agreed that if your attention is focused on the tiger you might end up reassessing the situation. The tiger might leave the scene, so that in the end, you might feel relief instead of fear. But what is not clear is how monitoring a situation that you assume, because you take your fear at face value, to be dangerous can entail that the fear itself raises the question whether there is really danger. There is thus clearly a tension between the claim that the focus of attention has the function to help monitoring what is taken to be dangerous, and Brady's thesis that emotions have the function to raise the question whether they are justified.

In general, it should also be underlined that different emotions come with different attentional patterns. When you feel interested by something, your attention focuses on that thing, but when you are bored at a concert, your attention will drift away (Eastwood et al. 2012). Disgust has also been shown to correlate with attentional focus (Charash and McKay 2002). But it would seem that when experiencing disgust at something, such as a corpse, there is often a conflict between wanting to look at what triggers disgust and looking away from it, so that our attention at least in part shifts away from the object of disgust. Indeed, it has been suggested that fear can have the same effect. Thus, Kenneth Hugdahl and Kjell Morten Stormark (2003) hold that we tend actively to avoid further processing of stimuli that are perceived as aversive by disengaging our attention from such stimuli and shifting attention to a different spatial location. Finally, even if some positive emotions do capture our attention, they appear to do so in a distinctive way in that they tend to widen the attentional focus (Fredrickson and Branigan 2005; Gupta 2019). If you are happy to have finished your workday, your attention will not rest on that workday but it will zoom out and all sorts of loosely related ideas and images will cross your mind. Now, in all those cases, it is difficult to hold that emotions help collecting information about their objects by maintaining the focus of attention on these objects. Being bored with a concert surely does not put you in a good epistemic position vis-à-vis the details of the concert, and neither does looking away from something out of disgust or fear, or else thinking about all sorts of things because you feel happy to have finished your workday. Given this, the claim that the function of attentional focus in emotions is to raise the question of justification by seeking considerations that bear on whether the emotion is accurate or not does not appear vindicated. In general, it would seem that the influence of emotions on attentional focus is no threat to the claim that emotion can provide *prima facie* justification.

7.6. Taking Stock

What we have seen in this chapter is that the justification thesis that flows from perceptual accounts is not only plausible in itself but appears well placed to resist the main objections it faces. This is not to say that it is fully vindicated, but we have at least some ground to accept it. The question to which we will turn next is whether the fact that we often base our evaluative beliefs on our emotions is a good thing from the practical point of view. Does it help us to act rationally or does it foster practical irrationality?

7.7. Summary

- The normative question whether emotions are good or bad for us divides into several ones: the question of how emotions affect the rationality of what we think, how they affect the rationality of what we do, and finally the question of how emotions affect the prudence and the morality of our actions.
- Regarding whether emotions affect the rationality of what we think, a central question is whether emotions can provide epistemic justification for evaluative beliefs.
- The account that flows from perceptual accounts of emotions is one according to which a belief regarding properties such as dangerousness, disgustingness or offensiveness are *prima facie* justified if they are based on the corresponding emotions. Such beliefs are *ultima facie* justified on condition that as far as you know your emotions are not misleading you.
- Another claim that goes well with perceptual accounts is that emotions are epistemically indispensable to our knowledge of evaluative features. Because emotions might not be sufficiently trustworthy, this claim does not entail that emotions provide *prima facie* justification.
- An important worry is whether emotions are sufficiently reliable to consist in sources of justification. In reply, either one can argue that emotions are sufficiently, if not very highly, reliable, or one can reject the reliabilist assumption behind the question and embrace evidentialism.
- Another worry is that by contrast to sensory perceptions, emotions appear to allow for normative why-questions, so that one might be tempted to

think that they have epistemic justification conditions that are on a par with those of evaluative beliefs. According to some, emotion could have justification conditions while affording a privileged route to evaluative knowledge. Another possibility is to hold that the sense in which emotions can be held to be justified does not prevent them from functioning as regress-blockers.

- This worry is tied with the question whether emotions have epistemic justification conditions and if they do, what such conditions would amount to. According to some, emotions are justified by their cognitive bases, but it is in fact not clear that emotions need the epistemic support of other states.
- A third worry comes from the close link between emotions and attention, for it might seem that by focusing our attention to their objects, emotions raise rather than silence justification questions. In reply, it can be argued that the function of this attentional focus is that of coping with something that is held to have an evaluative feature because the emotion is taken at face value.

7.8. Study Questions

1. Can you really be justified in believing that a film is admirable, say, on the basis on someone's testimony, or do you have to rely on your own experience of that film?
2. How does caffeine or alcohol affect your emotions? How could you determine whether such conditions interfere with your emotions or help you to have more accurate emotions?
3. What would explain that we have thermometers to measure temperatures but we lack similar devices for evaluative features such as offensiveness or disgustingness?

7.9. Further Readings

Brady, Michael S. 2013. *Emotional Insight: The Epistemic Role of Emotional Experience*. Oxford: Oxford University Press, chap. 3.

Deonna, Julien A., and Fabrice Teroni. 2012b. "From Justified Emotions to Justified Evaluative Judgements." *Dialogue* 51 (1):55–77.

Echeverri, Santiago. 2019. "Emotional Justification." *Philosophy and Phenomenological Research* 98 (3):541–566.

Elgin, Catherine Z. 2008. "Emotion and Understanding." In *Epistemology and Emotions*, edited by G. Brun, U. Dogluoglu and D. Kuenzle. Aldershot: Ashgate.

Goldie, Peter. 2004. "Emotion, Reason, and Virtue." In *Emotion, Evolution, and Rationality*, edited by Dylan Evans and Pierre Cruse, 249–267. New York: Oxford University Press.

Johnston, Mark. 2001. "The Authority of Affect." *Philosophy and Phenomenological Research* 63 (1):181–214.

Kauppinen, Antti. 2013. "A Humean Theory of Moral Intuition." *Canadian Journal of Philosophy* 43 (3):360–381.

Milona, Michael, and Hichem Naar. 2020. "Sentimental Perceptualism and the Challenge from Cognitive Bases." *Philosophical Studies* 177 (10):3071–3096.

Pelser, Adam C. 2014. "Emotion, Evaluative Perception, and Epistemic Justification." In *Emotion and Value*, edited by Sabine Roeser and Cain Todd, 107–123. Oxford: Oxford University Press.

Zagsebski, Linda. 2003. "Emotion and Moral Judgment." *Philosophy and Phenomenological Research* 66 (1):104–124.

8 Emotions and Practical Rationality

8.1. Introduction

Remember the tale of Medea, who killed her sons out of anger. This tragedy makes it clear that emotions can cause us to do things that are both bad for ourselves and hence imprudent, and bad for others and hence immoral. Medea's case also illustrates that emotions can trigger actions that conflict with our better judgment. She is horrified by the evil of what she plans to do, but to no effect. Medea blames her angry passions for having mastered her. More generally, emotions are often regarded as the source of akratic actions and indeed of actions that are characterized by practical irrationality.

Practical irrationality, in the sense at stake, is the kind of rationality that concerns what we do. Just as what we think is guided by requirements of rationality, such as the requirement not to have beliefs that contradict each other, our actions are guided by requirements of rationality. It is often considered, for instance, that rationality requires us to do what we judge, all things considered, to be the best action. Akratic actions, which by definition flout this requirement, would necessarily manifest practical irrationality. As a second example, consider procrastination. Procrastination consists in freely putting off something you consider to have sufficient reason not to put off. Given this, it is plausible that practical rationality requires agents to do now what they judge they have to do now instead of later. Finally, a requirement of practical rationality that is often considered fundamental is that agents ought to take the means they see as necessary to their ends.

Such requirements can be considered to be structural in that they depend on the coherence, broadly understood, of agents. There is an incoherence in acting against one's better judgment, just as there is an incoherence in not doing now what you judge you have to do now instead of later. Another family of requirements, which are sometimes considered to concern rationality, makes substantive demands that do not depend only on internal coherence. Consider the requirement to believe only what is true. Because the satisfaction of this requirement depends on how the world is, and not merely on how you take the world to be, this is a clear example of a substantive requirement. Similarly,

DOI: 10.4324/9781315542300-11

the requirement to act on reasons understood as facts that justify your action, by contrast to beliefs about such facts, would be a substantive rationality requirement.

It should be stressed that neither of these rationality requirements are identical with the requirement of prudence, understood in terms of what is good for the agent. It is true that acting in accordance with your better judgment can well promote your interest and thus be good for you, but of course, you can act in a way that is good for yourself while doing something you judge that is not, all things considered, the best. This might be so, for instance, because what you consider to be best, all things considered, depends on reasons that are distinct from self-regarding reasons, such as moral reasons. Similarly, depending on what your ends are, you can take the means necessary to your ends while failing to do what is good for you. This is for instance the case when your end is the good of someone else and what is required involves self-sacrifice. Again, procrastination is often bad for the agent – by putting off preparing for an exam you might end up not being ready for it – but it need not be, for what you put off might not tend to promote your own interest. You might, for instance, put off sending money to a charity even if you consider you should do it now rather than later.

Everyone can agree that emotions sometimes cause akratic actions as well as other forms of practical failures. Medea's rage caused her to kill her sons. Your fear of jumping into the lake might cause you not to jump even if you realize that jumping is required to get to the other side of the lake, which is what you want. Similarly, what causes you to procrastinate on a task might be the fear of not being up to that task. One interesting question is how emotions trigger practical failures. Another question is whether emotions generally interfere with our practical rationality or whether they can sometimes help us to be more rational from the point of view of practical reason. As we shall see, several philosophers, such as Nomy Arpaly (2000) and Karen Jones (2003), have argued that emotions can sometimes help us to overcome practical irrationality. Indeed, others have proposed that without emotions, decision and action would be badly hampered if not impossible. Thus, according to de Sousa (1987) and to Damasio (1994), emotions are key to decision-making.

Because akrasia has been central to philosophical discussions since antiquity and because it is also generally considered paradigmatic of practical irrationality, the discussion will focus on the role of emotions in akrasia. Before turning to akrasia, however, we will look at the intriguing case of so-called *arational actions*, that is, expressive actions, which are intentional but which are not done for a reason. After, this, we shall turn to the question of how emotions can trigger akratic actions. We will then consider the question of whether emotions cannot at least sometimes result in actions that are morally praiseworthy even if irrational, as well as the question whether akratic actions motivated by emotions are sometimes not only morally admirable, but also more rational than the ones that conform to the better judgment of the agent. Lastly, we will discuss the more ambitious thesis that emotions are necessary to decision-making.

8.2. Arational Actions

As we discussed in Chapter 5, some emotions, such as fear you feel when confronting a tiger, are closely tied to motivation in that they facilitate actions, but also in that they involve a desire, such as the desire to avoid harm, which sets a goal for the agent, for instance the avoidance of harm, and which will result in action, depending on the agent's deliberation. On this picture, running away can be considered the rational thing to do in that it furthers the agent's goal of avoiding harm. By contrast, some actions resulting from emotion appear to serve no goal at all. This is the case of some actions that express emotions. As Rosalind Hursthouse (1991) explains, examples of expressive actions include running, jumping, or leaping up to reach the leaves on trees out of joy, pulling one's hair out or rolling in a deceased person's clothes out of grief, covering one's face in the dark or when alone out of shame, or covering one's eyes when they are already shut out of horror. In all these cases, the agent might seem not to have a good reason to perform the action, such that one might tempted to accuse emotions of producing practical irrationality.

A case of expressive action that has been amply discussed is that of Jane, who out of hatred for Joan, tears at Joan's photograph with her nails and gouges holes in the eyes of Joan's portrait. According to Hursthouse (1991), who imagined the case to illustrate what she calls "arational actions" (1991, 58–59), Jane's action is intentional or voluntary, but what is special about it is that it does not appear to be performed for a reason. Hursthouse holds that insofar as such actions are not performed *against* the agent's reasons, they are not irrational. But neither are such actions rational, given the lack of reason the agent has for the action. Hursthouse argues that to make room for arational actions, one needs to abandon the thesis that intentional actions are necessarily done for a reason. More precisely, she assumes an account of reasons according to which acting on reasons amounts to acting on a desire plus some means–end belief and holds that arational actions are intentional even if they cannot be accounted for in terms of belief–desire explanations.

Cases such as that of Jane are intriguing. Even if they are not performed against the agent's practical reasons, such actions are surely verging on practical irrationality. Because they are intentional, one would expect that such actions are done in the light of some perceived good. Even if it has been challenged, the thesis that intentional action is done *under the guise of the good* is difficult to deny (see Tenenbaum 2013). But what good could Jane see in gouging the eyes in the picture of a person she hates? She might have considered the action to be instrumentally good, but this is far from necessarily the case. We can safely assume that she does not believe that destroying a photograph will hurt her rival, for instance. Moreover, even if she might do this in the belief that this is the best way to vent her anger, nothing forces us to assume that this is the reason why she performs the action. Could it be that Jane considers the action intrinsically good? To say the least, it is difficult to see what intrinsic good she might have seen in performing such an action. If one considers that practical rationality requires agents to do only that for which she has good reasons, one might well doubt that arational actions are fully rational. Even so, Jane's action appears intelligible, just as leaping up to reach the leaves of trees when feeling joy or rolling in a deceased person's clothes out of grief are. This is simply the kind of things we do when we are experiencing such emotions.

This is why it is tempting to try to explain such expressive actions in terms of a pairing of desire combined with a means–end belief, thereby making it rational. One possibility here is to argue with Michael Smith (1998) that given her hatred, Jane has the desire to gouge out the eyes in the photograph and the means–end belief being simply that by gouging out the eyes in the photograph, this is what she does. The action would be desired as such, and not as a means to some further end. The problem is that this explanation fails to make it clear why Jane's anger would dispose her to do such a bizarre thing as gouging out eyes in a photograph. Indeed, by rendering the action entirely rational, it fails to account for the intuition that such actions are less than perfectly rational.

According to Peter Goldie (2000), who, like Smith, wants to defend the belief–desire model of action explanation, Jane's action has to be explained not by a desire but by a wish, that is, a motivational state like a desire except that we believe we cannot satisfy it. Because of her hatred, Jane wishes she could scratch out Joan's eyes, something that we surely find intelligible given that when we hate something, we often want that thing to be destroyed. However, we can assume that Jane does not desire really to scratch out the eyes of real Joan, maybe because she is afraid of the consequences for herself or because she thinks it would be a morally bad thing to do. When she attacks the photograph instead, it is because she imagines that she is doing what she wishes, namely, scratching out Joan's eyes. The idea is that because the real action is not a realistic option, Jane finds herself with the symbolic desire to hurt the photograph. In Goldie's terms: "By acting out through expressive action, Jane is, in a symbolic way, acting out *just* what she knows she ought not to do" (2000, 131). This, according to Goldie, explains the bizarre desire to scratch out the eyes in the photograph, which in tandem with the belief that scratching out the eyes in the photograph is just doing so, explains the action.

What is attractive about this account of expressive actions is that it makes room for the sense that such actions are bizarre but nonetheless intelligible, given the intelligibility of wanting to destroy what one hates. A good question, however, is whether Goldie's account does make Jane's action too rational. If we ascribe to Jane the wish to scratch out the eyes in the photograph and the belief that by doing so she indeed does so, we have to conclude that she is in fact perfectly rational. But as we saw, it is difficult to see what good, whether intrinsic or instrumental, Jane could have seen in such an action. By trying to save belief–desire explanations of actions, Goldie's account arguably appears to read too much rationality into the case.

As Döring (2003; see also Betzler 2009) suggests, such cases can be better understood if one abandons the belief–desire model of action explanations and makes room for explanations in terms of emotions and their evaluative content.

As we have seen in Chapter 6, Döring favors a perceptual theory of emotions. Such a theory makes it possible to develop a different account of how emotions contribute to the explanation of action. As Döring writes, emotions "can rationalize actions because, like perceptions, they have a representational intentional content" (2003, 214). If one allows that emotions represent evaluative features, there is indeed room for action explanations in terms of such evaluative features. Suppose that Jane is afraid of Joan. Jane's action of avoiding Joan can be easily explained in terms of the fear Jane feels given that this fear represents her rival as dangerous. The perceived dangerousness of Joan gives Jane a reason to take measures to ensure her safety. Similarly, suppose Jane lashes out at the real Joan. We might explain Jane's action by invoking Joan's perceived hate-worthiness. Joan's perceived hate-worthiness would consist in a reason to lash out at her, however immoral that action is.

The question is whether this story transposes to the case of arational actions. How should one account for scratching out the eyes in the photograph? According to Döring (2003), Jane's action consists in a symbolic expression of her hatred, something which depends on cultural norms. If so, however, the question arises whether or not Jane needs to see the action in question as a good way symbolically to express her emotion. If she does, then the action can be taken to aim at some good. It would fail to count as arational. If not, then it would seem that one can wonder whether the action is really intentional. Given this, Jane's action could not be considered both intentional and arational.

What we need, it would seem, is an account of Jane's action that makes room for the fact that in some sense, because the action is intentional, she sees her action as good, while in another, she does not take her action to be good. This, in any case, appears plausible if one holds that intentional actions are done in the light of some perceived good. Given this, one could see the case as involving a conflict, which resembles cases of recalcitrance, between Jane's emotional perspective and her rational perspective. Given the symbolic transfer of her hatred to the photograph, we can assume that it appears to Jane that lashing out at the photograph of Joan is good in some way. However, it is plausible that Jane does not believe or judge that lashing out at the photograph is good in any sense of that term. As a result, the reason for which she acts is one she would disavow. Thus, however intentional and done in the light of some perceived good, the action is one for which there appears to be no reason.

Whether or not this suggestion is on the right lines, an important point, which is raised by Döring (2003), is that not all expressive actions involve symbolic replacement. You do not leap up to reach the leaves on trees in a kind of symbolic replacement of leaping to reach something else. In general, and this is something that Hursthouse (1991) stressed, what should be kept in mind is that expressive actions and in fact all actions that result from emotions are quite varied. Some expressive actions, such as sweating or trembling, are involuntary and non-intentional. Others, such as clenching one's fists, can be done involuntarily, but can also be controlled. Still others are done intentionally because we are in the grip of an emotion and simply want to do them. A good example here is that of jumping for joy. Then, there are actions that can be explained in terms of the evaluative features that emotions represent. In case of a conflict between the emotional and the rational perspective, cases of arational actions might arise. As we will shortly discuss, actions that result from emotion can clash not only with a specific judgment, but with the agent's judgment as what is to be done all things considered.

8.3. Emotions and Akrasia

Akratic actions (from the Greek *kratein*, which means control and the privative "a"), or weak-willed actions, are generally taken to involve a conflict between what we do and what we think we ought to do, such as when you have another glass of wine even though you judge that it would be better, all things considered, to refrain. You are perfectly aware, for instance, that having another glass of wine will result in a bad migraine, so that even if it would be pleasant to continue drinking, you consider that the better course of action, all things considered, is very clearly to refrain. Indeed, as far as you know, you have conclusive reasons for not performing that action. But as often happens, you have that other glass of wine in spite of your better judgment.

It is common to distinguish different kinds of akratic actions. One important distinction is between akratic actions that are free and ones that are not. According to a first possibility, thus, it is freely, and also intentionally, that we act against our better judgment. By contrast, other cases of akrasia would seem less than free and intentional. Medea's killing, for instance, appears to be a clear case of unfree akrasia, since from what she says, her rage forced her, against her will, to do the killing. In some sense, one can say that Medea was not really herself when acting on her anger, a point that raises the question of the relation between emotions and autonomy, to which we will come back.

The possibility of freely and intentionally acting against your better judgment makes for a number of puzzles regarding the nature of intentional action and the relation between practical judgment and action (see Stroud 2008). Basically, the question is how we can freely and intentionally opt for a course of action that we consider to be inferior. In fact, it is only rather recently, starting in the late 1960s, that the possibility of free intentional action performed in spite of the agent's better judgment started to be deemed possible (see Davidson 1969). However, most philosophers would now agree that we can (and indeed often do) freely and intentionally act against our better judgment. This type of akratic action, sometimes called "strict akrasia" can be defined in the following way:

> (Strict akrasia) An action is a strict akratic action if and only if (a) it is free and intentional, and (b) at the time at which the action is performed, the agent judges that there are decisive reasons for not performing that action, all things considered.

> (see Mele 1987; and also Davidson 1969)

The "better judgment", in this definition, is the judgment that the agent has, all things considered, decisive reasons for not performing the action in question, for instance because another action is considered superior. Such a judgment is called "better judgment" because it is based on what the agent takes to be all the relevant considerations. Whatever you have decisive reasons to do is what you ought to do. Thus, when you act against your better judgment, you act against the judgment that you ought not perform the very action that you perform.

One point to underline is that it is at the very moment of the action that the agent makes the better judgment. This marks off strict akrasia from another important form of practical irrationality, sometimes claimed to consist in weakness of will properly understood, and which involves an irrational change of heart, such as when upon waking up, you reconsider your resolution to go jogging at dawn and stay in bed in spite of having resolved to do so (see Holton 2009).

How would emotions cause strict akratic actions? One obvious suggestion here is that emotions involve motivations that cause the akratic action. In the case of Medea, it does indeed appear that the desire for revenge involved in her rage is the cause of her evil deed. In that case, it would seem that the cause is overwhelming, causing Medea to act against her will, so that the action could not be considered free. But emotions need not involve overwhelming motivations. Even intense anger could result in a motivation that causes you to act without forcing you to do so against your will. What it takes to act freely is debated, but it would seem that you can have a desire for revenge that does not deprive you of your freedom, while being strong enough to motivate you in spite of your better judgment. Given this, it appears plausible that insofar as they involve motivations, emotions can cause strict akratic actions.

An attractive suggestion here is that emotions can contribute to akrasia in virtue of the patterns of attention that they involve. According to de Sousa, by drawing attention to certain considerations, emotions interfere with our practical reasoning, so that we draw the irrational conclusion that the akratic action is the one to be done while judging that all our reasons taken together indicate that we ought to refrain. As de Sousa explains, it would seem that emotions are "perfectly tailored for the role of arbitrators among reasons" because "their essential role lies in establishing specific patterns of salience relevant to inferences" (1987, 200). The suggestion that by focusing on certain aspects of a situation, emotions influence our decisions is plausible, and quite clearly it is entirely compatible with the claim that the motivations that are involved in emotion have a role to play in the causation of akratic actions.

Following Donald Davidson's influential account (1969), de Sousa assumes that akrasia necessarily involves a reasoning error that occurs before the action. This is in fact far from obvious. It would seem that akrasia can, but need not involve such reasoning error. Consider again the question of whether you should have another glass of wine. We can easily assume that you carefully consider all your reasons for and against an action and that as a result, you judge that these reasons, taken together, indicate that you should refrain from having another glass. From this, you could well correctly infer that this action is out of the question, while nonetheless freely and intentionally having another glass. The akratic break, in such cases, lies between reasoning and motivation, and not between any previous steps in the reasoning. This, however, does not affect the general claim that emotions are instrumental in causing the akratic break in virtue of the patterns of attention that they involve. By drawing your attention to some specific aspects of a situation, an emotion can well affect what you will be motivated to do, whatever the conclusion of your reasoning regarding what you ought to do.

If this is on the right lines, emotions would be in a position to have particularly strong causal impact on what we do, an impact which would at least sometimes result in acting against our better judgment. However, the role of emotions in akrasia is arguably not merely causal. As we have seen when considering arational actions, the fact that emotions consist in evaluative representations makes it possible to explain actions in terms of the evaluative features that are represented. Emotions could thus shed light on the reasons for which akratic actions are done (Tappolet 2003). The idea is that insofar as evaluative features are tied to practical reasons, the evaluative features you are aware of in virtue of your emotions will explain your action. To keep things simple, consider again a case of fear. The fear you experience when considering a jump into the lake represents the jump as dangerous. Being dangerous is a reason, however partial, to refrain from jumping. It follows that your fear informs you about a reason you have not to jump. Thus, if you refrain from jumping in spite of your better judgment, the perceived danger is the reason that explains why you do not jump. This will not make it the case that refraining from jumping is the rational thing to do – remember that you judge that, all things considered, you have decisive reasons to take the jump – but it will help understanding why such action can be considered to be intentional in spite of going against our better judgment.

Cases of akrasia that involve emotions, like cases of arational actions, can be compared to cases of recalcitrance. Recalcitrance, we have seen, involves a conflict between your emotion and your specific evaluative judgment, such as when you fear the spider while judging that it is in fact innocuous. The conflict at stake in the case of akrasia is one between what you feel and what you judge, all things considered. You are afraid of the danger, while you judge that all things considered you have decisive reason to perform the feared action. As such, these two states represent compatible states of affairs. However, there is nonetheless a tension here. Given your fear, you will tend to have a general negative feeling toward the action and you will be reluctant to accomplish the action you see as dangerous, so that in the end, your emotion might well override your better judgment.

We have seen that emotions are powerful causes of strict akratic actions. But emotions do not merely have a causal role, since they also shed light on the reasons for which we perform such actions. The question is whether the influence of emotion is limited to producing actions that manifest practical irrationality. As we will see in the next section, cases of akrasia are again instructive.

8.4. Inverse Akrasia

Akratic actions traditionally were of special interest to philosophers because they were thought to consist not only in practical irrationality but also in imprudent and foremost in immoral actions. Thus, the cases of akrasia that were prominent in the discussions were cases in which agents are acting in spite of their moral judgments. Akrasia was seen as one of the main sources of immoral actions. The question then was whether it is possible to freely and intentionally act against the judgment that the course of action is morally bad and thus to be avoided. Assuming this traditional picture of akrasia, R. M. Hare (1952), for instance, denies that we can freely and intentionally act against our moral judgment. Hare held that it is a conceptual truth that moral judgments necessarily are followed by actions. If you failed to act on your moral judgment, it must be because like Medea you were not free to act or because you did not really judge that this was what you ought to do.

More recently, the focus has not only shifted to cases of akrasia that do not involve moral judgments, but also to cases in which the judgment against which the agent acts is flawed. When the judgment at stake concerns what is good for the agent, this arguably makes for cases in which the akratic action fails to be imprudent. Thus, if you mistakenly judge that you have conclusive reasons to do something dangerous but because you are afraid, you do not act on your judgment, you will have made the prudent choice. Similarly, in the case of actions performed in spite of a mistaken moral judgment, it would seem that the akratic action can well be moral despite being irrational. Such cases, which have been called "inverse akrasia" or indeed "moral inverse akrasia" to distinguish them from prudent akratic actions (Arpaly and Schroeder 1999, 163), have been at the center of discussions regarding the role of emotions in akrasia.

The case that has been prominent in the discussion of inverse akrasia is that of Mark Twain's character Huckleberry Finn (see Bennett 1974; and also Arpaly and Schroeder 1999). Huck has helped a slave, Jim, to escape from his owner on a raft down the Mississippi River. As they come close to where Jim will become a free person, Huck has second thoughts. Turning Jim in to the authorities, he thinks, is the right thing to do. However, when the opportunity to do so arises, Huck finds himself lying to slave hunters in order to protect Jim. Jonathan Bennett (1974), who construes the case as a conflict between bad morality and sympathy, describes the case as one in which sympathy wins over bad morality. Unless one is committed to moral relativism or the view that an agent should never act illegally, it can be agreed that this is a clear case in which the morally praiseworthy thing to do is not to turn in Jim. Huck's moral principles, which he uncritically acquired from rural Missouri, and according to which slave ownership is just another kind of ownership, are deeply flawed. Given this, it appears plausible that Huck's failure to turn Jim in is morally praiseworthy even if the action is performed against his better judgment and thus irrational. What happens, it would seem, is that his feeling of sympathy for Jim, by moving him to refrain from turning Jim in, gets him to take the morally right course of action.

Huck describes himself as being too weak – he hasn't "the spunk of a rabbit", as he says (quoted in Bennett 1974, 4) – to follow what his conscience says he ought to do, so it might be thought that his failure to turn Jim in was not a free action. One might thus argue that his sympathy for Jim forced him to act against his will. This, however, does not appear to be the best way to understand the case. In contrast with the case of Medea, where it appears indeed plausible that her rage forced her to act against her will, it would seem strange to suppose that Huck's sympathy took over and forced him to act against his will. We can readily assume that Huck was free to have done otherwise, but chose not to follow his conscience – that is, chose to act against his better judgment – out of sympathy for Jim.

Indeed, there is a strong consideration in favor of the claim that Huck's action was not forced upon him by his sympathy. What has to be stressed is that we not only are ready to praise the action as morally praiseworthy, but we are happy also to praise the agent, Huck, for what he has done. This is a point made by Arpaly and Schroeder (1999), who argue that inverse akrasia is incompatible with rationalist accounts of the self. They note that "[t]he reader of Twain's novel tends to see Huckleberry's action not as an accidental good deed done by a bad boy, but as indicative of the fact that Huckleberry is, in an important sense, a good boy, a boy with his heart in the right place" (1999, 163). But if we are ready to praise Huck for what he did, we cannot at the same time assume that what he did was forced upon him by his feelings of sympathy. Surely, he has to be considered to be himself the source of his actions for us to praise him.

The interesting upshot here is that by contrast to a rationalist account of the self, according to which responsible actions have to flow from the agent's better judgment, there are reasons to embrace an account of the self which allows that acting on our emotion can result in free actions for which we are responsible. More generally, as Arpaly and Schroeder argue (1999), it would seem that any account of the self that identifies selves with their rational capacities is not going to do justice to cases such as that of Huck. Actions that result from emotions rather than from the agent's better judgment can be considered, at least on some occasions, to consist in actions that are autonomous, in the sense that they take their source in the agent's self instead of being forced upon the agent by something external to the self (see Tappolet 2016). Autonomy, in this context, is understood as self-governance. You are autonomous when you determine your thoughts and actions instead of being at the mercy of forces that are external to your own self, such as threats and compulsions (see Buss and Westlund 2018). What is required for autonomous agency is both complex and controversial, but what a case like that of Huck suggests is that it would be wrong to believe that only actions resulting from the exercise of our reasoning capacities can be considered to be autonomous.

In any case, there are reasons to think that emotions are not only instrumental in causing akratic actions and more generally practical irrationality. When the better judgment is mistaken, emotions can also result in actions that are prudentially good, in the sense that they promote what is good for the agent. When the mistaken better judgment is a moral one, emotions can result in irrational albeit morally praiseworthy actions, for which the agent can be praised. In both cases, however, the actions remain irrational because they are done despite the agent's better judgment. A good question, to which we will turn now, is whether acting against a flawed better judgment necessarily manifests practical irrationality.

8.5. Rational Akrasia

Until relatively recently, it was taken for granted that acting against one's better judgment was necessarily irrational. This assumption has been challenged. According to a number of authors, such as Alison McIntyre (1990, see also Arpaly 2000 and Tappolet 2003), akratic actions need not be irrational, or more modestly might be more rational than acting on the better judgment.

Again, Huck's case is central to this debate. The argument is that in spite of consisting in an action that conflicts with his better judgment, Huck's action is the one that is grounded in Huck's practical reasons. The idea is that Huck's all things considered judgment is not only false, but that it also neglects important considerations that Huck could and indeed should have considered in this deliberation. Had Huck thought harder, he would have realized that Jim was his friend, that Jim was putting his trust in him, and that Jim had a legitimate desire for freedom. Moreover, had Huck taken these considerations into account, he would have seen that, all things considered, he had more reason to help Jim than to turn him in. Sadly, Huck failed to think about these considerations, so his better judgment fails to reflect his practical reasons. As we know, Huck's sympathy luckily prevents him from turning Jim in. Given this, it can be argued that his emotions helped Huck to take into account the reasons he neglected, thus making him more rational than if he had acted in accordance with his better judgment.

Arpaly (2000) imagines a similar case that involves a prudential choice. Emily, a chemistry Ph.D. student, feels restless, sad, and ill motivated. Her feelings cause her to abandon the chemistry program against her better judgment. When she thinks about these feelings, she judges that they are groundless, but in fact, the feelings are triggered by factors that are good reasons to envisage a different career, given her beliefs and desires, such as the fact that chemistry would not allow her fully to exercise her talents. As Arpaly puts it, "Emily [...] acts far more rationally in leaving the program than she would in staying in the program, not simply because she has good reasons to leave the program, but because she acts for these good reasons" (2000, 504–505). Arpaly compares the case of Emily with that of Alice, whose bad feelings arise because of lack of self-esteem, and argues that in leaving the program, Alice is twice irrational. Alice holds a false conviction in the face of the evidence she has and she leaves the program for bad reasons. Because Emily leaves the program for good reasons, the only irrationality involved in her case is her failure to give up the conviction that she should stick with the program. What saves Emily are her emotions. As Karen Jones puts it, it would seem that "an agent's emotions can be keyed-to her reasons in such a way that they enable the agent to track those reasons, while her all-things-considered judgment does not" (2003, 186).

According to McIntyre (1990), such possibilities arise because agents are not necessarily clear-sighted about the reasons they have, and as a result of their deliberation will fail to take into account all their practical reasons. How exactly this claim is understood depends on the account of practical reasons that is favored. If one thinks of practical reasons as external facts, it would seem obvious that one might be mistaken about one's reasons. For instance, if moral facts constitute practical reasons and it is a fact that it is morally wrong to turn Jim in, then it is clear that one can be mistaken about such facts. Huck would simply fail to acknowledge this moral fact in his deliberation. However, as McIntyre (1990; see also Arpaly 2000) argues, one can also follow Bernard Williams (1981) and assume that practical reasons are *internal*, in the sense that they depend on the agent's motivations, and nonetheless accept that we might be wrong about the reason we have. This is so because on any reasonable account, we can be wrong about our motivations and the reasons in which these motivations result, or else have false beliefs regarding the means to take for achieving what we want, so that what we infer concerning our reasons might be erroneous. This is where sometimes emotions can help. As McIntyre puts it, "an agent's sensitivity to considerations that are reasons might on some occasions outstrip his more intellectual ability to see that they are reasons and are such as justify a course of action" (1990, 390).

The claim that actions performed in spite of the agent's better judgment can be more rational than actions that conform to the better judgment has been disputed. The reason is that from the point of view of the agent, it would seem that the right thing to do is to follow the conclusion of their deliberation. Surely it would seem that to be rational Huck has no choice but to trust his own reasoning and the conclusion he draws. The same appears true of Emily, and indeed she considers her decision to withdraw from the chemistry program as irrational. Thus, it might appear tempting to claim with Döring that "an account of practical rationality [...] must be given in terms of subjective reasons: an agent is rational to the extent to which he is guided by his subjective reasons" (2010, 287). Subjective reasons, in this context, are practical reasons that agents believe they have, by contrast with objective reasons, which are the ones that agents really have. To be guided by subjective reasons, thus, is nothing else than being guided by one's better judgment.

The question is whether practical rationality requires an agent to follow their better judgment or whether the requirement is to act in terms of the practical reasons this agent has. Do we have to do what we believe we have conclusive reasons to do, or should we rather do what we have conclusive reasons to do? Given that better judgments might fail to take into account the reasons an agent has, there is room to argue that it is the second, substantive requirement that matters. The normative force of the first requirement, which asks agents to be guided by their better judgment, can be considered to derive from the second one, which concerns not our judgment but the reasons we have (Kolodny 2005). Given what you believe about your reasons, it will seem to you that what you have to do is this or that, but this might simply be wrong. Thus, to be rational, and not merely apparently so, you had better not follow an irrational better judgment, one which fails to take into account the reasons you have. If this is on the right lines, following one's emotions can be, on some occasions, a more reliable path to practical rationality, compared to following one's better judgment.

In sum, emotions would be far from only causing rational havoc. They could also, on some occasions, allow us to act in more rational ways. As we will discuss in the next section, the role of emotions in practical irrationality has been thought to be even more important. Emotions, it has been argued, are central to effective deliberation and decision-making.

8.6. Emotions and Decision-Making

As we have seen on several occasions, emotions bear a close relationship to attentional phenomena. When you are afraid of something, for instance, your attention will focus on the object of your fear as well as possible escape routes. According to de Sousa (1987), this characteristic of emotions allows them to play a crucial practical role. Pure reason, as such, would be unable to determine what we ought to attend to and to inquire about. In particular, pure reason would not be able to determine what information is relevant in order to take a decision. What we need to know is how to retrieve only what is necessary from the vast store of information we have. This is what de Sousa calls the "philosopher's frame problem" (1987, 193). Emotions, de Sousa argues, would be nature's way of dealing with that problem. Consider a robot sitting on a wagon on which a ticking bomb is attached, but who keeps on analyzing the many consequences of this option, determining for instance that pulling the wagon out of the room would not change the price of tea in China, instead of getting away (Dennett 1984). What de Sousa holds is that it would be thanks to fear that we would avoid the sad destiny of this robot.

According to de Sousa, emotions manage to do this because of their tie to attention. As he puts it, "an emotion limits the range of information that the organism will take into account, the inferences actually drawn from a potential infinity, and the set of live options among which it will choose" (1987, 195). Because of this, emotions make it possible "to control the crucial factor of salience among what would otherwise be an unmanageable plethora of objects of attention, interpretations, and strategies of inference and conduct" (1987, 249). Filling the gap of pure reason in the determination of belief and action is what de Sousa takes to be the biological function of emotions.

As Ramy Majeed (2019) explains, the role of emotion in determining the salience of information depends on the evaluative component of emotions. "[E]motions", he writes, "feel good or bad, and in virtue of that, their intentional objects are represented as also being good or bad; as being positive or negative" (2019, 58). This, he argues, helps explain why emotions have a biasing effect. The reason is that our attention is drawn to pieces of information that are represented as positive or negative, while we tend to neglect what is represented as neither positive nor negative.

A similar hypothesis has been proposed by Damasio (1994). According to Damasio, emotion feelings function as "somatic markers" that "have been connected, by learning, to predicted future outcomes of certain scenarios" (1994, 174). Somatic markers assist us in our deliberation by highlighting options as good or bad and by focusing attention on the negative or positive outcome of options, so that the number of considered options is limited. Put otherwise, emotions are biasing devices. Given this, emotions help to narrow down the range of options we consider, thus making up for the shortcoming of pure reason. As Damasio puts it: "a somatic state, negative or positive, caused by the appearance of a given representation, operates not only as a *marker for the value of what is represented, but also as a booster for continued working memory and attention*" (1994, 197–198). Somatic markers help narrow down the options we consider, but they also facilitate the cost–benefit analysis of our options, positive feelings moving us to favor options, while negative feelings move us to shun them. More generally, it is plausible that emotions play a central role in the assessment of our options. As Brady writes about the anticipation of shame or of pleasure, but also of comfort and discomfort, "[t]he anticipation of feeling such things is a central factor in [our] assignment of utility" to our options (2018, 77).

Damasio's evidence includes studies of patients who have suffered from brain lesions in the prefrontal lobe, which is crucial to the processing of emotions. One particularly telling case is that of his patient Elliot. Although being an intelligent, skilled, and able-bodied person, who had an enviable personal and professional status, Elliott was no longer capable of holding a job or of keeping up good relations with his family after having had to undergo surgery in order to remove a brain tumor. After the surgery, Elliott was no longer able to manage his time properly and make sensible decisions. More generally, "his ability to reach decisions was impaired, as was his ability to make an effective plan for the hours ahead of him, let alone to plan for the months and years of his future" (Damasio 1994, 37). Surprisingly, there was no change whatever in his general abilities. Elliott was, among other things, able to perform very well on reasoning tasks, even when the reasoning concerned moral or more generally practical issues. The problem is that even when he had considered several valid options, he still would be unable to decide what to do. This difficulty, according to Damasio, came from a change in his feelings: what once evoked strong positive or negative emotions no longer caused any reaction. The lack of emotional reactions prevented Elliott from assigning expected values to the options he considered, thus making "his decision-making landscape hopelessly flat" (1994, 51).

Biological evolution but also learning will determine what emotional biases each of us ends up with. As a result, someone might react with fear at the sight of a dog, however innocuous, while someone else will not be afraid at all of the same dog. Given this, some emotional biases are likely to result in actions that fail to be grounded in good reasons, thus fostering irrationality. This accounts for a good part of the irrationality that emotions produce. But if de Sousa and Damasio are right, the irrationality that emotions produce would be the price to pay to be able to make any decision. Without emotions, we would not be in any position to choose between options. As a result, it would be a big mistake to think that emotions must be kept out of our practical reasoning.

Against this picture, Jon Elster (1999), who emphasizes the irrationality of emotions and their role in biasing cognition, has argued that the account of rational-choice theory presupposed by de Sousa and Damasio is a caricature. Rational choice theory, he claims, does not presuppose that a rational agent would always consider all possible outcomes of all possible options. Instead of relying on their emotions, agents would do better to rely on rational methods to select the relevant information. A good question here is what other strategies a rational agent could use. Independently of how one answers that question, however, what appears to be plausible is that human beings, and also a good number of nonhuman animals, do in fact rely on their emotions to handle the problem that arises from the plethora of information. It should be also noted that the question of how to interpret the hypothesis that decision-making depends on somatic markers has given rise to heated debates (see Bartol and Linquist 2015). However, there is little doubt that insofar as they involve evaluations, emotions must play a central role in the identification of an agent's options.

Let us close with a note of caution. Before we conclude that emotions, in general, have the function to determine salience, thereby facilitating decision-making by reducing the number of options we consider, we should be careful to remind ourselves of the fact that emotions have different effects on attention. As we have seen (in Chapter 7, section 5), boredom makes your attention drift away, while feeling happy tends to widen the attentional focus. This is not to say that the impact of emotion on attention fails to play any role in decision-making. But because of the variety of the effects, the way emotions influence decision-making is bound to be more complex. It cannot consist merely in a focus of our attention on what we perceive, given our emotions, as good or bad.

8.7. Taking Stock

We started with the question of whether the traditional conception of emotions as sources of practical irrationality is warranted. When discussing expressive actions that are intentional but for which there seems to be no reason, that is, arational actions, we saw that emotions and the evaluative representations they involve might help explain what we do. Given this, arational actions can be understood in terms of a conflict between the perspective afforded by our emotions, such as our hatred, and our belief that the reason for which we act is not a good one. A similar structure appears to characterize akratic actions. The conflict, in such cases, is between our emotion and our better judgment.

As cases of akratic actions show, emotions can cause practical irrationality, and their power to do so, which stems from the motivational force of emotions as well as the influence they have on attention, is not to be underestimated. However, emotions can have more positive effects. As illustrated by the case of Huck, who helps Jim in spite of his better judgment, they can also result in akratic actions that are morally praiseworthy. Indeed, such cases arguably illustrate how emotions can help to act in ways that better agree with the agent's practical reasons, thus making the resulting action more rational, compared to acting in accordance with the agent's better judgment.

As a result, the verdict regarding the role of emotions in the production of practical irrationality is mixed. Sometimes emotions cause practical irrationality, but sometimes they help us to achieve practical rationality. However, quite independently of their role in the causation of actions, emotions appear to play an indispensable practical role. By focusing our attention on what is relevant and by marking options as good or bad, emotions make up for the shortcoming of pure reason.

8.8. Summary

- Arational actions, such as Jane's lashing out at a photograph of her rival out of hatred, are expressive actions that are intentional but are not done for a reason in that they cannot be explained in terms of the agent's desires and her belief. Insofar as emotions have representational content, it can be suggested that they help explain such actions, even if, in the end, the reason for which they are done is one the agent would disavow.
- Emotions are also involved in akratic actions, that is, actions that are performed in spite of the agent's better judgment. In some cases, emotions result in akratic actions that do not count as free and intentional, but in other cases, the resulting action appears clearly free and intentional. Again, insofar as emotions involve representational content, akratic actions can be explained in terms of the evaluative features that are represented.
- Emotions sometimes cause inverse akratic actions, that is, actions that are prudentially or morally praiseworthy in spite of conflicting with the agent's better judgment.
- In some cases, which involve better judgments that fail to be grounded in the agents' reasons, emotions can also enable agents to act according to the reasons they have.
- In addition, emotions arguably play an even more central role in practical rationality in that they make it possible for us to make choices. Because they focus the agent's attention on what is pertinent for deciding what to do, thus narrowing down the infinity of possible options so as to make choice manageable, and because they mark options as good or bad, emotions make up for the shortcomings of pure reason.

8.9. Study questions

1. Emotions are often blamed for causing akratic actions, but can emotions help us to stick by our better judgment?
2. Imagine that you are in Huck's situation. What would you have done and what would have been the correct course of action, on your view?
3. How do emotions affect other forms of practical irrationality, such as procrastination?

8.10. Further Readings

Arpaly, Nomy. 2000. "On Acting Rationally against One's Best Judgment." *Ethics* 110 (3):488–513.

Arpaly, Nomy, and Timothy Schroeder. 1999. "Praise, Blame and the Whole Self." *Philosophical Studies* 93 (2):161–188.

Damasio, Antonio. 1994. *Descartes' Error: Emotion, Reason and the Human Brain*. New York: Gossett/Putnam, chap. 3.

de Sousa, Ronald. 1987. *The Rationality of Emotion*. Cambridge, MA: MIT Press, chap. 7.

Döring, Sabine A. 2003. "Explaining Action by Emotion." *Philosophical Quarterly* 53 (211):214–230.

Friedman, Marilyn A. 1986. "Autonomy and the Split-Level Self." *Southern Journal of Philosophy* 24 (1):19–35.

Hursthouse, Rosalind. 1991. "Arational Actions " *Journal of Philosophy* 88 (2):57–68.

Jones, Karen. 2003. "Emotion, Weakness of Will, and the Normative Conception of Agency." In *Philosophy and the Emotions*, edited by Anthony Hatzimoysis, 181–200. Cambridge: Cambridge University Press.

Majeed, Raamy. 2019. "What Can Information Encapsulation Tell Us About Emotional Rationality?" In *The Value of Emotions for Knowledge*, edited by Laura Candiotto, 51–69. Basingstoke: Palgrave Macmillan.

McIntyre, Alison. 1990. "Is Akratic Action Always Irrational?" In *Identity, Character, and Morality*, edited by Owen Flanagan and Amelie O. Rorty, 379–400. Cambridge, MA: MIT Press.

9 Sentimentalism

9.1. Introduction

It appears hard to deny that emotions are connected, in some way or other, with the evaluative. As we noted early on, fear, disgust, and shame, for instance, appear closely connected to the fearsome (or the dangerous), the disgusting, and the shameful, respectively. On the positive side of the spectrum, admiration, attraction, and pride appear obviously connected to the admirable, the attractive, and the prideworthy, respectively. Features like the fearsome, the disgusting, and the shameful, but also the admirable, the attractive, and the prideworthy are clearly evaluative. These features are involved in assessments of things as good or bad. When you say of something that it is disgusting, for instance, you assess it as bad in some way. Saying that someone is admirable, by contrast, amounts to assessing that person as good in some way.

As a result, it is no surprise that, as we saw when discussing theories of emotions, most theories of emotions hold that emotions are closely connected with the evaluative. This is, of course, the case of evaluative theories and more specifically of perceptual theories, broadly understood, which we explored in Chapter 6. Furthermore, as we have also seen (in Chapter 7), it is also plausible that emotions provide *prima facie* justification for evaluative beliefs, that is, beliefs that consist in the attribution of evaluative features. Finally, as we saw in the previous chapter, insofar as our emotions represent evaluative features, acting on our emotions can be explained in terms of the evaluative features in light of which the action is performed.

But what in the world are evaluative features? As yet we have left things open regarding the nature of the evaluative. Are evaluative features objective properties in the world, on a par with the shape or mass of things? If so, what is their relation to natural properties, that is, the properties postulated by the natural as well as the social sciences? Another possibility is that evaluative features depend, in some way or other, on our subjectivity. One prominent suggestion, as we will see, is that evaluative features depend on our subjective reactions in a way that is similar to how colors are thought by many to depend on our color experiences. As will become apparent, there are different ways of understanding this analogy.

DOI: 10.4324/9781315542300-12

Depending on what evaluative features are, we might be forced to reconsider the relation between emotions and the evaluative. The main worry is that the theories of emotions we considered the most promising, that is, evaluative theories, may be committed to what could be an erroneous conception of evaluative features as objective properties of the world. If so, we would have to reconsider our understanding of what emotions are. In any case, before we have a better grasp of what evaluative features are, we have not sufficiently explained what emotions are. If emotions are supposed to be representations of evaluative features, it is crucial to know what these are.

To answer the question of what the evaluative consists in, we have to take a plunge into *metaethics*, that is, the part of moral philosophy that is concerned with the most abstract issues, such as the question of moral objectivity or the question whether moral judgments can be true. Interestingly, a number of metaethical theories emphasize emotions in their account of the evaluative. Moral facts, but also moral concepts and moral judgments as well as moral words and sentences, have been thought to involve, in one way or another, emotions or more generally affects. In fact, metaethical debates are, in large part, built around the opposition between *moral sentimentalism*, on the one hand, and *moral rationalism*, on the other. Moral sentimentalism, which can be traced back to Hume (1739–1740/2000), is the doctrine according to which, roughly, what we feel is the source of morality. By contrast, moral rationalism, which is associated with Kant (1785/1996), holds that morality is grounded in rationality.

More recently, it has become clear that the opposition between moral sentimentalism and moral rationalism should not be overstated. For instance, emphasizing the role of emotion in ethics is perfectly compatible with holding that moral judgments can be true or false, a claim that has traditionally been associated with moral rationalism. What is more, some sentimentalist theories, such as the theory according to which moral sentences express emotions instead of truth-assessable propositions, appear premised on questionable assumptions about the nature of emotions as mere feelings.

In this chapter, we will examine a longstanding debate regarding the evaluative and its relation to emotions. After a first section aimed at clarifying the notion of sentimentalism, we will discuss different theories of evaluative features that link them to emotions, starting with so-called *simple subjectivism* (Prinz 2007) before turning to *ideal observer theories* (Lewis 1989; Kauppinen 2014), which attempt to make room for the objectivity of the evaluative. After this, we will focus on so-called *neo-sentimentalist accounts*, which can be traced back to Franz Brentano (1889/2009) and are still very much alive both in their reductive versions (D'Arms and Jacobson 2000b, Forthcoming) and in their non-reductive versions, which are also known as *sensibility theories* (McDowell 1985; Wiggins 1987).

9.2. Kinds of Sentimentalism

It will be useful to start with a clarification. One question philosophy has traditionally been interested in is that of the nature of value. "What is value?", philosophers are fond of asking. Because the term "value" has several meanings, however, this question can be taken in different ways. Talk of value often concerns goods, such as pleasure, freedom, or justice, which we ought to promote in our lives or possibly in general. We may, for instance, think that justice is a value that ought to be promoted in our society. Talk of values can also bear on the ideals that guide our actions. We say for instance that democracy and autonomy are Western values, and we can say of someone that reliability and integrity are her personal values.

Values in the sense of goods or of ideals are highly interesting in their own right, but metaethical debates concern values in another sense. What metaethical theory attempts to capture is the fundamental question of the nature of what we ascribe to an object when we say that it is good, that it is bad, or else admirable or disgusting, etc. It would seem that when we say that something is good or admirable, for instance, what we say is that this thing in question has an evaluative property, that is, that it has goodness or admirableness. The question is whether this is the case, and if it is the case, the next question is what kind of property that might be.

Another clarification that is in order concerns the distinction between two broad families of normative concepts: the evaluative, on the one hand, and the deontic (from the Greek *deon*, meaning that which is binding), on the other (Mulligan 1998; Tappolet 2014). The central deontic notions are the obligatory, the permissible, and the forbidden. Deontic concepts are used in judgments concerning what we *ought* or *ought not* to do, be it from the moral point of view or from some different point of view, such as the legal point of view. By contrast, evaluative concepts are used to assess the worth of things. As such, evaluative concepts do not directly concern what we ought to do. Even so, what is good or bad bears on what we ought to do. The reason for this is that according to all moral theories, what we ought to do at least sometimes depends on whether the consequences are good or bad. It is thus likely that deontic and evaluative concepts are closely related and that therefore both count as normative concepts.

It follows from the distinction between the evaluative and the deontic that moral sentimentalism can concern either both the evaluative and the deontic domain, or only one of the two. In fact, things are even a bit more complicated. Strictly speaking, moral sentimentalism is concerned only with a subset of the evaluative and the deontic domain, namely, the moral subset. The question of what counts as *moral* is a tricky one. A common assumption is that morality is concerned with what we owe to others, or with what is good or bad for others as opposed to what is good for the agent. What is controversial is whether one has moral duties to oneself. In any case, it is clear that the evaluative and the moral need not coincide. Evaluative features such as the admirable or the disgusting, for instance, need not be moral. You can be morally admirable, for instance because you helped save a drowning child at great cost to yourself. But you can also be admirable in ways that have little to do with morality, such as when you are admirable because you are a great pianist. Similarly, something, like a rotten cheese, can be disgusting without being morally disgusting. Thus, sentimentalism regarding the evaluative is not equivalent to moral sentimentalism.

To further clarify what sentimentalism amounts to, let me introduce a few other distinctions that concern metaethics. It is generally agreed that metaethical or, more generally, metanormative questions divide into four different groups, which each give rise to a distinct set of questions. To simplify, let us focus on the moral domain. There are questions regarding the nature of moral facts. Consider the putative fact that pain is bad. *Moral ontology*, for instance, is concerned with the question of whether this alleged fact is an objective moral fact, which exists independently of our reactions and our judgments. According to moral realism, the answer is that moral facts can be objective in that sense, while anti-realism denies this. Moral constructivism, by contrast, holds that the objectivity of moral facts results from a process of subjective or intersubjective construction. Ontological questions are connected but distinct from questions concerning *moral semantics*, which concern the meaning, or more generally the function, of moral language. One of the main aims here is to determine whether moral sentences differ from sentences that seek to describe how things are. Questions regarding the function of moral language should not be confused with questions about the nature of moral judgments, understood as psychological states instead of sentences, and the concepts that such judgments involve. Questions about moral judgments are the focus of *moral psychology*. One central question in moral psychology is the question whether *moral internalism* is true, that is, whether moral judgments are internally, or necessarily, tied to motivation, so that when you judge that you ought to do something, you necessarily are motivated to act accordingly, something which typically results in action. If you hold that moral judgments have this necessary connection to motivation, you will have to deny that you can make a moral judgment without being motivated accordingly, thereby denying the possibility of akratic actions. Finally, a last set of questions concerns what we can know or be justified in believing regarding morality. Thus, *moral epistemology* looks into the question of whether moral knowledge and moral epistemic justification might be a possibility.

Sentimentalism takes very different shapes depending on what specific part of metaethics it concerns (for an overview, see Kauppinen 2022). Regarding moral ontology, for instance, a moral sentimentalist holds that moral facts depend, in one way or another, on affects, whether there are emotions or sentiments. On one version of this thesis, moral facts are *projections* of our moral attitudes, an idea that Hume expressed when he said that by contrast with reason, "taste has a productive faculty, and gilding or staining all natural objects with the colours, borrowed from internal sentiment, raises in a manner a new creation" (1751/1948, 269, see also Blackburn 1998). Such *ontological moral sentimentalism* is distinct from *semantic moral sentimentalism*, the view that emotions play a prominent role in moral semantics. *Emotivists* or more generally *expressivists*, such as A. J. Ayer (1936), Charles Stevenson (1937), and more recently Simon Blackburn (1998) and Allan Gibbard (1990), have for instance argued that moral sentences are on a par with interjections, such as "booh!" or "hurray!" in that they express subjective reactions instead of propositions that could be true or false. As to moral judgments, they have been thought to be caused by emotional reactions (Haidt 2001) or else to consist in emotions or more generally affects (Blackburn 1998; Prinz 2007). This kind of *psychological moral sentimentalism* differs not only from ontological and semantic sentimentalism, but also from a fourth kind of sentimentalism, which concerns moral knowledge. *Epistemological moral sentimentalism* holds that moral knowledge or else the epistemic justification of moral beliefs depends on emotions.

It should be clear that the same kind of theoretical options can be defended regarding the normative generally, whether it concerns the evaluative or the deontic. Indeed, as we have seen in Chapter 7, emotions can be seen as affording epistemic justification and possibly evaluative knowledge. To hold such a view amounts to embracing a form of *epistemological sentimentalism*. In contrast to most other forms of sentimentalism, however, epistemological sentimentalism is in principle not committed to sentimentalism regarding values. On the contrary, the assumption could well be that emotions allow us to get in touch with an independently existing evaluative reality that has nothing to do with our responses. This makes it clear that in spite of sharing some affinities, the different forms of sentimentalism are logically independent.

With these clarifications in mind, let us focus on one specific type of sentimentalism, which has attracted a lot of attention: sentimentalism about evaluative facts and the properties they involve. This debate, we now know, is one that concerns the ontology of evaluative facts, whether or not these are moral.

9.3. Simple Subjectivism

Evaluative theories of emotions, as we have seen, hold that emotions involve representations of things as having specific evaluative features, or values, such as fearsomeness (or danger), disgustingness, or admirableness. What are these values? Let us focus on admirableness. Because of the lexical connection between the term "admirable" and the term "admiration", it might seem obvious that something on the following line must hold:

1. x is admirable if and only if x causes admiration in some observer.

Thomas Hobbes appears to have had this kind of view in mind even if strictly speaking the following passage concerns the words: "But whatsoever is the object of any man's appetite or desire; that is it which he for his part calleth *good*: and the object of this hate, and aversion, *evil*; and of his contempt, *vile* and *inconsiderable*" (1651/2012, Book 1, Chap. 6).

An account of values along these lines is often called *simple subjectivism*. Because it amounts to saying that something is admirable insofar as it is admired by someone or other, it is the simplest way to tie the admirable to admiration. The subjectivity (or *response-dependence*, as it is often called) of the account comes from the fact that what is admirable or not is thought to depend entirely on whether some observer or other feels admiration for it. Whether something is admirable would be determined by what the observer feels. Indeed, the very existence of the admirable would depend on what observers feel. This makes the account relativist, for the admirable and more generally all values are held to be relative to the emotional reactions that particular individuals feel.

Simple subjectivism is generally considered to be entirely hopeless. It seems obvious that a landscape can stay admirable even if it stops causing admiration in you, maybe because you are no longer focusing on the view. Our emotional reactions are simply too fickle to be seen as determinants of what has value. One way to handle this problem is to introduce psychological dispositions into the definition. The claim, thus, would be that the admirable exclusively depends on what an individual is disposed to admire. More generally, value could be thought to consist in what an observer is disposed to feel. Because what a person is disposed to admire is in principle less fickle than what she happens to admire at a particular moment, this suggestion improves on the initial proposal. This is how the theory would apply to the case of the admirable:

2.   x is admirable if and only if the observer is disposed to feel admiration at x.

A theory along these lines has been defended by Jesse Prinz (2007) regarding right and wrong. According to Prinz, such moral properties can be defined in terms of the dispositions to undergo a number of related emotions, that is, in terms of sentiments of approbation and disapprobation. The sentiment of disapprobation regarding lying, for instance, consists in the disposition to feel self-blame emotions, such as shame or guilt, when you tell a lie, or else other-blame emotions, such as disappointment or moral anger, but also contempt or disgust for someone else who lies. Given this, Prinz defines what is right and wrong in the following way: "An action has the property of being morally wrong (right) just in case there is an observer who has a sentiment of disapprobation (approbation) toward it" (2007, 92).

Another solution to the fickleness problem consists in specifying values in terms of what things are *disposed* to cause. Again, the advantage of involving dispositions is that they are more stable than our emotional reactions. So, to no longer feel admiration, for example because you are no longer looking at the landscape, is compatible with that landscape still being disposed to cause admiration in you. This yields the following biconditional:

3.   x is admirable if and only if x is disposed to cause admiration in some observer.

Having, like Hobbes, more the semantics than the ontology in mind, Edvard Westermarck nonetheless appears to subscribe to a version of this kind of account when he writes that "[t]o name an act good or bad, ultimately implies that it is apt to give rise to an emotion of approval or disapproval in him who pronounces that judgment" (1906, 4). Such a dispositional account of values remains entirely subjectivist, since whether something is disposed to cause admiration in someone depends largely on who that person is. As this formulation brings out, this account is relativist. What is disposed to cause admiration in me – Alpine landscapes, for instance – need not, of course, be disposed to cause admiration in you, who might be left entirely cold by the sight of such landscapes.

Now, were it not for G. E. Moore (1912/2005), Westermarck's definition of values would probably have been forgotten. The irony is that the passage in which Moore mentions Westermarck spells out a serious objection to his account. The objection aims not at the ontological thesis about values, but at the claim, also defended by Westermarck, that judgments about right and wrong are judgments about what feelings something tends to cause. To judge that an action is wrong would be to judge that it tends to cause a feeling of moral indignation or disapprobation in me. As Moore underlines, the problem is that this view makes it impossible to disagree regarding what is wrong. That I judge that a particular action tends to cause disapproval in me is fully compatible with the judgment that the same action does not tend to cause disapproval in you. Both judgments can be true, so there is no disagreement. The problem, as Moore notes, is that it certainly appears that there can be moral disagreements.

This objection also makes trouble for the thesis regarding the nature of values. This is so because the view that values consist in dispositions to cause feelings is naturally thought to entail that judgments about values are judgments about dispositions to cause feelings. Given this, when I judge that something is good, what I judge is that this thing is disposed to cause a particular positive feeling in me. Similarly, when you judge that something is good, what you judge is that this thing is disposed to cause a particular feeling in you. And again, the problem is that this makes disagreement about values impossible. To judge that something tends to cause some reaction in one person does not contradict the judgment that this same thing does not tend to cause that reaction in another person or else that this another person has an entirely different reaction.

The same problem arises with the account that Prinz (2007) proposes. It appears natural to assume that on his account, to judge that something is wrong is to judge that one disapproves of it, in the sense that one is disposed to undergo a number of negative emotions. But since a different observer can well be disposed very differently, my judgment that something is wrong is perfectly compatible with your judgment that this thing is not wrong. In fairness, it must be said that Prinz's overall account is somewhat more complicated, because he holds that the judgments of right and wrong are in fact emotions. According to him, to judge that one's lying is wrong would consist in shame or guilt at one's lie, where that emotion represents the action as being such as to cause the sentiment of disapprobation in oneself. However, this more complicated story does not make a difference regarding the possibility of disagreement. What is represented by the moral judgment, whether it is an emotion or not, is that one has a specific sentiment towards it, one that others need not share. Prinz is ready to accept this consequence, but the price of having to deny the possibility of disagreements regarding matters of right and wrong might well seem too high.

Another, related problem with such dispositional accounts is that they have a hard time accounting for mistakes concerning values. Insofar as values are determined by what we tend to feel or by what feelings tend to be triggered by things, the only kind of mistakes we can make concern what we tend to feel or what feelings tend to be triggered. But these are usually not things about which we make a lot of mistakes. Because of this, these accounts do not seem to make room for the full range of mistakes we are prone to make regarding values. Consider a paradigmatic case of wrong action, such as torturing puppies for fun. According to Prinz, someone who approves such actions does not make any mistake about the wrongness of the action. This is hard to believe.

A final problem with both the dispositional accounts under scrutiny is that we would have to conclude that one and the same thing is both admirable and not admirable, something which is hard to believe. Insofar as I am disposed to admire a landscape but you are not, the landscape will be both admirable and not admirable. Similarly, insofar as a landscape tends to cause admiration in me and not in you, it will be both admirable and not admirable. The subjectivist could suggest here that things are not admirable, but only admirable-for-me and admirable-for-you, thereby introducing a strong form of relativism regarding values. This might be the way to go, but before adopting what appears quite a revisionary account of values, which entail that all values are relative, we have to examine accounts that improve on simple subjectivism.

9.4. Ideal Observer Theories

A natural move to improve on simple subjectivism is to take inspiration from the case of colors and appeal to the notion of normality. So-called *secondary qualities*, such as colors, are often thought to consist in dispositions to trigger responses, such as visual experiences. In contrast to simple subjectivism, the responses in question are specified as those that normal subjects would experience in standard circumstances, such as sufficient light. For example, red would be the disposition to cause experiences of red in a normal subject, given standard circumstances. Similarly, one can hold that values are dispositions to cause certain response in normal subjects, given standard circumstances. In the case of the admirable, we would have the following definition:

4. x is admirable if and only if x is disposed to cause admiration in a normal observer, given standard circumstances.

On a common reading, which is inspired by a common account of secondary qualities, normality is understood in empirical terms. One could for instance define what is normal, in that sense, as what is statistically most common. As D'Arms and Jacobson (2000b) point out, no such account is likely to succeed. The problem, simply, is that no such account, and indeed none of the accounts we have discussed so far, "can capture the normative aspects of these judgments" (2000b, 726). By contrast to the judgment that something is admirable, which entails that you have reasons to do certain things, such as spending time exploring a work of art you admire, the judgment that something is disposed to cause admiration in a normal observer, given standard circumstances, has no normative force. Suppose that what is at stake is statistical normality. What you would judge is that the thing in question is disposed to cause admiration in most people. That this is so, however, does not entail anything about what you ought to do. It is not reason-giving.

One tempting amendment here, which can be traced back to Adam Smith (1759/2002), is to appeal not to a normal observer but to an *ideal* observer (see Firth 1951; Lewis 1989; Kauppinen 2014). This gives us the following account of the admirable:

5. x is admirable if and only if x is disposed to cause admiration in an ideal observer, in standard conditions.

Ideal observer theories allow for a good measure of objectivity, since even if there is a dependence on subjective responses of a kind, the admirable does not depend on what some random observer feels. Because of this, they constitute a clear improvement both on simple subjectivism and on definitions involving an empirical understanding of normality. Thus, ideal observer theories can make room for disagreement, since we can disagree about what an ideal observer would admire. This approach also readily makes room for mistakes about whether something is admirable, for you might be wrong about what an ideal observer would admire. And things would not turn out to be both admirable and not admirable, since the verdict of the observer is the one that counts to determine whether something is admirable. Note, however, that this advantage would be lost, if one were to allow different ideal observers to have different responses. In any case, insofar as it is the emotional response of an observer characterized as ideal that is at stake, it would seem that to judge that something is admirable should have normative force. Surely the verdict of an ideal observer has some weight in what I ought to feel and do.

The hard question, of course, is how we should understand the term "ideal" in this context. If what is a stake is a definition of the admirable, that is, a reduction of what is admirable to what an ideal observer feels, we can immediately rule out one interpretation. What can be excluded is that an ideal observer is simply one that gets things right in terms of values. As D'Arms and Jacobson (2000b) note, this would make the definition badly circular. Indeed, it would amount to accepting that the admirable, or more generally values, exist independently of any observer.

The problem is that this epistemological reading is in fact very natural. As David Enoch (2005) has pointed out, it appears difficult to justify the introduction of idealizing conditions otherwise than by the thought that an ideal observer is better placed to track independently existing values. Idealization is naturally called for to avoid mistakes regarding independently existing facts. Enoch gives the example of a watch. It is a good idea to look at your watch to know the time, but because the batteries might be low, it makes sense to require that your watch's batteries be charged, thus introducing a moderate amount of idealization. However, this move makes sense only if you suppose that your watch more or less reliably tracks time. As Enoch writes, "[t]he natural rationale for idealization [...] thus only applies to cases where the relevant procedure or response is thought of as tracking a truth independent of it" (2005, 764). Because ideal observer theories cannot appeal to such a rationale, the move to idealization appears objectionably *ad hoc*.

In reply, Antti Kauppinen (2014) has argued that the rational for idealization can be practical. What justifies the appeal to what an ideal observer feels is that we are interested in having solutions to practical problems and not in finding out about independently existing facts. The problem with non-idealized responses, he argues, is that they cause practical problems. To solve such problems, we have to discount some of our responses, thereby treating certain responses as authoritative, thereby endorsing them as ideal, in the sense that they are optimal for solving the practical problems in question. What are the practical problems that Kauppinen envisages? According to him, what will happen if we define values in terms of our uncorrected responses is that we will end up with outcomes that we do not desire and are motivated to avoid. As he puts it, with uncorrected responses, "we face mutual recrimination, boredom, dissatisfaction, and unhappiness. For example, acting on just any desire may result in ill health, garish wallpaper, a broken marriage and a distrustful community" (Kauppinen 2014, 580). The problem with this reply is that things like ill health, garish wallpapers, broken marriages and distrustful communities seem bad whether or not ideal observers happen to approve of them. It is thus not clear that Kauppinen's reply manages to do without objective values, which exist independently of ideal observers.

What are the other options to understand the notion of an ideal observer? There are, in fact, two options. The first consists in spelling out what makes an observer ideal at least partially in evaluative terms, such as kindness and impartiality. The other possibility consists in defining what an ideal observer is in non-evaluative terms, such as, for instance, being fully informed regarding non-evaluative facts. The problem, as has been noted by Russ Shafer-Landau (2003), is that this makes for a dilemma. On the first horn, the problem is that to avoid an infinite regress we will have to presuppose that some evaluative properties, such as the property of being kind, cannot be defined in terms of the responses of an ideal observer. But this makes for a circular account. On the other horn, the problem is that it is not clear that the responses of the ideal observer will have the authority to determine the extension of evaluative properties. Why should we put our trust in an observer who is not kind and impartial, say? One might also doubt that the normativity of values can be preserved if the characteristics of the ideal observer are spelled out in non-evaluative terms. Why should we care that such an observer with a number of natural characteristics admires something? After all, in spite of what we are told, it is very intuitive that such an observer could be wrong.

The obvious move to make room for the normativity of values is explicitly to invoke a normative notion in the definition of values. This takes us to neo-sentimentalist accounts.

9.5. Neo-sentimentalism

Neo-sentimentalism is often formulated as a thesis that concerns evaluative concepts and judgments (D'Arms and Jacobson 2000b). But neo-sentimentalism can also concern the nature of evaluative properties (D'Arms and Jacobson Forthcoming) and this ontological form of neo-sentimentalism will be our focus here. The basic idea of this approach is that values have to be understood in terms of subjective responses that are normatively endorsed, that is, responses that are endorsed as *fitting*, or else appropriate, correct, merited, rational, grounded in reasons, etc. These dimensions of endorsement are not exact equivalents, but to simplify, we will mostly focus on fittingness.

Neo-sentimentalism sometimes is proposed as an account of the generic notions of the good and the bad. Thus, Brentano famously wrote: "In the broadest sense of the term, the good is that which is worthy of love, that which can be loved with a love that is correct" (1889/2009, 11). Brentano understood love not as a specific emotion or a specific sentiment but as including all positive emotions, which he characterized as belonging to the sphere of inclination or pleasure. Even so, contemporary neo-sentimentalists most often focus on a specific range of values, sometimes called "sentimental values" or "affective values", and claim that they can be understood on the same pattern as the property of being admirable. These values include all those that correspond to kinds of emotion, such as disgustingness, shamefulness, or fearsomeness. Taking up the example of the admirable, here is how neo-sentimentalism can be formulated:

6.   x is admirable if and only if admiration is fitting in response to x.

Because it explains values such as admirableness in terms of our responses and because such responses play a central role in determining when something is admirable, such an account holds that values are subjective (or response-dependent). However, insofar as such an account makes ample room for disagreement regarding values as well as error concerning values, it also allows for values to be objective. As John McDowell (1985), who holds that sentimental values are to be explained in terms of affective responses that are *merited* by objects, explains, values thus understood can be both subjective and objective, in some sense of these terms. They are objective in the sense that they are not "mere figments of [our] subjective states" (McDowell 1985, 114). Thus, something can well cause admiration in you while it is not, as such, admirable, for admiration would not be a fitting response to that thing.

Quite generally, there are two main ways of conceiving of neo-sentimentalism. On one approach, the *no-priority view* characteristic of so-called *sensibility theories* (McDowell 1985; Wiggins 1987) – an account to which we will come back – the aim is not to give a reductive analysis of values. Thus, because the claim is not that admirableness reduces to fitting admiration, no priority should be given to the right-hand-side of the biconditional. Instead, such a biconditional is proposed as an illuminating account – an *elucidation* as opposed to an *analysis*, as it is sometimes put – of how admirableness and admiration are related to each other.

On a second approach, which is our focus in this section, neo-sentimentalist biconditionals are offered as reductive analyses of values. It follows that the endorsement in question cannot be spelled out in evaluative terms. A fitting response cannot, on pain of circularity, be taken to be a response that is good in some way. According to most of those who aim to provide a reductive analysis of values, the endorsement, therefore, has to be deontic. (But see Mulligan 1998 for a naturalistic reduction.) Fitting responses are thus standardly taken to be responses that in some sense or other we *ought* to have. Another possibility is to reduce values to responses that we have reasons to have.

Because neo-sentimentalism understands values in terms of emotions or more generally affective responses, it is not identical with *fitting attitude theories*, which propose to understand values in terms of normatively endorsed attitudes, whether these attitudes are affective or not. Moreover, neo-sentimentalism and fitting attitude theories more generally are close cousins of the so-called *buck-passing* account of value offered by Scanlon (1998), and according to which values are primarily explained in terms of normatively endorsed actions, rather than endorsed emotions. Neo-sentimentalism is thus but one version of a more general approach that aims at explaining values in terms of the deontic. Even so, both fitting attitudes theories and neo-sentimentalism, and indeed also buck-passing accounts, share at least some difficulties as well as two important attractions.

One important attraction of neo-sentimentalism is that it appears to demystify values in that it would explain why values are related to what we ought to do. As Wlodek Rabinowicz and Toni Rønnow-Rasmussen explain, such an approach removes the air of mystery from the "compellingness" of values, because "there is nothing strange in the prescriptive implications of value ascription if value is explicated in deontic terms" (Rabinowicz and Rønnow-Rasmussen 2004, 391–392). This is directly related to a second attraction of neo-sentimentalism. By reducing values to fitting attitudes such as emotions, we have an explanation of why values are action-guiding, in the sense that they give rise to motivation (Danielsson and Olson 2007). This is so because of the close link between emotions and motivations. As we underscored, many emotions typically come with motivations. Thus, even if it is not committed to moral internalism, that is, to the thesis that evaluative judgments are necessarily related to motivation, neo-sentimentalism entails that there is at least often an internal or necessary relation between values and motivation.

The main objection to the neo-sentimentalist analysis is called the "wrong kind of reasons" objection (Rabinowicz and Rønnow-Rasmussen 2004; see also D'Arms and Jacobson 2000b). Even if it generalizes to all versions of neo-sentimentalism, it is easiest to explain in terms of the version of the account that is spelled out in terms of reasons for emotions. On such an account, to be admirable is to be such that there is sufficient reason to feel admiration. The problem arises because there are many kinds of reasons that we can have for and against our responses and only some of these reasons have to do with the value of things. Here is a famous example imagined by Rabinowicz and Rønnow-Rasmussen (2004): suppose an evil demon threatens to inflict severe punishment on you if you do not admire him. Given this, you have a pretty good prudential reason to admire the demon. But clearly, this does not tend to make him admirable, so the prudential reason you have to admire him has nothing to do with the admirableness of the demon. This example involves prudential reasons, but it can be modified to involve moral reasons. If the demon promises to end a pandemic if you admire him, you will have a moral reason to admire him. But again, it would seem that this moral reason to feel admiration has little to do with the admirableness of the demon. In the sense relevant to the neo-sentimentalist analysis, you do not have sufficient reason to admire him. As D'Arms and Jacobson (2000a) stress, it would be a "moralistic fallacy" to infer that because it is morally right or wrong to feel an emotion, that emotion is therefore fitting or unfitting in the sense relevant to the definition of value.

As such, this does not appear to make for any problem. It would seem easy to distinguish prudential and moral reasons from the reasons that are relevant to the admirableness or more generally the value of things. The problem, however, is that the neo-sentimentalist owes us a general and principled account of how to distinguish the wrong kinds of reasons from the right kinds of reasons, where only the latter are the ones that bear on the value of things. And the tricky thing is that insofar as the ambition of the neo-sentimentalist is to reduce evaluative properties, such a general account cannot simply appeal to the value of things to specify what the right kind of reasons are. One cannot, for instance, say that reasons of the right kind to admire someone are those that are grounded in that person's admirableness.

Not a small book could be written about the different replies to the wrong kind of reasons objection along with the different criticisms these replies have been subjected to (for a thorough overview, see Nye 2017). To get a sense of this debate, let us consider an important reply that has been made. It consists in distinguishing between *object-given reasons* and *state-given reason* and argues that only the former are reasons of the right kind (Parfit 2001/2018). In contrast to object-given reasons, a state-given reason concerns the value of having the response to an object, for instance the prudential or moral value of admiring the demon. Object-given reasons are limited to the features of the object that is evaluated. As noted by Rabinowicz and Rønnow-Rasmussen (2004; see also D'Arms and Jacobson Forthcoming), an important problem with the suggestion that only object-given reasons are of the right kind is that in some cases, what appears to be a reason of the wrong kind depends on the very features of the object. It can be the properties of the demon, such his being vain and vindictive and his therefore being liable to lash out if you fail to admire him that is the reason to admire him, but since these properties do not tend to make him admirable, they consist in reasons of the wrong kind. Similarly, that a joke is cruel might be a reason not to be amused by it, but this appears compatible with there being sufficient reason of the right kind to be amused by the joke. This, in any case, is so if we allow for jokes that are funny in spite of being cruel.

Whether or not that solution to the wrong kind of reasons objection works, one aspect of the discussion needs emphasizing. As Andrew Reisner (2009) notes, the methodology that is used to set up the objection and to discuss the alleged solutions is based on our intuitions regarding values. The right kind of reasons, we are told, are those that have to do with the value of things. The problem with the demon-induced reason to admire him, we are told again, is that in spite of there being some reason to admire him, the demon is not admirable. This is in any case is the intuition that we are supposed to have. What appears to come first, then, are the values and the intuitions we have regarding them. This strongly suggests that the reason we have to admire (or not to admire) someone is nothing but the fact that the person is (or is not) admirable. It thus would seem natural to hold that if there is a reason to admire a person, it is *because* that person is admirable, and not *vice versa*. But if this is the case, attempts to reduce values to normatively endorsed attitudes are bound to fail. For according to the reductive analysis, what would have to be true is that if someone is admirable, it is because there is a reason or because it is fitting to admire that person, where that reason cannot be that the person is admirable.

What transpires is that the neo-sentimentalist analysis fails because it gives the wrong answer to the *Euthyphro dilemma*. In Plato's famous *Euthyphro* (2002), Socrates famously asks whether the pious is loved by the gods because it is pious or whether it is pious because it is loved by the gods. Transposed to the case of value and more specifically to the case of the admirable, the question is whether we admire something because it is admirable or whether something is admirable because we admire it. More precisely, within the neo-sentimentalist framework, the question is whether admiration is fitting because something is admirable or whether something is admirable because admiration for it is fitting. Neo-sentimentalists hold the latter, but it is far from clear that this is correct. What appears right is rather that admiration for someone is fitting because that person is admirable. This, in any case, is what realists about values would say. Whether realism about values is correct is, of course, debatable, but the problem for neo-sentimentalism is that its answer to the Euthyphro dilemma clashes with the assumptions about values that appear to drive the discussion of the wrong kind of reason objection.

The question is what follows regarding the nature of values. Should we simply jettison the neo-sentimentalist approach and claim that values are natural or maybe even non-natural objective properties of things that have nothing to do with our feelings? This will not sound right if one thinks of values, such as the admirable or the shameful, that are evidently connected to emotions. In the next section, we will explore a different way to understand the relation between emotions and values.

9.6. Sensibility Theories

Up to now, we have focused on reductive accounts of value. However, as we have seen above, so-called sensibility theorists, such as David Wiggins (1987) and John McDowell (1985), propose a non-reductive version of neo-sentimentalism. The central idea is that properties such as admirableness, shamefulness, or disgustingness are inextricably tied to the exercise of human sensibility while not being reducible to any relational property involving such a sensibility. Thus, non-reductive neo-sentimentalism agrees with reductive neo-sentimentalism that something is admirable if and only if admiring that thing is fitting. However, it denies that the property of being admirable is the property of being the object of fitting admiration. What is proposed is a no-priority reading of the biconditional, according to which it has neither to be read as a definition of what the admirable amounts to, nor as a definition of what admiration consists in. As McDowell (1987) explains, our responses and the evaluative properties are "siblings" rather than parents and children, in the sense that neither our responses nor the evaluative properties have metaphysical priority.

How are we to understand the notion of being a metaphysical sibling? More pointedly, how could an evaluative property that is not defined in terms of our responses be closely related to these responses? If the admirable is not the property of making admiration fitting, how could it be closely related to admiration? How could that property be a metaphysical sibling of admiration? A plausible answer is that properties such as admirableness, while not reducible to fitting responses, are nonetheless ones that are picked out by concepts that are response-dependent, in the sense that they are conceptually tied to the concepts of the relevant emotional responses. Importantly, that a concept is response-dependent does not entail that it is reducible to the concept of fitting responses. On a no-priority reading, neither the concept of value nor the concept of the fitting response is prior to, or more fundamental than, the other. What it means is that evaluative concepts and the concepts of fitting emotional responses are conceptually tied to each other without being reducible to each other. Simply put, the suggestion is that the property of being admirable, disgusting, shameful, etc., are non-relational, or monadic, properties, but the concepts *admirable*, *disgusting*, *shameful*, etc., are nonetheless response-dependent.

How are we to understand this idea? Wiggins (1976) offers a helpful analogy when considering the Euthyphro dilemma. He considers the example of redness and holds that it can both be true that redness is a monadic property while being in some sense a "relative" property. It is a relative property because the category of color is an anthropocentric category: "The category corresponds to an interest that only takes root in creatures with something approaching our own sensory apparatus" (1976, 107). This makes the concept of redness a response-dependent one, that is, one that has to be explained in terms of our visual responses. The crucial point to understand is that this claim is perfectly compatible with the claim that redness is a monadic property. Thus, the property of redness is both objective and subjective. It is objective in the sense that we see things as red because they are red. But it is also subjective, or response-dependent, because the concept is anthropocentric, that is, things count as red only because we share a specific sensory apparatus, which allows us to discriminate red things. Accordingly, both answers to the Euthyphro questions are true. We see things as red because they are red, and things count as red because we see things as red.

The same story can be told about values. The idea is that it is both true that we admire something because it is admirable and that something is admirable because we admire it. It is true that we admire something because it is admirable for the simple reason that admirableness is a monadic property, to which we aim to respond when we feel admiration, and indeed to which we successfully respond when our admiration is fitting. However, admirableness is also response-dependent, in the sense that the corresponding concept is anthropocentric: we have this concept only because we are beings susceptible to feeling admiration. Paraphrasing Wiggins (1976), we can say that feeling admiration is required for there to be such as a thing as the perspective from which admirableness is there to be perceived.

Interpreted in this way, neo-sentimentalism has no trouble handling the wrong kind of reason objection. The right kind of reason, or the right kind of fittingness, is the one that depends on the objective value of things. A response of admiration regarding something is fitting insofar as, and because, that thing is admirable. This easily rules out responses of admiration to demons that fail to be admirable as well as responses of amusement to jokes that fail to be funny.

Here is how we might make this explicit in the neo-sentimentalist biconditional:

7. x is admirable if and only if admiration is fitting in response to x, and admiration is fitting in response to x because x is admirable.

By now, however, the major difficulty of this approach should have started to become obvious. The difficulty consists in the blatant circularity of the proposal. Insofar as the fittingness of a response is defined by an appeal to values, it seems that we are locked in a tight and unhelpful circle. If you are attracted by the reductive version of neo-sentimentalism it is clear that this will not do for you. However, sensibility theorists will remind us that they are not attempting to offer a reductive analysis. The aim is rather to elucidate the concept of admirableness by pointing out its relations to other concepts. Because there is no priority between the concept of the admirable and that of admiration, a circle is just to be expected. Still, one might wonder whether there is any gain in knowledge given the tight circularity of the biconditional. Is such a biconditional any better than the claim that something is a cat if and only if the belief that it is a cat is true? This is surely a true statement, but it is also an utterly uninteresting one. Why should a similarly circular statement concerning values be of interest?

We can again turn to Wiggins for an answer. His answer points towards the epistemology of values. What is of interest, according to him, is that "when we consider whether or not x is good or right or beautiful, there is no appeal to anything that is more fundamental than [...] human sentiments [...]" (Wiggins

1987, 189). Because the concept of the good, the right and the beautiful are not as closely related to our emotions, these examples might not be the best ones. However, the point appears particularly plausible in the case of values such as the admirable. When we consider whether something is admirable, there surely is no way to appeal to anything more fundamental than our feelings of admiration. This does not mean that these feelings are always right, of course. Rather, it means that we have to start with what we feel even to raise the question of whether or not something is admirable. This is why one would not have sufficiently elucidated the concept of the admirable without spelling out its tie with admiration.

More discussion would be needed to dispel the doubts that one might have. We would need to compare the present account of values with theories according to which values are not connected in any way to emotions. Furthermore, we would need to spell out the relation between evaluative properties and natural properties. Is the admirable identical with a particular natural property or maybe more plausibly with a disjunction of natural properties? Or might there be a weaker relation, such as the relation of dependence between the admirable and natural properties called "supervenience", which roughly consists in the fact that there could be no difference at the evaluative level without differences at the natural level? These are highly interesting questions, but even before considering them, it cannot be denied that the non-reductive version of neo-sentimentalism is an attractive conception of values such as the admirable, the disgusting or the shameful. The question is where this leaves us regarding emotions.

9.7. Taking Stock

The question we started with was whether we would need to reconsider our conclusions regarding what emotions are once we have made up our mind about the nature of values. The good news is that if non-reductive neo-sentimentalism is on the right track, this will not be necessary. Non-reductive neo-sentimentalism and broadly perceptual theories of emotions, including the receptive theory, make for a neat fit (see Tappolet 2016). Insofar as emotions are evaluative representations, that is, representations that are correct on condition things are admirable, disgusting, or shameful, for instance, it is no mystery that fittingness can be understood in terms of values, in the sense that fitting admiration is simply admiration regarding what is admirable. As we are now in a position to see, it is plausible that fittingness is nothing but representational correctness.

As noted in the introduction to this chapter, one worry with perceptual theories of emotions is that they are committed to an improbable objectivist account of values. Insofar as the theory of values that appeared more plausible holds that evaluative properties are objective in the strong sense of being monadic properties, the perceptual theorist need not worry. For those who are not persuaded, the question is what other theories of values are compatible with perceptual theories. A good candidate, it would seem, is an error theory according to which we talk and feel as if there are objective values even if this nothing but an illusion (see Mackie 1977).

All this is particularly good news if one considers how reductive neo-sentimentalists try to avoid the circularity that would be involved in their account if emotions were evaluative representations. The strategy that works best to avoid that kind of circularity consists in embracing motivational theories (see D'Arms and Jacobson Forthcoming). Thus, had we concluded that the reductive approach to values is the best, we would have had to reconsider our argument against motivational theories.

Before we finish this chapter, let us think again about the opposition between sentimentalism and rationalism as it applies to values. The upshot of our discussion is that a version of sentimentalism appears plausible. What should be underscored, however, is that this version of sentimentalism is one that holds that insofar as our emotions might fail to be fitting, we can be wrong about values. Insofar as the possibility of representational error is a hallmark of rationalism, it follows that the divide between the two broad approaches is much less important than what one might have initially thought.

9.8. Summary

- The term "value" can refer to good things or ideals, but also to evaluative properties of things or people, such their admirableness or their goodness. Evaluative concepts are distinct from deontic concepts, such as the concept of the obligatory.
- Moral sentimentalism and more generally sentimentalism about the evaluative or the deontic take different shapes depending on what parts of metaethics are concerned: ontological sentimentalism, semantic sentimentalism, such as emotivism, psychological sentimentalism and epistemological sentimentalism.
- *Simple subjectivism* holds that something has value if and only if it causes or is disposed to cause a certain emotion in the observer, or if and only if the observer is disposed to feel that emotion. The most important problem with this approach is that it cannot account for the fact that we can disagree about values.
- *Ideal observer theories* hold that something has value if and only if it is disposed to cause a certain emotion in an ideal observer. This account improves on simple subjectivism in that it makes room for disagreement. One problem is that such theories struggle to justify the introduction of idealization conditions. Another problem is that it faces a dilemma: either they allow that ideal observers are characterized by evaluative features, so that they face circularity, or they deny this, and as a result it is not clear that the responses of ideal observers have any authority.
- *Neo-sentimentalism* in its reductive version holds that values reduce to emotions endorsed as fitting. The main attraction of this approach is that it promises to explain the normativity of values. Neo-sentimentalism faces the wrong-kind-of-reason objection, an objection that makes it transparent that

it is difficult not to assume that fitting emotions are those that respond to independently existing values.

- *Sensibility theories* have no ambition to reduce values to fitting emotions. They hold that values are monadic properties, even if the concepts that pick out those values are anthropocentric and response-dependent, in the sense that they are conceptually tied with the concepts corresponding to our responses.
- Sensibility theories of values make for a good fit with evaluative theories of emotions and in particular with perceptual accounts.

9.9. Study Questions

1. What kind of account of emotions is compatible with the thesis that moral sentences are expressions of emotions and cannot be assessed in terms of truth or falsity?
2. Would different ideal observers agree in their responses, and if not, what does this entail regarding the compatibility of ideal observer theories and relativism?
3. The cruelty of a joke is a reason of a kind not to feel amusement at the joke, but does the cruelty make it such that the joke is less funny, so that you have less reason of the right kind to be amused by it?

9.10. Further Readings

D'Arms, Justin, and Daniel Jacobson. 2000. "Sentiment and Value." *Ethics* 110 (4):722–748.

Enoch, David. 2005. "Why Idealize?" *Ethics* 115 (4):759–787.

Firth, Roderick. 1951. "Ethical Absolutism and the Ideal Observer." *Philosophical and Phenomenological Research* 12 (3):317–345.

Howard, Nye. 2017. "The Wrong Kind of Reasons." In *The Routledge Handbook of Metaethics*, edited by Tristram McPherson and David Plunkett, 340–354. New York: Routledge.

Kauppinen, Antti. 2014. "Fittingness and Idealization." *Ethics* 124 (3):572–588.

Lewis, David. 1989. "Dispositional Theories of Value II." *Proceedings of the Aristotelian Society* Supp. Vol. 63 (1):113–137.

McDowell, John. 1985. "Values and Secondary Qualities." In *Morality and Objectivity*, edited by Ted Honderich, 110–129. London: Routledge.

Rabinowicz, Wlodek, and Toni Rønnow-Rasmussen. 2004. "The Strike of the Demon: On Fitting Pro-Attitudes and Value." *Ethics* 114 (3):391–423.

Reisner, Andrew E. 2009. "Abandoning the Buck Passing Analysis of Final Value." *Ethical Theory and Moral Practice* 12 (4):379–395.

Wiggins, David. 1987. "A Sensible Subjectivism." In *Needs, Values, Truth: Essays in the Philosophy of Value*, 185–214. Oxford: Blackwell.

10 Ethics and the Emotions

10.1. Introduction

Emotions can cause great harm. As the case of Medea illustrates (Chapter 7), people can kill out of rage, and the same is true of jealousy or envy. They can lie or cheat out of envy and they can fail to help out of fear or disgust. It is true that some emotions, such as compassion or love, can have more positive consequences, but often enough, even such emotions will result in actions that fail to be morally good. Out of ill-placed compassion, for instance, you might interfere with someone's project to become autonomous. Indeed, it would seem that emotions of any imaginable kind have the potential to result in morally questionable actions. Sadness might make you fail to notice the needs of others, indignation might make you deaf to someone's rightful plea, amusement might make you forget about the cruelty of an action, and even an emotion as innocent as surprise could manifest a prejudice and result in an offensive remark. On top of this, it appears that at least some emotions appear wrong quite independently of their consequences. For instance, it can be argued that envy, jealousy or hate should never be felt because such feelings are wrong even when they fail to result in any harm.

Accordingly, it might be tempting to imagine that morally perfect agents should be like the *Star Trek* character Data in that they would not feel any emotion. Alternatively, if they could not help feeling emotions, these feelings would lack influence on their thoughts and actions. On such a radically rationalist picture, which even the Stoics and Immanuel Kant would find exaggerated (see Chapter 1), morally perfect agents would have to know what morality requires, they would have to reason perfectly from their moral principles to practical conclusions via some empirical premises, and then they would have to be motivated accordingly, never swayed by any emotion.

Only few of us would be tempted by such an ideal, if only because it appears out of reach for human beings. Indeed, most contemporary moral theorists would agree that to act well, you must feel emotions. Interestingly, this is true of advocates of all three major approaches in normative ethics, that is, deontology, consequentialism, and virtue ethics. Consider *deontology*, an approach mainly inspired by Kant (1785/1996) and according to which an action is right insofar

DOI: 10.4324/9781315542300-13

as it is in accordance with moral duty, to which we have to conform whatever the consequences of our actions. Deontologists and in particular Kantians, such as Marcia Baron (1995), Nancy Sherman (1997), and Carla Bagnoli (2003), have been keen to emphasize the role of emotions such as respect for the moral law but also love and compassion in moral agency. Moral agency, they hold, does not reduce to acting on moral principles, but can include emotions.

The same is true of consequentialism, the approach of which classical utilitarianism as defended by Jeremy Bentham (1789/1961) and John Stuart Mill (1863/1998) is the historical forerunner. Some contemporary consequentialists define right actions in terms of motives that have the best consequences (Adams 1976), but even so-called *act consequentialists*, who hold that the right action is the one that promotes the good, have stressed the importance of character in moral agency. Thus, consequentialists would for most part agree that motivation springing from fellow-feelings such as compassion or sympathy are central to moral agency (see Railton 1984; Pettit 2015).

These developments in the deontological and consequentialist camps can be seen as resulting from the increasing importance of the third main approach in normative ethics, namely *virtue ethics* (Anscombe 1958, Hursthouse 1999, Annas 2011). The core claim of virtue ethics is that the central notion in ethics is that of virtues. Thus, unless they follow Anscombe (1958) and jettison the notion of right action altogether, virtue ethicists hold that the right action has to be defined in terms of virtuous agency. Standard virtue ethics claims that the right action is the one that a virtuous agent would do in the circumstances (see Hursthouse 1999). More generally, the claim is that moral agency requires virtues. Because they consider that virtues involve emotions, virtue ethicists hold that emotions play an important role in moral agency.

All these normative theorists agree that emotions play an important role in moral agency. What they disagree about is the exact role emotions play. We will examine the question of how emotions feature in moral agency by focusing on the role of emotions in virtues, starting with the Aristotelean conception of virtues as developed by Rosalind Hursthouse (1999) and Julia Annas (2011). As we shall see, the standard interpretation of Aristotle places knowledge at the core of virtues. After presenting this interpretation, which we will call the Socratic interpretation, we will discuss two objections that can be raised against it. After this, we will turn to the view, defended among others by Gopal Sreenivasan (2020), according to which emotions are the core of virtues. As we will see, this conception makes room for an argument to the effect that virtues are essential to happiness and flourishing.

10.2. Aristotelian Virtue Theory

Because it has deeply shaped contemporary debates, it will be useful to start with a brief sketch of Aristotle's account of moral virtue in *The Nicomachean Ethics*. Aristotle defines virtues (*aretê* in Ancient Greek, a term that means excellence) as entrenched character traits that merit praise. Virtues, he thought, are essential to the happiness or flourishing (*eudaimonia*) of human beings, which Aristotle thought was the highest good. Aristotle distinguishes between virtues that are moral (or "ethical" as he would have preferred to put it) and intellectual virtues, which concern theoretical and practical reasoning. Denying that virtues are simply natural traits we are born with, Aristotle held that ethical virtues are character traits that depend on education, which he conceived in terms of the acquisition of habits. Examples of ethical virtues that Aristotle had in mind are honesty, courage, generosity, and justice.

According to Aristotle, ethical virtues are character traits that set agents to act but also to react in specific ways. Thus, even though ethical virtues are not emotions, they importantly involve emotional dispositions. More precisely, Aristotle held that virtues involve dispositions to experience right emotions. Aristotle conceives of right emotions as ones that strike a mean or are, as he also puts it, "intermediate" between two extremes. Here is how he expresses this thought:

> For instance, both fear and confidence and appetite and anger and pity and in general pleasure and pain may be felt both too much and too little, and in both cases not well; but to feel them at the right times, with reference to the right objects, toward the right people, with the right motive, and in the right way, is what is both intermediate and best, and this is characteristic of virtue.
> (*The Nicomachean Ethics*, 1106b20–25)

The courageous agent, for instance, experiences neither too much nor too little fear, by contrast to both the coward, who feels too much fear, and the overconfident and rash agent, who feels little or no fear at all.

The claim that virtues involve right emotions is embraced by contemporary Aristotelians. Thus, Hursthouse holds that virtues involve dispositions to feel emotions, where "these emotions will be felt on the *right* occasions, toward the *right* people and objects, for the *right* reason [...]" (1999, 108). According to contemporary Aristotelians, however, dispositions to experience emotions are just one aspect of ethical virtues. A common claim, which they both endorse and attribute to Aristotle, is that ethical virtues consist in *multitrack dispositions* not only to experience right emotions, but also to act in certain ways – honestly, justly, etc. – and to have a variety of mental states, such as desires, perceptions, and expectations. Here is how Hursthouse expresses this idea:

> A full Aristotelian concept of virtue is the concept of a complex character trait, that is, a disposition that is well entrenched in its possessor and, as we say, "goes all the way down." The disposition, far from being a single-track disposition to do, say, honest actions, or even honest actions for certain reasons, is multitrack involving many other actions [sic] as well: desires, emotions and emotional reactions, perceptions, attitudes, interests, and expectations.
> (Hursthouse 2006, 101)

Hursthouse (1999) gives the example of an honest person. An honest person, she claims, will reliably tend to avoid dishonest deeds such as cheating. She will reliably do honest ones, such as telling the truth. Moreover, she will do these things in characteristic ways, that is, for instance, readily and unhesitatingly. In addition, she will be distressed if those near and dear to her are dishonest, she will be unresentful of honest criticism, shocked and angered by acts of dishonesty and delighted when honesty triumphs. The honest person, then, is characterized by a multitrack disposition that involves the disposition to experience a range of emotions.

A good question here is how the different parts of the disposition that constitute an ethical virtue relate to each other. Is one of the dispositional strands central or are all of them on an equal footing? This question relates directly to the question of the role of knowledge in ethical virtue. Aristotle thought that ethical virtues require a specific cognitive ability, which he viewed as a virtue of the intellect as it is concerned with actions, namely, practical wisdom (*phronesis*). Practical wisdom is the ability to reason well about practical matters. It involves having a proper appreciation of the different goods that make for a happy or flourishing life, such as friendship or pleasure, and of how they fit together. Aristotle held that, by contrast to what is the case with amiable natural dispositions we are born with, ethical virtues involve practical wisdom.

How, exactly, are we to understand the interaction between practical wisdom and the other components of virtues? Let us consider what can be dubbed, for reasons that soon will become clear, the "Socratic interpretation" of the Aristotelian account.

10.3. The Socratic Interpretation

A prominent way to understand the role of practical wisdom consists in holding that the ability to reason well about practical questions constitutes the core of ethical virtues (Hursthouse 1999; Annas 2011). According to this conception, the set of dispositions that constitute a specific ethical virtue hang together because they flow from the exercise of practical reasoning. It would be insofar as you reason correctly regarding practical matters that you will be in a position to do the right things and to experience the right emotions. This is how Hursthouse expresses this idea: "Each of the virtues involves getting things right, for each involves *phronesis*, or practical wisdom, which is the ability to reason correctly about practical matters" (1999, 12). Thus, even if virtues involve both an emotional and an intellectual component, the intellectual component is the fundamental one. In a nutshell, the core of ethical virtues would consist in the ability to properly exercise one's practical reason.

What needs to be underlined is that virtues are not merely thought to involve practical wisdom understood as the general ability to weigh different goods in light of how they contribute to happiness or flourishing. What the exercise of each particular virtue requires is a specific judgment concerning a specific good. This is made clear by Liezl Van Zyl when she writes: "The virtuous person doesn't just happen to care about certain things; instead, she cares about the right things and has the right desires. This requires a judgment that certain things are truly good or important and therefore worth protecting or pursuing" (2018, 23). Similarly, Michael Brady holds that "virtuous motivation centrally and essentially involves an evaluative element" (2005, 87), which takes precedence over what he considers to be motivational elements, such as desires and emotions. Thus, the benevolent person is someone who values the welfare of others and is thus motivated to act accordingly, while the honest agent values truth and is hence motivated to tell the truth. Indeed, virtuous agents do not merely act on random evaluative judgments. Their evaluative judgments constitute knowledge. Thus, Brady claims that "the benevolent person is someone who knows that promoting the welfare of others is intrinsically valuable, the truthful or honest person knows that truth is intrinsically good and falsehood intrinsically evil" (2005, 99), and so forth for other virtues.

The result is an understanding of virtues that is, in essence, the one attributed to Socrates, according to whom virtue is knowledge and vice is ignorance (see Plato's *Protagoras*). On this account, virtues are excellences of character that centrally consist in states of knowledge. They involve dispositions to experience emotions, but these dispositions are not central. Evaluative knowledge is more fundamental than emotional dispositions, because to be right, emotions need to be responsive to the agent's evaluations. Thus, the dispositions to experience emotions are dispositions to respond to evaluative knowledge as it is mobilized in specific contexts. As we have seen, the honest agent knows that truth is intrinsically good and falsehood intrinsically bad. When confronted with someone who does not care at all about truth and misleads others to believe falsehoods, honest agents will therefore form a negative evaluative judgment about this person, a judgment in response to which they will feel emotions such as outrage or contempt.

The main argument of what can be called the Socratic interpretation of the Aristotelian account is based on yet another Aristotelian thesis, namely, that virtuous actions have to be done for the right reasons (see for instance Hursthouse 1999; Annas 2011). The virtuous agent, Aristotle claims, "must choose to act the way he does, and he must choose it for its own sake [...]." (*The Nicomachean Ethics*, 1105a28–34) The courageous agent, for instance, will save a drowning child at the risk of his own limbs not because this is a way to impress others, but because it will save the child. This suggests that virtuous agents not only choose what is required, but that they also know the reason why they should choose the right action. What appears required is that virtuous agents have the relevant evaluative knowledge. How could you know what the right reasons are if you fail to have the relevant evaluative knowledge?

One might wonder how close to Aristotle the Socratic interpretation really is. Did Aristotle really hold that virtues are excellences of character that centrally consist in states of knowledge? As we will see, it is not the only way to understand Aristotle. More generally, the question is whether the Socratic interpretation is really convincing as a theory of virtues. Let us turn to the main objections that can be raised against this account.

10.4. The Objection from Modesty

A first objection against the Socratic interpretation is that not all virtues require knowledge. As Julia Driver (2001) has argued, some virtues, which she calls "virtues of ignorance", appear to require that one ignores a number of things. Driver discusses blind charity, impulsive courage, forgiveness and trust, as well as modesty. Let us focus on modesty. According to Driver, modesty is a virtue that requires that the agent underestimate, to some extent, her self-worth. Thus, a modest person needs to think that she is somewhat less good than she actually is. Suppose you are the very best pianist in the world. If you are modest, you would fail to fully recognize that you are the best pianist in the world. It follows that you need to have a false belief about yourself. Given this, you are not in a position to know that you act modestly when you do so, for instance by not boasting about your talent. Indeed, you would not be in a position to act modestly for the right reasons. In general, Driver argues that such examples show that "[k]nowledge of virtue-making factors is not a necessary condition for virtue." (2001, xv).

Defenders of the Socratic interpretation can reply that a virtue like modesty involves knowledge. Modesty, for instance, would involve an accurate understanding of the significance of ones' achievements (see Van Zyl 2018). Being modest would require knowing that you are the best pianist in the world while understanding the limits of this fact. You would be aware that luck and opportunity has played an important part in your achievements. Moreover, you would understand that this is not the only dimension of assessment that counts. You might be excellent at classical music, but other pianists might be better than you are when it comes to playing jazz or blues, for instance. You would also realize that being the best pianist in the world does not entail that you are good at everything. Maybe you are not very good as a cook or as a philosopher, after all. Most importantly, if you are modest, you will see that being the best pianist in the world does not make you the best person in the world. Self-worth does not depend on a person's achievements in one domain. Given this, knowing that you are the best pianist in the world appears compatible with the virtue of modesty.

The question is whether one could not be modest without having these beliefs about the limit of one's achievement. Even if the value of understanding the limits of one's achievements is undeniable, it might seem too demanding a feat for the virtue of modesty. One interesting suggestion is that what matters for modesty is neither ignorance nor complex knowledge about the limit of one's achievements. Rather, immodesty and modesty would be a matter of caring about certain things. Thus, Fred Schueler argues that "[s]omeone who is genuinely modest is someone who doesn't care whether people are impressed with her for her accomplishments" (1997, 478). This formulation is not entirely satisfactory, for as Driver (2001) notes, one might fail to care about whether others are impressed by one's achievements simply because one feels contempt for them, and this surely does not appear particularly modest. There is, however, a more plausible suggestion in the vicinity. As Arpaly and Schroeder (2013) argue, modest agents can well know what qualities they have, but what is crucial is that they do not care about how well they rank. Whether or not they know their ranking, they do not attach any importance to this fact. In particular, they do not value being ranked high. As a result, even if modesty often leads to ignorance about one's own merits as a side effect – if you do not care about how you are ranking you are less likely to seek information regarding how well you rank – ignorance would not be required for modesty. However, knowledge regarding one's achievements and its limits would not be required either. The interesting point is that on this account, modesty would depend on caring and not on entertaining thoughts regarding the limits of one's achievements.

A good question is what constitutes caring in this context. Arpaly and Schroeder (2013, see also Frankfurt 1982) consider caring to be a matter of desiring certain outcomes. However, an attractive account of caring consists in the claim that caring is a multitrack disposition to experience a number of emotions, depending on how what we care for fares (Helm 2001; Shoemaker 2003; Naar 2018). A person who cares about how she ranks among pianists is disposed to be happy should she rank high, to hope that she will move up and fear that she might move down the ranking, to be envious about those who rank higher, and so on. As David Shoemaker notes, the principal characteristics of caring, is that "in caring for X, I am rendered vulnerable to gains and losses – to emotional ups and downs – corresponding to the up-and-down fortunes of X" (2003, 91).

This suggests that the mistake the immodest person makes is an affective one. She cares for something that is not worthwhile. By contrast, the modest person does not make that affective mistake. She might care about the value of music, about being an accomplished musician, and so forth, but she is not interested in whether or not she beats other pianists, something that does indeed appear to be unimportant.

10.5. The Objection from Over-Intellectualization

As the discussion of modesty suggests, the main concern with the Socratic interpretation is that it over-intellectualizes virtues. It would seem that in most cases, when we act out of courage or generosity, say, we do so without reflecting on what to do. As Annas remarks, virtuous agents appear to "respond directly and immediately to situations in a way that often contrasts with the more inhibited thoughtful response of the less virtuous" (2011, 28). The generous person will respond to the need of others at once, without pausing to think about what is to be done. When asked what motivated them, courageous agents will typically mention features of the situation, such as that the child was about to be swept away. This suggests that virtuous agents are not typically moved by explicit thought concerning the value of what they do. Virtuous agents simply appear to see situations as requiring action, independently of any deliberation about what to do. Indeed, many cases are such that deliberation would be counterproductive. When there is a child about to be swept away, it is surely not the time to begin a survey of one's options in order to reach a conclusion about what to do in the light of what one values. There is thus good reason to doubt that virtuous actions require evaluative knowledge.

Annas (2011) offers a solution that appears plausible. She draws on Aristotle's suggestion that virtues are similar to skills, in the sense that "both are practical and both can be learned only by practice, by doing what needs to be done" (2011, 16). According to Annas, the role knowledge plays in virtues is analogous to the one it plays in skills such as that of playing the piano. To develop virtues, we need to make use of conscious practical reasoning, just as when we learn how to play the piano. We learn from role models and teachers, by imitating what they do, by following instructions, but also by understanding why they do what they do. All this takes conscious effort and reasoning – the giving and receiving of reasons, as Annas puts it – but once someone has mastered the skill of making virtuous decisions, she can deploy this skill without having to deliberate about what to do. However, because of the way the skilled person has acquired her skill, she "will be able to 'give an account' of what [she] does, which involves being able to explain why [she] is doing what [she] is doing" (2011, 20). Thus, Annas' account does not have any difficulty holding that virtue is a disposition not only to act well but to do so for the right reasons.

The analogy with skills, and in particular with musical skills, is attractive. A good question is whether it makes room for the Socratic claim that the core of virtue is evaluative knowledge. In particular, what is not clear is that we need to assume that the knowledge possessed by the virtuous agent is propositional knowledge that this or that – truth, the welfare of others, etc. – has intrinsic value. Indeed, to assume this would not make for a plausible account of the learning of a skill. When you learn to play the piano, you do not learn general propositional truths about why this or that has to be done that way, which you then internalize, so as to be able to play without thinking about these truths. You train how to move your fingers over the keyboard, of course, but the main thing is that you learn something that involves affects. Importantly, you learn how to express what you feel, but also what you have to feel at the different moments of a musical piece. As Annas (2011) notes, there are many skills whose deployment does not involve feelings – "a skilled potter can produce pots, and a skilled plumber can fix leaks in an unconcerned way" (2011, 66) – but what she fails to realize is that even the skilled potters and plumbers learned to care about what they do.

This suggestion ties well with another Aristotelian theme featured in the *Nicomachean Ethics*, namely that moral education is, at least in good part, the education of the emotions. Thus, explicitly endorsing Aristotle, Bernard Williams holds that

> [i]f [moral] education does not revolve round such issues as what to fear, what to be angry about, what – if anything – to despise, where to draw the line between kindness and a stupid sentimentality – [he does] not know what it is. [...] [A]s Aristotle perceived, we are concerned with something not so aptly called the inculcation of principles, but rather the education of the emotions.
> (1973, 225)

As a result, it will not come as a surprise that the main alternative to the Socratic interpretation is one according to which emotions are the core of virtues.

10.6. Sreenivasan's Theory of Virtues

Following Aristotle's claim that right emotions are characteristic of virtue, many have argued that emotions lie at the core of virtues. Kristján Kristjánsson, for instance, holds that "emotional reactions constitute essential ingredients in virtues" (2018, 20), a claim he attributes to Aristotle (see also Roberts 1989; 2013; Achtenberg 2002). More precisely, because virtues are dispositions, the thought is that emotional dispositions form the core of virtues. There is a variety of ways this suggestion can be developed. In this section, we will focus on a recent account developed in great detail by Sreenivasan (2020) and according to which a number of virtues have emotional dispositions – emotion traits, in his terms – at their core. The virtues Sreenivasan aims at capturing are virtues like kindness, courage, and compassion. He doubts that the virtue of justice fits the same pattern.

Sreenivasan sets out to answer the question of what virtuous agents must be like in terms of their psychological makeup. His answer is that emotions are central and indispensable to virtues like kindness, courage, and compassion, in the sense that dispositions to experience emotions "are required for exemplars of virtue to pass the most basic test of the central dimension of virtue" (2020, 33). This "central test" of virtue (2020, 24), as he calls it, involves consistently making correct practical judgments about situations calling for virtue, something that puts the agent in a good position reliably to act well. For instance, to qualify as having the virtue of compassion you must consistently make correct judgments about what to do across a variety of situations that call for compassion. You must judge that you ought to help an old man to reassemble his shopping that he accidentally spilled all over the sidewalk, that you ought to give something to eat to the starving child, or that you ought to visit a sick friend, assuming that these situations call for compassion. The claim, then, is that to pass the central test of virtue, exemplars of virtues such as kindness, courage or compassion need to possess specific emotion traits. More precisely, such virtues involve a modified or, more precisely, a *morally rectified* emotion trait.

Whatever exactly is involved in moral rectification, what is clear is that a rectified emotion trait is not defined as one that flows from correct moral judgment. On the contrary, the morally rectified trait is what allows the virtuous agent to make correct practical judgment. This makes for an important difference with the Socratic picture of what is involved in virtue. But if morally rectified emotions traits are not traits that conform with the verdict of moral judgment, what are they?

The natural move to understand the notion of morally rectified emotion traits is to ask what emotions are taken to be. Even though he claims not to have any particular objection to perceptual theories of emotions, Sreenivasan is officially neutral regarding this question. His case rests on claims about emotions and their relation to attention. As we have seen (in Chapter 8), de Sousa holds that "an emotion limits the range of information that the organism will take into account, the inferences actually drawn from a potential infinity, and the set of live options among which it will choose" (de Sousa 1987, 195). Building on de Sousa's insight, Sreenivasan proposes two pairs of relatively uncontroversial claims regarding the function of emotions, one regarding *input* salience, concerning what triggers emotions, and the other regarding *output* salience, concerning how to respond to things that have triggered an emotion.

Here is the first pair of claims:

a) Emotions control input salience, and
b) Emotions exhibit a significant degree of plasticity in their control of input salience.

According to these claims, emotions have the function to focus the subject's attention selectively and highlight the relevance of certain things, such as danger, noxiousness, loss, and so forth for each kind of emotion. In addition to this, the range of things on which an emotion focuses someone's attention can change. As Sreenivasan puts it, "the eliciting conditions (or triggers) for a given emotion are not fixed, but admit of change (to a certain extent)" (2020, 53). Thus, specific eliciting conditions can be added – you can learn to fear new things, which did not trigger fear in you – while others get subtracted – some things that you used to fear will no longer trigger that emotion. As a result, an individual's emotional dispositions are plastic. This second point is well taken, for as we discussed (in Chapter 3), even biological determinists agree that emotional dispositions are in part shaped by both our environment and our culture.

The second pair of claims concerns the role of emotions in focusing the attention on the responses to be made to one's environment:

c) Emotions control output salience, and
d) Emotions exhibit a significant degree of plasticity in their control of output salience.

The thought is that by controlling output salience, emotions control "the salience of some specific response(s) within the range of possible responses the subject might have or make" (2020, 60). In the case of fear, for instance, these responses typically, but not necessarily, are actions, such as flight, fight, or other forms of self-protection. As we underlined (again in Chapter 3), it is uncontroversial that our environment and our culture shape our emotional dispositions by influencing their associated action tendencies.

Taken together, the four claims about emotions entail that emotion traits are perfectly tailored to play the central role in virtues that Sreenivasan envisages. By controlling input and output salience, emotions importantly influence how we respond to specific situations, and because they are plastic both at the input and the output level, they can be educated so as to become better responses to situations. As we will shortly see, Sreenivasan directly appeals to this point in his arguments, to which we now turn. Discussing these arguments will allow us to understand the notion of morally rectified emotion traits.

10.7. Sreenivasan's Arguments

One of the three arguments that Sreenivasan offers starts with the intuitive premise that virtuous action requires that an agent be aware of the morally salient features of a situation. Virtuous agents need to be consistently "tuned in to the moral world" (2020, 133). Given this, it is easy to see that experiencing an emotion is likely to help the agent to be virtuous. As Sreenivasan notes, because they exert control of both input and output salience, "emotions are well suited to explaining why certain features of the world are consistently salient to a given agent (and why certain responses consistently follow from the salience of those features)" (2020, 134).

This claim is well illustrated by the virtue of compassion. The emotion that underlies the virtue of compassion Sreenivasan calls "sympathy". Drawing on Peter Goldie (2000), Shaun Nichols (2004), and Daniel Batson (2011), Sreenivasan characterizes *sympathy* by contrasting it with *empathy* and *personal distress*. Empathy is generally taken to consist in a process that results in the vicarious sharing of homologous affect, such as when you share someone's else sadness or joy. It is thought to involve imaginatively putting yourself in the shoes of someone else. Personal distress, on the other hand, is generally taken to consist in a feeling that is not always homologous and is self-oriented. You are distressed by the distress or trouble of others. Unlike empathy, sympathy does not require homology – what you experience can but need not be of the same sort as what the person for whom you feel sympathy experiences, and indeed, you may feel sympathy for someone who is in trouble but who does not feel anything, for example because that person has lost consciousness. Unlike personal distress, which is focused on one's own welfare, sympathy is other-oriented. Sympathy comes with an altruistic motivation, which has as its ultimate goal the improvement not of one's own welfare but of someone else's welfare. Sympathy, or indeed what is often called "compassion", is thus an emotion that is elicited by the fact that someone is in distress (or in trouble, but to simplify, I will only mention distress) and it motivates the agent to help the person with the aim of improving that person's welfare. Because when you experience sympathy, your attention is focused on the person in distress, their distress will be salient. Compared to someone who does not feel anything, you are certainly more likely to notice that this person needs help. Thus, someone who is disposed to feel sympathy is thereby disposed to be better at noticing that other people are in need for help. This makes it plausible to assume that a sympathy trait is a central component of the virtue of compassion.

A second argument in favor of the claim that emotion traits are central to virtues like kindness, courage, or compassion is that experiencing emotions is necessary to perform the virtuous actions in the right way. The specific requirement Sreenivasan proposes concerns the emotion expressed by the action.

In the case of the virtue of compassion, the compassionate act "must sincerely express the agent's sympathy" (2020, 15). This, in any case, is how an exemplar of virtue would perform the action. As is illustrated by the case of the old man who accidentally spills his shopping over the sidewalk, we expect that if you are a moral exemplar who helps reassemble the shopping, you do so in a manner that expresses your sympathy with the old man. As Sreenivasan notes, this might take different forms, just as there are different ways to fail the requirement, for instance by offering one's help while wearing a blank face and ignoring the old man. This requirement is clearly plausible and there is no doubt that a sympathy trait will make it likely that an agent satisfies the requirement.

These arguments give plausibility to the view that a virtue like compassion centrally involves a morally rectified sympathy trait. If you have a morally rectified sympathy trait, surely you will be better at noticing when others are in distress and surely you will endeavor to help them in a way that expresses sympathy.

However, we still do not have a firm grasp on what makes a sympathy trait morally rectified. What we are told is that "the point of modifying ordinary sympathy is to rectify it morally, i.e., to remedy its liabilities to moral error" (2020, 148). Tying this point to the claims regarding the plasticity of emotions, Sreenivasan holds that at the input side, ordinary sympathy's liabilities to error "can be morally rectified by adding or subtracting suitable eliciting conditions to someone's trait" (2020, 155). He discusses empirical findings on racial biases that make it plausible that "the input side of sympathy is plastic enough that out-group distress *can* be added as an eliciting condition for someone's trait" (2020, 162). This suggests that a morally rectified sympathy trait is a disposition to experience sympathy regarding cases that share a property, namely being in distress, in virtue of which these cases constitute appropriate eliciting conditions.

Given this explanation of what moral rectification consists in, it is plausible to hold that a morally rectified emotion trait is in fact nothing but a disposition to experience emotions that fit their eliciting conditions. A morally rectified sympathy trait would consist in the disposition to experience emotions of sympathy that accurately target distress, whether this distress is that of in-group or out-group persons. As we have seen, Sreenivasan does not want to commit himself to any specific theory of emotions. However, what we now are in a position to understand is that there is good reason to claim that the theory that best matches his account is one according to which emotions have evaluative representational content.

Indeed, Sreenivasan's third and last argument for his account appears to take a leaf from perceptual theories of emotions. What he argues is that "deferring to the feelings of an exemplar of virtue is sometimes the best way to figure out what the morally right thing to do is in a given practical situation" (2020, 168). This, he claims, is explained by the fact that the authority of virtuous agents derives from the proto-authority of their emotional responses. The advice of an exemplar of compassion, for instance, is one you should listen to because it is based on the exemplar's experience of sympathy when imagining the case that you are confronted with. Sreenivasan insists that for the argument to work, it is crucial to assume that the emotions that have proto-authority are not triggered in error. In the case of sympathy, thus, it is crucial that the agent's sympathy is not triggered in the absence of someone being in distress. As Sreenivasan parenthetically notes, "[t]hese misfirings are the emotional equivalent of an illusion" (2020, 187). These claims strongly suggest that the account of emotion that is presupposed is one according to which emotions have evaluative representational content.

If this is on the right track, what we have here is an account according to which some virtues centrally involve dispositions to experience fitting emotions. The virtue of compassion, on this interpretation, is one that centrally involves a sympathy trait that consists in a disposition to experience emotions of sympathy that are fitting, where fittingness is a matter of representing its object correctly. How exactly should we conceive of the content of the evaluation involved in sympathy? A first suggestion might be simply that sympathy is fitting when its intentional object is in distress. To underscore the negative value of distress, however, it seems plausible that sympathy in fact represents the distress as bad. On this suggestion, sympathy would be modeled on pain, which arguably represents a bodily disturbance as bad (see Bain 2011).

In any case, understood this way Sreenivasan's account of compassion and similar virtues is attractive. The question is whether this account captures everything that is important in the psychological makeup of the virtuous agent. In particular, one might wonder whether the focus on dispositions to experience fitting emotions of one specific kind, such as sympathy, does not leave aside the fact that virtues appear to involve multitrack emotional dispositions. This is the question to which we now turn.

10.8. The Importance of Caring

Sreenivasan's account of compassion holds that this virtue centrally involves a morally rectified sympathy trait, that is, a disposition to experience emotions of sympathy that are fitting. The core of compassion would be a singletrack emotional disposition. When we discussed the Aristotelian account of virtues, by contrast, we saw that according to some, like Hursthouse, virtues instead involve multitrack emotional dispositions (1999). Honesty, for instance, was thought to involve the disposition to feel distressed if confronted with dishonesty, unresentful at honest criticism, shocked and angered by acts of dishonesty, delighted when honesty triumphs, and so forth.

Theories of virtues according to which emotional dispositions are central can thus follow either of the two following models:

1. (Singletrack model) A virtue centrally involves a singletrack emotional disposition to experience fitting emotions of one specific kind.
2. (Multitrack model) A virtue centrally involves a multitrack emotional disposition to experience a specific set of fitting emotions.

As our discussions of compassion and of honesty show, both models are attractive. One might think that they are in competition and that one should be preferred to the other. What I will try to show is that the intuitions underlying the two models, properly understood, are, in fact, compatible.

Let us look more closely at the multitrack model. On that model, having a virtue will essentially amount to having a sentiment that consists in being vulnerable to the gains and losses of some object, be it truth or welfare. As a result, having a virtue essentially amounts to caring. If you are honest, for instance, you care about truth, in the sense that you are vulnerable to the gains and losses of truth. By contrast, the dishonest person does not care about truth. Similarly, as we saw when discussing immodesty, the dishonest person makes an affective mistake. The dishonest person fails to care for something that is worthwhile.

One attractive feature of the multitrack model is that it makes room for the plausible thought, which Brady (2005) underscores, that virtues centrally involve evaluations. The reason for this is that caring in fact amounts to a form of valuing (Seidman 2009). If you are honest, you care for truth and thus value truth, something which explains why you are motivated to tell the truth and more generally to act honestly. Similarly, if you are a benevolent agent you value the welfare of others insofar as you care about the welfare of others – you will be happy when things go well for others, sad when they do not go well for others, and so on, something which explains why you are motivated to help others in need.

With this in mind, we can ask whether all virtues should not be understood on the multitrack model. In particular, should our prime example of singletrack virtue, compassion, not better be understood as involving a multitrack emotional disposition? It would seem, after all, that benevolence and compassion are very similar. Indeed, one might think "benevolence", as the term is used by Brady, and "compassion" are but two names for the same virtue. What Sreenivasan tells us about compassion confirms this thought. According to him the virtue of compassion is "characteristically oriented [...] toward the goodness of another person's welfare" (2020, 141). This makes clear that the value to which compassion is taken to respond is just the same as the one to which benevolence is taken to respond: it is the goodness or value of others' welfare. Given this, the question is whether compassion need not involve more than simply a corrected sympathy trait. Would we not expect that compassionate agents are ones who care for others' welfare in that they not only will feel sympathy when they incur loss to their welfare, but who also rejoice when others do well? Who will hope that others' welfare improves, or be upset when others get intentionally harmed? In other words, it would seem that the virtue of compassion has to involve a multitrack emotional disposition.

The worry that should arise here concerns the emotion of sympathy. Surely this emotion, which in fact is sometimes called "compassion" (Goldie 2000; Nussbaum 2001), has a special role to play in the virtue of compassion. To make room for this thought, what needs to be understood is that not all components of a multitrack emotional disposition need to have an equal standing. What can be suggested is that multitrack emotional dispositions consist in structured bundles of singletrack dispositions. Given this, it is possible that one or the other singletrack disposition that is part of such a bundle plays a special role. What appears true in the case of compassion, in particular, is that the sympathy trait plays a special role in the multitrack emotional disposition that lies at the core of that virtue. Put otherwise, the sympathy trait appears to be the signature trait of that virtue.

The question is what that special role might be. One possibility is that what makes some singletrack dispositions special lies at the ontological level. Maybe the sympathy trait is in some way or other more fundamental, ontologically speaking, than the other parts of the compassion bundle. Whether or not this is so, what is plausible is that the sympathy trait and its manifestations have epistemic priority. On this suggestion, it would be mainly on the basis of someone's manifestations of the disposition to experience sympathy toward people in distress that we tell that someone has the virtue of compassion. This might be because we take the sympathy trait to be more fundamental from an ontological point of view. Maybe the virtue of compassion is thought to be primarily constituted by a sympathy trait, the other dispositions of the bundle being considered less important.

In any case, there is room for the claim that virtues centrally involve multitrack emotional dispositions in which the disposition to feel a particular kind of emotion plays a special role. Put differently, virtues can be thought to be sentiments that consists in caring about some value, such as truth or welfare, where this caring at least sometimes involves an emotional disposition, such as a sympathy trait in the case of the virtue of compassion, which constitutes its signature trait.

One might wonder whether all virtues involve a special trait as part of the multitrack emotional disposition or whether there are two kinds of virtues. One might also wonder whether all virtues involve emotional dispositions at all. Considering these questions would require that we have a grasp of what character traits are virtues, something that presupposes an account of what makes a trait a virtue. According to a prominent suggestion, which can again be traced back to Aristotle, virtues are character traits that are necessary for happiness or flourishing. In the next section, we will address the question of how virtues relate to happiness.

10.9. Virtues and Happiness

Many virtue theorists hold that being virtuous necessarily contributes to the happiness of the virtuous agent (for instance Hursthouse 1999; Annas 2011). Some believe that being virtuous is both necessary and sufficient for happiness. Because of the hardship that even virtuous agents have to endure, Aristotle's more modest claim, according to which virtue is necessary but not sufficient for happiness, appears easier to defend. However, even this more modest claim might seem doubtful when one thinks of vicious agents. It is not obvious that their lack of honesty, of compassion, of courage, and so forth, contribute to their unhappiness. On the contrary, as has been pointed out by many, it would rather seem that the exercise of vices contributes to their happiness. For instance, Daniel Haybron (2008) discusses the case of the Emperor of the Mongol Empire, Genghis Khan (c. 1158–1227), who appears to have led a happy and flourishing life even though he was responsible for the slaughter of tens of millions. In any case, the actions that typically flow from virtues such as compassion or courage can surely lead to self-sacrifice instead of happiness or flourishing. At best, virtue and happiness appear to be only contingently connected: in some circumstances, the exercise of virtue increases happiness, but there is no necessary connection between virtue and happiness.

Interestingly, once the account of virtues as centrally consisting in emotional dispositions is in place, there is room for an argument to the effect that virtue and happiness are necessarily connected. The claim, more precisely, is that it is because of their nature that virtues tend to be beneficial for individuals. Before we look at the argument for this conclusion, it is necessary to clarify the concept of happiness. The term "happiness" is in fact used in two different senses (see Haybron 2008). In one sense, "happiness" refers to a positive psychological state. There are different accounts of what that state consists in, ranging from *hedonism*, the view that happiness, in that sense, consists in a positive balance of pleasures, to *life satisfaction accounts*, according to which psychological happiness is a question of satisfaction with one's life. By contrast, the second sense, the term "happiness" is synonymous with "well-being" and "flourishing". And it is also the sense that corresponds to the notion of *eudaimonia* we find in Aristotle. In this sense, you are happy when you lead a life in which things go well for you. According to some, psychological happiness is the main ingredient of a flourishing life. But this is just one among many possible accounts (for a useful overview, see Fletcher 2016). In any case, it follows that the question of how virtues relate to happiness splits into two questions. On the one hand, there is the question of how virtues relate to happiness in the first sense, that is, *psychological happiness*, and on the other hand, there is the question of how virtues relate to happiness in the second sense, which we will call *flourishing*.

Let us look at the question of how virtues might relate to psychological happiness. There are several ways to draw the connection, depending on what psychological happiness is taken to be. Let us focus on an attractive account of psychological happiness that makes the connection especially tight. This account is the *emotional state theory* defended by Daniel Haybron (2008; see also Rossi 2018). According to this theory, psychological happiness consists in a positive balance of emotional or more generally of affective states. Individuals are happy, in that sense, when the positive affective states they experience, whether these are emotions of joy, hope, or admiration, or moods such as elation or calm, counterbalance the negative affective states they might feel.

Given this conception of psychological happiness, it is easy enough to see how virtues relate to happiness and unhappiness. Insofar as the core of virtues are emotional dispositions, each time an emotional disposition manifests itself, that is, each time the agent experiences an emotion as a result of her emotional disposition, her state of psychological happiness or unhappiness will be affected.

Now, because virtue results in fitting emotions, it follows that the emotions that constitute the psychological happiness or unhappiness of the agent are all fitting. Thus, when it results from virtues, the psychological happiness or unhappiness in question can itself be considered to be overall fitting, in the sense that they match evaluative reality. Given this, it is possible to argue that virtues necessary relate to flourishing. The reason is that according to a plausible account of flourishing, fitting happiness is an essential component of flourishing. Since it is neutral with respect to the possibility of other components, this claim is compatible with a number of accounts of flourishing. It is for instance compatible with so-called objective list accounts of flourishing, according to which flourishing is a matter having access to a plurality of goods, such as pleasure, friendship, and knowledge. On such an account, fitting happiness might be considered to be just another of the objective goods that are required for a flourishing life. However, insofar as they agree that fitting happiness plays an essential role in self-fulfilment, the claim that fitting happiness is an essential component of flourishing is also compatible with self-fulfilment theories (Haybron 2008).

Now, if we put these different claims together, what we obtain is that insofar as virtues result in fitting emotions, so that they result in overall fitting happiness, virtues result in flourishing. Put differently, we have the following argument (see Rossi and Tappolet 2016):

1. Virtues are constituted by dispositions to experience fitting emotions.
2. Fitting emotions are constituents of fitting happiness
3. Fitting happiness is a constituent of flourishing.

If the premises of this argument are granted, we can infer that the virtues that have emotional dispositions as their core and which result in positive emotions tend to make a person's life go well for her. To make good the claim that virtues are necessarily related to flourishing, what needs to be added is the requirement that the dispositions in question result in fitting emotions that are positive. Thus, what should be specified is that it is only when the external conditions are favorable that the possession of virtues can result in a flourishing life. A world in which virtuous agents are confronted with dishonesty or distress, for instance, will tend to make them psychologically unhappy and will affect their flourishing. However, a world in which they are surrounded by honesty, truth, or happiness, will tend to make them happy and will contribute to their flourishing.

We amply discussed the first premise of the argument. Not so for the second and the third premise, which clearly involve substantial and controversial claims. Nonetheless, whether this argument is on the right lines or not, what it shows is the fruitfulness of the account of virtues that places emotional dispositions at its core.

10.10. Taking Stock

We started both this chapter and this part of the book with Medea's rage and its destructive consequences. In spite of this, we saw that emotions can be good for us in several ways. We discussed the question of whether emotions can positively affect the rationality of what we think and concluded, in Chapter 7, that it is plausible to hold that our beliefs concerning features such as dangerousness or disgustingness are *prima facie* justified when they are based on the corresponding emotions. Such beliefs might even be *ultima facie* justified when, as far as you know, these emotions are not misleading you. We also discussed how emotions can, in certain circumstances, positively influence the rationality of what we do. It is true that emotions can result in actions that conflict with the agent's better judgment, but we saw that when this judgment is flawed, such actions might in fact be prudentially or even morally praiseworthy. Indeed, in some cases, akratic actions flowing from emotions might agree with the agent's practical reasons. What is more, we saw that there is reason to believe that emotions are good for us in that their impact on attention makes it possible for us to make choices.

In this chapter, we turned to the question of whether emotions could be good from the point of view of morality. What emerged was an account of virtues as character traits that have at their core emotional dispositions, where such emotional dispositions constitute caring for specific values, such as truth or the welfare of others.

The conclusion is that emotions are Janus-faced: they can be good or bad for us. In particular, it is only when they are fitting that they are part and parcel of virtuous moral agency. In light of this, the question that appears most urgent is how we could set about having emotions that are fitting. The fundamental question is how we could make it happen that the emotions we feel change for the best. This is the question to which we will turn in the two final chapters.

10.11. Summary

- Aristotelian virtue theorists hold that virtues are complex character traits that consist in dispositions to experience right emotions but also to have a variety of other mental states, including desires.
- On the Socratic interpretation, the core of virtue is constituted by knowledge of what is good, such as truth or others' welfare, or bad, such as dishonesty or distress.
- One problem with the Socratic interpretation comes from the fact that some virtues, such as modesty, appear to require ignorance rather than knowledge. It is not clear that this problem cannot be handled, but what appears to be the case is that a virtue like modesty is, in fact, rather a matter of what we care for than of what we know.
- Another objection to the Socratic interpretation is that it appears to over-intellectualize virtues. A promising reply to this objection consists in understanding virtues as kinds of skills.

- By contrast with the Socratic interpretation, many philosophers hold that emotional dispositions are the core of virtues. Sreenivasan, for instance, argues that the emotion of sympathy and more specifically a morally corrected sympathy trait is central to the virtue of compassion.
- On reflection, there is no incompatibility between the claim that virtues consist in multitrack emotional dispositions, which consist in caring for some values such as the welfare of others, and the claim that some singletrack emotional dispositions, such as a sympathy trait, play a special role.
- The claim that virtues have emotional dispositions as their core allows for an argument to the effect that, when things are favorable, virtues contribute to psychological happiness, understood as the positive balance of affective states, as well as to flourishing, understood in terms of fitting affective states.

10.12. Study Questions

1. Would you want to live with an agent who conforms to the radical rational ideal of moral agency, according to which a perfect moral agent feels no emotions? And if not, why not?
2. Is there something wrong in feeling a nasty emotion like envy, jealousy or schadenfreude (that is, pleasure in others' suffering) in cases in which this does not result in any harmful action? If so, why?
3. Recall Huck's morally admirable action of helping Jim out of sympathy in spite of his better judgment. Would you count him as morally virtuous, or is there something missing?

10.13. Further Readings

Anscombe, G. E. M. 1958. "Modern Moral Philosophy." *Philosophy* 33 (124):1–19.

Aristotle. 1983. *The Nicomachean Ethics.* Translated by W. D. Ross. Oxford: Oxford University Press, esp. books II, III and VI.

Annas, Julia. 2011. *Intelligent Virtue.* New York: Oxford University Press, chaps. 2 and 3.

Brady, Michael S. 2005. "The Values of the Virtues." *Philosophical Studies* 125:85–113.

Driver, Julia. 2001. *Uneasy Virtue.* Cambridge: Cambridge University Press, chap. 2.

Hursthouse, Rosalind. 1999. *On Virtue Ethics.* Oxford: Oxford University Press, chaps. 1 and 5.

Rossi, Mauro, and Christine Tappolet. 2016. "Virtue, Happiness, and Wellbeing." *The Monist* 99 (2):112–127.

Sreenivasan, Gopal. 2020. *Emotion and Virtue.* Princeton, NJ: Princeton University Press, especially chaps. 2 and 3.

Van Zyl, Liezl. 2018. *Virtue Ethics: A Contemporary Introduction.* New York: Routledge, especially chaps. 2 and 4.

Williams, Bernard A. O. 1973. "Morality and the Emotions." In *Problems of the Self,* 207–229. Cambridge: Cambridge University Press.

Art and the Shaping of Emotions

11 Emotion Regulation and Music

11.1. Introduction

Remember the last film you watched. Maybe you were thrilled by the almost unbearable suspense or else you were moved to tears by the hardships the protagonist had to endure. Films and more generally fictions can make us feel all sorts of emotions, ranging from fear, sadness, and anger to hope, admiration, and amusement, to name only a few possibilities. Similarly, music can move us to tears but it can also fill us with joy. Quite generally, even if some of the emotions we feel in response to art are negative, there is little we enjoy more than watching a good film, reading a good novel, or listening to good music. Because of this, art is an important source of happiness.

A good question here is how it is possible that works of art, and more specifically works of fiction, can cause emotions. How is it possible that we are moved by the fate of fictional character, since we are aware this character does not suffer for real. This puzzle, which is known as *the paradox of fiction*, has attracted a great deal of attention. Works of art not only cause emotions, but they are commonly thought to express emotions or more generally affective states. A brightly colored painting or an up-beat tune can express joy, while dark colors or somber music is often taken to express sadness. Indeed, we readily talk of joyful and sad music, just as we can characterize a painting as joyful or sad. These issues again raise difficult questions. What is it for a piece of music to be sad or joyful? And what in the world could it be for it to express sadness, given that a piece of music cannot, in any literal sense, be sad. Here too, we appear to be faced with a puzzle. We characterize works of art in terms of states such as sadness or joy, and we hold that works of art can express states. But even if we normally hold that to express a mood it is necessary to be in that mood, that is, to be literally sad or joyful, we do not hold that works of art literally experience emotions or moods. Sad music and more generally art that is expressive of negative moods or emotions raise a further puzzle. The question is how to explain the appeal of art that expresses negative moods or emotions. In particular, what seems puzzling is that we frequently listen to sad music even if it appears that sad music induces sadness. This *paradox of sad music* appears to have the same structure as the

DOI: 10.4324/9781315542300-15

paradox of tragedy, first raised by Aristotle (2013), which concerns the appeal of tragedies that cause us to feel aversive emotions, such as horror.

These puzzles are interesting in themselves and quite generally, the manifold connections between art and the emotions have fascinated philosophers (see Levinson 1997; Matravers 2007; Naar 2013a). Considering how art and emotions are related is also important for grasping a further issue, that is, the question of emotion regulation. To put it simply, this is because art is an important tool we use to regulate our emotions.

As we have seen early on, the regulation question is, with the essence question and the normative question, one of the three questions philosophers have been interested in. The regulation question asks to what extent and how emotion regulation is possible. The aim of this chapter is to explore the issue of emotion regulation by focusing on music as a regulation tool, while the next chapter discusses literature and sentimental education. We start with an overview of the science of emotion regulation. We then turn to the question of how music, and more specifically how listening to music serves to regulate our emotions. In order to answer this question, we will look at the different ways in which listening to music can induce emotions. Because some of these affective states are negative, this raises the question of why we would want to listen to music that has such negative effects. This will bring us to the paradox of sad music, which we will examine in detail. The last section looks into how music can afford experiences of flow, thereby directly contributing to happiness.

11.2. The Science of Emotion Regulation

As we have seen when surveying the history of the philosophy of emotions (in Chapter 1), philosophers of the past were keenly aware that some of our emotions are harmful and that more generally, our emotions need to be shaped. Accordingly, they made several intriguing suggestions concerning how to regulate our emotions. Aristotle, for instance, held that the acquisition of virtue requires the education of emotions, something which involves habituation. According to him, we need to become habituated to feel emotions on the right occasions. The Stoics, who were much more critical of emotions than Aristotle, since they thought that most of our emotions consist in deeply mistaken judgments, proposed a variety of methods to eradicate emotions, ranging from cognitive therapy to habituation and even musical therapy, which they conceived, intriguingly, as having a rational impact on the soul (see Scade 2017). Similarly, Aquinas as well as Descartes suggested that we could control our emotions by means of reflection, for instance by imagining the cause of the emotion in a different light.

Contemporary psychologists have but added to what is already quite a varied list of emotion regulation methods. James Gross (1998, 2014), a leading figure in emotion regulation science, underscores the variety of emotion regulation types. In his introductory survey, Gross (2014) proposes to understand emotions as involving a *situation-attention-appraisal-response* sequence. On this view, any emotion starts with a situation – the snake slithering into your tent, for instance – that compels attention and that gets appraised by you, something which gives rise to a multisystem response, comprising experiential, behavioral and neuro-biological changes. Consider the example of the snake. We can assume that you perceive the snake. Now, this will result into an emotional response on condition that your attention is captured by the snake's movements and that you appraise the snake as a threat. It is noteworthy that in many cases, this emotional response produces a change in the situation that gave rise to it – you chase the snake away, for instance. The emotional sequence is thus characterized by a feedback loop.

Let us underscore that this sequential model is meant to be compatible with a number of emotion theories. In particular, the model can be spelled out in terms of the receptive theory, according to which emotions consists in felt evaluations which depend on cognitive bases (see Chapter 6). In terms of the receptive theory, the sequence starts with a real or imaginary situation, which attracts your attention. The grasp of the situation, be it a visual perception, a belief or some other similar state, constitutes the cognitive basis of your felt evaluation. Moreover, depending on the kind of emotion and the kind of circumstances, that felt evaluation will give rise to a number of responses, such as facial expressions and motivations.

Gross distinguishes between several types of emotion regulation on the basis of this sequential model. A crucial distinction, to start with, is that between intra-personal *emotion regulation*, such as when you attempt to control your anger by going on a walk, and interpersonal *emotion regulation*, such as when you try to calm a friend's anger by taking your friend on a walk. In the first case, the goal of the regulation concerns yourself, while in the second, the goal concerns your friend's anger. Intrapersonal emotion regulation is particularly important in the development of children and more specifically in the moral education of chil-dren at the hands of parents or teachers. But it also features prominently in our everyday social interactions among adults, as illustrated in the example of your attempt to deal with your friend's anger.

Interestingly, emotions, or at least their expressions, can serve as tools by which we attempt to regulate other people's emotions. You can for instance make your anger at your friend for having broken a vase intentionally manifest by shouting at your friend, thereby getting the friend to feel guilt, regret, or even fear. Indeed, such cases are not limited to human interactions. Insofar as a dog barking aggressively at another dog does so with the intention to induce fear, such a case can be seen as a case of emotion regulation. Intrapersonal emotion regulation can also start with emotions. If you manage to feel amused at your-self for fearing to do something, such as disclosing your love to someone, you might be able significantly to reduce the fear, thereby allowing you to overcome that fear.

Another set of distinctions proposed by Gross (2014) concerns what feature of emotions are impacted on by a regulation process. The several dimensions that can be affected involve the magnitude, the duration, as well as the offset of the multisystem response. Emotion regulation can for instance increase or decrease the intensity of your anger, but it can also affect your facial expression or the actions you take in the wake of your anger. Emotion regulation thus can result in different modulations of the whole emotional sequence.

According to Gross (2014), these distinctions are at play in five families of emotion regulation processes, which concern the four elements of the emotional sequence: *situation selection, situation modification, attentional deployment, cognitive change,* and *response modulation.* Thus, situation selection and situation modification, when feasible, concern the first element of the whole sequence. Attentional deployment strategies concern the second element. A good example of this kind of strategy is distraction, such as when you try to forget an event that irritates you by watching a film. A striking example of an interpersonal version of this strategy is that of Iago's successful efforts to arouse Othello's jealousy. As Ronald de Sousa (1987) points out, Iago's stratagem is to direct Othello's attention to what appears to be evidence of Desdemona's infidelity. A third family of processes involves cognitive changes, which aim at impacting the appraisal element. Such cognitive changes can consist in modifying how you think about a situation, such as when you manage to convince yourself that an exam is a welcome challenge and not a threat. What results is a *reappraisal* of the situation. Finally, the fifth family of response modulation strategies aims at directly changing the multisystem emotional response. Going for a walk, breathing deeply or having a strong drink are examples of this kind of strategy, for such activities can all be used to modulate your physiological changes as well as your felt experience. As we have seen early on (in Chapter 3), facial expressions appear to depend on display rules, which explain intercultural differences observed in such expressions. Facial expressions are thus also possible targets of regulation strategies. In particular, expressive suppression, which involves trying to inhibit our facial, or more generally our expressive behavior, is a common form of regulation strategy.

Given the wide variety of strategies, a good question concerns the advantages and disadvantages they involve. Some strategies have been shown to be more effective than others. As Gross discusses (Gross 1998, 2014), some strategies also tend to be costlier than others. For instance, suppression, which aims at reducing emotion-expressive behavior, has been shown to have more problematic consequences than reappraisal, which is a strategy that aims at changes earlier in the emotional sequence. For instance, suppression tends, among other things, to decrease positive but not negative emotions, while reappraisal leads to decreased levels of negative experience and increased levels of positive emotions.

Another complexity in emotion regulation comes from the fact that the goals of regulation efforts can be very different. There are, of course, hedonic motivations. We often aim at lowering the intensity and duration of negative emotions, such as sadness or fear, just as we often aim at increasing the intensity and duration of positive emotions. But in other cases, the goals of regulation are not hedonic. You might want to intensify the anger you feel because you think this will help you in confronting your boss. In this case, you have instrumental reasons to feel strong anger and this is what motivates your attempt to get yourself to experience anger. Or you might want to lessen your amusement at a funny situation that happens to take place during a funeral. The reason for this might be that you prefer to comply with the social convention according to which one should feel sad at a funeral, or else you might be motivated by the thought that you do not want to hurt the close family of the deceased by what would be perceived as a lack of concern.

A point that is not at the forefront of the science of emotion regulation is that emotion regulation might aim quite generally at feeling fitting emotions. This, in any case, would be our goal if one were to adopt an Aristotelian account of virtue, which places fitting emotions at the heart of virtues (see Chapter 10). On such a conception, emotion regulation would amount to a kind of *education*, since the changes in the emotions that are envisaged aim exclusively at feeling proper or fitting emotions. We will consider issues regarding education in Chapter 12. Let us now turn to how we can change what we currently feel by getting involved with art, and in particular by listening to music.

11.3. The Emotional Effects of Music

It is no secret that many of us turn to art to regulate our emotions. When we try to get rid of a negative emotion, such as sadness at a missed opportunity, some of us watch a film, others read a novel, and many of us listen to music. Indeed, as Patrick Juslin and John Sloboda (2010) stress, studies suggest that the most common motive for listening to music is to influence our emotions, that is, to change what we feel, to enjoy or comfort ourselves or else to relieve stress. Indeed, there are reasons to think that musical therapy is nothing but the systematization of what we do when listening to music (for an overview of music therapy, see Thaut and Wheeler 2010).

Now, it is a bit of a mystery how music can evoke emotions in us. Hence it is also a bit of a mystery that we can regulate our emotions by listening to music. To see why it seems a mystery that music can cause us to feel emotions, let us look at the emotions we feel toward fictions. As noted above, it appears puzzling that something that you think is a mere fiction can cause you to feel emotions. In normal circumstances, when you discover that there is nothing to be afraid of, your fear subsides. In the case of fiction, however, we feel all sorts of emotions, such as compassion and fear for characters we know to be fictional. Thus, the question is whether such emotions are genuine. Even so, it is clear that we experience affective states in response to fiction (see Chapter 12).

Not so in the case of music. The reason why it is especially difficulty to understand how listening to a piece of music can cause emotions is that music is not a representational art. Unlike a film or a novel, music does not tell us stories about things and people. Of course, a piece of music can be accompanied by a text or a title, so that a narrative element complements the music. As such, however, a piece of music does not describe or depict anything. Think of a purely instrumental piece of music that happens to have no title. Such a piece is quite likely to trigger emotions in listeners in spite of not having any narrative element.

Let us look at how emotions could be caused by music. A first point here is that, as Stephen Davies (2010), notes, some of the ways in which music causes emotions are entirely non-mysterious. First, a piece of music can be charged with contingent personal associations, such as when it is the piece that was played at your wedding, say, so that each time you hear it you are filled with happy memories. Such associations can also be shared among a group or a culture. Think of what hockey fans associate with the national anthem, which they hear at the beginning of each game. When hearing the anthem on another occasion, hockey fans are surely likely to feel exhilaration in spite of there being no hockey game to win or lose. Furthermore, evaluative features of a musical piece, such as its repetitive boringness or a surprising rhythm change can give rise to emotions such as boredom or surprise. In addition, features of the musical performance are likely to cause emotions. Think for instance about how you react to a particularly beautiful execution of a difficult passage. Insofar as such emotions consist in reactions to things and their evaluative features, they are by no means mysterious.

Two further causal routes from music to emotions are worth mentioning. The first is the *entrainment effect* of music (see Juslin and Västfjäll 2008; Scherer 2013; Trost and Vuilleumier 2013). Because music involves rhythm, listening to a music is likely to produce emotions or more generally affective states by directly influencing the peripheral nervous system. We have all experienced not being able to stand still when listening to dance music. What needs underscoring is that this entrainment effect can result in affective states. Think of how listening to an up-beat rhythm not only makes you move your body accordingly, but also makes you feel elated. It is likely that this entrainment effect is also what motivates soccer players, for instance, to listen to loud rock music in order to fire themselves up before a game.

Furthermore, as Klaus Scherer (2013) notes, listening to music can also give rise to emotions because of a process of *empathy*, that is, a process that involves imaginatively putting yourself into the shoes of someone else and feeling the kind of emotion that the other person feels. Emotions elicited through empathy are particularly important in the case of live music, where seeing a musician who expresses emotions is likely to give rise to matching emotions. But imaginatively putting yourself into the shoes of the composer can also result in feelings.

Finally, as neurologist Isabelle Peretz (2010) argues, there are reasons to think that music can cause emotions by co-opting emotion circuits in the brain that have evolved for emotional responsiveness to vocal expressions. As she notes, there is remarkable invariance across both individuals and cultures in judgments regarding whether music is joyful or scary. Hence, even if individual experience and culture play a role in how we respond to music, the tendency to respond emotionally appears innate. According to Peretz, "[i]nfants' musical emotion could emerge from an innate propensity to respond to the emotional tone of the voice [...]" (2010, 103). This appears to be a plausible hypothesis, which is likely to explain why music we perceive as sad, for instance, can on some occasion, cause sadness.

These are all relatively non-mysterious ways in which music can impact what we feel. There is yet another way that music can affect us, one which concerns how the listener responds to the music's expressiveness. Music is commonly thought to be happy, sad, and sometimes even angry. The question of musical expressiveness has attracted a lot of philosophical attention, and it will prove useful to consider this question before discussing this last way in which music can cause emotions. Consider the funeral march from Beethoven's *Third Symphony*, which counts as a paradigmatic example of a piece of music that expresses sadness. Since a symphonic movement does not literally feel any emotions, the fact that it appears to express a state such as sadness is puzzling. A number of theories have been proposed to address this question, among which *arousal theories* (Matravers 1998; Cochrane 2010), *persona theories* (Levinson 1996; Robinson 2005) and *resemblance theories* (Kivy 1980; Davies 1994, 2010).

According to arousal theories, the expression of emotions in music is to be understood in terms of the emotions caused in the audience. In a nutshell, sad music is music that arouses sadness, happy music causes happiness, scary music causes fear, and so forth for other emotions that are expressed. The main difficulty with this approach concerns cases in which the audience does not appear to feel anything even though the piece of music in question clearly expresses feelings. In reply, arousal theorists argue that the aroused response can be extremely faint, consisting merely in the feelings associated with attenuated bodily changes or even with a mere neural simulation of such changes. Even so, it is hard to believe that music can express sadness only insofar as we feel even some minimal degree of sadness. In a move that parallels accounts of evaluative features that invoke dispositions (see Chapter 9), one could argue that sad music is such as to be disposed to cause sadness in certain circumstances. The question, then, would be how to spell out these circumstances. Should we say that sad music causes sadness in standard circumstances and normal listeners? Or should we say that it would be fitting to feel sad when we listen to sad music? Such suggestions do not seem very plausible and the reason is that even if people differ in their attitudes to sad music, sad music is often sought by some people because it makes them feel good (see Sizer 2019).

By contrast, persona theories deny that we need to feel anything when listening to expressive music. They hold that for a piece of music to count as expressive of an emotion, it is necessary that we hear the piece as expressing the emotion of an imagined human person, that is, the music's persona. When listening to sad music, what we do is imagine a persona in the music who is feeling sadness, and so forth for other kinds of emotions. Now, it is clear that we can and sometimes do imagine a person in the music we listen to. The worry with this approach, however, is that these kinds of imaginings do not seem necessary to grasp the expressiveness of a musical piece. We surely can recognize that a piece of music is sad without attributing the sadness in question to some imaginary being.

This is why resemblance theories, which hold that music resembles the way in which human beings give expression to their emotions, appear to be more plausible as a general account of musical expressiveness. What such theories claim is that musical pieces are taken as expressing emotions in virtue of the resemblance between their dynamic structure and the structures observed in the behavior of human beings. Not only is there a perceived resemblance between melodies and vocal expression, but the contours of musical pieces also bear a perceived resemblance to bodily movements. As Davies puts it, "music resembles gaits, carriages, or comportments that are typically expressive of human occurrent emotions [...]" (2010, 33). According to Davies, this is a general phenomenon in the sense that we often see things as expressing emotions on the basis of how they look or more generally of how they appear to us. Indeed, seeing emotional expression in things that are devoid of emotions is something we are often impelled to do. For instance, because the hanging branches of willow trees are seen as resembling, in some relevant way, the appearance of sad people, we cannot help but see willow trees as looking sad. Similarly, most of us see dogs of the Saint Bernard breed as expressing sadness in virtue of its hanging eyebrows and sloping jowls.

With this in mind, let us return to the question of how music can cause emotions. As such, the arousal theory, which takes as its starting point that music can arouse emotions, is compatible with several accounts of how the expressiveness of music results in emotions. Consider for instance Tom Cochrane, who defends an arousal theory that takes on board elements of the persona and the resemblance theory. He holds that "music hijacks the simulation mechanism which recognizes the actions and emotions of others" (2010, 203), a claim that is very close to the idea that music co-opts the emotional systems that evolved to respond to human voices (see Peretz 2010). According to Cochrane, what happens in the case of music is akin to what happens in emotional contagion, something which he holds involves the so-called *mirror neurons*, that is, the neurons that fire both when we perform an action and when we perceive another person performing that action. When we start to feel fear or amusement at the sight of someone's fear or amusement, we are in fact unconsciously imitating the expressive responses of that person. A similar account is open to the persona theorist, who can hold that the emotions we are caused to feel when listening to music derive, by emotional contagion, from the ones that the persona in the music is imagined to have. The idea of contagion is particularly easy to associate with the resemblance theory of musical expression. And indeed, Davies (2010, 2013) offers an emotional contagion account and suggests that we "catch", via a process of emotional contagion, the emotion that is expressed in the musical piece, and which we perceive in the contour of the musical piece. This gives rise to emotions that mirror the emotions expressed in the music. Thus, music that expresses sadness will, by contagion, make us sad. However, unlike a full-blown emotion of sadness, the sadness that we feel in that case is not directed at any particular object. As Davies explains, "if the listener does mirror the music's expressiveness, that response is caused by and tracks the music, but does not take the music, or any other thing, as its emotional object" (2010, 37). This suggests, as Jenefer Robinson (2005) claims, that in fact, the affective states that are caused by music by a process of emotional contagion are not emotions, but moods.

We have uncovered several ways that music can cause emotions and have seen, in particular, that music can trigger moods that mirror the ones expressed by a musical piece. What should be underscored here is that what the listener feels is likely to result from the interaction of several affective states, produced by different causal mechanisms. For example, a piece of music can trigger happy memories by association with a happy event but also have an up-beat rhythm that entrains you to move accordingly and feel elated. In any case, it is undeniable that we often know the effect of listening to a particular piece of music has on how we feel, and we often deliberately use this knowledge in order to induce the desired effects in us.

This explains how we can use music to change how we feel. But this is not the end of the story. Indeed, the affective states we feel thanks to a process of contagion give rise to a well-known puzzle, known as the paradox of sad music.

11.4. The Paradox of Sad Music

Why would we ever want to listen to sad music if doing so tends to make us sad? After all, we normally try to avoid feeling sad. Here is how this paradox of sad music can be spelled out (see Davies 1994; Sizer 2019):

1. Sad music induces sadness;
2. Sadness is an unpleasant affective state, which we tend to avoid;
3. Yet we deliberately listen to sad music.

There are a number of solutions to this paradox, some of which are parallel to the solutions proposed to the paradox of negative emotions in art, which asks why we ever would want to attend a tragedy, read a sad novel, or watch a film that involves tragic events (see Chapter 12).

The most common approach consists in accepting the three assumptions that form the paradox while attempting to show that they are not incompatible. The main suggestion on these lines consists in arguing that the negative effect of having to experience negative affective states is largely compensated by the benefits of so doing. Solutions that focus on compensation can be traced by to Aristotle (2013), who famously held that tragedy allows *catharsis*. The horror and pity we feel when attending to the tragic destiny of the heroes as displayed on the stage allows us to purge negative emotions. Clearly, the same can be envisaged in the case of music. As Jerrold Levinson (1982) suggests, responding with grief to music might allow "one to bleed off in a controlled manner a certain amount of harmful emotion with which one is afflicted" (1982, 338). Indeed, Levinson holds that a variety of other rewards compensate for the pain of the negative affective states caused by music. In fact, according to Levinson, at least some of the many benefits afforded by listening to music, such as the reward of savoring the feel of emotions that are detached from real-life distress or the reward of a sense of communion with the composer, cannot be obtained in the absence of negative affective states. How convincing is this solution? It would seem that even if music can offer such rewards, it is not something that happens in all the cases in which we listen to a piece of music that expresses negative affective states and are hence liable to cause similarly negative affective states.

A similar compensatory solution starts by pointing out that many things that we value come with negative aspects. Endurance races, such as marathons, are a good example. Those who value such activities cannot deny that preparing and running a marathon, for instance, is something that involves both positive and negative aspects. However, in the eyes of the marathon runner, the disvalue of the pain they feel, for instance, is largely compensated by the overall value of the endeavor. Accordingly, it can be suggested that something similar happens in the case of music. Thus, Davies (1994, 2010) holds that our goal is to understand and appreciate the music, and this is something we value even if it is something that can involve the experience of negative emotions. The value of the whole is thus taken to compensate for the disvalue of the part that consists in the experience of sadness. This solution appears to point in the right direction in that it focuses on the value of listening to music. However, even if there is no doubt that discerning the melodic structure of a piece, say, can afford intense pleasure, it is questionable whether many of us have the goal of understanding music when listening to music.

In fact, it is not obvious that we have to accept the propositions that form the paradox. It might seem to be an advantage of Davies' view, or indeed of any solutions in terms of compensation that they are in a position to handle not only the case of sad music but all cases of music that cause negative emotions, whatever these might be. Still, there is something particular about the case of sad music that a wholesale solution fails to capture. Sad music is in fact particularly attractive at least to some of us, and there seems to be something wrong in the thought that listening to sad music results in a negative experience, which needs to be compensated in some ways.

Let us therefore look into the solutions to the paradox that propose to solve it by denying the assumptions that form it, starting with the second assumption. According to Laura Sizer (2019), the sadness induced by sad music is not altogether unpleasant. Taking on board Levinson's (1997) claim that the sadness felt with respect to sad music and sad fiction is divorced from everyday care and concerns and thus more pure or unencumbered compared to ordinary sadness, Laura Sizer holds that the sadness caused by sad music not only reinforces the sort of focused attention on the music that allows us fully to engage with it, but can also be uniquely positive and comforting. The question here is whether it is the sadness itself that constitutes the positive experience or whether the sadness induced by music should not rather be seen as part of an overall pleasant experience or else resulting in a pleasant experience. Unless the sadness induced by music is itself pleasant in some ways, the solution on offer in fact amounts to a compensatory solution. Now, according to one study (Vuoskoski et al. 2012), listening to sad music causes responses of sadness that are not experienced as negative or unpleasant, by contrast to the emotional responses to scary music, which are rated as clearly unpleasant. This might seem to strengthen the case against the second assumption of the paradox. However, it might just as well suggest that we should question the first assumption. Can it really be sadness that is induced by music if what is experienced is not unpleasant? Let us consider this question.

A number of authors have questioned the claim that sad music generally induces sadness. Nobody would doubt that listening to sad music can, on some occasions, trigger sadness. But the question is whether it typically does cause sadness. Peter Kivy (1990, 2006), for one, holds that music can cause neither what he calls "garden-variety emotions" nor moods. Kivy grants that beauty and other positive aesthetic properties can trigger feelings of awe, but according to him, these feelings are not related to the affect expressed in music. Because his argument presupposes a controversial account of emotions, according to which emotions presuppose propositional attitudes such as beliefs and desires, it is less than persuasive. In general, the conclusion that music can cause neither emotions nor moods seems difficult to believe.

The problem with the flat denial that sad music typically causes sadness is that it appears to fly in the face of empirical studies, according to which the ratings of experienced sadness were significantly higher than the rating for other emotions (but see Zentner et al. (2008) for divergent results, according to which sad music is perceived as expressive of sadness, but not as causing an experience of sadness). A more plausible strategy, therefore, is to hold that sad music induces a response that is in some way similar to sadness, but nonetheless consists in a positive affective state. And in fact, recent empirical work suggests that the typical response to sad music is the feeling of being moved. According to Vuoskoski and Eerola (2017), who take their inspiration from studies regarding our reaction to sad films (see Hanich et al. 2014), the feeling of being moved plays a central role in the enjoyment we take in sad music. On their view, the music-induced sadness contributes to the enjoyment we take in sad music by intensifying the feeling of being moved. A good question here is what the feeling of being moved consists in. As Vuoskoksi and Eerola note, that kind of feeling is typically induced by critical life events, such as birth, death, and marriage, but also by exposure to artwork and to nature.

A closer look at the nature of the feeling of being moved suggests that instead of seeing it as a piece in the mechanism that takes us from sadness to enjoyment, we should in fact take it as a unified response to sad music. In a nutshell, what seems plausible is that sad music typically causes not sadness but the feeling of being moved. Let us look at a recent account of the feeling of being moved offered by Julien Deonna (2020; see also 2018; Cova and Deonna 2014). According to Deonna, being moved is a distinct emotion, which involves all the characteristics of paradigmatic emotions, such as intentional objects and appraisals. He holds that this emotion consists in "the experience of being struck by the goodness of some specific positive value being exemplified" (2020, 190). To illustrate this, let us consider a case of being moved by the birth of a child. What happens when you are moved by the birth of a child is that you are struck by the momentous value of life that is exemplified in this event.

What is of particular interest for the present discussion is that people reporting on their experience of being moved tend to say that it is an overall pleasant experience, even if it nonetheless involves both positive and negative feelings. It is as if being moved can countenance some sadness along the joy felt in response to the goodness of some value. The explanation for the mixed nature of how being moved can feel is that quite often, the value that is exemplified is set against a negative background. Think of a case in which you are moved by the courage of a soldier who sacrificed his life to save his comrades. In such a case, the value of courage is made especially salient against the dark background of the soldier's death. Because being moved has often this kind of mixed feel, there is reason to think that it is the typical response we have when listening to beautiful but sad music. The suggestion that seems likely is that when we listen to sad music that is beautiful, we typically feel moved by the music. The claim that sad music typically triggers feelings of being moved would mean, according to the account offered by Deonna, that when listening to sad music, we are struck by value of the beauty that is exemplified in this particular piece of music.

Insofar as being moved involves a feel of sadness, this suggestion can easily explain why people often think that listening to sad music makes them feel sad. But because it is an overall positive emotion, we can also explain why they hold that their experience is not a negative or unpleasant one. Moreover, we can see why sad music is more likely to move us, compared to happy or scary music. It is plausible that grasping the sadness expressed in the music is likely to induce an emotion that involves a mixed feel, involving some sadness. Indeed, the sadness perceived in the music serves as the dark background that makes the beauty of the music salient.

Let us note here that this solution generalizes to other art forms that express sadness. Even if the mechanisms that are involved are likely to be different in that our affective responses need to be mediated by an understanding of the narrative, sad films and, more generally, sad narratives often move us in similar ways to the way sad music moves us. Given that being moved is a positive emotion that is part of the pleasure that sad narratives give us, there is therefore no mystery in the fact that we tend to be fond of such sad narratives (Cova, Deonna, and Sander 2017). A good question, to which we will return in the next chapter, is whether this solution can solve the paradox of negative emotion, whatever the kind of negative emotion that is involved.

Being moved by music is certainly one of the great joys of listening to music, and we have seen reasons to think that sad music is especially well placed to induce this emotion. But it is not the only one. Let us therefore turn to another way of conceiving the enjoyment we take in music.

11.5. Music, Flow, and Happiness

There is no doubt that many of us enjoy listening to music, whether it is sad, happy, or expressive of some other affective states. The hypothesis we will consider in this section is that listening to music can cause an experience of *flow*, as described by Mihaly Csikszentmihalyi (1975, 1990). As we will see, flow is arguably a specific kind of enjoyment, that is, enjoyment we take in certain kinds of activities (Tappolet 2022). The activities which can induce flow are quite varied and include rock climbing, sailing, chess, video games, dancing, painting, sculpting, composing, and writing. Interestingly, if it is true that listening to music can induce flow experiences and flow is a kind of enjoyment, we can see why music is one of the main sources of happiness. If listening to music is liable to cause this kind of enjoyment, we have a good explanation of why listening to music makes us happy. Accordingly, we also would have an explanation of why we often listen to music. In many cases, it would simply be because we want to achieve the simple goal of improving how we feel. In such cases, listening to music amounts to emotion regulation aimed at increasing our psychological happiness.

Music has been associated with flow since the beginning of flow research (see Csikszentmihalyi 1975). Even if a good part of his work focuses on composing music and playing a musical instrument, Csikszentmihalyi also considers the effects of listening to music. Thus, he illustrates his claim that flow requires the perception of a challenge that matches your ability in the following way: "a piece of music that is too simple relative to one's listening skills will be boring, while music that is too complex will be frustrating. Enjoyment appears at the boundary between boredom and anxiety, when the challenges are just balanced with the person's capacity to act" (1990, 52).

To see that listening to music is, in fact, particularly well placed to induce flow, let us look at what flow consists in. In an early characterization, Csikszentmihalyi describes flow, which he also calls the "optimal experience," as "the holistic sensation that people feel when they act with total engagement" (1975, 36). According to him, the agent in a state of flow experiences action "as a unified flowing from one moment to the next, in which he is in control of his actions, and in which there is little distinction between self and environment, between stimulus and response or between past, present, and future" (1975, 36).

According to Csikszentmihalyi and more generally to flow researchers (Csikszentmihalyi 1975; Nakamura and Csikszentmihalyi 2012; Engeser and Schiepe-Tiska 2012), experiences of flow depend on the following two conditions:

- Perceived challenges that match existing skills; and
- Clear proximal goals and immediate feedback about progress.

Furthermore, the experience of flow is thought to have the following characteristics:

- Intense and focused concentration on what one is doing, to the point that the rest of the world seems to be cut off;
- Merging of action and awareness, in which a person is aware of her action, but not aware of herself as separate from what she is doing;
- Loss of reflective self-consciousness, such that considerations about the self become irrelevant;

- Feeling of control of one's action and over the demands of the environment, a sense of mastery in that one feels that one can deal with the situation;
- Distortion of temporal experience, such that, typically, the time passes faster than normal; and finally,
- Experience of the activity as intrinsically rewarding, so that there is no need for external goals or rewards.

Somewhat surprisingly, an intuitively important aspect fails to figure in current lists of characteristics. By all accounts, an important characteristic of flow is that it involves enjoyment. This surely explains why flow is experienced as intrinsically rewarding. Indeed, the importance of enjoyment is clear from the beginning of flow research. Csikszentmihalyi, for one, had initially set out to study the nature and conditions of enjoyment. In his first book, he thus writes that flow "is the crucial component of enjoyment" (1975, 11), the activities that cause flow being experienced as highly enjoyable. What is more, the questionnaires in the studies that lead to Csikszentmihalyi's 1975 publication already use enjoyment of the experience as an indicator of intrinsic reward. Since he allows for other, more passive kinds of enjoyment, flow is associated with a specific form of enjoyment, which Csikszentmihalyi considers to be the highest.

As stated above, what is crucial to flow is the perceived balance between the challenge involved in the activity and the skills of the individual, something that results in the sense of control and mastery. When the challenge is experienced as too demanding, given an individual's skill at the activity, anxiety is the result. When the challenge is perceived as not demanding enough, given the individual's skills at the activity, the individual will feel boredom. "Flow", by contrast, "is experienced when the perceived opportunities for action are in balance with the actors' perceived skills" (Nakamura and Csikszentmihalyi 2012, 94). Flow is thus directly opposed to anxiety and boredom, two states that commonly count as affective. To be anxious at some activity or to be bored by some activity is, by most accounts, to feel an emotion toward this activity. This suggests that flow itself is also an emotion.

The same conclusion follows from a closer look at the characteristics of flow. What becomes clear is that flow experiences share the hallmark of emotions (see Chapter 2). Flow experiences are typically characterized by phenomenal properties, for not only do they involve a feeling of control and of mastery, but they are described as involving an experience of the activity as intrinsically rewarding. Flow experiences also typically involve motivation, such as the desire to carry on with the activity, or to return to it later. There is no doubt, in addition, that flow experiences have intentional objects. They are directed at the activities which give rise to the experience of flow. Given this, it is easy to see that flow experiences involve an appraisal. The activity in question is appraised positively, as intrinsically rewarding. It follows from this that flow experiences are tied to a formal object. Because it is a kind of enjoyment, the formal object of flow is arguably nothing but the property of being enjoyable, where this property is attached to activities that present a challenge that match one's skills.

If this is on the right track, flow is a distinct emotion. More specifically, it is a kind of enjoyment, namely, the enjoyment we take in particular activities. Because it is a positive emotion, flow can be taken to contribute directly to psychological happiness. As we discussed (in Chapter 10), psychological happiness is best understood as consisting in a positive balance of emotional or more generally of affective states (Haybron 2008). Given this, experiencing flow will by itself have a positive impact on the balance of your affective states. It will thus increase your happiness, or at least decrease your unhappiness.

On this account, it is easy to understand why, quite often, we listen to music in order to feel better. This is because music is particularly well placed to give rise to experiences of flow. Think again of the marks of flow and remember what you felt when listening to your favorite music. When you are engrossed by the music to which you listen, your attention is caught entirely by the music, to the point that the rest of the world seems to disappear. There appears to be no distance anymore between a self of yours, the listening, and the music. This merging into the music makes you lose interest in yourself as an object of reflective self-consciousness. Moreover, temporal experience gets importantly distorted in that you are not aware of spending hours listening to the music. And of course, you deeply enjoy yourself and are in no need of a further external reward to continue listening to that music.

One might wonder, at this stage, how it can be that listening to music can induce flow. On the face of it, one might think that listening to music is not enough of an activity to cause flow experiences. Or indeed, one might argue that even if listening is indisputably an activity, it does not afford enough of a challenge. Maybe listening to some music – think of Igor Stravinsky's *Rite of Spring* or of *Anthropology* as played by Charlie Parker, for instance – is a bit of a challenge, but surely, we also enjoy listening to a good blues tune or even to some very simple lullabies. As we have seen, Csikszentmihalyi thought that the music had to be neither too simple nor too complex, relative to the listener's skills. This makes it sound as if listening to music is like a mathematical problem, however. Solving mathematical problems surely can induce flow, but it would seem that there is something distinctive about music that an analogy with problem solving misses.

In fact, it appears that we can preserve the grain of truth that the music should not be too simple or too complex, thereby providing a listener's experience that consists in challenges that match the skills of the listener. The suggestion is that listening to music involves, at least in those cases in which it causes flow, what can be described as an *inner dance*. Let us first consider overt movement. As we have already underscored, music often creates an urge to move. As Sizer notes, "before the creation of that peculiar Western music tradition, the concert hall, which expects music listeners to sit still while they listen to music, music and movement were regularly linked" (2019, 258). As we have seen when discussing the different mechanisms by which music can cause emotions, entrainment plays an important role, and this entrainment often gives rise to bodily movements. A second mechanism that is important in this context is that of musical expectancy (see Meyer

1956; Huron 2006). Listeners come to music with a number of expectations, which depend on their familiarity with the piece and their acquaintance with the style of the piece. Depending on how the music unfolds, these expectations will be confirmed or violated, and it is noteworthy that listeners prefer music that is not overly predictable, lest they become bored by it. What happens when we listen to music results from the combined effects of entrainment and of the listener's musical expectations (see Trost and Vuilleumier 2013). In all likelihood, it is the combination of these effects that makes it possible to dance along with the music to which we listen, and not simply to be caused to tap our foot or move our body by what we hear. Insofar as dancing to music is an activity that involves a challenge and for which you need skills, dancing is the perfect candidate to explain how listening to music can induce experiences of flow.

Now, it is clear that we do not always dance or even tap our foot when listening to music. However, there is reason to think that even if there is no overt dance or movement that takes place, listening to music can cause what can be thought as a kind of inner dance. This is what Ray Jackendoff (1992) suggests, and it is noteworthy that he explicitly makes the link with affective states. Jackendoff considers that the correlation of music and dance suggests that "musical affect – the emotional response to music – arises through the music's entraining the body representations, whether or not one actually dances to the music – that is, whether or not the body representations are actually translated into motor patterns" (1992, 16). Inner dance, on this suggestion, consists in a sequence of body representations in the listener, which need not translate into overt movements. On this suggestion, the challenge involved in listening to music, which is of course rarely conscious, consists in to being able to perform this outer or inner dance well, synchronizing with the musical pace. If a piece of music is too complex, you will trip and start feeling anxious, but if it is too simple or you have heard it too often, there will not be enough of a challenge and you will become bored.

If this is on the right lines, we have uncovered what could well be the main attraction of listening to music, whatever affect it expresses. Happy, sad, and even scary music can induce experiences of flow. Whether a piece of music has this effect or not depends on your familiarity with the music and its style, as well as the skills you bring to the table. Given this we can see why personal musical tastes differ. In some cases, the effects can, of course, be conjoined, such as when sad music not only induces the emotion of being moved but also triggers the experience of flow. No wonder that we often turn to music to regulate our emotions.

11.6. Taking Stock

We explored the way art, and in particular music, can be used to regulate our emotions. As we saw, music, and in particular music that is seen as expressive of emotions and moods, has the power to make us feel intense affective states, some of which are extremely pleasant. Sad music, for instance, far from always causing an unpleasant experience of sadness, often causes the emotion of being moved, which is a positive emotion we experience when we are struck by the beauty of the music. Generally, listening to music can cause us to experience flow, which is, arguably, a kind of enjoyment we take in activities. Thus, when we choose to listen to music we select a tool that has a powerful effect on what we feel. A good question, to which we will turn in the next chapter, is how music compares to other forms of art, such as film and literature, in terms of emotion regulation.

11.7. Summary

- Emotion regulation consists in the shaping of our emotions, for instance regarding when and for how long one experiences an emotion or how one expresses that emotion.
- Emotion regulation can be intrapersonal in that it targets your own emotions, or interpersonal in that it targets the emotions of someone else.
- There are five families of emotion regulation, which concern the different elements of an emotional sequence: selection situation, situation modification, attentional deployment, cognitive change, and response modulation.
- The goals of emotion regulation can involve hedonic rewards, but you can also have other reasons to want to regulate your emotions.
- Music can induce emotions in several ways, for instance by evoking personal associations or by presenting features such as being boringly repetitive or by being admirably played, but also by a mechanism of entrainment, by empathy, and by contagion, among others.
- Sad music can induce the emotion of being moved, which is an overall pleasant emotion we feel when we are struck by the beauty of the music, which is made salient by the darkness of its sadness. That sad music is well placed to cause this emotion explains why many of us are fond of sad music.
- In general, listening to music often causes experiences of flow, which consists in a kind of enjoyment that concerns activities that are perceived as challenges that match our skills.

11.8. Study Questions

1. Remember the last time you tried to get rid of some negative emotions, such as anger or disgust. What emotion was it, what kind of strategies did you use, and were they successful?
2. Think of scary music, such as the soundtrack of the *Alien* trilogy. Does scary music make for a paradox on the lines of the paradox of sad music, and if so, how can we solve that paradox?
3. What music would you recommend to a friend in order to promote that person's happiness, and how would you justify that choice?

11.9. Further Readings

Cochrane, Tom. 2010. "A Simulation Theory of Musical Expressivity." *Australasian Journal of Philosophy* 88 (2):191–207.

Davies, Stephen. 2010. "Emotions Expressed and Aroused by Music: Philosophical Perspectives." In *Handbook of Music and Emotion: Theory, Research, Applications*, edited by Patrick N. Juslin and John A. Sloboda, 15–43. Oxford: Oxford University Press.

Deonna, Julien A. 2020. "On the Good That Moves Us." *The Monist* 103 (2):190–204.

Gross, James J. 2014. "Emotion Regulation: Conceptual Foundations." In *Handbook of Emotion Regulation*, edited by James J. Gross, 3–20. New York: Guilford Press.

Levinson, Jerrold. 1982. "Music and Negative Emotion." *Pacific Philosophical Quarterly* 63 (4):327–346.

Matravers, Derek. 2007. "Musical Expressiveness." *Philosophy Compass* 2 (3):373–379.

Nakamura, Jeanne, and Mihaly Csikszentmihalyi. 2012. "Flow Theory and Research." *Oxford Handbook of Positive Psychology*:195–206.

Robinson, Jenefer. 2013. "Three Theories of Emotion: Three Routes for Musical Arousal." In *The Emotional Power of Music: Multidisciplinary Perspectives on Musical Arousal, Expression, and Social Control*, edited by Tom Cochrane, Bernadino Fantini and Klaus R. Scherer, 155–168. Oxford: Oxford University Press.

Sizer, Laura. 2019. "Sad Songs Say So Much: The Paradoxical Pleasures of Sad Music." *Journal of Aesthetics and Art Criticism* 77 (3):255–266.

Tappolet, Christine. 2022. "Sailing, Flow, and Happiness." In *The Sailing Mind*, edited by Roberto Casati, 17–29. Cham: Springer.

12 Sentimental Education and Fiction

12.1. Introduction

We have seen that music is a powerful tool to induce and regulate emotions. Other forms of art have a similar potential. This is particularly striking in the case of narrative art forms, such as films or novels, to which we often turn to regulate our emotions. Watching a romantic drama such as *Casablanca* or reading a novel such as *Anna Karenina* is prone to move us. Furthermore, when we are immersed in a film or a novel, we experience the particular kind of enjoyment that consists in the experience of flow. We all know the experience of being entirely focused on what we read, forgetting about the rest of the world, and simply enjoying the intrigue. There is reason, thus, to think that narrative art is an important source of happiness. In this, the experience of narrative art forms is no different from listening to music.

There is, however, an important difference between music and narrative art in terms of how they affect us. What we are prone to react to are the stories conveyed by such art forms. Watching films or reading novels make us experience a variety of emotions, ranging from curiosity about what is going to happen and amusement at some incongruous remark, to emotions such as fear, hope, or sadness, depending on how the plot unfolds.

As we have seen in the last chapter, a puzzle here is how it can be the case that we feel emotions in response to fictional characters and events, since we seem to be fully aware that such emotions do not concern real characters and events. In this chapter, we will look into what is known as the *paradox of fiction*. We will also consider the question of how it can be that we are fond of narrative art that appears to cause highly negative emotions, such as fear and disgust, which we generally tend to avoid. The question is whether the solution to the *paradox of tragedy*, and more generally the solution to the *paradox of negative emotion*, is of the same kind as the solution to the *paradox of sad music* we discussed.

In the previous chapter, we focused on how we can regulate our emotion by listening to music, and we discussed several ways that music can induce emotions and more generally affective states, such as moods. Our main concern in this chapter, by contrast, is whether art can contribute to the development of our emotional dispositions and indeed of our sentiments, thereby allowing for an

DOI: 10.4324/9781315542300-16

education of our sentiments. The claim that narrative art, and in particular literature, importantly contribute to our moral development is a common one (Nussbaum 1990, 2001; Robinson 2005). Before we understand how narrative art might achieve such a feat, however, there is room for skepticism. On the face of it, it is simply not obvious that people who spend a lot of time reading novels or watching films are morally superior.

We start with the discussion of what sentimental education consists in, as compared to emotion regulation. We then discuss what changing emotional dispositions consist in. After this, we examine the main strategies that allow one to achieve such changes. In order to understand how fiction could help to achieve such changes, we examine the power of fiction to cause emotions, something which requires exploring the paradox of fiction. To complete our understanding of the relation between fiction and emotions, we then turn to the paradox of tragedy. Finally, focusing on the case of literature, we discuss whether narrative art is in a good position to provide us with an education of our sentiments.

12.2. What Is Sentimental Education?

The thought that emotions need to be educated, which can be traced back to Aristotle (1983), is not only central to virtue ethics and more generally to virtue theory (Hursthouse 1999; Kristjánsson 2018; Sreenivasan 2020). It is also bound to play an important role in any ethical approach that holds that what we do depends on the emotions we experience. For instance, it is natural for an advocate of consequentialism to claims that we should often rely on feelings of compassion because this is what promotes the good. Given this, such a consequentialist can but hope that there is an educational process by which we can get ourselves to experience compassion more often. But what exactly is involved in the education of emotions, and how does it differ from the regulation of emotions?

We saw that emotion regulation consists in the shaping of our emotions with respect to when, how, and for how long one experiences an emotion, as well as what behavioral and neurobiological changes are involved (Gross 2014). Emotion regulation can concern any element of the emotional sequence that takes us from a situation to a multisystem response involving experiential, behavioral, and neurobiological changes, via attentional focus and appraisal. Understood this way, regulation concerns *emotional episodes*, that is, emotions we experience on particular occasions. As was made clear early on (see Chapter 2), emotional episodes are distinct from *emotional dispositions*, such as the disposition to feel fear when you see a bear. Emotional dispositions might also be susceptible to change. Indeed, they might be susceptible to change in response to targeted strategies.

It is therefore useful to contrast emotion regulation, which concerns emotional episodes, with the education of emotional dispositions. We will call this way of shaping emotions "sentimental education" (see Robinson 2005). Ordinarily, sentimental education is taken to concern the sentiment of love, such as illustrated in Gustave Flaubert's influential 19th century novel, *Sentimental Education*. In this chapter, however, we will use the term to refer not only to the education of love but to the education of emotional dispositions of all sorts, whether single- or multitrack.

The main difference between regulation and education concerns their goals. As we saw, emotion regulation allows for a great variety of goals, such as the hedonic and strategic goals. By contrast, the notion of education is narrower. When educating ourselves with respect to our emotions, we aim at experiencing emotions that are *proper*, in the sense that the emotions answer to some normative standard.

In fact, given the contrast between the goal of experiencing proper emotions and the multiple other goals we can have when attempting to change the emotions we feel, as well as the contrast between the shaping of emotional episodes – what we have called "emotions" – and the shaping of emotional dispositions, we can distinguish between four ways of shaping what we feel: (a) the regulation of emotional episodes, that is, *emotion regulation*, (b) the education of emotional episodes, that is, *emotion education*, (c) the shaping of emotional dispositions, which is like emotion regulation in that it can take on any goal and can thus be dubbed "*sentimental regulation*", and finally, (d) the education of emotional dispositions, that is, *sentimental education* (see Table 12.1).

Insofar as the goal of experiencing proper emotions is one of the several goals that one can have when regulating one's emotions, changes aimed at the experience of proper emotions are, in fact, a subcategory of the changes we can envisage regarding our emotions. As a result, the education of emotional episodes is a kind of emotion regulation. Similarly, changes aimed at having proper emotions by intervening at the level of emotional dispositions are a subcategory of changes in our sentiments aimed at any goal whatsoever. It follows that sentimental education is but one of the forms that the shaping of sentiments can take. Even so, because it is of central ethical concern, we will focus on sentimental education in the remainder of the chapter.

But what counts as *proper* emotions, exactly? One possibility is to hold that proper emotions are the ones recommended by the social norms of the group to which one belongs. Such norms can have social cooperation as a broad aim, but they certainly need not have this aim. Indeed, in some cases, such norms result in quite unwelcome consequences. Think of social norms according to which a specific group has to feel submissive fear when interacting with the dominant members of that society. A good example here are the norms regarding what to feel that have become internalized by women in patriarchal societies. Even if the process by which such sexist norms have become internalized can be thought

Table 12.1 The different forms that the shaping of emotions can take

	Emotional episodes	**Emotional dispositions**
Any goal	(a) Emotion regulation	(c) Sentimental regulation
Goal of proper emotions	(b) Emotion education	(d) Sentimental education

to consist in a kind of sentimental education, it is surely not one that we would want to recommend.

A more attractive suggestion consists in the thesis that proper emotions are the ones that are morally good. Sentimental education would aim at emotions that are morally good (Kristjánsson 2018). This is certainly a worthy ideal, but to understand what is required one would need a substantial moral theory. From our perspective, however, what makes sense is to focus on emotions that are proper in the sense of being *fitting*, where fittingness is understood as representational correctness. On this understanding, fitting emotions match how things are in terms of their evaluative features. For instance, a fitting emotion of fear is one that is felt in response to a dangerous or fearsome object, and a fitting emotion of admiration is one that is felt in response to something or someone admirable. This is the notion of fittingness that is central to the Aristotelian account of virtue that we discussed earlier, and according to which emotional dispositions constitute the core of virtues (see Chapter 10). In the remainder of this chapter, we will assume that sentimental education aims at fitting emotions.

12.3. Sentimental Education as Calibration

The question of sentimental education is often framed as one that concerns children (see Kristjánsson 2018). To be sure, the sentimental education of children is of utmost importance. The emotional dispositions of children are likely to be more malleable than those of adults, so if we hope to have a positive impact on people's emotional dispositions, we should try to do so as early as we can. However, there is reason to believe that the emotional dispositions of adults also allow for changes. For instance, studies on racial biases involving adult participants show that real-life experience with racial outgroup members, such as living in the same society, can reduce racial biases in our emotional reactions (Zuo and Han 2013). As Gopal Sreenivasan (2020) explains, this study shows that distress felt by members of an outgroup can be added, given relevant cultural experience, as an eliciting condition for what he calls the trait of sympathy, which he holds is central to the virtue of compassion (see Chapter 10). Examples such as this show that sentimental education is a process that can unfold over the entire lifespan of an individual.

As we saw early on, both biological determinists (Ekman 1999; Griffiths 1997; Tooby and Cosmides 2000) and social constructionists (Averill 1980; Harré 1986; Armon-Jones 1986) agree that emotional dispositions are malleable (see Chapter 3). Biological determinists hold that emotions depend on innate features that result from evolutionary selection but they allow that emotional dispositions are shaped by our environment and by our culture. Social constructionists, who hold that emotions are the product of social practices, allow for even more malleability since they emphasize the cross-cultural variability of emotions.

The question of what is involved in sentimental education is distinct from the developmental question of how emotional dispositions are set up in the first place. It will nonetheless be useful to look at the developmental question.

As we discussed, biological determinists hold that infants come into the world with dispositions to feel emotions such as fear when confronted with certain objects. If Antonio Damasio (1994) is right, fear at loud noises is innate. As a result of learning preparedness (Seligman 1970), infants would easily be able to add items to the list of things that they are innately disposed to fear. They would thus quickly learn to associate spiders and heights with fear. While more effort is needed in order to learn to fear guns and electric outlets, say, there is no doubt that we can also learn to fear such things as well.

At the other spectrum, social constructionists focus on social factors. A prominent possibility here is to hold that infants are born with dispositions to feel responses that fall short of being full-blown emotions. It is only when these responses become associated with socially transmitted scripts that they become full-blown emotions. According to Ronald de Sousa (1987), such responses become full-blown emotions after being associated with *paradigm scenarios*, that is, with situation types that go back to childhood, and that specify the characteristic of the emotion that corresponds to such situations. On this account, emotions depend on socially transmitted scripts, which tie situation types with reactions. As de Sousa explains, the association with paradigm scenarios is seen as depending on the acquisition of emotion terms. For example, small children will learn the term "fear" by associating specific responses with scenarios such as thunderstorms. According to de Sousa, paradigm scenarios are highly contextual and socially informed, even if they are in no way arbitrary. On the contrary, paradigm scenarios "are drawn first from our daily life as small children and later reinforced by the stories, art, and culture to which we are exposed" (1987, 182). Over time, paradigm scenarios become richer as the lists of things that are associated with fear change.

These developmental questions are both interesting and suggestive, but they are largely independent of the question of how sentimental education can be achieved. This is because neither of the two stories tell us how we go from being disposed to fear a class of objects, whether or not this disposition is innate, to being disposed to fear a broader or a narrower class of objects. Both the biological determinist story and social constructionist story offered by de Sousa allow for such changes. Moreover, they both agree that emotional dispositions are the result of the interaction of biological and cultural forces. But we still have to figure out how changes in our emotional dispositions can come about. Clearly, de Sousa's claim that the associations with particular classes of objects are reinforced by stories, art, and culture is suggestive. The question is how the assocation with the the initial class might come about.

As we have seen, there are two mechanisms that can be seen at work in the cultural shaping of emotional dispositions: *blending* and *cognitive elaboration* (see Chapter 3, Section 7). Blending consists in the processes of morphing together two or more emotional responses to produce a distinct emotional response (Plutchik 1980; Prinz 2004). The emotion the Ifaluk people call *fago*, for instance, can be seen to consist in a blend of love, compassion, and sadness (Lutz 1988). Cognitive elaboration is a process that involves the combination of a cognitive component, such as a belief, and an emotion so as to give rise to a new kind of emotion (Johnson-Laird and Oatley 2000). Indignation is a good example of an emotion that seems to result from cognitive elaboration or *recalibration*, as Prinz (2004) calls it. Thus, indignation is plausibly seen as the recalibration of anger by the belief that there is an injustice. Similarly, guilt can be understood as the recalibration of an emotion such as distress by the belief that one has done something wrong. Because emotions resulting from recalibration can be felt in spite of the fact that one does not have the beliefs that served in the recalibration, there is reason to think that cognitively elaborated emotions do not require one to have the belief in question. Once the learning process is achieved, you will feel guilt at certain situations even if you do not believe that you did something wrong, or indeed, even if you believe there is nothing wrong that you did.

Blending and cognitive elaboration are likely to play an important role in the cultural shaping of our emotions. But these processes are not the more basic ones. The most basic process is the one that allows to add or retract from the set of things that trigger an emotional response. Let us call this basic process "calibration", so as to mark the distinction with the two other processes. By contrast with calibration, both blending and cognitive elaboration work on distinct emotional dispositions to give rise to a new emotional disposition.

This is easy to see with blending, which takes a number of distinct kinds of emotions to make a new blend. To illustrate this, let us consider again *fago*. What happens when this blend comes into existence is that elements of the different emotional dispositions at stake – the dispositions to feel love, to feel compassion and to feel sadness – blend so as to constitute a new emotional disposition, with its own phenomenological and motivational profile, as well as its own set of triggers. This process leaves the original emotional dispositions untouched.

Cognitive elaboration similarly involves changes concerning existing emotional dispositions. It takes an emotional disposition of a specific kind, with its own sets of triggers, in order to produce a new kind of emotional disposition. For instance, the disposition to feel anger at some situations will, *via* cognitive elaboration, give rise to the disposition to feel indignation at another set of situations. Again, the initial emotional disposition will not be affected. The agent holds on to the disposition to feel anger when faced with some stimuli, but acquires a new disposition, the one that is tied to injustice and which results in feelings of indignation. By contrast, calibration is a process that does not result in a new emotional disposition. It starts with the disposition to feel fear and produces changes in the set of things that trigger the reaction of fear.

Calibration, then, is the process by which emotional dispositions change in terms of the set of stimuli that are associated with the response at stake. Interestingly, this process can be conceived of as a learning process. Indeed, we saw early on (in Chapter 2, Section 6) that emotional dispositions can be understood as consisting in standing states that involve implicit representations as to what kind of things are dangerous, disgusting, etc. Given this, calibration can be seen as resulting in implicit evaluative knowledge regarding what kind of things are dangerous, disgusting, etc. This at least is what calibration amounts to when things go well and the process does not result in distortions. If by some bad luck, you become disposed to fear innocuous things, such as common house spiders, it surely cannot be said that you have acquired evaluative knowledge.

But how exactly does calibration come about?

12.4. From Conditioning to Social Learning

As explained by neuroscientists Andreas Olsson and Elizabeth Phelps in their influential survey article, "Social Learning of Fear" (2007; see also Rachman 1977), there appear to be three ways that changes in our emotional disposition to feel fear can arise: *conditioning*, *observational learning*, and *instructed learning*. Conditioning is a process that involves directly experiencing an aversive stimulus. Fear conditioning, the study of which goes back to Pavlov's work on conditioned reflexes (1927), consists in the pairing of a naturally aversive stimulus with a neutral stimulus. When successful, an association between the reaction of fear and the representation of the conditioned stimulus is formed. For instance, if a dog bites you, something which is naturally painful and aversive, you are likely to form an association between the dog and the aversive experience, so that when seeing that dog again, or indeed seeing dogs in general, you will feel fear. In other terms, you will have acquired a disposition to feel fear directed at dogs, thereby adding this particular set of stimuli to what triggers your fear. Learning can also depend on positive reinforcement, and there is no reason to doubt that this can also be a way to calibrate emotions. The experience of fear, or indeed any emotion, with respect to a set of stimuli could thus be reinforced by the presence of a reward, such as praise by your parents.

As Olsson and Phelps (2007) emphasize, however, learning what to fear on the basis of experiencing aversive stimuli can both be risky and unreliable. It involves the risk of getting seriously hurt by aversive stimuli. Similarly, learning based on experience involving other negative emotions, such as anger or disgust, involves the risk of getting hurt. Moreover, the fact that you rely on a limited number of experiences, some of which can be misleading, such as when what hurts you is in fact generally innocuous, the learning process might well fail to be reliable. By contrast, acquiring fears indirectly, through social transmission, does not involve the risk of getting hurt by the aversive stimulus. Insofar as social transmission is based on group knowledge, it will also be more reliable. Social learning based on observation of others thus allows avoidance of the shortcomings of conditioning.

Observational learning is well illustrated by how rhesus monkeys learn to fear snakes (Chapter 3, Section 2). Young individuals learn to be afraid of snakes by observing fear reactions directed at snakes in conspecifics (Öhman and Mineka 2001). As Olsson and Phelps (2007) note, the ability to detect and respond appropriately to signs of fear, such as facial expressions, which is found in humans but also in many non-human animals, including primates but also birds, mice, and cats, is likely to have significant selective evolutionary advantage. It allows for fast learning of how to react to new forms of danger. For instance, a study shows how on the basis of the observation of the bad experience of a few individuals crows, which were captured, banded and then released by individuals wearing a particular mask, crows in a perimeter of more than one kilometer, including young crows, learned to fear individuals wearing that mask even if they had not witnessed the initial capturing scene (Cornell, Marzluff, and Pecoraro 2012).

Fear is highly contagious, as one may put it. Indeed, as Olsson and Phelps (2007) report, merely watching a film of someone expressing fear at something can induce the association necessary to the acquisition of fear toward this type of stimulus. Moreover, in the case of human beings, receiving information about another person's disposition to feel fear, such as spider phobia, can induce that same disposition even in the absence of observation. However, what needs to be emphasized is that the learning process in both human and non-human animals is mediated by other factors, such as familiarity or relatedness with the individual who is observed as well as the social status of that person. Such factors are taken to indicate that the individual you observe is trustworthy. It follows that there is a selection in whose reactions you are going to imitate, so that you will acquire emotional dispositions that are similar to only a subset of the people around you. Crucially, this explains the importance of role models in emotional learning. The individuals you perceive to be role models are the paradigm figures, whom you look up to and imitate.

The third learning process listed by Olsson and Phelps (2007) is specific to creatures who share a language. It relies on information that is conveyed verbally, whether or not the stimulus is present, such as when parents tell their child that it is dangerous to touch electrical outlets. This way of learning fear is clearly prominent among humans. As Olsson and Phelps (2007) report, "experimental studies on children involving storytelling reveal that verbal instructions can be a strong stimulus for fear learning" (Olsson and Phelps 2007, 1099; see also Field, Argyris, and Knowles 2001). These studies are of particular interest here because they involve asking children to imagine that two puppets are monsters and the learning was induced either by a video providing positive or negative interaction with the puppets or by providing positive or negative verbal information about these monsters, thereby showing that learning by verbal communication can be as efficient as learning by observation.

Even if this fear acquisition mechanism is different from the two others in that it involves verbal communication, it nonetheless results in changes at the level of the fear disposition. Also, as in the case of fear learning based on observation, one would expect that learning based on verbal communication is mediated by factors such as familiarity, relatedness, and the social status of the informer. Surely you will trust an informer more if you believe the informer to be a familiar figure of authority. Thus, we can expect children to put more trust in what their parents tell them about dangers, compared to the trust they put in complete strangers.

These three learning pathways need not be restricted to the case of fear. On the contrary, they are likely to be found generally, whatever the kind of emotional disposition at stake. Dispositions to experience disgust, anger, sadness, but also joy, admiration, or hope, to name just a handful of examples, can surely be modified on the basis of direct experience, either aversive or appetitive, as well as by observation and verbal information. With this in mind, let us turn to the question of how fiction can affect what we feel.

12.5. The Paradoxical Power of Fiction

There seems to be little question that watching films or reading novels tends to cause a variety of emotions in us. As Jenefer Robinson writes: "A good story makes us curious and suspenseful about what is going to happen; it makes us laugh and cry; it may make us feel fear and anger, horror and disgust, love and compassion, and indeed the whole repertoire of emotions in our culture" (2005, 105). Indeed, it would seem that there is no limit to the kinds of emotions fiction can induce.

In some respects, works of fiction cause emotions in the same way as musical pieces do. Thus, a film or a novel often causes emotions in us by virtue of being associated with emotionally charged events, such as being the first film you ever watched. Films and novels can also cause emotional reactions by virtue of their evaluative features, such as the quality of their cinematography or the beauty of their prose. However, the details of how fiction causes emotions are bound to differ from the case of music. The reason is that in contrast to what holds in the case of music, what moves us are the events and the characters in the fiction. As Robinson (2005) notes, there is a horrifying moment is Shakespeare's tragedy *Macbeth*, when Macduff learns that Macbeth has had Lady Macduff and all their children murdered. In addition to the horror we feel at the thought of these murders, we are also horrified and repulsed by Macbeth himself. And as Kendall Walton (1978) famously illustrated, we can even feel what seems to be fear for ourselves when watching a film. Thus, Charles appears to feel fear when the green slime in the film suddenly appears to ooze toward him. As Derek Matravers (1998) notes, however, fear, and more generally emotions felt for one-self, are very unusual in fiction. Because the slime inhabits the fictional world and not the real world, it cannot threaten Charles for real. There is thus something anomalous in Charles' reaction, and by giving the impression of oozing onto Charles, the behavior of the slime is similarly irregular.

Arguably the most potent way that fiction arouses emotions depends on our engagement with characters. Consider Tolstoy's novel *Anna Karenina*. What triggers a raft of emotions when we read Tolstoy's novel is the fate of the main character, Anna Karenina. We feel compassion for Anna Karenina when she is prevented from seeing her son whom she loves dearly, and we feel fear for her when she starts thinking about suicide. In general, what appears distinctive about many of the emotions we feel when watching films or reading novels is that they concern characters for whom we care, with whom we identify at least to a certain extent. In fact, in order to feel emotions for fictional characters, what appears necessary is that we empathize with these characters. Quite generally, as Keith Oatley (1999) notes, it is our imaginative involvement with fiction that drives our emotions. Thus, it is insofar as we imaginatively engage with Anna Karenina and empathize with her, in the sense that we adopt her perspective and share to some degree her experience, that we will tend to feel emotions for her (see John 2017).

Moreover, as Robinson (2005) stresses, the way the story is told has an important role to play in getting us involved in fiction. In particular, form can encourage the reader to become involved with the characters in the story. For instance, by using a stylistic device, such as a striking metaphor, the writer can make us focus on a particular feature, thereby influencing what we feel regarding a character. More generally, depending on the information we are given about a character, we will tend to identify with that character, thereby making empathy more likely.

Fictions appears well placed to cause emotions of virtually any kind. But is this really so? How can it be the case that fictions are in a position to evoke emotions at all, given that fictional characters and events do not exist for real? This question gives rise what is known as the paradox of fiction (Radford 1975; Levinson 1997; Naar 2013a). This paradox involves three propositions:

1. We experience emotions directed at fictional characters and situations.
2. In order to experience an emotion toward an intentional object, one must believe that this intentional object exists.
3. We do not believe that fictional characters and situations exist.

Most solutions to the paradox involve rejecting one of the three theses in this triad. Thus, the possibility this paradox raises is that what we experience regarding fictions are not genuine emotions. The best-known solution involving the denial of the first premise is that offered by Walton (1978). What Walton holds is that it is not literally true that we experience emotions directed at fictions. What we do when watching a film or reading a novel consists in engaging in a pretense, which is comparable to make-believe games in which children engage, such as when they pretend to bake cookies using cakes of mud. This suggests that the emotions we feel within such pretenses are themselves pretenses. Charles would not genuinely feel fear at the green slime. Instead, he would be engaging in a game of make-believe that involves pretending to be experiencing fear. Note that according to Walton, this does not mean that Charles is not experiencing anything, for even if his fear is not a genuine emotion, Walton holds that it is a *quasi-emotion*, which involves some of the characteristics of genuine fear. Charles, for instance, feels his heart pounding and his muscles tensed.

According to Walton, however, Charles' state is crucially different from ordinary fear. This is because Charles neither judges that there is danger nor has any corresponding motivation – Charles does not run out of the theater to save his life. The problem with this argument is that as we have seen (in Chapter 6), it does not appear that judgments are required for emotions. You simply do not need to judge that you are in danger to be afraid. Moreover, as we discussed (in Chapter 5), the link between emotions and motivation is not as strong as Walton assumes. In general, emotions directed at fiction appear to be similar to those we experience toward true stories, such as when we watch a documentary or read the news. In most of these instances, we are not in a context of a direct confrontation with the reported reality, so that it is no surprise that the emotions we experience do not give rise to actions. But as Matravers (1998) stresses, this surely does not count against the claim that such emotions are perfectly genuine.

Walton's main reason for the claim that Charles's fear is a quasi-emotion is that Charles does not take the slime to exist: "The fact that Charles is fully aware that the slime is fictional is [...] good reason to deny that what he feels is fear" (1978, 6). Thus, it is mainly because Walton subscribes to the second premise of the paradox that he denies that emotions directed at fictions are genuine. But how plausible is the claim that we need to believe in the existence of the intentional object of our emotion?

In fact, the most plausible solution to the paradox consists in rejecting the second proposition of the paradox. As Robinson holds, "[e]motions do not require belief in their 'objects' to get off the ground" (2005, 151). Insofar as one drops the requirement that you have to believe in the existence of the object of your emotion in order to have an emotion, the question is what replaces that belief. One common reply is that it is sufficient to entertain the thought that something exists to feel an emotion (Lamarque 1981; Carroll 1990). Similarly, one can hold that emotions directed at fictions involve imagining that something is the case (Novitz 1980). Charles would simply need to entertain the thought or else imagine that the slime is on its way to destroy him in order to experience fear directed at the slime. Generally, it is well accepted that imagining an event can cause an emotional reaction (see Damasio 1994; Oatley 1999; Gallese 2001). As Damasio (1994) explains, merely imagining meeting a friend can give rise to an emotion. Indeed, the same neurological networks are activated whether we engage in fiction or are confronted to reality (Clay and Iacoboni 2012).

A further question concerns the rationality of emotions directed at fiction. How could such emotions be rational since there is nothing to be afraid and nobody at risk? An attractive suggestion is that the emotions in question are premised on beliefs about what happens in the fiction (Teroni 2019). When fearing for Anna Karenina's life, we do not believe that Anna Karenina really exists and is threatened by a genuinely existing danger. Rather, what we believe is that she exists in the fiction and that she is threatened in the fiction. Our fear, thus, would be rational insofar as it is based on and adjusted to the belief about what is the case in the fiction. The interesting point here is that fearing for Anna Karenina would be fitting with respect to what happens to her, given that in the fiction, her life is at risk. By contrast, if by some sort of mental confusion, we felt fear for Anna Karenina on the basis of the belief that she will marry Vronsky and be forever happy, the fear would be neither fitting nor rational, given the mismatch between the belief and the emotional reaction.

If this is on the right lines, not only we can feel full-blown emotions toward fictional entities, but such emotions often are perfectly rational. However, another worry regarding our engagement with fiction is likely to arise. Why is it the case that we are keen to read novels and watch films even though doing so appears to trigger a great many negative emotions?

12.6. The Paradox of Negative Emotions

The paradox of negative emotions, which encompasses the paradox of tragedy, has the same structure as the paradox of sad music. As we saw, the paradox of sad music is that even though sad music appears to cause sadness, and sadness is an unpleasant affective state that we tend to avoid, we nonetheless deliberately listen to sad music (see Chapter 11, Section 4). The paradox of negative emotions can be formulated in terms of a similar triad of incompatible propositions (see Levinson 1997; Smuts 2009; Naar 2013a):

1. Fictions such as tragedies and thrillers cause negative emotions.
2. Negative emotions are aversive affective states, which we tend to avoid.
3. We deliberately engage with fictions such as tragedies and thrillers.

The question raised, basically, is how it can be the case that we want to engage with fictions even though doing so seems to cause aversive affective states, which we normally tend to avoid. Think about tragedies and thrillers, or else melodramas and horror movies. These forms of art all seem to cause intensively negative emotions, such as pity, fear, and disgust. And yet many of us freely engage with such works of fiction.

A good many philosophers have argued that the three propositions forming the paradox are in fact entirely compatible. What they propose is an explanation in terms of some benefit that compensates for the negative emotions we experience. The claim is that even though engaging with fictional works causes aversive emotions, doing so brings important benefits that largely compensate for the aversiveness. A variety of benefits thought to be strong enough to compensate for the experience of negative emotions has been proposed in the literature. Thus, Aristotle (2013) proposed that attending tragedies allowed for *catharsis*, that is, the purging of negative emotions such as horror and pity. The advantage of purging negative emotions in the context of fiction is that you can do this safely, without having to come close to anything that could really hurt you. How plausible is this proposed solution? The main problem is that this explanation of why we engage in fictions such as tragedies and thrillers does not seem to account for the fact that people do not regard their engagement with such fictions as consisting in a means to some further good. Rather, people who consume tragedies or horror films appear to enjoy every moment of it and thus appear to find the experience intrinsically attractive. This same problem mars other solutions in terms of compensation, such as the claim that engaging with fictions that cause negative emotions might be worthwhile because it affords valuable knowledge regarding human existence (Packer 1989; Nussbaum 2001). The problem is that we do not, in general, treat our engagement with fiction such as tragedies and thrillers as instrumental to some compensatory good. Quite often, we engage with such fictions because we find this intrinsically attractive.

How plausible, then, are the propositions that form the paradox? Are emotions such as fear or disgust not necessarily aversive, maybe? According to some, we need to reject the second proposition and deny that the emotions we feel in response to fictions such as tragedies and thrillers are aversive (Walton 1990; Neill 1992; Levinson 1982). According to a first explanation, emotions do not involve valence, in the sense that emotions are neither pleasant nor unpleasant. What can be unpleasant is the intentional object of the emotion – the bear attacking you – not the emotion itself. The main problem with the suggestion that emotions such as fear and disgust have no valence is that it runs counter to common experience. We commonly take the experience of fear or disgust directed at imagined objects to be unpleasant and aversive. According to a second explanation, negative emotions directed at fictions are not aversive because they are experienced in the absence of any real-life applications (Levinson 1982). Again, the worry is that this claim goes against common experience. When we experience fear simply on the basis of imagining that a bear is attacking us, our fear might be milder compared to an encounter with a real bear, but the negative phenomenology does not seem different. Moreover, the suggestion fails to account for the fact that some people avoid engaging in fictions that cause negative emotions.

Similarly, Aaron Smuts (2009) argues that we should reject the second proposition. He claims that what we are interested in when engaging in fictions such as tragedies and thrillers is what he calls "rich experiences", which involve a host of negative emotions, such as extreme distress, disgust, anger, fear, and horror. Experiencing such emotions without having to deal with real world problems is something that we find desirable even if it involves unpleasantness. As Smuts writes, "[a]rt safely provides us the opportunity to have rich emotional experiences that are either impossible or far too risky to have in our daily lives" (2009, 74). The question, however, is why we would find having such rich negative experiences attractive. If we could choose, would we not rather prefer the experience of a rich array of positive emotions, like joy and amusement? Insofar as single negative emotion appears unattractive, it would seem that experiencing a group of them would not make for a better experience.

This seems to leave us with only one option, namely, rejecting the first proposition. Do fictions like tragedies and thrillers really cause negative emotions in those who engage with them? David Hume (1957/1985b) intriguingly suggested that unpleasant emotions we experience when attending a tragedy can be converted into a positive experience, given the aesthetic pleasure afforded by the tragedy. The idea is that if the aesthetic pleasure is strong enough, the mixed emotion we experience when attending a tragedy will be positive. What is necessary for this is that the aesthetic pleasure is sufficiently strong to give rise to an overall positive experience. Now, it is plausible that part of our response to fictions is mediated by our reactions to aesthetic features of the work of art itself. However, the question of how different reactions combine to give rise to an overall emotional experience is difficult. And even if in some cases, something like Hume's conversion takes place, so that we end up experiencing an overall positive emotional reaction when engaging in fictions such as tragedies, it is hard to believe that it affords a general solution to the paradox.

What in fact appears plausible is that we have to adopt a pluralist solution (Naar 2013a; Strohl 2019). Depending on the case, there will be different explanations of what makes our engagement with fictions such as tragedies worth our while. In some cases the reward consists in some expected goods, such as knowledge, that our engagement makes possible, while in other cases, our engagement is motivated by the positive experience it affords us. This piecemeal approach is supported by the case of sad fiction. As we noted (in Chapter 11), sad fiction is like sad music in that it tends to arouse the emotion of being moved, which we have seen is an overall positive emotion, which we find attractive (Hanich et al. 2014; Cova, Deonna, and Sander 2017). Given this, it is plausible to hold that being moved is what we seek when we read sad novels or watch a melodrama. What about thrillers? Thrillers in fact bear the solution on their sleeves: what fans of thrillers want is obviously to experience thrill, which we would all agree is a pleasant experience, which is correlated to but distinct from fear (see Buckley 2016). In the case of horror movies, Noel Carroll (1990) might be right when he claims that we, or at least fans of this genre, have a fascination with monsters, such as vampires and werewolves, which violate our categorical schemes. As Carroll notes, these violations are disturbing, but they can also hold us spellbound, commanding and retaining our attention, triggering curiosity and thrill.

With this in mind, let us finally turn to the question of whether fiction can make us morally better, more virtuous agents.

12.7. Literature and the Education of Sentiments

Engaging with fiction, and in particular reading novels, has often been thought to help us become morally better agents. Most often the claim concerns specific kinds of fiction. Thus, Martha Nussbaum (1990, 2001) has argued that reading realistic novels of the 19th century, such as Henry James' *The Golden Bowl*, is something which can help us acquire moral knowledge. Indeed, according to Nussbaum, realistic novels are better placed than moral treatises to provide us with moral knowledge. By contrast to realistic novels, moral treatises only afford an intellectual grasp of propositions, which cannot do justice to the complexity of human life. As Robinson (2005) stresses, the moral knowledge that Nussbaum envisages is taken to depend on the emotions we feel when engaging with fiction. Robinson herself argues that the emotional process of engaging with fiction contributes to our moral education. What Robinson holds is that a good novel encourages readers to reflect upon the education of the characters' emotions as well as upon their own emotional reactions to the plot, something which allows readers to have a better understanding of life.

As she underscores herself, what Robinson has in mind, however, is more an "education by the emotions" (2005, 156) than an education *of* the emotions, let alone an education that aims at calibrating emotional dispositions. Robinson nonetheless gives an important hint as to how novels can impact our emotional dispositions. As we have seen, she points out that even if the world of fiction has been crafted by the novelist, the way we emotionally react to the fictional world is the same as we emotionally react to the real world. This suggests that the calibration of emotional dispositions that results from our engagement with fiction is no different from calibration in real life. We have seen that calibration can result from three distinct processes: *conditioning*, *observational learning*, and *instructed learning*. Let us look at how these processes could take place in the context of novels.

Conditioning consists in the pairing of an unconditioned aversive or appetitive stimulus with a neutral stimulus. Because you are not in a position to experience real stimuli in the word of fiction, it might seem that conditioning by fiction is ruled out from the start. However, insofar as you can have aversive or appetitive experience when engaging in fiction, there is room to argue that conditioning by fiction is a possibility. As a reader, you will not encounter a real dog, but you might encounter a dog in the fiction. Suppose the dog is a neutral stimulus, and as yet you are not disposed to feel fear directed at dogs. Depending on how the story unfolds, you might undergo an aversive experience. The dog may badly hurt a child and because you empathize with the child's distress, you experience distress. This might result in the association of dogs with aversive experiences and hence in the acquisition of a disposition to feel fear when you encounter dogs.

It is even easier to see how social learning based on observation can arise in the context of fiction. As we have seen in the case of fear, individuals learn to fear new types of things by observing the bad experiences of others with objects of that type. Indeed, observing the mere expression of fear can be sufficient to have an impact. Now, when reading novels, you have a front seat for observing how characters in the story emotionally react to situations. Depending on factors that encourage trust, such as familiarity or social status, that the character is presented as having, you are likely to acquire a disposition to have similar emotional reactions. This, it would seem, is a major way that novels, but also films, influence our emotional dispositions.

The third way of affecting the reader's disposition, namely instructed learning, is also one that plays an important role in the way fiction is liable to change us. The process is one that depends on the sharing of information regarding evaluative features. This is clearly something that can happen in the context of reading fiction. As we saw, storytelling involving positive or negative information about puppets can influence how children think and react to puppets. In such a case, it is the narrator who is providing information. In other cases, the evaluative information is provided by the characters in the fiction. Suppose you are reading a novel in which some character gives voice to an evaluative opinion. Insofar as you trust that character, and this is something that will depend on how the character is presented in the story, you will tend to treat the character as a reliable informant, and this can well give rise to a change in your emotional disposition.

An obvious worry that will arise here is that these different ways in which fiction contributes to the calibration of your emotional dispositions can well result in dispositions that are deeply flawed. Depending on the kind of novels you engage with, you might end up with overall fitting emotional dispositions, but you could just as well come to acquire dispositions to feel fear at innocuous things, for instance. Insofar as what you read can induce being afraid of the members of a minority, for instance, there is a real risk of distortion. What should be stressed here is that learning by engaging in fiction does not involve more risk than learning by engaging in the real world. The quality of the emotional disposition you acquire by observational learning and by instructed learning depends on the quality of emotional dispositions of the individuals you observe and who inform you. Calibration is risky whether you use the real world or fictional worlds as a model.

But can novels not be more helpful than this? We have seen that we often tend to empathize with the characters in a fiction, thereby adopting their perspective and experiencing emotions that are in principle similar to the ones the character experiences. Thus, a common suggestion which is inspired by Nussbaum's work (1990, 2001; also see Duncan, Bess-Montgomery, and Osinubi 2017; Maxwell 2018), is that reading novels, or at least reading novels that tend to engage you emotionally, allows you to expand your ability to empathize with the plight of others, thereby making you a better person. The assumption here is that empathy is linked to altruistic motivation. Thus, the more you will be disposed to empathize with others, the more you will tend to help them when they are in need.

Now, there is evidence that empathy correlates with prosocial or altruistic motivation (Batson 2011). And indeed, there is also evidence that reading novels that encourage empathizing tends to make you more empathetic in real life. For instance, an interesting study showed that reading novels can be a powerful strategy to improve outgroup attitudes (Vezzali et al. 2015). The study, which involved reading passages from J. K. Rowling's *Harry Potter* books, showed that strong identification with Harry Potter, an orphan who is close to stigmatized groups in the novel, resulted in more empathy with stigmatized groups, such as immigrants and homosexuals. In general, readers of fiction tend to do better on tasks that serve to test empathy, compared to readers of non-fiction (Mar, Oatley, and Peterson 2009). In fact, reading emotionally engaging fiction appears to increase empathy in readers, by contrast to the reading of non-fiction (Bal and Veltkamp 2013). Interestingly, the increase in empathy appears characterized by a "sleeper effect", the observed effect being more important when tested a week later. In short, there are good reasons to believe that empathy directed at fictional characters spills over to the real world.

This is in itself an interesting result. But what should we conclude from this with respect to the question of the calibration of emotional dispositions? To answer this question, we need to examine the relation between empathy and emotional dispositions. The term "empathy" allows for different meanings, but in the present context, empathy is assumed to consist in an imaginative process that results in the vicarious sharing of homologous affects (see Chapter 10, Section 7). When you empathize with someone who feels joy, for instance, you will imagine what it is like to be in that other person's situation and you will feel an emotion that mirrors that person's joy. As such, empathy is distinct from an emotion that concerns the person, such as sympathy, which represents the distress of that person as bad, and which tends to motivate us to relieve that other person's distress. Empathy is also distinct from the disposition to experience emotions directed at others. In particular, it is distinct from the disposition to experience sympathy.

However, what needs to be underscored is that though distinct, empathy is likely to encourage sympathy. As Nussbaum (2001) notes, empathy helps us to understand what others feel. Empathy, she holds, "is a very important tool in the service of getting a sense of what is going on with the other person, and also of establishing concern and connection" (2001, 330–331). Moreover, as Nussbaum also notes, empathy helps to focus our attention on the other person's plight. Given this, it appears plausible to hold that empathy and the disposition to experience sympathy are correlated. The more you are prone to empathize with others, the more you will tend to notice when others are in distress. Insofar as sympathy represents someone's distress as bad, the disposition to feel sympathy can be taken to involve the implicit representation that distress in general is bad. So, what happens when you have heightened empathy is that you are likely to note many more instances of distress, and if you have the disposition in question, you will feel sympathy more often. To put it simply, empathy plays the role of a distress detector.

If this account is on the right lines, fiction that encourages empathy would play an important role even if it does not contribute to the calibration of our sentiments. Empathy as such is often criticized for its shortcomings (see Prinz 2011; Bloom 2017). Reading fiction would allow us to overcome an important shortcoming that characterizes empathy in that it would widen the cases of distress we consider. However, it should be clear that not all fiction will have this effect. In some cases, engaging in fiction reinforces out-group biases. In the same way as calibration by novels is a risky process and depends on the quality of the novel, it would seem that the training of empathy afforded by novels involves a moral risk.

In any case, the take-home lesson is that reading novels, and particularly novels that engage you emotionally, will have an important impact on your emotional dispositions. Whether they contribute to your sentimental education or have a distorting effect, however, will depend on what kind of novels you happen to read, something which is mostly a matter of luck.

12.8. Taking Stock

The question we started with in this chapter was whether works of fiction can contribute not only to the regulation of our occurrent emotions but to the education of our emotional dispositions, that is to efforts that aim at having emotions that are fitting. We saw that the education of our emotional dispositions was a matter of calibrating emotional dispositions, something which can be done by conditioning but also by social learning, involving either observation of others' emotional reactions or by explicit verbal instruction. Looking into how works of fiction cause emotions, we concluded that they do so in much the same way as real situations, imagining that something is the case being sufficient to cause an emotional reaction. Because of this, there are reasons to think that calibration via fiction depends on the same mechanisms as real-world calibration. Calibration via fiction is thus a powerful, if risky, way to change our emotional dispositions and thereby change the kind of person we are.

12.9. Summary

- *Sentimental education*, which is an important step in an individual's moral education, is distinct from *emotion regulation* in that it concerns emotional dispositions and it aims at experiencing emotions that are proper.
- Both biological determinists and social constructionists agree that emotional dispositions are malleable.
- Blending and cognitive elaboration are distinct from calibration, which is the process by which emotional dispositions change in terms of the set of stimuli associated with a response.
- Calibration can be achieved in three ways: conditioning, observational learning, and instructed learning.
- Fictions cause emotions in much the same way as the real world causes emotions, and these emotions are genuine emotions, which can be rational.
- We engage in fictions such as tragedies and thrillers that seem to cause negative emotions sometimes because of expected compensatory goods but also because such works cause us to experience emotions such as being moved or being thrilled.
- Engaging in fiction and in particular reading novels has important effects on the calibration of our emotional dispositions, since conditioning, observational learning, and instructed learning can take place within the context of fiction.
- Whether calibration via novels results in sentimental education will depend on the quality of the novel.
- Reading novels that engage us emotionally results in an increase in empathy, which is conducive to altruistic motivation.
- Empathy is distinct both from the emotion of sympathy and from the disposition to feel sympathy, but insofar as it serves as a distress detector, it plays an important role in determining when we feel sympathy.

12.10. Study Questions

1. What would be an example of a change concerning your emotional dispositions but does not amount to sentimental education?
2. Stoics recommended the eradication of some emotions. What would be required to eradicate anger in terms of changes in your sentiments? Is this eradication of anger something that is psychologically realistic, assuming it is a desirable aim?
3. How do we come to have fictional role models, and are there methods of choosing such role models that are more reliable than others?

12.11. Further Readings

Cova, Florian, Julien Deonna, and David Sander. 2017. "'That's Deep!': The Role of Being Moved and Feelings of Profundity in the Appreciation of Serious Narratives." In *The Palgrave Handbook of Affect Studies and Textual Criticism*, edited by Donald R. Wehrs and Thomas Blake, 347–369. Cham, Switzerland: Springer International.

John, Eileen. 2017. "Empathy in Literature." In *Routledge Handbook to Philosophy of Empathy*, edited by Heidi L. Maibom, 306–316. Abingdon: Routledge.

Kristjánsson, Kristján. 2018. *Virtuous Emotions*. Oxford: Oxford University Press, chap. 9.

Maxwell, Bruce. 2018. "The Link Between Fiction and Empathy as a Trait of Moral Character." In *The Theory and Practice of Virtue Education*, edited by Tom Harrison and David Ian Walker, 126–139. New York: Routledge.

Nussbaum, Martha C. 1990. *Love's Knowledge: Essays on Philosophy and Literature*. Oxford: Oxford University Press, chap. 4.

Prinz, Jesse. 2011. "Against Empathy." *Southern Journal of Philosophy* 49 (1):214–233.

Radford, Colin. 1975. "How Can We Be Moved by the Fate of Anna Karenina?" *Aristotelian Society* Supp. 49 (1):67–80.

Robinson, Jenefer. 2005. *Deeper Than Reason: Emotion and Its Role in Literature, Music, and Art*. Oxford: Oxford University Press, chaps. 4–6.

Smuts, Aaron. 2009. "Art and Negative Affect." *Philosophy Compass* 4 (1):39–55.

Walton, Kendall L. 1978. "Fearing Fictions." *Journal of Philosophy* 75 (1):5–27.

Conclusion

The philosophy of emotions, and affective sciences more generally, have made huge progress in the last 50 years. Indeed, recent measures of publications show an exponential trend in emotion research, understanding emotions, and affective phenomena being thought by more and more disciplines, ranging from psychology to sociology and economics, to be key to understanding human affairs. As has recently been argued, it appears that in the wake of behaviorism and cognitive sciences, the present time is that of the rise of *affectivism* (Dukes et al. 2021).

The number of research efforts invested in understanding emotions is testimony to the importance of emotions. It is often repeated that emotions, in all their variety, are pervasive and indeed essential features of our lives. We have considered the nature of emotions and seen that emotions are best understood as felt evaluations, that can be assessed in terms of how they fit the world. We have discussed the sometimes positive, sometimes negative role of emotions in theoretical and practical rationality. We have surveyed theories of values and virtues according to which emotions are central to our evaluations and to our virtues. We have looked at the role of music in the regulation of emotions and that of fiction in the education of sentiments. These are important questions, even if they are only a few of the hugely interesting questions in the philosophy of emotions.

After a long journey such as this one, the hope is that you, my dear reader, have enough in terms of motivation but also of conceptual tools to continue on your own through the thorny but exciting field of questions that emotions raise.

DOI: 10.4324/9781315542300-17

References

Achtenberg, Deborah. 2002. *Cognition of Value in Aristotle's Ethics: Promise of Enrichment, Threat of Destruction.* Albany, NY: State University of New York Press.

Adams, Robert Merrihew. 1976. "Motive Utilitarianism." *Journal of Philosophy* 73 (14):467–481.

Annas, Julia. 2011. *Intelligent Virtue.* New York: Oxford University Press.

Anscombe, G. E. M. 1958. "Modern Moral Philosophy." *Philosophy* 33 (124):1–19.

Aquinas, Thomas. 1268–1273/1981. *Summa Theologica.* Translated by Fathers of the English Dominican Province. 5 vols. New York: Benziger Bros.

Aranguren, Martin. 2017. "Reconstructing the Social Constructionist View of Emotions: From Language to Culture, Including Nonhuman Culture." *Journal of the Theory of Social Behaviour* 47 (2):244–260.

Archer, John. 1979. "Behavioural Aspects of Fear." In *Fear in Animals and Man*, edited by Wladyslaw Sluckin, 56–85. New York: Van Nostrand Reinhold.

Aristotle. 1983. *The Nicomachean Ethics.* Translated by W. D. Ross. Oxford: Oxford University Press.

Aristotle. 2007. *Rhetorics.* Translated by William Rhys Roberts. Oxford: Clarendon Press.

Aristotle. 2013. *Poetics.* Translated by Anthony Kenny. Oxford: Oxford University Press.

Armon-Jones, Claire. 1985. "Prescription, Explication and the Social Construction of Emotion." *Journal for the Theory of Social Behaviour* 15 (1):1–22.

Armon-Jones, Claire. 1986. "The Thesis of Constructionism." In *The Social Construction of Emotions*, edited by Rom Harré, 32–56. Oxford: Blackwell.

Arnold, Magda B. 1960. *Emotion and personality.* New York: Columbia University Press.

Arpaly, Nomy. 2000. "On Acting Rationally Against One's Best Judgment." *Ethics* 110 (3):488–513.

Arpaly, Nomy, and Timothy Schroeder. 1999. "Praise, Blame and the Whole Self." *Philosophical Studies* 93 (2):161–188.

Arpaly, Nomy, and Timothy Schroeder. 2013. *In Praise of Desire.* New York: Oxford University Press.

Audi, Robert. 2011. *Epistemology: A Contemporary Introduction to the Theory of Knowledge, Third edition.* Abingdon: Routledge.

Averill, James R. 1980. "A Constructivist View of Emotion." In *Emotion: Theory, Research and Experience,* Vol. I. *Theories of emotion*, edited by Robert Plutchik and Henry Kellerman, 305–339. New York: Academic Press.

Averill, James R. 1985. "The Social Construction of Emotion: With Special Reference to Love." In *The Social Construction of the Person*, edited by Kenneth J. Gergen and Keith E. Davis, 89–109. New York: Springer Verlag.

Ayer, Alfred Jules. 1936. *Language, Truth, and Logic*. London: Victor Gollancz.

Bagnoli, Carla. 2003. "Respect and Loving Attention." *Canadian Journal of Philosophy* 33 (4):483–516.

Bain, David. 2011. "The Imperative View of Pain." *Journal of Consciousness Studies* 18 (9–10):164–185.

Bain, David. 2014. "Pains That Don't Hurt." *Australasian Journal of Philosophy* 92 (2):305–320.

Bal, P. Matthijs, and Martijn Veltkamp. 2013. "How Does Fiction Reading Influence Empathy? An Experimental Investigation on the Role of Emotional Transportation." *Public Library of Science One* 8 (1):1–12.

Ballard, Brian Scott. 2021. "Content and the Fittingness of Emotions." *Philosophical Quarterly* 71 (4):845–863.

Baron, Marcia. 1995. *Kantian Ethics Almost without Apology*. Syracuse, NY: Cornell University Press.

Barrett, Lisa Feldman. 2006. "Are Emotions Natural Kinds?" *Perspectives on Psychological Science* 1 (1):28–58.

Barrett, Lisa Feldman. 2017. *How Emotions are Made. The Secret Life of the Brain*. Boston, MA: Houghton Mifflin Harcourt.

Bartol, Jordan, and Stefan Linquist. 2015. "How Do Somatic Markers Feature in Decision Making?" *Emotion Review* (1):81–89.

Batson, C. Daniel. 2011. *Altruism in Humans*. New York: Oxford University Press.

Beall, Anne, and Robert Sternberg. 1995. "The Social Construction of Love." *Journal of Social and Personal Relationships* 12 (3):417–438.

Beck, Jacob. 2012. "The Generality Constraint and the Structure of Thought." *Mind* 121 (483):563–600.

Beck, Jacob. 2019. "Perception is Analog: The Argument from Weber's Law." *The Journal of Philosophy* 116:319–349.

Bedford, Errol. 1956–1957. "Emotions." *Proceedings of the Aristotelian Society* 57:281–304.

Bennett, Jonathan. 1974. "The Conscience of Huckleberry Finn." *Philosophy* 49 (188):123–134.

Ben-Ze'ev, Aaron. 2001. *The Subtlety of Emotions*. Cambridge, MA: MIT Press.

Bentham, Jeremy. 1789/1961. *An Introduction to the Principles of Morals and Legislation*. Garden City, NJ: Doubleday.

Bermúdez, José Luis, and Arnon Cahen. 2015. "Nonconceptual Mental Content." In *The Stanford Encyclopedia of Philosophy*, edited by Edward N. Zalta, 1–48, URL = https://plato.stanford.edu/archives/fall2015/entries/content-nonconceptual/.

Betzler, Monika. 2009. "Expressive Actions." *Inquiry* 52 (3):272–292.

Blackburn, Simon. 1998. *Ruling Passions: A Theory of Practical Reasoning*. Oxford: Oxford University Press.

Bloch, R. Howard. 1992. *Medieval Misogyny and the Invention of Western Romantic Love*. Chicago: University of Chicago Press.

Block, Ned. 1995. "On a Confusion about a Function of Consciousness." *Behavioral and Brain Sciences* 18:227–287.

Bloom, Paul. 2017. "Empathy and Its Discontents." *Trends in Cognitive Sciences* 21 (1):24–31.

Brady, Michael S. 2005. "The Values of the Virtues." *Philosophical Studies* 125:85–113.

Brady, Michael S. 2013. *Emotional Insight: The Epistemic Role of Emotional Experience*. Oxford: Oxford University Press.

Brady, Michael S. 2018. *Emotion: The Basics*. Abingdon: Routledge.

Brentano, Franz. 1874/1995. *Psychology from an Empirical Standpoint*. Translated by Antos C. Rancurello, D. B. Terrel and Linda L. McAlister. London: Routledge.

Brentano, Franz. 1889/2009. *The Origin of our Knowledge of Right and Wrong*. Translated by Roderick Chisholm and Elizabeth Schneewind. New York: Routledge and Kegan Paul.

Briggs, Jean L. 1970. *Never in Anger: Portrait of an Eskimo Family*. Cambridge, MA: Harvard University Press.

Broad, C. D. 1954. "Emotion and Sentiment." *Journal of Aesthetics and Art Criticism* 13 (2):203–214.

Brody, Leslie. 1999. *Gender, Emotion, and the Family*. Cambridge, MA: Harvard University Press.

Buckley, Ralf C. 2016. "Qualitative Analysis of Emotions: Fear and Thrill." *Frontiers in Psychology* 7 (1187).

Buddhaghosa, Bhadantācariya. 1984. *The Path of Purification (Visuddhimagga)*. Translated by Bhikkhu Ñāṇamoli. Kandy, Sri Lanka: Buddhist Publication Society.

Buss, Sarah, and Andrea Westlund. 2018. "Personal Autonomy." In *The Stanford Encyclopedia of Philosophy*, edited by Edward N. Zalta. URL = https://plato.stanford.edu/archives/spr2018/entries/personal-autonomy/.

Camras, Linda A. 1994. "Basic Emotions and Expressive Development." *Cognition and Emotion* 6:269–284.

Cannon, Walter B. 1927. "The James–Lange Theory of Emotions: A Critical Examination and an Alternative Theory." *American Journal of Psychology* 39:106–124.

Carroll, Noel. 1990. *The Philosophy of Horror*. New York: Routledge.

Charash, Michael, and Dean McKay. 2002. "Attention Bias for Disgust." *Journal of Anxiety Disorders* 16 (5):529–541.

Clay, Zanna, and Marco Iacoboni. 2012. "Mirroring Fictional Others." In *The Aesthetic Mind: Philosophy and Psychology*, edited by Elizabeth Schellekens and Peter Goldie, 313–329. Oxford: Oxford University Press.

Clore, Gerald L. 1994a. "Why Emotions are Felt." In *The Nature of Emotion*, edited by Paul Ekman and Richard J. Davidson, 103–111. New York: Oxford University Press.

Clore, Gerald L. 1994b. "Why Emotions Are Never Unconscious." In *The Nature of Emotions: Fundamental Questions*, edited by Paul Ekman and Richard J. Davidson, 285–292. New York: Oxford University Press.

Clore, Gerald, and Karen Gasper. 2000. "Feeling is Believing: Some Affective Influences on Belief." In *Emotions and Beliefs: How Feelings Influence Thoughts*, edited by Nico H. Frijda and Antony S. R. Manstead, 10–44. Cambridge: Cambridge University Press.

Cobos, Pilar, Maria Sanchez, Carmen Garcia, Maria Nevies Vera, and Jaime Vila. 2002. "Revisiting the James versus Cannon Debate on Emotion: Startle and Autonomic Modulation in Patients with Spinal Cord Injuries." *Biological Psychology* 61 (3):251–269.

Cochrane, Tom. 2010. "A Simulation Theory of Musical Expressivity." *Australasian Journal of Philosophy* 88 (2):191–207.

Cohon, Rachel. 2018. "Hume's Moral Philosophy." In *The Stanford Encyclopedia of Philosophy*, edited by Edward N. Zalta. URL = https://plato.stanford.edu/archives/fall2018/entries/hume-moral/.

Coles, Nicholas A., Jeff T. Larsen, and Heather C. Lench. 2019. "A Meta-Analysis of the Facial Feedback Literature: Effects of Facial Feedback on Emotional Experience Are Small and Variable." *Psychological Bulletin* 145 (6):610–651.

Cornell, H. N., J. M. Marzluff, and S. Pecoraro. 2012. "Social Learning Spreads Knowledge about Dangerous Humans Among American Crows." *Proceeding of the Royal Society B* 279 (1728):499–508.

Cova, Florian, and Julien A. Deonna. 2014. "Being moved." *Philosophical Studies* 169 (3):447–466.

Cova, Florian, Julien Deonna, and David Sander. 2017. "'That's Deep!': The Role of Being Moved and Feelings of Profundity in the Appreciation of Serious Narratives." In *The Palgrave Handbook of Affect Studies and Textual Criticism*, edited by Donald R. Wehrs and Thomas Blake, 347–369. Cham, Switzerland: Springer International Publishing.

Cowan, Robert. 2016. "Epistemic Perceptualism and Neo-Sentimentalist Objections." *Canadian Journal of Philosophy* 46 (1):59–81.

Crane, Tim. 1992. "The Nonconceptual Content of Experience." In *The Contents of Experience*, edited by Tim Crane. Cambridge: Cambridge University Press.

Csikszentmihalyi, Mihaly. 1975. *Beyond Boredom and Anxiety*. San Francisco, CA: Jossey-Bass.

Csikszentmihalyi, Mihaly. 1990. *Flow: The Psychology of Optimal Experience*. New York: Harper and Row.

D'Arms, Justin, and Daniel Jacobson. 2000a. "The Moralistic Fallacy: On the 'Appropriateness' of Emotions." *Philosophy and Phenomenological Research* 61 (1):65–90.

D'Arms, Justin, and Daniel Jacobson. 2000b. "Sentiment and Value." *Ethics* 110 (4):722–748.

D'Arms, Justin, and Daniel Jacobson. 2003. "The Significance of Recalcitrant Emotion (or Anti-Quasi-Judgmentalism)." In *Philosophy and the Emotions*, edited by Anthony Hatzimoysis, 127–145. Cambridge: Cambridge University Press.

D'Arms, Justin, and Daniel Jacobson. Forthcoming. *Rational Sentimentalism*. Oxford: Oxford University Press.

Damasio, Antonio. 1994. *Descartes' Error: Emotion, Reason and the Human Brain*. New York: Gossett/Putnam.

Danielsson, Sven, and Jonas Olson. 2007. "Brentano and the Buck-Passers." *Mind* 116 (463):511–522.

Darwin, Charles. 1872. *The Expressions of the Emotions in Man and Animals*, 1st ed. New York: Philosophical Library.

Davies, Stephen. 1994. *Musical Meaning and Expression*. Ithaca, NY: Cornell University Press.

Davies, Stephen. 2010. "Emotions Expressed and Aroused by Music: Philosophical Perspectives." In *Handbook of Music and Emotion: Theory, Research, Applications*, edited by Patrick N. Juslin and John A. Sloboda, 15–43. Oxford: Oxford University Press.

Davies, Stephen. 2013. "Music-to-Listener Emotional Contagion." In *The Emotional Power of Music*, edited by Tom Cochrane, Bernadino Fantini and Klaus R. Scherer, 169–196. Oxford: Oxford University Press.

Davidson, Donald. 1969. "How Is Weakness of the Will Possible?" In *Moral Concepts*, edited by Joel Feinberg, 93–113. Oxford: Oxford University Press.

Deigh, John. 1994. "Cognitivism in the Theory of Emotions." *Ethics* 104 (4):824–854.

Deigh, John. 2014. "William James and the Rise of the Scientific Study of Emotion." *Emotion Review* 6 (1):4–12.

Dennett, Daniel C. 1984. "Cognitive Wheels: The Frame Problem of AI." In *Minds, Machines and Evolution*, edited by Christopher Hookway, 129–151. Cambridge: Cambridge University Press.

Dennett, Daniel C. 1991. *Consciousness Explained*. Boston, MA: Little, Brown and Co.

Deonna, Julien A. 2018. "The Emotion of Being Moved." In *Shadows of the Soul: Philosophical Perspectives on Negative Emotions*, edited by Christine Tappolet, Fabrice Teroni and Anita Konzelmann Ziv. New York: Routledge.

Deonna, Julien A. 2020. "On the Good that Moves Us." *The Monist* 103 (2):190–204.

Deonna, Julien A., and Klaus R. Scherer. 2010. "The Case of the Disappearing Intentional Object: Constraints on a Definition of Emotion." *Emotion Review* 2 (1):44–52.

Deonna, Julien A., and Fabrice Teroni. 2012a. *The Emotions: A Philosophical Introduction*. Abingdon: Routledge.

Deonna, Julien A., and Fabrice Teroni. 2012b. "From Justified Emotions to Justified Evaluative Judgements." *Dialogue* 51 (1):55–77.

Deonna, Julien A., and Fabrice Teroni. 2014. "In What Sense Are Emotions Evaluations?" In *Emotion and Value*, edited by Sabine Roeser and Cain Todd, 15–31. Oxford: Oxford University Press.

Deonna, Julien A., and Fabrice Teroni. 2015. "Emotions as Attitudes." *Dialectica* 69 (3):293–311.

Deonna, Julien A., and Fabrice Teroni. 2016. "Getting Bodily Feelings into Emotional Experience in the Right Way." *Emotion Review* 9 (1):55–63.

Descartes, René. 1649/1989. *The Passions of the Soul*. Translated by Stephen H. Voss. Indianapolis, IN: Hackett.

de Sousa, Ronald. 1987. *The Rationality of Emotion*. Cambridge, MA: MIT Press.

de Sousa, Ronald. 2011. *Emotional Truth*. New York: Oxford University Press.

de Sousa, Ronald. 2015. *Love: A Very Short Introduction*. Oxford: Oxford University Press.

Dewey, John. 1985. "The Theory of Emotion. (I) Emotional Attitudes." *Psychological Review* 1 (6):12–32.

Díaz, Rodrigo. 2019. "Using fMRI in Experimental Philosophy: Exploring the Prospects." In *Methodogical Advances in Experimental Philosophy*, edited by Eugen Fischer and Curtis Mark. London: Bloomsbury.

Díaz, Rodrigo. 2022. "Emotions and the body: Testing the Subtraction Argument." *Philosophical Psychology* 35 (1):47–65.

Doi, Takeo. 1973. *The Anatomy of Dependence: The Key Analysis of Japanese Behavior*. Translated by John Bester. Tokyo and New York: Kodansha International.

Dokic, Jérôme, and Stéphane Lemaire. 2015. "Are Emotions Evaluative Modes?" *Dialectica* 69 (3):271–292.

Döring, Sabine A. 2003. "Explaining Action by Emotion." *Philosophical Quarterly* 53 (211):214–230.

Döring, Sabine A. 2007. "Seeing What to Do: Affective Perception and Rational Motivation." *Dialectica* 61 (63):363–394.

Döring, Sabine A. 2010. "Why Be Emotional?" In *The Oxford Handbook of Philosophy of Emotion*, edited by Peter Goldie, 283–301. Oxford: Oxford University Press.

Dretske, Fred. 1988. *Explaining Behavior: Reasons in a World of Causes*: MIT Press.

Driver, Julia. 2001. *Uneasy Virtue*. Cambridge: Cambridge University Press.

Dukes, Daniel, Kathryn Abrams, Ralph Adolphs, Mohammed E. Ahmed, Andrew Beatty, Kent C. Berridge, Susan Broomhall, Tobias Brosch, Joseph J. Campos, Zanna Clay, Fabrice Clément, William A. Cunningham, Antonio Damasio, Hanna Damasio, Justin D'Arms, Jane W. Davidson, Beatrice de Gelder, Julien Deonna, Ronnie de Sousa, Paul Ekman, Phoebe C. Ellsworth, Ernst Fehr, Agneta Fischer, Ad Foolen, Ute Frevert, Didier Grandjean, Jonathan Gratch, Leslie Greenberg, Patricia Greenspan, James J. Gross, Eran Halperin, Arvid Kappas, Dacher Keltner, Brian Knutson,

David Konstan, Mariska E. Kret, Joseph E. LeDoux, Jennifer S. Lerner, Robert W. Levenson, George Loewenstein, Antony S. R. Manstead, Terry A. Maroney, Agnes Moors, Paula Niedenthal, Brian Parkinson, Ioannis Pavlidis, Catherine Pelachaud, Seth D. Pollak, Gilles Pourtois, Birgitt Roettger-Roessler, James A. Russell, Disa Sauter, Andrea Scarantino, Klaus R. Scherer, Peter Stearns, Jan E. Stets, Christine Tappolet, Fabrice Teroni, Jeanne Tsai, Jonathan Turner, Carien Van Reekum, Patrik Vuilleumier, Tim Wharton, and David Sander. 2021. "The Rise of Affectivism." *Nature Human Behaviour* 5:816–820.

Duncan, Charles, Georgene Bess-Montgomery, and Viktor Osinubi. 2017. "Why Martha Nussbaum is Right: The Empirical Case of the Value of Reading and Teaching Fiction." *Interdisciplinary Literary Studies* 19 (2):242–259.

Eastwood, John, Alexandra Frischen, Mark Fenske, and Daniel Smilek. 2012. "The Unengaged Mind: Defining Boredom in Terms of Attention." *Perspectives on Psychological Science* 7:482–495.

Echeverri, Santiago. 2019. "Emotional Justification." *Philosophy and Phenomenological Research* 98 (3):541–566.

Ekman, Paul. 1972. *Emotions in the Human Face*. New York: Pergamon Press.

Ekman, Paul. 1994. "Moods, Emotions, and Traits." In *The Nature of Emotion: Fundamental Questions*, edited by Paul Ekman and Richard J. Davidson, 56–58. New York: Oxford University Press.

Ekman, Paul. 1997. "Should We Call It Expression or Communication?" *Innovations in Social Science Research* 10:333–344.

Ekman, Paul. 1999. "Basic Emotions." In *Handbook of Cognition and Emotion*, edited by Tim Dalgleish and Mick J. Power, 45–60. Chichester, UK: Wiley.

Ekman, Paul, and Wallace V. Friesen. 1971. "Constants across Cultures in the Face and Emotion." *Journal of Personality and Social Psychology* 17:124–129.

Ekman, Paul, Robert W. Levenson, and Wallace V. Friesen. 1983. "Autonomic Nervous System Activity Distinguished Among Emotions." *Science* 221 (4616):1208–1210.

Elgin, Catherine K. 1996. *Considered Judgment*. Princeton, NJ: Princeton University Press.

Elgin, Catherine Z. 2008. "Emotion and Understanding." In *Epistemology and Emotions*, edited by G. Brun, U. Dogluoglu and D. Kuenzle, 33–49. Aldershot: Ashgate.

Ellsworth, Phoebe C. 1994. "William James and Emotion: Is a Century of Fame Worth a Century of Misunderstanding?" *Psychological Review* 101 (2):222–229.

Elster, Jon. 1999. *Alchemies of the Mind: Rationality and the Emotions*. Cambridge: Cambridge University Press.

Engeser, Stefan, and Anja Schiepe-Tiska. 2012. "Historical Lines and an Overview of Current Research on Flow." In *Advances in Flow Research*, edited by Stefan Engeser, 1–22. New York: Springer.

Enoch, David. 2005. "Why Idealize?" *Ethics* 115 (4):759–787.

Euripides. 2011. *Medea and Other Plays*. Translated by Peter Burian and Peter Shapiro. Oxford: Oxford University Press.

Evans, Jonathan St. B. T., and Keith E. Stanovich. 2013. "Dual-Process Theories of Higher Cognition: Advancing the Debate." *Perspectives on Psychological Science* 8 (3):223–241.

Faucher, Luc, and Christine Tappolet. 2002. "Fear and the Focus of Attention." *Consciousness and Emotion* 3 (2):105–144.

Faucher, Luc, and Christine Tappolet. 2008. "Facts and Values in Emotional Plasticity." In *Fact and Value in Emotion; Consciousness and Emotion Book Series*, edited by Louis Charland and Peter Zachar, 101–137. Amsterdam: John Benjamins.

Fehr, Beverley, and James A. Russell. 1984. "Concept of emotion viewed from a proto-type perspective." *Journal of Experimental Psychology: General* 113 (3):464–486.

Fernàndez-Dols, José-Miguel, and María-Angeles Ruis-Belda. 1995. "Are Smiles Signs of Happiness? Gold Medal Winners at the Olympic Games." *Journal of Personality and Social Psychology* 69:1113–1119.

Field, A., N. G. Argyris, and K. A. Knowles. 2001. "Who's Afraid of the Big Bad Wolf: A Prospective Paradigm to Test Rachman's Indirect Pathways in Children." *Behaviour Research and Therapy* 39 11:1259–1276.

Firth, Roderick. 1951. "Ethical Absolutism and the Ideal Observer." *Philosophical and Phenomenological Research* 12 (3):317–345.

Fisher, Helen. 2004. *Why We Love: The Nature and Chemistry of Romantic Love.* New York: Henry Holt & Co.

Fletcher, Guy. 2016. *The Philosophy of Well-Being: An Introduction.* New York: Routledge.

Frank, Robert H. 1988. *Passions within Reason: The Strategic Role of the Emotions.* New York: Norton.

Frankfurt, Harry. 1982. "The Importance of What We Care About." *Synthese* 53 (2):257–272.

Fredrickson, Barbara L., and Christine Branigan. 2005. "Positive Emotions Broaden the Scope of Attention and Thought-Action Repertoires." *Cognition and Emotion* 19 (3):313–332.

Freud, Sigmund. 1915/1984. "The Unconscious." In *The Pelican Freud Library,* Vol. 11. *On Metapsychology: The Theory of Psychoanalysis,* edited by A. Richards, 159–222. Harmondsworth, UK: Penguin.

Friedman, Marilyn A. 1986. "Autonomy and the Split-Level Self." *Southern Journal of Philosophy* 24 (1):19–35.

Fridlund, Alan J. 1994. *Human Facial Expression: An Evolutionary View.* San Diego, California: Academic Press.

Frijda, Nico H. 1986. *The Emotions.* Cambridge: Cambridge University Press.

Frijda, Nico H. 1994a. "Varieties of Affect: Emotions and Episodes, Moods and Sentiments." In *The Nature of Emotion: Fundamental Questions,* edited by Paul Ekman and Richard J. Davidson, 59–67. Oxford: Oxford University Press.

Frijda, Nico H. 1994b. "What is the Function of Emotions?" In *The Nature of Emotion: Fundamental Questions,* edited by Paul Ekman and Richard J. Davidson, 112–122. New York: Oxford University Press.

Frijda, Nico H. 2005. "Emotion Experience." *Cognition and Emotion* 19 (4):473–497.

Frijda, Nico H. 2007. *The Laws of Emotion.* Mahwah, NJ: Erlbaum.

Frijda, Nico H. 2010. "The Psychologists' Point of View." In *Handbook of Emotions, 3rd Edition,* edited by Michael Lewis, Jeannette M. Haviland-Jones and Lisa Feldman Barrett, 68–87. New York: Guilford Press.

Gallese, Vittorio. 2001. "The 'Shared Manifold' Hypothesis: From Mirror Neurons to Empathy." *Journal of Consciousness Studies* 8 (5–7):33–50.

Gendron, Maria, Carlos Crivelli, and Lisa Feldman Barrett. 2018. "Universality Reconsidered: Diversity in Making Meaning of Facial Expressions." *Current Directions in Psychology* 27 (4):211–219.

Gibbard, Allan. 1990. *Wise Choices, Apt Feelings: A Theory of Normative Judgment.* Cambridge, MA: Harvard University Press.

Goldie, Peter. 2000. *The Emotions: A Philosophical Exploration.* Oxford: Oxford University Press.

Goldie, Peter. 2004. "Emotion, Reason, and Virtue." In *Emotion, Evolution, and Rationality*, edited by Dylan Evans and Pierre Cruse, 249–267. New York: Oxford University Press.

Goldie, Peter. 2011. "Grief: A Narrative Account." *Ratio* 24 (2):119–137.

Grahek, Nikola. 2007. *Feeling Pain and Being in Pain*. 2nd ed. Cambridge, MA: MIT Press.

Greenspan, Patricia. 1988. *Emotions and Reasons: An Enquiry into Emotional Justification*. London: Routledge.

Griffiths, Paul E. 1997. *What Emotions Really Are: The Problem of Psychological Categories*. Chicago: University of Chicago Press.

Gross, James J. 1998. "The Emerging Field of Emotion Regulation: An Integrative Review." *Review of General Psychology* 2:271–299.

Gross, James J. 2014. "Emotion Regulation: Conceptual Foundations." In *Handbook of Emotion Regulation*, edited by James J. Gross, 3–20. New York: Guilford Press.

Gupta, Rashmi. 2019. "Positive Emotions Have a Unique Capacity to Capture Attention." In *Progress in Brain Research*, edited by Narayanan Srinivasan, 23–46. Amsterdam: Elsevier.

Haack, Susan. 2003. *Defending Science – Within Reason: Between Scientism and Cynicism*. Amherst, MA: Prometheus Books.

Haidt, Jonathan. 2001. "The Emotional Dog and Its Rational Tail: A Social Intuitionist Approach to Moral Judgment." *Psychological Review* 108 (4):814–834.

Hanich, Julian, Valentin Wagner, Mira Shah, Thomas Jacobsen, and Winfried Menninghaus. 2014. "Why We Like to Watch Sad Films: The Pleasure of Being Moved in Aesthetic Experiences." *Psychology of Aesthetics, Creativity, and the Arts* 8:130.

Hare, Richard M. 1952. *The Language of Morals*. Oxford: Clarendon Press.

Harré, Rom. 1986. "An Outline of the Social Constructionist Viewpoint." In *The Social Construction of Emotions*, edited by Rom Harré, 2–14. Oxford: Blackwell.

Haybron, Daniel M. 2008. *The Pursuit of Unhappiness: The Elusive Psychology of Well-Being*. New York: Oxford University Press.

Heim, Maria. 2013. *The Forerunner of All Things: Buddhaghosa on Mind, Intention, and Agency*. New York: Oxford University Press.

Helm, Bennett W. 2001. *Emotional Reason: Deliberation, Motivation and the Nature of Value*. Cambridge: Cambridge University Press.

Helm, Bennett W. 2015. "Emotions and Recalcitrance: Reevaluating the Perceptual Model." *Dialectica* 69 (3):417–433.

Hobbes, Thomas. 1651/2012. *Leviathan*. Oxford: Oxford University Press.

Hohmann, George W. 1966. "Some Effects of Spinal Chord Lesions on Experienced Emotional Feelings." *Psychophysiology* 3:143–156.

Hugdhal, Kenneth, and Kjell Morton Stormack. 2003. "Emotional Modulation of Selective Attention: Behavioral and Psychophysiological Measures." In *Handbook of Affective Sciences*, edited by Tim Dalgleish and Mick J. Power, 276–291. Oxford: Oxford University Press.

Hume, David. 1739–1740/2000. *A Treatise of Human Nature*. Edited by David Fate Norton and Mary J. Norton. Oxford: Clarendon Press.

Hume, David. 1751/1948. "An Enquiry Concerning Human Understanding." In *Hume's Moral and Political Philosophy*, edited by H. D. Aiken. New York: Hafner Press.

Hume, David. 1757/1985a. "Of the Standard of Taste." In *Essays: Moral, Political and Literary,* 221–230, edited by Eugene F. Miller, 231–258. Indianapolis, IN: Liberty Fund.

Hume, David. 1757/1985b. "Of Tragedy." In *Essays: Moral, Political and Literary*. Indianapolis, IN: Liberty Fund, 1985.

Hupka, Ralph B. 1991. "The Motive for the Arousal of Romantic Jealousy: Its Cultural Origin." In *The Psychology of Jealousy and Envy*, edited by Peter Salovey, 252–270. New York: Guilford Press.

Huron, David. 2006. *Sweet Anticipation: Music and the Psychology of Expectation.* Cambridge, MA: MIT Press.

Hursthouse, Rosalind. 1999. *On Virtue Ethics.* Oxford: Oxford University Press.

Hursthouse, Rosalind. 2006. "Are Virtues the Proper Starting Point for Morality?" In *Contemporary Debates in Moral Theory*, edited by James Dreier, 99–112. Malden, MA: Blackwell.

Hursthouse, Rosalind. 1991. "Arational Actions." *Journal of Philosophy* 88 (2):57–68.

Irons, David. 1894. "Prof. James' Theory of Emotion." *Mind* 3 (9):77–97.

Izard, Carroll E. 1971. *The Face of Emotion.* New York: Appleton-Century-Crofs.

Jackendoff, Ray S. 1992. *Languages of the Mind: Essays on Mental Representation.* Cambridge, MA: MIT Press.

Jackson, Frank. 1982. "Epiphenomenal Qualia." *Philosophical Quarterly* 32:127–136.

Jackson, Frank. 1998. *From Metaphysics to Ethics: A Defence of Conceptual Analysis.* Oxford: Oxford University Press.

Jacobson, Daniel. 2011. "Fitting Attitude Theories of Value." In *The Stanford Encyclopedia of Philosophy*, edited by Edward N. Zalta. URL = https://plato.stanford. edu/archives/spr2011/entries/fitting-attitude-theories/

James, William. 1884. "What Is an Emotion?" *Mind* 9:188–205.

James, William. 1890. *The Principles of Psychology.* New York: Dover.

Jaworski, William. 2018. "Mind–Body Theories and the Emotions." In *The Ontology of Emotions*, edited by Hichem Naar and Fabrice Teroni, 14–36. Cambridge: Cambridge University Press.

Jenkins, Carrie. 2017. *What Love Is and What It Could Be.* New York: Perseus Books.

John, Eileen. 2017. "Empathy in Literature." In *Routledge Handbook to Philosophy of Empathy*, edited by Heidi L. Maibom, 306–316. Abingdon: Routledge.

Johnson-Laird, P. N., and Keith Oatley. 2000. "Cognitive and Social Construction in Emotions." In *Handbook of Emotions*, 2nd ed., edited by Michael Lewis and Jeannette M. Haviland-Jones, 458–475. New York: Guilford Press.

Johnston, Mark. 2001. "The Authority of Affect." *Philosophy and Phenomenological Research* 63 (1):181–214.

Jones, Karen. 2003. "Emotion, Weakness of Will, and the Normative Conception of Agency." In *Philosophy and the Emotions*, edited by Anthony Hatzimoysis, 181–200. Cambridge: Cambridge University Press.

Juslin, Patrick N., and John A. Sloboda. 2010. "Introduction: Aims, Organization, and Terminology." In *Handbook of Music and Emotion: Theory, Research, Applications*, edited by Patrick N. Juslin and John A. Sloboda, 3–12. Oxford: Oxford University Press.

Juslin, Patrik N., and Daniel Västfjäll. 2008. "Emotional responses to music: The need to consider underlying mechanisms." *Behavioral and Brain Sciences* 31 (5):559–575.

Kahneman, Daniel. 2011. *Thinking, Fast and Slow.* New York: Farrar, Straus and Giroux.

Kant, Immanuel. 1785/1996. *Groundwork of the Metaphysics of Morals.* Translated by Mary J. Gregor. Cambridge: Cambridge University Press.

Kant, Immanuel. 1797/2018. *The Metaphysics of Morals.* Translated by Mary J. Gregor. Cambridge: Cambridge University Press.

Kauppinen, Antti. 2013. "A Humean Theory of Moral Intuition." *Canadian Journal of Philosophy* 43 (3):360–381.

Kauppinen, Antti. 2014. "Fittingness and Idealization." *Ethics* 124 (3):572–588.

Kauppinen, Antti. 2022. "Moral Sentimentalism." In *The Stanford Encyclopedia of Philosophy*, edited by Edward N. Zalta. URL = https://plato.stanford.edu/archives/spr2022/entries/moral-sentimentalism/.

Kenny, Anthony. 1963/2003. *Action, Emotion and Will*. London: Routledge.

Kivy, Peter. 1980. *The Corded Shell: Reflection on Musical Expression*. Oxford: Oxford University Press.

Kivy, Peter. 1990. *Music Alone: Philosophical Reflections on the Purely Musical Experience*. Ithaca, NY: Cornell University Press.

Kivy, Peter. 2006. "Mood and Music: Some Reflections for Noël Carroll." *Journal of Aesthetics and Art Criticism* 64 (2):271–281.

Knuuttila, Simo. 2004. *Emotions in Ancient and Medieval Philosophy*. New York: Oxford University Press.

Kolodny, Niko. 2005. "Why Be Rational?" *Mind* 114 (455):509–563.

Kragel, Philip A., and Kevin S. LaBar. 2013. "Multivariate Pattern Classification Reveals Autonomic and Experiential Representations of Discrete Emotions." *Emotion* 13 (4):681–690.

Kragel, Philip A., and Kevin S. LaBar. 2016. "Decoding the Nature of Emotion in the Brain." *Trends in Cognitive Sciences* 20 (6):444–455.

Kriegel, Uriah. 2014. "Towards a New Feeling Theory of Emotion." *European Journal of Philosophy* 2 (3):420–442.

Kristjánsson, Kristján. 2018. *Virtuous Emotions*. Oxford: Oxford University Press.

Lamarque, Peter. 1981. "How Can We Fear and Pity Fictions?" *British Journal of Aesthetics* 21:291–304.

Lazarus, Richard S. 1991. *Emotion and Adaptation*. New York: Oxford University Press.

Ledoux, Joseph E. 1994. "Emotional Processing, but not Emotions, Can Occur Unconsciously." In *The Nature of Emotion: Fundamental Questions*, edited by Paul Ekman and Richard J. Davidson, 291–292. New York: Oxford University Press.

Ledoux, Joseph E. 1996. *The Emotional Brain*. New York: Simon and Schuster.

Levinson, Jerrold. 1982. "Music and Negative Emotion." *Pacific Philosophical Quarterly* 63 (4):327–346.

Levinson, Jerrold. 1996. *The Pleasures of Aesthetics*. Ithaca, NY: Cornell University Press.

Levinson, Jerrold. 1997. "Emotion in Response to Art: A Survey of the Terrain." In *Emotion and the Arts*, edited by Mette Hjort and Sue Laver, 20–34. New York: Oxford University Press.

Levy, Robert I. 1984. "The Emotions in Comparative Perspective." In *Approaches to Emotions*, edited by Klaus R. Scherer and Paul Ekman, 397–412. Hillsdale, NJ: Erlbaum.

Lewis, C. S. 1936. *The Allegory of Love*. Oxford: Oxford University Press.

Lewis, David. 1989. "Dispositional Theories of Value II." *Proceedings of the Aristotelian Society* Supp. Vol. 63 (1):113–137.

Lindquist, Kristen A., and Lisa Feldman Barrett. 2008. "Constructing Emotion: The Experience of Fear as a Conceptual Act." *Psychological Science* 19 (9):898–903.

Lindquist, Kristen A., Tor D. Wager, Hedy Kober, Eliza Bliss-Moreau, and Lisa Feldman-Barrett. 2012. "The Brain Basis of Emotion: A Meta-Analysis Review." *Behavioral and Brain Sciences* 35:121–143.

Livingston, Paisley. 2019. "Lange vs James on Emotion, Passion, and the Arts." *Royal Institute of Philosophy* Supp. Vol. 85:39–56.

Lutz, Catherine A. 1988. *Unnatural Emotions: Everyday Sentiments on a Micronesian Atoll and their Challenges to Western Theory*. Chicago: University of Chicago University Press.

Lyons, Jack. 2016. "Epistemological Problems of Perception." In *The Stanford Encyclopedia of Philosophy*, edited by Edward N. Zalta. URL = https ://plato.stanford.edu/archives/spr2017/entries/perception-episprob/.

Lyons, William. 1980. *Emotion*. Cambridge: Cambridge University Press.

Lyons, William. 1999. "The Cognition–Emotion Debate: A Bit of History." In *Handbook of Cognition and Emotion*, edited by Tim Dalgleish and Mick J. Power, 21–44. Chichester: John Wiley & Sons.

Mackie, John Leslie. 1977. *Ethics: Inventing Right and Wrong*. New York: Penguin.

MacPherson, Fiona. 2012. "Cognitive Penetration of Colour Experience: Rethinking the Issue in Light of an Indirect Mechanism." *Philosophy and Phenomenological Research* 84 (1):24–62.

Majeed, Raamy. 2019. "What Can Information Encapsulation Tell Us About Emotional Rationality?" In *The Value of Emotions for Knowledge*, edited by Laura Candiotto, 51–69. Basingstoke: Palgrave Macmillan.

Mar, Raymond A., Keith Oatley, and Jordan B. Peterson. 2009. "Exploring the Link between Reading Fiction and Empathy: Ruling out individual Differences and Examining Outcomes." *Communications* 34:407–428.

Massin, Olivier. Forthcoming. "The Reactive Theory of Emotions." *European Journal of Philosophy*.

Matravers, Derek. 1998. *Art and Emotion*. Edinburgh: Edinburgh University Press.

Matravers, Derek. 2007. "Musical Expressiveness." *Philosophy Compass* 2 (3):373–379.

Matsumoto, David, and Bob Willingham. 2009. "Spontaneous Facial Expressions of Emotion of Congenitally and Non-Congenitally Blind Individuals." *Journal of Personality and Social Psychology* 96 (1):1–10.

Maxwell, Bruce. 2018. "The Link Between Fiction and Empathy as a Trait of Moral Character." In *The Theory and Practice of Virtue Education*, edited by Tom Harrison and David Ian Walker, 126–139. New York: Routledge.

McDowell, John. 1985. "Values and Secondary Qualities." In *Morality and Objectivity*, edited by Ted Honderich, 110–129. London: Routledge.

McDowell, John. 1987. Projection and Truth in Ethics. Edited by the Department of Philosophy. Lawrence, KS: University of Kansas Press.

McIntyre, Alison. 1990. "Is Akratic Action Always Irrational?" In *Identity, Character, and Morality*, edited by Owen Flanagan and Amelie O. Rorty, 379–400. Cambridge, MA: MIT Press.

Mead, Margaret. 1928. *Coming of Age in Samoa*. New York: William Morrow.

Mele, Alfred R. 1987. *Irrationality: An Essay on 'Akrasia', Self-Deception, and Self-Control*: New York: Oxford University Press.

Mengzi. 2008. *Mengzi: With Selections from Traditional Commentaries*. Translated by Bryan W. Van Norden. Indianapolis, IN: Hackett Publishing.

Meyer, Leonard. 1956. *Emotion and Meaning in Music*. Chicago: University of Chicago Press.

Mill, John Stuart. 1863/1998. *Utilitarianism*. New York: Oxford University Press.

Millikan, Ruth G. 2004. *Varieties of Meaning: The 2002 Jean Nicod Lectures*. Cambridge, MA: MIT Press.

Milona, Michael. 2016. "Taking the Perceptual Analogy Seriously." *Ethical Theory and Moral Practice* 19 (4):897–915.

Milona, Michael, and Hichem Naar. 2020. "Sentimental Perceptualism and the Challenge from Cognitive Bases." *Philosophical Studies* 177 (10):3071–3096.

Mitchell, Jonathan. 2017. "The Epistemology of Emotional Experience." *Dialectica* 57 (1):57–84.

Mitchell, Jonathan. 2019a. "The Intentionality and Intelligibility of Moods." *European Journal of Philosophy* 27 (1):118–135.

Mitchell, Jonathan 2019b. "Pre-emotional Awareness and the Content-Priority View." *Philosophical Quarterly* 69 (277):771–794.

Mitchell, Jonathan. 2020. "The Bodily-Attitudinal Theory of Emotion." *Philosophical Studies* 178 (8):2635–2663.

Mitchell, Jonathan. 2021. *Emotions as Feelings Towards Values*. Oxford: Oxford University Press.

Montague, Michelle. 2009. "The Logic, Intentionality, and Phenomenology of Emotion." *Philosophical Studies* 145 (2):171–192.

Moore, G. E. 1912/2005. *Ethics*. Oxford: Oxford University Press.

Moors, Agnes. 2013. "On the Causal Role of Appraisal in Emotion." *Emotion Review* 5 (2):132–140.

Moors, Agnes. 2017. "Integration of Two Skeptical Emotion Theories: Dimensional Appraisal Theory and Russell's Psychological Construction Theory." *Psychological Inquiry* 28 (1):1–19.

Müller, Jean Moritz. 2019. *The World-Directedness of Emotional Feeling: On Affect and Intentionality*. Cham, Switzerland: Palgrave Macmillan.

Mulligan, Kevin. 1998. "From Appropriate Emotions to Values." *The Monist* 81 (1):161–188.

Mulligan, Kevin. 2009. "Emotions and Values." In *The Oxford Handbook of Philosophy of Emotion*, edited by Peter Goldie, 475–500. Oxford: Oxford University Press.

Naar, Hichem. 2013a. "Art and Emotion." In *The Internet Encyclopedia of Philosophy*. https://iep.utm.edu/.

Naar, Hichem. 2013b. "A Dispositional Theory of Love." *Pacific Philosophical Quarterly* 94 (3):342–357.

Naar, Hichem. 2018. "Sentiments." In *The Ontology of Emotions*, edited by Hichem Naar and Fabrice Teroni, 149–168. Cambridge: Cambridge University Press.

Naar, Hichem. 2019. "Emotion: Animal and Reflective." *Southern Journal of Philosophy* 57 (4):561–588.

Naar, Hichem. Forthcoming. "What Ontology for Emotions?" In *Routledge Handbook of Emotion Theory*, edited by Andrea Scarantino. New York: Routledge.

Nakamura, Jeanne, and Mihaly Csikszentmihalyi. 2012. "Flow Theory and Research." In *Oxford Handbook of Positive Psychology*:195–206. New York: Oxford University Press.

Neill, Alex. 1992. "On a Paradox of the Heart." *Philosophical Studies* 65:53–65.

Nesse, Randolph N. 1990. "Evolutionary Explanations of Emotions." *Human Nature* 1(3):261–289.

Nichols, Shaun. 2004. *Sentimental Rules: On the Natural Foundations of Moral Judgment*. Oxford: Oxford University Press.

Novitz, David. 1980. "Fiction, Imagination and Emotion." *The Journal of Aesthetics and Art Criticism* 38 (3):279–288.

Nussbaum, Martha C. 1990. *Love's Knowledge: Essays on Philosophy and Literature*. Oxford: Oxford University Press.

Nussbaum, Martha C. 2001. *Upheavals of Thought: The Intelligence of Emotions*. Cambridge: Cambridge University Press.

Nye, Howard. 2017. "The Wrong Kind of Reasons." In *The Routledge Handbook of Metaethics*, edited by Tristram McPherson and David Plunkett, 340–354. New York: Routledge.

Oatley, Keith. 1999. "Why Fiction May be Twice as True as Fact: Fiction as Cognitive and Emotional Simulation." *Review of General Psychology* 3 (2):101–117.

Öhman, Arne, and Susan Mineka. 2001. "Fears, Phobias, and Preparedness: Toward an Evolved Module of Fear and Fear Learning." *Psychological Review* 8:483–522.

Olsson, Andreas, and Elizabeth A. Phelps. 2007. "Social Learning of Fear." *Nature Neuroscience* 10 (9):1095–1102.

Pacherie, Elisabeth. 2001. "The Role of Emotions in the Explanation of Action." *European Review of Philosophy* 5: 55–90.

Packer, Mark. 1989. "Dissolving the Paradox of Tragedy." *Journal of Aesthetics and Art Criticism* 47:212–219.

Panksepp, Jaak. 1998. *Affective Neuroscience: The Foundations of Human and Animal Emotions.* New York: Oxford University Press.

Panksepp, Jaak. 2000. "Emotions as Natural Kinds in the Brain." In *Handbook of Emotions, 2nd ed.*, edited by Michael Lewis and Jeannette M. Haviland-Jones, 137–156. New York: Guilford Press.

Parfit, Derek. 2001/2018. "Rationality and Reasons." In *Exploring Practical Philosophy: From Action to Values*, edited by Dan Egonsson, Jonas Josefsson, Björn Petersson and Toni Rønnow-Rasmussen, 17–41. London: Routledge.

Pavlov, Ivan P. 1927. *Conditioned Reflexes.* Oxford: Oxford University Press.

Pelser, Adam C. 2014. "Emotion, Evaluative Perception, and Epistemic Justification." In *Emotion and Value*, edited by Sabine Roeser and Cain Todd, 107–123. Oxford: Oxford University Press.

Peretz, Isabelle. 2010. "Towards a Neurobiology of Musical Emotions." In *Handbook of Music and Emotion: Theory, Research, Applications*, edited by Patrick N. Juslin and John A. Sloboda, 99–126. Oxford: Oxford University Press.

Perler, Dominik. 2018. *Feelings Transformed: Philosophical Theories of the Emotions, 1270–1670.* Translated by Tony Crawford. New York: Oxford University Press.

Pettit, Philip. 2015. *The Robust Demands of the Good: Ethics with Attachment, Virtue, and Respect.* Oxford: Oxford University Press.

Pitcher, George. 1965. "Emotion." *Mind* 74 (July):326–346.

Plato. 1974. *The Republic.* Indianapolis, IN: Hackett.

Plato. 1995. *Phaedrus.* Indianapolis, IN: Hackett.

Plato. 2002. "Euthyphro." In *Five Dialogues: Euthyphro, Apology, Crito, Meno, Phaedo.* Edited by John M. Cooper, 1–44. Indianapolis, IN: Hackett.

Plato. 2009. *Protagoras.* Translated by C. C. W. Taylor. Oxford: Oxford University Press.

Plutchik, Robert. 1980. *Emotion: A Psychoevolutionary Synthesis.* New York: Harper and Row.

Price, Anthony William. 2009. "Emotions in Plato and Aristotle." In *The Oxford Handbook of Philosophy of Emotion*, edited by Peter Goldie, 121–142. Oxford: Oxford University Press.

Price, Carolyn. 2006. "Affect without Object: Moods and Objectless Emotions." *European Journal of Analytic Philosophy* 2 (1):49–68.

Price, Carolyn. 2015. *Emotion.* Cambridge: Polity Press.

Prinz, Jesse J. 2004. *Gut Reactions: A Perceptual Theory of the Emotions.* New York: Oxford University Press.

Prinz, Jesse J. 2006. "Is Emotion a Form of Perception?" In *The Modularity of Emotion, Canadian Journal of Philosophy* Supp. Vol. 32:137–160.

Prinz, Jesse. 2007. *The Emotional Construction of Morals.* New York: Oxford University Press.

Prinz, Jesse. 2011. "Against Empathy." *Southern Journal of Philosophy* 49 (1):214–233.

Rabinowicz, Wlodek, and Toni Rønnow-Rasmussen. 2004. "The Strike of the Demon: On Fitting Pro-Attitudes and Value." *Ethics* 114 (3):391–423.

Rachman, Stanley. 1977. "The Conditioning Theory of Fear-Acquisition: a Critical Examination." *Behaviour Research Therapy* 15 5:375–387.

Radford, Colin. 1975. "How Can We Be Moved by the Fate of Anna Karenina?" *Aristotelian Society* Supp. Vol. 49 (1):67–80.

Railton, Peter. 1984. "Alienation, Consequentialism, and the Demands of Morality." *Philosophy and Public Affairs* 13 (2):134–171.

Ratcliffe, Matthew. 2005. "William James on Emotion and Intentionality." *International Journal of Philosophical Studies* 13 (2):179–202.

Rawls, John. 1971. *A Theory of Justice: Justice within a Liberal Society*. Cambridge, MA: Cambridge.

Reisenzein, Rainer. 1996. "Emotional Action Generation." In *Processes of the Molar Regulation of Behavior*, edited by Wolfgang Battmann and Dutke Stephan, 151–165. Lengerich, Germany: Pabst Science.

Reisenzein, Rainer, and Achim Stephan. 2014. "More on James and the Physical Basis of Emotion." *Emotion Review* 6 (1):35–46.

Reisenzein, Rainer, Markus Studtmann, and Gernot Horstmann. 2013. "Coherence between Emotion and Facial Expression: Evidence from Laboratory Experiments." *Emotion Review* 5 (1):16–23.

Reisner, Andrew E. 2009. "Abandoning the Buck Passing Analysis of Final Value." *Ethical Theory and Moral Practice* 12 (4):379–395.

Roberts, Robert C. 1989. "Aristotle on Virtues and Emotions." *Philosophical Studies* 56 (3):293–306.

Roberts, Robert C. 2003. *Emotions: An Essay in Aid of Moral Psychology*. Cambridge: Cambridge University Press.

Roberts, Robert C. 2013. *Emotions in the Moral Life*. Cambridge: Cambridge University Press.

Robinson, Jenefer. 2005. *Deeper than Reason: Emotion and Its Role in Literature, Music, and Art*. Oxford: Oxford University Press.

Rorty, Amelie O. 1978. "Explaining Emotions." In *Explaining Emotions*, edited by Amelie Rorty, O., 127–151. Berkeley, CA: University of California Press.

Rossi, Mauro. 2018. "Happiness, Pleasures, and Emotions." *Philosophical Psychology* 31 (6):898–919.

Rossi, Mauro. 2021. "A Perceptual Theory of Moods." *Synthese* 198 (8):7119–7147.

Rossi, Mauro, and Christine Tappolet. 2016. "Virtue, Happiness, and Wellbeing." *The Monist* 99 (2):112–127.

Rossi, Mauro, and Christine Tappolet. 2019. "What Kind of Evaluative States Are Emotions? The Attitudinal Theory vs. the Perceptual Theory of Emotions." *Canadian Journal of Philosophy* 49 (4):544–563.

Rossi, Mauro, and Christine Tappolet. In preparation. "Valuings as Sentiments."

Russell, James A. 1994. "Is There Universal Recognition of Emotion from Facial Expressions? A Review of the Cross-Cultural Studies." *Psychological Bulletin* 115:102–141.

Russell, James A. 2003. "Core Affect and the Psychological Construction of Emotion." *Psychological Review* 110 (1):145–172.

Salmela, Mikko. 2011. "Can Emotion be Modelled on Perception?" *Dialectica* 65 (1):1–29.

Sartre, Jean-Paul. 1962. *Sketch for a Theory of the Emotions*. New York: Methuen.

Scade, Paul. 2017. "Music and the Soul in Stoicism." In *Selfhood and the Soul: Essays on Ancient Thought and Literature in Honour of Christopher Gill*, edited by Richard Seaford, John Wilkins and Matthew Wright. New York: Oxford University Press.

Scanlon, Thomas. 1998. *What We Owe to Each Other*. Cambridge, MA: Harvard University Press.

Scarantino, Andrea. 2010. "Insights and Blindspots of the Cognitivist Theory of Emotions." *The British Journal for the Philosophy of Science* 61:729–768.

Scarantino, Andrea. 2014a. "Basic Emotions, Psychological Construction, and the Problem of Variability." In *The Psychological Construction of Emotion*, edited by Lisa Feldman Barrett and James A. Russell, 334–376. New York: Guilford Press.

Scarantino, Andrea. 2014b. "The Motivational Theory of Emotions." In *Moral Psychology and Human Agency*, edited by Daniel Jacobson and Justin D'Arms, 156–185. New York: Oxford University Press.

Scarantino, Andrea, and Ronald de Sousa. 2018. "Emotion." In *The Stanford Encyclopedia of Philosophy*, edited by Edward N. Zalta. URL = https://plato.stanford.edu/archives/sum2021/entries/emotion/.

Schachter, Stanley, and Jerome E. Singer. 1962. "Cognitive, Social, and Physiological Determinants of Emotional States." *Psychological Review* 69 (5):379–399.

Scherer, Klaus R. 1984. "On the Nature and Function of Emotion: A Component Process Approach." In *Approaches to Emotions*, edited by Klaus Scherer and Paul Ekman, 293–318. Mahwah, NJ: Erlbaum.

Scherer, Klaus R. 1994. "Emotion Serves to Decouple Stimulus and Response." In *The Nature of Emotion: Fundamental Questions*, edited by Paul Ekman and Richard J. Davidson, 127–130. New York: Oxford University Press.

Scherer, Klaus R. 2004. "Feelings Integrate the Central Representation of Appraisal-driven Response Organization in Emotion." In *Feelings and Emotions*, edited by Antony S. R. Manstead, Nico Frijda and Agneta Fischer, 136–157. Cambridge: Cambridge University Press.

Scherer, Klaus R. 2005. "What Are Emotions? And How Can They Be Measured?" *Social Science Information* 44 (4):695–729.

Scherer, Klaus R. 2009. "The Dynamic Architecture of Emotion: Evidence for the Component Process Model." *Cognition and Emotion* 23:1307–1351.

Scherer, Klaus R. 2013. "How Music Creates Emotion: A Multifactorial Process Approach." In *The Emotional Power of Music: Multidisciplinary Perspectives on Musical Arousal, Expression, and Social Control*, edited by Tom Cochrane, Bernadino Fantini and Klaus R. Scherer, 121–145. Oxford: Oxford University Press.

Schueler, G. F. 1997. "Why Modesty Is a Virtue." *Ethics* 107 (3):467–485.

Searle, John R. 1983. *Intentionality*. Cambridge: Cambridge University Press.

Seidman, Jeffrey. 2009. "Valuing and Caring." *Theoria* 75 (4):272–303.

Seligman, Martin E. P. 1970. "Phobias and Preparedness." *Behaviour Therapy* 2 (3):307–320.

Seneca. 2010. *Anger, Mercy, Revenge*. Translated by Robert A. Kaster and Martha C. Nussbaum. Chicago: University of Chicago Press.

Shafer-Landau, Russ. 2003. *Moral Realism: A Defence*. New York: Oxford University Press.

Shapiro, Lisa. 2020. "Descartes and Spinoza on the Primitive Passions." In *Freedom, Action, and Motivation in Spinoza's Ethics*, edited by Noa Naaman-Zauderer, 62–81. New York and Abingdon: Routledge.

Sherman, Nancy. 1997. *Making a Necessity of Virtue: Aristotle and Kant on Virtue*. Cambridge: Cambridge University Press.

Shoemaker, David W. 2003. "Caring, Identification, and Agency." *Ethics* 114 (1):88–118.

Siegel, Erika. H., Molly K. Sands, Wim Van den Noortgate, Paul Condon, Yale Chang, Jennifer Dy, Karen S. Quigley, and Lisa Feldman Barrett. 2018. "Emotion Fingerprints or Emotion Populations? A Meta-Analytic Investigation of Autonomic Features of Emotion Categories." *Psychology Bulletin* 144 (4):343–393.

Siegel, Susanna. 2017. *The Rationality of Perception*. New York: Oxford University Press.

Silva, Laura. 2021. "The Epistemic Role of Outlaw Emotions." *Ergo* 8 (23):664–691.

Sizer, Laura. 2019. "Sad Songs Say So Much: The Paradoxical Pleasures of Sad Music." *Journal of Aesthetics and Art Criticism* 77 (3):255–266.

Smith, Adam. 1759/2002. *The Theory of Moral Sentiments*. Cambridge: Cambridge University Press.

Smith, Craig, and Leslie Kirby. 2004. "Appraisal as a Pervasive Determinant of Anger." *Emotion* 4:133–138.

Smith, Joel. 2014. "Are Emotions Embodied Evaluative Attitudes?" *Disputatio* 6 (38):93–106.

Smith, Michael A. 1998. "The Possibility of Philosophy of Action." In *Human Action, Deliberation and Causation*, edited by Jan Bransen and Stefaan Cuypers, 17–41. Dordrecht, Netherlands: Kluwer.

Smuts, Aaron. 2009. "Art and Negative Affect." *Philosophy Compass* 4 (1):39–55.

Solomon, Robert C. 1976/1993. *The Passions: Emotions and the Meaning of Life*. Indianapolis, IN: Hackett.

Solomon, Robert C. 2003. *Not Passion's Slave: Emotions and Choice*. New York: Oxford University Press.

Solomon, Robert C. 2007. *True to Our Feelings: What Our Emotions Are Really Telling Us*. New York: Oxford University Press.

Soteriou, Matthew. 2018. "The Ontology of Emotion." In *The Ontology of Emotions*, edited by Hichem Naar and Fabrice Teroni, 71–89. Cambridge: Cambridge University Press.

Sreenivasan, Gopal. 2020. *Emotion and Virtue*. Princeton, NJ: Princeton University Press.

Stevenson, Charles Leslie. 1937. "The Emotive Meaning of Ethical Terms." *Mind* 46 (181):14–31.

Strawson, Galen. 1994. *Mental Reality*. Cambridge, MA: MIT Press.

Strohl, Matthew. 2019. "Art and Painful Emotion." *Philosophy Compass* 14 (1):1–12.

Stroud, Sarah. 2008. "Weakness of Will." In *The Stanford Encyclopedia of Philosophy*, edited by Edward N. Zalta. URL = https://plato.stanford.edu/archives/win2021/entries/weakness-will/.

Superson, Anita. 2020. "Feminist Moral Psychology." In *The Stanford Encyclopedia of Philosophy*, edited by Edward N. Zalta. URL = https://plato.stanford.edu/archives/sum2020/entries/feminism-moralpsych/.

Tappolet, Christine. 2003. "Emotions and the Intelligibility of Akratic Action." In *Weakness of Will and Practical Irrationality*, edited by Sarah Stroud and Christine Tappolet, 97–120. Oxford: Clarendon Press.

Tappolet, Christine. 2012. "Emotions, Perceptions, and Emotional Illusions." In *Perceptual Illusions. Philosophical and Psychological Essays*, edited by Clotilde Calabi, 207–224. Basingstoke, UK: Palgrave Macmillan.

Tappolet, Christine. 2014. "The Normativity of Evaluative Concepts." In *Mind, Values, and Metaphysics. Philosophical Essays in Honor of Kevin Mulligan, Vol. II*, edited by Anne Reboul, 39–54. Cham, Switzerland: Springer.

Tappolet, Christine. 2016. *Emotions, Values, and Agency*. Oxford: Oxford University Press.

Tappolet, Christine. 2018. "The Metaphysics of Moods." In *The Ontology of Emotions*, edited by Hichem Naar and Fabrice Teroni, 169–186. Cambridge: Cambridge University Press.

Tappolet, Christine. 2020. "Emotions Inside Out: The Nonconceptual Content of Emotions." In *Concepts in Thought, Action, and Emotion: New Essays*, edited by Christoph Demmerling and Dirk Schroeder, 257–276. New York: Routledge.

Tappolet, Christine. 2022. "Sailing, Flow and Happiness." In *The Sailing Mind*, edited by Robert Casati, 17–29, Cham, Switzerland: Springer.

Tenenbaum, Sergio. 2013. "Guise of the Good." In *The International Encyclopedia of Ethics*, edited by Hugh LaFollette. Chichester, UK: Wiley-Blackwell.

Teroni, Fabrice. 2007. "Emotions and Formal Objects." *Dialectica* 61 (3):395–415.

Teroni, Fabrice. 2019. "Emotion, Fiction and Rationality." *British Journal of Aesthetics* 59 (2):113–128.

Thaut, Michael H., and Barbara L. Wheeler. 2010. "Music Therapy." In *Handbook of Music and Emotion: Theory, Research, Applications*, edited by Patrick N. Juslin and John A. Sloboda. Oxford: Oxford University Press.

Tooby, John, and Leda Cosmides. 1990. "The Past Explains the Present: Emotional Adaptations and the Structure of Ancestral Environments." *Ethology and Sociobiology* 11:375–424.

Tooby, John, and Leda Cosmides. 2000. "Evolutionary Psychology and the Emotions." In *Handbook of Emotion*, 2nd ed., edited by Michael Lewis and Jeannette M. Haviland-Jones, 91–116. New York: Guilford Press.

Trost, Wiebke, and Patrik Vuilleumier. 2013. "Rhythmic Entrainment as a Mechanism for Emotion Induction by Music: A Neurological Perspective." In *The Emotional Power of Music: Multidisciplinary Perspectives on Musical Arousal, Expression, and Social Control*, edited by Tom Cochrane, Bernadino Fantini and Klaus R. Scherer, 213–225. Oxford: Oxford University Press.

Tuske, Joerg. 2016. "The Concept of Emotion in Classical Indian Philosophy." In *The Stanford Encyclopedia of Philosophy*, edited by Edward N. Zalta. URL = https://plato.stanford.edu/archives/fall2021/entries/concept-emotion-india/.

Van Norden, Bryan W. 2019. "Mencius." In *The Stanford Encyclopedia of Philosophy*, edited by Edward N. Zalta. URL = https://plato.stanford.edu/archives/fall2019/entries/mencius/.

Van Zyl, Liezl. 2018. *Virtue Ethics: A Contemporary Introduction*. New York: Routledge.

Vezzali, Loris, Sofia Stathi, Dino Giovannini, Dora Capozza, and Elena Trifiletti. 2015. "The Greatest Magic of Harry Potter: Reducing Prejudice." *Journal of Applied Social Psychology* 45:105–121.

Virág, Curie. 2017. *The Emotions in Early Chinese Philosophy*. New York: Oxford University Press.

Vuoskoski, Jonna K., and Tuomas Eerola. 2017. "The Pleasure Evoked by Sad Music Is Mediated by Feelings of Being Moved." *Frontiers in Psychology* 8 (439):1–11.

Vuoskoski, Jonna K., William F. Thomson, Doris McIlwain, and Tuomas Eerola. 2012. "Who Enjoys Listening to Sad Music and Why?" *Music Perception: An Interdisciplinary Journal* 29:311–317.

Walton, Kendall L. 1978. "Fearing Fictions." *Journal of Philosophy* 75 (1):5–27.

Walton, Kendall L. 1990. *Mimesis as Make-Believe*. Cambridge: Cambridge University Press.

Weiskrantz, Lawrence. 1986. *Blindsight: A Case Study and Implications*. New York: Oxford University Press.

Wells, Adrian, and Gerald Matthews. 1994. *Attention and Emotion: A Clinical Perspective*. Hove, UK: Lawrence Earlbaum Associates.

Westermarck, Edvard. 1906. *The Origin and Development of the Moral Ideas*, Vol. I. Freeport, NY: Books for Libraries Press.

Wheatley, Thalia, and Jonathan Haidt. 2005. "Hypnotic Disgust Makes Moral Judgments More Severe." *Psychological Science* 16:780–4.

Whiting, Demian. 2009. "The Feeling Theory of Emotion and the Object-Directed Emotions." *European Journal of Philosophy* 19:281–303.

Wierzbicka, Anna. 1992. *Semantics, Culture, and Cognition: Universal Human Concepts in Culture-Specific Configurations*. New York: Oxford University Press.

Wierzbicka, Anna. 1999. *Emotions across Languages and Cultures: Diversity and Universals*. Cambridge: Cambridge University Press.

Wiggins, David. 1976. "Truth, Invention, and the Meaning of Life." *Proceedings of the British Academy* 62:332–378.

Wiggins, David. 1987. "A Sensible Subjectivism." In *Needs, Values, Truth: Essays in the Philosophy of Value*, 185–214. Oxford: Blackwell.

Williams, Bernard. 1973. "Morality and the Emotions." In *Problems of the Self*, 207–229. Cambridge: Cambridge University Press.

Williams, Bernard. "Internal and External Reasons." In *Moral Luck*, 101–113. Cambridge: Cambridge University Press, 1981.

Wilson, Eric Entrican, and Lara Denis. 2018. "Kant and Hume on Morality." In *The Stanford Encyclopedia of Philosophy*, edited by Edward N. Zalta. URL = https://plato. stanford.edu/archives/fall2021/entries/kant-hume-morality/.

Wittgenstein, Ludwig. 1953. *Philosophical Investigations*. Translated by R. Rhees and A. Kenny. Oxford: Blackwell.

Wollheim, Richard. 1999. *On the Emotions*. New Haven, CT: Yale University Press.

Wong, David B. 2019. "Moral Sentimentalism in Early Confucian Thought." In *Ethical Sentimentalism: New Perspectives*, edited by Remy Debes and Karsten R. Stueber, 230–249. Cambridge: Cambridge University Press.

Zagzebski, Linda 2003. "Emotion and Moral Judgment." *Philosophy and Phenomenological Research* 66 (1):104–124.

Zajonc, Robert B. 1984. "On the Primacy of Affect." *American Psychologist* 39 (2):117–123.

Zentner, Marcel, Didier Grandjean, and Klaus R. Scherer. 2008. "Emotions Evoked by the Sound of Music: Characterization, Classification, and Measurement." *Emotion* 8 (4):494–521.

Zuo, Xiangyu, and Shihui Han. 2013. "Cultural Experiences Reduce Racial Bias in Neural Responses to Others' Suffering." *Culture and Brain* 1 (1):34–46.

Index